ESSENTIALS
OF CHINESE ACUPUNCTURE

Compiled by
Beijing University of Chinese Medicine
Shanghai University of Traditional Chinese Medicine
Nanjing University of Traditional Chinese Medicine
The Institute of Acupuncture and Moxibustion of China Academy of
Traditional Chinese Medicine

FOREIGN LANGUAGES PRESS
BEIJING

First Edition 1980
Second Edition 1993
Second Printing 2005

Home Page:
  http://www.flp.com.cn
E-mail Addresses:
  info@flp.com.cn
  sales@flp.com.cn

ISBN 7-119-00240-6

© Foreign Languages Press, Beijing, 1993

Published by Foreign Languages Press
24 Baiwanzhuang Road, Beijing 100037, China

Distributed by China International Book Trading Corporation
35 Chegongzhuang Xilu, Beijing 100044, China
P.O. Box 399, Beijing, China

Printed in the People's Republic of China

This bronze figure showing acupuncture points is a reproduction of one cast in 1443 A.D., during the Ming Dynasty.

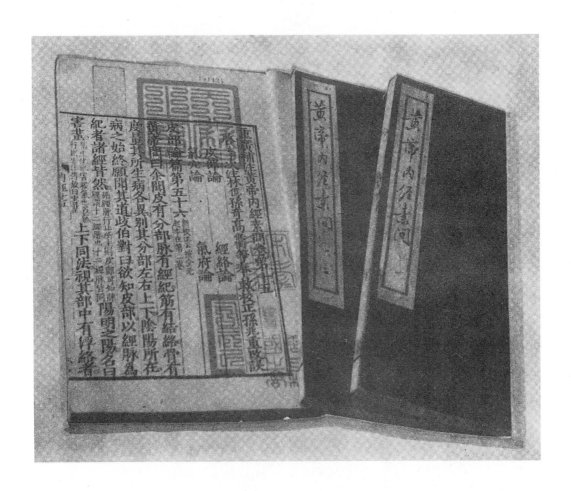

Huangdi Neijing (Canon of Medicine), compiled in 500-300 B.C., is the earliest extant medical book in China in which acupuncture is described.

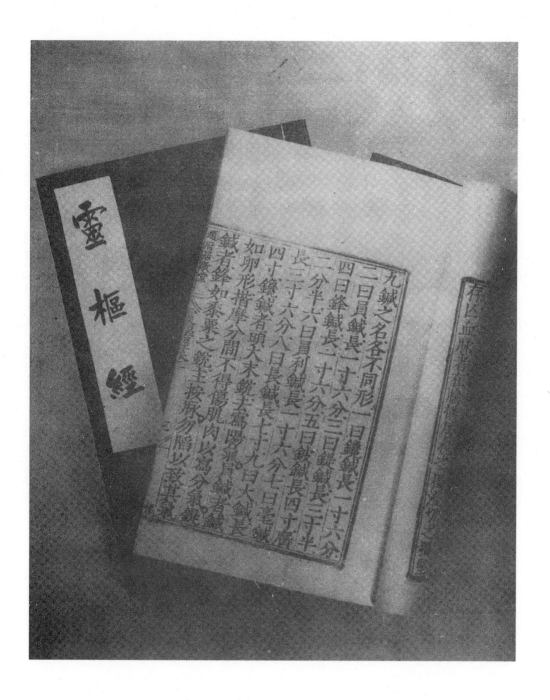

Lingshu, also known as *Canon of Acupuncture*, is a part of
Huangdi Neijing. It contains the earliest records of using
nine different acupuncture instruments, the "Nine Needles"

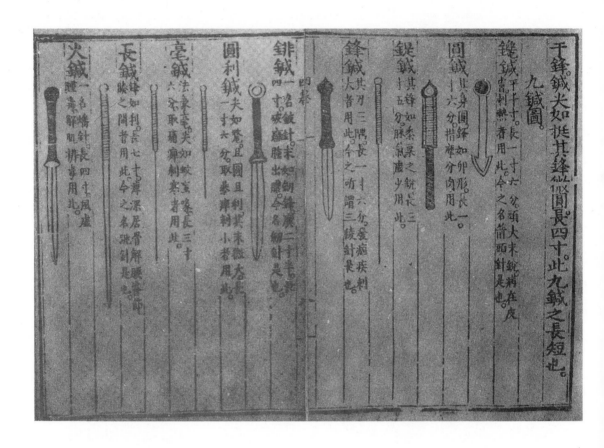

In *Zhenjiu Dacheng* (*Compendium of Acupuncture and Moxibustion*) compiled in 1601, nine kinds of needles and their clinical applications are recorded.

Contents

i

v

vii

PREFACE

1. This book is written in three parts. Part I in seven chapters introduces the basic theories of traditional Chinese medicine. This consists of the theory of *yin-yang*, the five elements, *zang-fu* (the viscera), channels and collaterals, *qi* (vital energy), blood, body fluid, etiology, diagnosis, and differentiation of syndromes. To emphasize theory at the beginning of the book is to lay a sound foundation for the study of acupuncture and moxibustion—an integral part of traditional Chinese medicine—taking this theory as a guide in clinical practice.

2. Part II consists of three chapters. It gives a general sketch of the channels and points, detailing the courses of the 12 channels, the extra channels, the points of each channel and the extraordinary points. The source material of the 12 regular channels is taken from *An Essay on Channels from Lingshu* (*Lingshu Jingmaipian* 灵枢经脉篇), and that of the 8 extra channels is taken mainly from *A Classic of Difficult Questions* (*Nanjing* 难经). As to the location of the points, *A Classic of Acupuncture and Moxibustion* (*Zhenjiu Jiayijing* 针灸甲乙经) has been consulted, and the *Illustrated Manual on the Points for Acupuncture and Moxibustion as Shown on the Bronze Figure* (*Tongren Shuxue Zhenjiu Tujing*、铜人俞穴针灸图经), the *Compendium of Acupuncture and Moxibustion* (*Zhenjiu Dacheng* 针灸大成),etc. have been referred to. The localization of the points is explained according to anatomical landmarks on the body surface and the locating methods that have been long in use in clinical practice. For precision, the regional anatomy including vasculature and innervation of each point are mentioned. These may also serve as references for the readers.

3. Part III deals with acupuncture and moxibustion therapy. The first chapter lays stress on acupuncture technique using the filiform needle and methods using other types of needle, as well as moxibustion technique. Manipulation methods in acupuncture and moxibustion introduced in this book are easy to master and practical for clinical use. Difficult and rare methods are not presented. The second chapter gives a general description of acupuncture therapy, while the third is devoted to treatment of common diseases and disorders. The treatment of 52 common diseases (and disorders) with acupuncture are minutely discussed as to etiology, pathology differentiation, the principle and method of treatment, and prescription of points, with detailed explanation showing the close relation of theory and practice.

The names of the diseases (or disorders) and their description are according to traditional Chinese medicine. For the sake of clarity, a note is given below each disease (or disorder) to explain its counterpart or the disease in which it might be manifest in terms of modern medicine.

4. In compiling this book we quote as little as possible from the ancient classics, while certain necessary original passages have been interpreted into modern language with sources given.

Some names of points though different when written in Chinese characters have the same spelling latinized. In such cases we add anatomical prefixes to distinguish them. Examples are Neck-Futu and Femur-Futu, Nose- Juliao and Femur-Juliao, Ear-Heliao and Nose-Heliao, etc.

5. Points of each channel are numbered according to their locating order. The first point of the Lung Channel for example is written as Zhongfu(Lu.1), the 14th point of the Liver Channel as Qimen (Liv. 14), etc.

6. This volume concludes with an appendix of two chapters. The first is on ear acupuncture therapy in which the relation between the auricle and channels, collaterals and viscera, the anatomical structure of the surface of the auricle, auricular points and clinical application are discussed. The second chapter gives a brief account of acupuncture analgesia including its special features and technique. Some examples of selection of points for pain suppression are given.

The Editor
March 10, 1979

FOREWORD

Essentials of Chinese Acupuncture is a translation of Zhongguo Zhenjiuxue Gaiyao (中国针灸学概要) published in 1964 and re-edited recently. This book features a clear presentation of the basic theories of traditional Chinese medicine so as to initiate readers to an understanding of traditional Chinese medicine in general and share its benefits in their clinical practice and study of acupuncture and moxibustion.

The theory of traditional Chinese medicine is totally different from that of modern medicine and has a unique system of its own. Some of the terms are rather difficult to express in other languages, nor is it easy to find an exact translation of the original. Some words that convey the concept of the Chinese terms convey it only in part. To present traditional Chinese medicine factually and faithfully, and as clearly as possible, we have observed the following points in our translation.

Some of the terms with extensive implications and basic meaning, such as *yin, yang, xu, shi, zang-fu, qi, sanjiao*, etc. are latinized and printed in italics. This is done in order not to distort the original expression and to preserve its traditional significance. The equivalent is given in brackets after the word when deemed necessary.

Such terms as blood, body fluid, phlegm, pericardium, heart, liver, spleen, lung, and kidney are translated literally though they carry a much broader meaning in the Chinese than in the context of modern medicine, and the reader should not limit them to their strict anatomical meaning. They may stand for the function of the tissue or organ concerned. Weakness of spleen, for instance, may mean a pathological condition of the digestive tract or an etiological factor of edema; over- activity of the liver may refer to functional disease, etc. There will be supplementary and comprehensive explanation in such cases.

Though care has been taken in translation and explanation, certain errors and misconceptions are likely to occur, and we ask our readers to point out for us any weaknesses in our work.

Translator
March 10, 1979

FORWARD
TO THE SECOND EDITION

Essentials of Chinese Acupuncture has been in use as the textbook for the introductory course in Beijing, Shanghai and Nanjing International Acupuncture Training Centers since it was re-edited and published in June 1979. Over the years that it has been in use, its clear and simple presentation has proved invaluable in the teaching of foreign doctors. Presented in an easily understandable form, it is well-suited to the needs of those who are just beginning their studies of acupuncture and moxibustion. We trust that the new edition, freed from its most obvious errors, will continue to make a worthwhile contribution to intenational acupuncture training.

China Beijing International Acupuncture Training Center
China Shanghai International Acupuncture Training Center
China Nanjing International Acupuncture Training Center
Proofreaders for English edition:
Xue Kuiyang and Lu Xiaozhen
March 1, 1993

INTRODUCTION

Acupuncture and moxibustion are important component procedures in traditional Chinese medicine which prevent and treat disease by puncturing certain points on the body with needles or applying heat with ignited moxa wool. Of marked efficacy and requiring but simple equipment, they have been widely popular in China and elsewhere for thousands of years.

The initiation and development of the art of acupuncture and moxibustion have undergone a long historical process. They are summaries of experience of the Chinese labouring people of many centuries in their struggle against disease. As early as in the Stone Age, people used needles fashioned of stone for curative purposes. These are known as *bian** and are a rudiment of acupuncture. When human society entered the Bronze and then the Iron Age, needles made of these metals were substituted for the stone *bian*. And with the development of social productive technique, needling instruments were constantly improved, providing conditions for the further refinement of acupuncture. Moxibustion originated after the introduction of fire into man's life. It is assumed that while warming themselves by the fire, people in ancient times accidentally found relief or disappearance of certain pain or illness when definite areas of the skin were subjected to burning. Moxa leaves were later chosen as the material for cauterization as they are easily lit and the heat produced is mild and effective in removing obstruction of channels and collaterals. And so the art of moxibustion was established.

The earliest extant medical classic in China, Huangdi Neijing** (黄帝内经 *Canon of Medicine*), was compiled between 500-300 B.C. It is a summary of the medical experience and theoretical knowledge prior to the Warring States period. The book, which consists of two parts, *Suwen* and *Lingshu*, describes the basic theories of traditional Chinese medicine, such as *yin-yang*, the five elements, *zang-fu*, channels and collaterals, *qi* (vital energy), and blood, etiology, pathology, diagnostic methods and differentiation of syndromes , as well as basic knowledge concerning acupuncture points and needling methods. Following *Neijing*, there appeared quite a number of treatises on acupuncture and moxibustion written in different dynasties, among which

---

* Phonetic transcription of the Chinese character 砭 , a word with "stone" as radical.
** Referred to hereafter simply as *Neijing*.

representative ones are:

Zhenjiu Jiayijing (针灸甲乙经 *A Classic of Acupuncture and Moxibustion*, 265 A.D.) compiled by Huangfu Mi of the Jin Dynasty on the basis of *Neijing, Nanjing* (难经 *A Classic of Difficult Questions*), and others. These books give a comprehensive description of the basic theories and knowledge of acupuncture and moxibustion, laying a foundation for the development of acupuncture and moxibustion into an independent branch of traditional Chinese medicine.

Tongren Shuxue Zhenjiu Tujing (铜人俞穴针灸图经 *Illustrated Manual on Points for Acupuncture and Moxibustion Shown on a Bronze Figure*, 1026 A.D.) was compiled by Wang Weiyi, an acupuncturist of the Song Dynasty, after thoroughly checking the acupuncture points of the fourteen channels. The next year, i.e., A.D. 1027, Wang Weiyi sponsored the casting of two life- size bronze figures marked with acupuncture points, a momentous event in the development of acupuncture and moxibustion.

Zhenjiu Zishengjing (针灸资生经 *A Classic of Acupuncture and Moxibustion Therapy*) published in A. D. 1220 was compiled by Wang Zhizhong of the Song Dynasty. This is a book in which the author comprehensively cites materials on acupuncture and moxibustion of the past era and combines them with his own clinical experience.

Shisijing Fahui (十四经发挥 *The Enlargement of the Fourteen Channels*, A.D. 1341) is a work by Hua Boren of the Yuan Dynasty. The book discusses systematically the courses and distribution of the twelve regular channels, of the Ren Channel and the Du Channels, as well as discussing the acupuncture points relating to them. It is a valuable reference book for the study of the theory of channels and collaterals.

Zhenjiu Dacheng (针灸大成 *Compendium of Acupuncture and Moxibustion*, A.D. 1601) is a work by Yang Jizhou, an acupuncturist of the Ming Dynasty. Here, the author systematically collected the literature and source material on acupuncture and moxibustion of past generations and presented methods of treatment secretly handed down to him by his ancestors. It has been an indispensable reference book in studying acupuncture and moxibustion in the nearly four centuries since its publication.

Historical records document the spread of Chinese acupuncture and moxibuston to other countries at a very early date. Their practice was introduced to Korea in the 6th century, going to Japan in the same period when a monk named Zhi Cong travelled eastward by sea, carrying with him *Mingtangtu* (明堂图 *Illustrated Manual of Channels, Collaterals and Acupuncture Points*), *Zhenjiu Jiayijing* and other medical books. In the late 17th century, acupuncture and moxibustion methods spread further to Europe. All of this actively promoted the medical and cultural exchange between China and other countries of the world.

From 1840 up to the eve of China's liberation, the country was under the reactionary rule of semi-feudalism and semi-colonialism. Her science and culture were devastated and traditional Chinese medicine, including acupuncture and moxibustion, was on the verge of extinction. After the founding of the People's Republic of China, enlightened by the Party's policy concerning traditional Chinese medicine as formulated by China's great leader and teacher Chairman Mao Zedong, Chinese medicine and pharmacology rejuvenated, and acupuncture and moxibustion became popular throughout the country. Acupuncture analgesia, a new technique of anaesthesia and new achievement in the field of acupuncture, was creatively developed on the basis of experience in relieving pain by needling. During the proletarian cultural revolution, owing to interference and sabotage by the "gang of four", acupuncture and moxibustion together with other branches of science suffered once again. With the downfall of the "gang of four", science and technology revived. Under the leadership of the Chinese Communist Party the prospects are again bright for further development in the field of acupuncture and moxibustion. Friendly contacts and academic exchanges between Chinese people and those of various other countries have increased in recent years. Many foreign friends have come to China to investigate and study acupuncture and moxibustion methods. We have revised the book *Essentials of Chinese Acupuncture* as to include our teaching experience gained in the recent years of our acupuncture courses for foreign doctors, and present this volume as a textbook on acupuncture and moxibustion. Sponsored by the Ministry of Public Health of the People's Republic of China, the work should facilitate technical exchange and promote international friendship.

The book consists of three parts. Part I is devoted to a general description of the basic knowledge of traditional Chinese medicine. In Part II, channels, collaterls and acupuncture points are introduced. Part III dwells on acupuncture and moixbustion therapy. Ear acupuncture therapy and acupuncture analgesia are also dealt with. Popular in style with fairly concise presentation, the book is written with the intention of maintaining an integral theoretical system of Chinese acupuncture and moxibusiton so as to give readers a comprehensive concept of Chinese acupuncture. Like any other branch of science, a basic knowledge is prerequisite to practice. For further study, it is advisable to combine theory with practice for perfection of the art. Finally, we sincerely hope that readers will offer their comments and suggestions with a view to a yet more useful next revision.

PART I

A GENERAL DESCRIPTION OF THE BASIC KNOWLEDGE OF TRADITIONAL CHINESE MEDICINE

T RADITIONAL Chinese medicine, a summary of the experience of the Chinese labouring people in struggling against disease for thousands of years, is invaluable for its rich practical knowledge and a unique integrated theoretical system established since ancient times.

The basic knowledge of traditional Chinese medicine mainly includes the theories of *yin-yang*, the five elements, *zang-fu*, channels and collaterals, *qi**, blood and body fluid, etiology, methods of diagnosis, and differentiation of syndromes.

Acupuncture and moxibustion are important component parts of traditional Chinese medicine. Like its other branches, they have developed on the basis of traditional Chinese medical principles. Part I therefore gives a general description of the basic knowledge of traditional Chinese medicine.

---

* *Yin-yang, zang-fu* and *qi* are phonetic transcriptions of Chinese characters whose equivalents will be given respectively in Chapters I, II and IV.

CHAPTER I

YIN-YANG AND THE FIVE ELEMENTS

The theories of *yin-yang* and the five elements were two kinds of outlook on nature in ancient China. They involved a naive concept of materialism and dialectics and actively promoted natural science in China. Ancient physicians applied these two theories in their field, which greatly influenced the formation and development of the theoretical system of traditional Chinese medicine and have guided clinical work up to the present.

I. Yin-Yang

The theory *yin-yang* holds that every object or phenomenon in the universe consists of two opposite aspects, namely, *yin* and *yang*, which are at once in conflict and in interdependence; further, that this relation between *yin* and *yang* is the universal law of the material world, the principle and source of the existence of myriads of things, and the root cause for the flourishing and perishing of things.

The theory of *yin-yang* mainly expounds the opposition, interdepending, inter-consuming-supporting and inter-transforming relation of *yin* and *yang*. These relationships between *yin* and *yang* are extensively used in traditional Chinese medicine to explain the physiology and pathology of the human body and serve as a guide to diagnosis and treatment in clinical work.

1. The opposition and interdependence of *yin* and *yang*

The opposition of *yin* and *yang* generalizes the contradiction and struggle of the two opposites within an object or a phenomenon. Ancient scholars used water and fire to symbolize the basic properties of *yin* and *yang*. That is to say, the basic properties of *yin* simulate those of water, including coldness, downward direction, dimness, etc., while the basic properties of *yang* are like those of fire, including hotness, upward direction, brightness, etc. From this, it can be inferred that anything that has the characteristics of quiescence, coldness, lower position (or downward direction), interior position (or inward direction), dimness, asthenia, inhibition, slowness, or which is substantial, etc., pertains to *yin*; whereas anything that is moving, hot, in an upper position (or moving in an upward direction), exterior position (or outward), bright, sthenic, excited, rapid, non-substantial etc., belongs to *yang*.

Since the *yin-yang* nature of a thing exists only by comparison, and moreover that a thing can be divided infinitely, its *yin-yang* nature is by no means absolute, but is relative. In some circumstances the two opposites of a thing may change, and so the *yin-yang* nature of the thing also changes. There exist the conditions of a *yin* aspect developing within *yin*, *yang* within *yang*, *yang* complicated with *yin*, and *yin* complicated with *yang*. This concept conforms with objective reality.

The tissues and organs of the human body may pertain either to *yin* or *yang* according to their relative locations and functions. Viewing the body as a whole, the trunk surface and the four extremities, being on the exterior, pertain to *yang*, while the *zang-fu* organs* are inside the body and are *yin*. Viewing the body surface and the four extremities alone, the back pertains to *yang*, while the chest and abdomen pertain to *yin*; the portion above the waist pertains to *yang* and that below pertains to *yin*; the lateral aspect of the four extremities pertains to *yang* and the medial aspect to *yin*; the channels running along the lateral aspect of an extremity pertain to *yang*, while those along the medial aspect pertain to *yin*. When speaking of the *zang-fu* organs alone, the *fu* organs with their main function of transmitting and digesting food pertain to *yang*; while the *zang* organs with their main function of storing vital essence and vital energy pertain to *yin*. Each of the *zang-fu* organs itself can again be divided into *yin* or *yang,* e.g., the *yin* and the *yang* of the kidney, the *yin* and the *yang* of the stomach, etc. In short, however complex the tissues and structures of the human body and their functional activities, they can be generalized and explained by the relation of *yin* and *yang*.

The interdepending relation of *yin* and *yang* means that each of the two aspects is the condition for the other's existence and neither of them can exist in isolation. For instance, without daytime there would be no night;

---

* Zang-fu organs correspond to viscera in modern medicine. For details, see Chapter II.

without excitation there would be no inhibition. Hence, it can be seen that *yin* and *yang* are at once in opposition and in interdependence; they rely on each other for existence, coexisting in a single entity. The movement and change of a thing are due not only to the opposition and conflict between *yin* and *yang* but also to their relationship of interdependence and mutual support.

In physiological activities, the transformation of substances into function or vice versa verifies the theory of the interdepending relation of *yin* and *yang*. Substance pertains to *yin* and function to *yang*, the former being the basis of the latter, while the latter is the reflection of the existence of the former and also the motive force for the production of the former. Only when there are ample nutrient substances can the functional activities of the *zang-fu* organs be healthy. Contrariwise, only when the functional activities of the *zang-fu* organs are sound are they able constantly to stimulate the production of nutrient substances. The coordination and equilibrium between substance and function are the vital guarantee of physiological activities. Hence we find in *Neijing*: "Yin is installed in the interior as the material foundation of *yang*, while *yang* remains on the exterior as the manifestation of the function of *yin*."

2. The inter-consuming-supporting and the inter-transforming relation of *yin* and *yang*

Consuming implies losing or weakening; supporting implies gaining or strengthening. The two aspects of *yin* and *yang* within a thing are not fixed, but in a state of constant motion. Owing to their mutual conflict and support, the losing or gaining of one aspect will inevitably influence the other. For instance, consuming of *yin* leads to gaining of *yang*, while consuming of *yang* results in gaining of *yin*. On the other hand, gaining of *yin* leads to consuming of *yang*, and gaining of *yang* results in consuming of *yin*. The functional activities of the human body require a certain amount of nutrient substances, resulting in a process of consuming of *yin* and gaining of *yang*, whereas the formation and storing of nutrient substances depends upon the functional activities and weakens the functional energy to a certain degree, causing a process of gaining of *yin* and consuming of *yang*. But such mutual consuming-supporting does not result in absolute equilibrium. Under normal conditions these opposites maintain a relative balance, while under abnormal conditions preponderance or discomfiture of *yin* or *yang* occurs.

In the inter-consuming and inter-supporting process, when there is any manifestation of losing the relative balance of *yin* and *yang* and failing to resume the balance, there results a preponderance or discomfiture of either *yin* or *yang*. This is the causative factor of the occurrence of disease. That is, whenever *yin* or *yang* is in a state of preponderance or discomfiture, it becomes an etiological factor. For instance, preponderance of harmful *yin* will consume *yang*, and discomfiture of *yang* will lead to a preponderance of *yin*, either of which may initiate a cold syndrome; on the other hand, preponderance of harmful *yang* will consume *yin*, and discomfiture of *yin* will cause a preponderance of *yang*, either of which stimulates a heat syndrome. However, the syndromes of cold or heat due to a preponderance of harmful factors pertain to the *shi* (实 excess) type, while those of cold or heat due to lowering the general resistance pertain to the *xu* (虚 deficiency) type.* These two types of syndromes are different in nature and the principles of treatment are consequently also different; i.e., the reducing (泻 *xie*) method for syndromes of the *shi* (excess) type and the reinforcing (补 *bu*) method for those of the *xu* (deficiency) type. (Fig. 1.)

Since the occurrence of a disease is the outcome of imbalance between *yin* and *yang*, all the methods of treatment should aim at reconciling the two and restoring them to a condition of relative balance. In acupuncture treatment, points on the right side may be selected to treat disorders of the left side and vice versa, while points on the lower portion of the body may be selected to treat disorders of the upper portion and vice versa. All these methods are based on the concept of regarding the body as an organic whole, and the aim of treatment is to readjust the relation of *yin* and *yang* and promote circulation of *qi* and blood.

The inter-transformation of *yin* and *yang* means that in certain circumstances and at a certain stage of development, each of the two aspects of *yin* and *yang* within a thing will transform itself into its opposite, i.e., *yin* transforms into *yang* and *yang* into *yin*. Whether the transformation actually takes place depends upon whether there exists the possibility of change in the thing itself. Given this possibility, the external conditions are also indispensable.

The development and change of a thing require a process, and the external conditions for transformation maturing gradually. The inter-

---

* *Xu* (deficiency) and *shi* (excess) are two principles in differentiation of syndromes. *Xu* (deficiency) implies lowered body resistance due to hypofunction or insufficiency of certain materials; *shi* (excess) indicates a pathological condition in which the exogenous etiological factor is violent while the general resistance of the body is still intact.

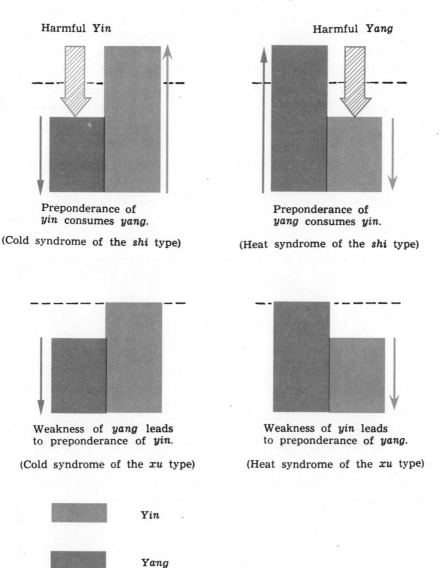

Equilibrium of *yin* and *yang*

Harmful *Yin*

Harmful *Yang*

Preponderance of
yin consumes *yang*.

(Cold syndrome of the *shi* type)

Preponderance of
yang consumes *yin*.

(Heat syndrome of the *shi* type)

Weakness of *yang* leads
to preponderance of *yin*.

(Cold syndrome of the *xu* type)

Weakness of *yin* leads
to preponderance of *yang*.

(Heat syndrome of the *xu* type)

Yin

Yang

Fig. 1. Preponderance and discomfiture of *yin* and *yang*.

transformation between *yin* and *yang* follows this rule. According to *Nei-jing*: "There must be quiescence after excessive motion; extreme *yang* will become *yin*." And, "The generation of a thing is due to transformation; the degeneration of a thing is due to transmutation." This is precisely the meaning of the old saying: "Once a certain limit is reached, a change to the opposite direction is inevitable," and the quantitative changes lead to qualitative change.

The inter-transformation of *yin* and *yang* is the universal law governing the development and change of things. The alternation of the four seasons is an example. Spring with its warmth sets in when the cold winter has reached its height, and the cool autumn arrives when the hot summer has reached its climax. The change in the nature of a disease is another example. A patient with continued high fever in an acute febrile disease may have a lowering of body temperature, pallor and cold extremities with weak and thready pulse, indicating that the nature of the disease has changed from *yang* to *yin*, and then the method of treatment for this patient should be changed accordingly.

The above is a brief introduction to the theory of *yin-yang*, with some examples to illustrate its application in traditional Chinese medicine. In short, the relation of inter-opposing, inter-depending, inter-consuming-supporting and inter-transforming of *yin* and *yang* can be summarized as the law of the unity of opposites. Further, these four relationships between *yin* and *yang* are not isolated from one another but interconnected, one influencing the others and each being the cause or effect of the others.

II. THE FIVE ELEMENTS

The theory of the five elements holds that wood, fire, earth, metal and water are basic materials constituting the material world. There exists among them an interdependence and inter-restraint which determines their state of constant motion and change.

The theory of the five elements basically explains the inter-promoting, inter-acting, over-acting and counter-acting relationship among them. Its application to traditional Chinese medicine is in classifying into different categories natural phenomena plus the tissues and organs of the human body and the human emotions and interpreting the relationship between the physiology and pathology of the human body and the natural environment with the law of the inter-promoting, inter-acting, over-acting and counter-acting of the five elements. This theory is used as a guide in medical practice.

1. Attribution of things to the five elements

Man lives in nature. The natural environment, such as weather changes and geographic conditions, greatly influences his physiological activities. This fact is manifest in man's dependence on the environment, but also in his adaptability to the environment. This is known as correspondence between man and nature. Proceeding from this recognition, traditional Chinese medicine comprehensively connects the physiology and pathology of the *zang-fu* organs and tissues with many important natural environmental factors. These factors are classified into five categories on the basis of the five elements. Similes and allegories are used to explain the complicated links between physiology and pathology as well as the correlation between man and the natural environment. The following table shows the five categories of things classified according to the five elements. (Tab. 1.)

2. The inter-promoting, inter-acting, over-acting and counteracting relation of the five elements

Promoting here implies promoting growth. The order of promoting is that wood promotes fire, fire promotes earth, earth promotes metal, metal promotes water, and water in turn promotes wood. In this interpromoting relation of the five elements, each is in the position of "being promoted" and of "promoting", the promoting element being thought of as the "mother" and the promoted element as the "son", forming what is known as the "mother-son" relationship. Wood for example is promoted by water, which is the "mother" of wood, while fire is the "son" of wood, being promoted by wood.

Acting here connotes bringing under control or restraint. In the interacting relation of the five elements, the order is that wood acts on earth, earth acts on water, water acts on fire, fire acts on metal, and metal in turn acts on wood. In this relationship, each of the five elements occupies the position of "being acted on" and "acting on". Wood for example is acted upon by metal, while it acts on earth.

In the complicated correlation among things, neither promotion of growth nor control is dispensable. Without promotion of growth there would be no birth and development; without control, excessive growth would result in harm. For instance, wood promotes fire and also acts on earth, while earth in turn promotes metal and acts on water. In the promotion of growth there thus resides control, and in control there exists promotion of growth. They are in opposition and also co-operation,

Tab. 1. The Five categories of things classified according to the five elements.

Five Elements	Human Body					Nature					
	Zang	Fu	Five Sense Organs	Five Tissues	Emotions	Seasons	Environmental factors	Growth & Development	Colours	Tastes	Orientations
Wood	Liver	Gall bladder	Eye	Tendon	Anger	Spring	Wind	Germination	Green	Sour	East
Fire	Heart	Small intestine	Tongue	Vessel	Joy	Summer	Heat	Growth	Red	Bitter	South
Earth	Spleen	Stomach	Mouth	Muscle	Meditation	Late summer	Dampness	Transformation	Yellow	Sweet	Middle
Metal	Lung	Large intestine	Nose	Skin & hair	Grief & melancholy	Autumn	Dryness	Reaping	White	Pungent	West
Water	Kidney	Urinary bladder	Ear	Bone	Fright & fear	Winter	Cold	Storing	Black	Salty	North

and so a relative balance is maintained between promoting and acting, which ensures the normal growth and development of things. In case of excess or insufficiency in the five elements there will appear phenomena of abnormal inter-acting known as over-acting or counter-acting.

Over-acting takes the form of launching an attack when a counterpart is weak. Clinically, this is conventionally called inter-acting. For example, "wood over-acting on earth, can also be called "wood acting on earth". The order of over-acting is the same as that of acting except that over-acting is not a normal inter-action but a harmful one occurring under certain conditions. Counter-acting implies preying upon (other elements). The order is just opposite to that of inter-acting. (Fig. 2.)

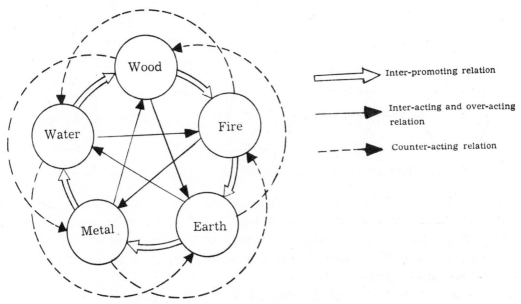

Fig. 2. Inter-promoting, inter-acting, over-acting and counter-acting relations among the five elements: Wood, Fire, Earth, Metal, and Water.

The phenomena of over-acting and counter-acting caused by excess or insufficiency of any one of the five elements often manifest themselves simultaneously. For instance, when wood is in excess it not only over-acts on earth, it also counter-acts on metal. Another example. When wood is in insufficiency, it is over-acted on by metal and counter-acted on by earth at the same time. (Fig. 3.)

The theory of the five elements applies in the medical field in using the inter-promoting, inter-acting, over-acting and counter-acting relation of the five elements to expound the interdepending and inter-restrain-

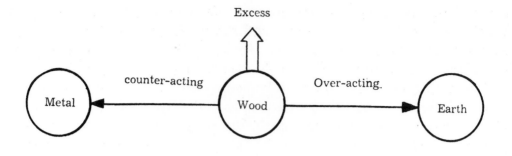

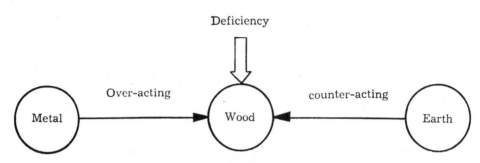

Fig. 3. Over-acting and counter-acting among the five elements.

ing relation among the *zang-fu* organs, sense organs and tissues, and also the correlation between man and nature. The theory is used mainly, however, to explain the changes, etiology and mechanism of the disease.

When an internal organ is inflicted, other organs may be affected, or the disease may spread or change into another kind of disease. Analysed according to the theory of the five elements, the complex changes that occur in disease all come under the following four conditions: over-acting, counter-acting, disorder of the "mother affecting the son" and vice-versa. Lung trouble for example may be due to disorder of the lung itself. But if the lung is affected by disorder of spleen, the disease is referred to as a disorder of the "mother affecting the son". If it is due to disorder of the kidney, it is known as disorder of the "son affecting the mother". Pulmonary disease may in some cases be caused by cardiac disorders, and this is known as fire over-acting on metal. If it is due to impairment of the liver, it is explained as wood counter-acting on metal. These five categories of the five elements and their inter-promoting, inter-acting, over-acting and counter-acting relation are also used in ascertaining pathological conditions. For instance a greenish tinge in the complexion accompanied with a preference for sour food suggests liver trouble; a florid complexion accompanied by a bitter taste in the mouth suggests heart trouble. Disorder of the spleen accompanied by a greenish complexion implies wood (liver) over-acting on earth (spleen); the condition of a patient suffering from heart trouble and whose complexion is abnormally dark may be explained as water (kidney) acting on fire (heart). If the above correlation of a disease is studied thoroughly the findings may be taken as a guide in treating the disease and preventing it from affecting another part of the body. Its possible transformation into other diseases may be controlled, so that the course of treatment can be shortened and the disease cured in an early stage.

In short, the theories of *yin-yang* and the five elements are two outlooks on nature in ancient China, both encompassing rudimentary concepts of materialism and dialectics and to some extent reflecting the objective law of things. They are of practical significance in explaining physiological activities and explaining pathological changes in guiding medical practice. In clinical application the two are usually related with and supplement each other and cannot be entirely separated. As for shortcomings in the two theories, by adhering to the scientific attitude of dialectical and historical materialism, we can continue making progress in our medical practice and promote the further development of traditional Chinese medicine in the light of constantly summing up our experience.

CHAPTER II

ZANG-FU (Internal Organs)

The term *zang-fu* in traditional Chinese medicine refers to the gross anatomical entities of the internal organs. At the same time, it is also a generalization of the physiological functions of the human body. The heart, liver, spleen, lung, kidney and pericardium grouped together are known as the six *zang* organs. Their main physiological functions are manufacturing and storing essential substances including vital essence, *qi* (vital energy), blood and body fluid. The small intestine, gall bladder, stomach, large intestine, urinary bladder and *sanjiao* are known collectively as the six *fu* organs. Their main functions are to receive and digest food, absorb nutrient substances, and transmit and excrete wastes. There are in addition extraordinary *fu* organs including the brain and the uterus.

The *zang* organs are different in function from the *fu*, but the difference is only relative. In physiological activities, a structural and functional connection as well as co-ordination exists not only among the *zang* and the *fu* organs as separate entities, but also among the *zang* and *fu* organs collectively, and even among the *zang-fu* organs on the one hand and the five sense organs and five tissues* on the other. The theory of *zang-fu* taking the five *zang* organs (six including the pericardium) as core explains the peculiarity of traditional Chinese medicine, i.e. the concept of regarding the body as an integral whole physiologically and pathologically.

I. THE ZANG ORGANS

1. Heart

The channel of the heart, located in the thorax, leads to the small intestine, and heart is thus externally and internally related to the small

---

*See Tab. 1.

intestine. (Each *zang* organ is linked with a *fu* organ by a channel, a situation known as external-internal relation.) The heart also opens into the tongue. (Each *zang* organ opens into a sense organ which indicates a close structural or physiological and pathological relationship between the internal organs and the sense organs.) The main physiological functions of the heart are controlling blood and vessels and housing the mind.

(1) Controlling blood and vessels. Vessels are the site of blood containment and circulation, the impulse of the heart sending blood incessantly through the vessels to nourish the whole body. When blood supply is sufficient and blood circulation normal, the complexion will be rosy and lustrous, and vitality full. The tissues and organs are well nourished and function properly.

(2) Housing the mind. The heart is considered the main organ governing mental activities and generalizing the physiological function of the brain. Spirit, consciousness, memory, thinking and sleep are all dominated by this function of the heart.

The two functions of the heart have a mutual effect and correlation. According to *Neijing*: "The heart dominates the vessels and the vessels supply the mind."

(3) Opening into the tongue. The two functions of the heart, i.e., controlling blood and vessels and housing the mind, are closely related to the colour, form, motility and sense of taste of the tongue. This is also expressed as "the tongue is the mirror of the heart".

2. Liver

The liver is situated in the right hypochondriac region, its channel connecting with the gall bladder relating it externally-internally with the gall bladder. The liver opens into the eye. Its main physiological functions are storing blood, maintaining patency for the flow of *qi* (vital function), and controlling the tendons.

(1) Storing blood. The liver possesses the function of storing blood and regulating the volume of circulating blood. During rest, part of the blood remains in the liver, while during vigorous activity blood is released from the liver to increase the volume of blood in circulation to the required amount. The liver, therefore, along with the heart, supplies the tissues and organs with blood, and it influences menstruation as well.

(2) Maintaining patency for the flow of *qi* (vital functions) means that the liver is responsible for harmonious and unobstructed functional activities of the human body, including the following three aspects:

— 23 —

a. The liver is related to emotional activities, especially depression and anger. Prolonged mental depression or a fit of anger may weaken the liver so that it is unable to promote the unrestrained and free flow of *qi*. Conversely, dysfunction of the liver is often accompanied by emotional changes such as mental depression and irascibility.

b. The harmonious and free-flowing functional activity of the liver promotes the functioning of the other *zang-fu* organs, channels and collaterals, especially those of the spleen and stomach in digestion and absorption.

c. This function of the liver also affects bile secretion, its storage in the gall bladder and excretion into the intestines.

(3) Controlling the tendons. The *yin* and blood of the liver nourish the tendons, keeping them in a normal state of contraction and relaxation. When the liver is supplied with ample *yin* and blood, the tendons are strong and free in extension and flexion.

(4) Opening into the eye. Each *zang-fu* organ has a certain influence on the function of the eye. However, because the liver stores blood and its channel directly communicates with the eye, it has a closer relation to ocular function, such as vision and movement of the eye, than other *zang-fu* organs.

3. Spleen

The channel of the spleen connects with the stomach, relating the spleen externally-internally to the stomach. It opens into the mouth. The main physiological functions of the spleen are governing transportation and transformation, controlling blood and dominating the muscles.

(1) Governing transportation and transformation. Transportation implies transmission. Transformation implies digestion and absorption. The spleen has the function of digesting food, absorbing its essential substances with a part of the fluid supplied, and transmitting them to the heart and the lung from where they are sent to nourish the whole body. Normal functioning of the spleen is required for good appetite, normal digestion and absorption, good nourishment and normal transmission of fluid.

(2) Controlling blood. The spleen has the function of keeping the blood circulating inside the vessels and preventing it from extravasation.

(3) Dominating the muscles. Normal functioning of the spleen in transportation and transformation enables the muscles to receive adequate nourishment from the food essentials and thus maintains muscle thickness and strength.

(4) Opening into the mouth. The spleen and the mouth co-ordinate functionally in receiving, transporting and transforming food. When the function of the spleen in governing transportation and transformation is normal, the appetite will be good and the lips will be red and lustrous.

The qi of the spleen has the further function of holding and keeping the internal organs in their normal positions.

4. Lung

The lung, situated in the thorax, has its channel connecting with the large intestine and it is therefore externally-internally related to the large intestine. It opens into the nose. Its main physiological functions are dominating qi (air) and controlling respiration, regulating water passages and dominating the skin and hair.

(1) Dominating qi (air) and controlling respiration. The lung is a respiratory organ. Through its function of dispersing a.d descending*, it inhales clean qi to supply the body's functions and exhales waste qi. This is what is known as the function of "getting rid of the stale and taking in the fresh". As the function of the lung greatly influences the functional activities of the whole body, the lung is said to dominate the qi (vital functions) of the entire body.

(2) Regulating water passages. The dispersing and descending function of the lung regulates water passages, promoting water metabolism. Its dispersing function turns a part of the body fluid into sweat to be excreted, while its descending function continuously sends a part of the body fluid down to the kidney and on to the urinary bladder to be excreted as urine.

(3) Dominating the skin and hair. Here the skin and hair signify the entire body surface. The lung disperses the essentials of food to the body surface, giving lustre to the skin, gloss and luxuriance to the hair, and regulating the opening and closing of the pores.

---

* Traditional Chinese medicine holds that the lung, owing to its dispersing nature, can promote the diffusion of qi (vital energy, air), blood and body fluid into every portion of the body, interiorly and exteriorly. Dysfunction of the lung in dispersing may lead to tightness of the chest, nasal obstruction, cough and expectoration.

The lung is also described as having a descending nature by virtue of its location in the upper part of the body. It is said that normally all internal organs situated in the upper part of the body have a descending nature, while those in the lower part have an ascending nature. The descending nature of the lung promotes regular breathing and smooth circulation of body fluid, sends qi (including breath) downward and so provides the conditions for the undisturbed performance of lung function. Failure in this descending nature may cause coughing, asthma, etc.

(4) Opening into the nose. The nose is the "gateway" of respiration. Unobstructed breathing and a keen sense of smell depend on good function of the lung.

5. Kidney

The kidney locates at either side of the lumbus. Its channel connects with the urinary bladder, with which it is externally-internally related. It opens into the ear. Its main physiological functions are (1) storing essential substances and dominating human reproduction, growth and development; (2) producing marrow which collects in the head forming the brain, dominating the bones and manufacturing blood; (3) dominating body fluid, and (4) receiving *qi* (air).

(1) Storing essence and dominating reproduction, growth and development. The essence in the kidney, also referred to as the *yin* of the kidney, consists of two parts: congenital essence inherited from the parents and acquired essence transformed from the essential substances of food. The vital essence of the kidney is an important aspect of the *qi* (vital functions) of the kidney, greatly influencing the function of the kidney in reproduction, growth and development. *Neijing* gives a precise description of the physiological function of the kidney in the process of birth, growth, full development and senility: At the age of about 14 for women and 16 for men, the *qi* of the kidney flourishes. Women will have the onset of menstruation, and men will have seminal emission, both signifying the power of reproduction. When women reach the age of 28 and men around 32, the *qi* of the kidney is at its height, the body grows and develops, reaching the prime of life. When women reach the age of 49 and men around 64, the *qi* of the kidney starts to decline, the body begins to wither and at the same time the function of reproduction gradually fails.

(2) Producing marrow, forming up the brain, dominating the bones and manufacturing blood. The kidney stores essence which can produce marrow (including spinal cord and bone marrow). The upper part of the spinal cord connects with the brain, while the bone marrow nourishes the bones and manufactures blood. The supply to the brain, the solidity of the bone, and the adequacy of the blood are therefore all closely related to the condition of the essence of the kidney.

(3) Dominating water metabolism. The part of fluid sent down by the descending function of the lung reaches the kidney. There it is divided by the *yang* function of the kidney into two parts: clear and turbid. The clear fluid (i.e., the part which is useful) is retained, and the turbid fluid

(i.e., the waste part) flows into the urinary bladder to form urine which is excreted.

(4) Receiving *qi* (air). Respiration is accomplished mainly by the lung, but the kidney helps through its function of controlling reception of *qi* (air). The distribution of the clean *qi* inhaled by the lung to the whole body depends not only on the descending function of the lung but also on the kidney's function of reception and control.

(5) Opening into the ear. The auditory function is dependent upon the nourishment from the *qi* of the kidney. Deafness in aged people is mainly due to deficiency of the *qi* of the kidney.

6. Pericardium

The pericardium is a membrane surrounding the heart. Its channel connects with *sanjiao*, with which it is externally-internally related. Its main function is to protect the heart. The pericardium is not generally regarded as an independent organ but as an attachment to the heart.

II. *FU* ORGANS

1. Small intestine

The small intestine is situated in the abdomen, its upper end connected by the pylorus with the stomach and its lower end communicating with the large intestine through the ileocecum. Its channel connects with the heart, with which it is externally-internally related. Its main function is to receive and temporarily store partially digested food in the stomach. Further digesting the food and absorbing the essential substance and a part of the water in food, the small intestine transfers the residues with a considerable amount of fluid to the large intestine.

2. Gall bladder

The gall bladder is attached to the liver, with which its channel connects and with which it is externally-internally related. Its main function is to store bile and continuously excrete it to the intestines to help digestion. This function of the gall bladder is closely related to the function of the liver in promoting patency of vital energy. It is therefore said that the liver and gall bladder preside over the unrestraint and patency of vital energy.

3. Stomach

The stomach is situated in the epigastrium, its upper outlet connected by the cardia with the esophagus, and its lower outlet communicating with the small intestine through the pylorus. Its channel connects with the spleen, with which it is externally-internally related. Its main function is to receive and decompose food. That is to say, the stomach receives and temporarily stores the food mass coming from the mouth through the esophagus while partially digesting it and then sending it downward to the small intestine. That is why the function of the stomach is normal when its *qi* is descending and abnormal when its *qi* is ascending. The stomach and spleen act in co-operation and are the main organs carrying on the functions of digestion and absorption. It is said that the spleen and stomach are the source of health.

4. Large intestine

The large intestine is situated in the abdomen, its upper end connected with the small intestine by the ileocecum and its lower end communicating with the exterior of the body through the anus. Its channel connects with the lung, with which it is externally-internally related. The main function of the large intestine is to receive the waste material sent down from the small intestine and, in the process of transporting it to the anus, absorb a part of its fluid content and then turn it into feces to be excreted by the body.

5. Urinary bladder

The urinary bladder is situated in the lower abdomen. Its channel connects with the kidney, with which it is externally-internally related. Its main function is the temporary storage of urine and its discharge from the body when a certain amount has accumulated. This function of the urinary bladder is accomplished with the assistance of the *qi* (function) of the kidney.

6. *Sanjiao*

The channel of *sanjiao* connects with the pericardium with which it is externally-internally related. *Sanjiao* is not a substantial organ, but a generalization of part of the functions of some of the *zang-fu* organs located in different sections of the body cavity.

Sanjiao is divided into three parts:

(1) Upper *jiao* (portion) (representing the chest) is a generalization of the function of the heart and lung in transporting *qi* and blood to nourish various parts of the body. It is like an all-pervading vapour.

(2) Middle *jiao* (portion) (representing the epigastrium) is a generalization of the function of the spleen and stomach in digestion and absorption. This may be compared to soaking things in water to cause decomposition and dissolution of substances.

(3) Lower *jiao* (portion) (representing the hypogastrium) is a generalization of functions of the kidney and urinary bladder in controlling water metabolism as well as storage and excretion of urine. It is like an aqueduct, a pathway for the flowing of water.

III. EXTRAORDINARY ORGANS

A brief introduction to the brain and the uterus is given as follows:

1. Brain

As early as in the book *Neijing* there were descriptions of the brain, one of which is as follows: "The brain is a sea of marrow. Its upper part is under the scalp of the vertex, point Baihui (Du 20) and its lower part reaches point Fengfu (Du 16)." Subsequently a further understanding of the brain was obtained; that is, it was recognized in *Yixue Yuanshi* (医学原始 *Origin of Medical Science*) that "the sense organs, i.e., the ears, eyes, mouth and nose, are in the head close to the brain. Owing to their highest and most obvious position, they may perceive objects, which will impress the brain directly and remain in the brain". Also, it was suggested in *Yilin Gaicuo* (医林改错 *Medical Correction*) that thinking and memorization are the main functions of the brain. As mentioned previously, the essence of the kidney produces marrow that forms the brain. The filling of the "sea" of marrow depends on the essence of the kidney. Furthermore, the heart, which houses the mind, and the liver, which dominates the unrestraint and patency of vital functions, are also related to mental activities. A tenet of traditional Chinese medicine, therefore, is that mental activity is dominated by various organs, the heart being the main one.

2. Uterus

The function of the uterus is to preside over menstruation and nourish the fetus. Internal organs and channels related to the function of the uterus are as follows:

(1) Kidney. The uterus is connected with the kidney, and only when the essence of the kidney is ample can the menstrual period recur regularly, and the impregnation and growth of the fetus be possible.

(2) Liver. The liver performs the function of storing blood and regulating the volume of circulating blood, which is also responsible for normal menstruation.

(3) Ren Channel and Chong Channel. Both originate in the uterus. The Ren Channel regulates the functions of all the *yin* channels and nourishes

the fetus. The Chong Channel has the function of regulating the *qi* and blood of the twelve regular channels. The *qi* and blood of the twelve regular channels pass into the uterus through the two channels, affecting the amount of menstrual flow and its cycle.

CHAPTER III

CHANNELS AND COLLATERALS

The channels and collaterals are distributed all over the human body, linking the interior *zang-fu* organs with the various tissues and organs of the superficial portion of the body to make the body an organic integrity. In the network of the channels and collaterals, the channels are the main trunks which pertain to the respective *zang-fu* organs, while the collaterals are their minor branches distributed over the entire body.

I. NOMENCLATURE AND CLASSIFICATION

The system of channels and collaterals mainly consists of the twelve regular channels, the eight extra channels and the fifteen collaterals. The twelve regular channels, together with the Ren Channel and the Du Channel of the eight extra channels, form the fourteen channels, along each of which are points for applying acupuncture and moxibustion.

The complete name of each of the twelve regular channels is composed of three parts: (1) hand or foot, (2) *yin* or *yang* (*yin* is again divided into Taiyin, Shaoyin and Jueyin, and *yang* into Taiyang, Yangming and Shaoyang), and (3) a *zang* or a *fu* organ. The hand or foot in the name of a channel depends on whether the channel starts or terminates at the hand or the foot, while *yin* or *yang* and a *zang* or a *fu* organ are determined by whether it takes its course along the medial or the lateral aspect of the limb, and which *zang* or *fu* organ it pertains to. For instance, the channel which terminates at the hand, runs along the medial aspect of the upper limb and pertains to the lung is named the Lung Channel of Hand-Taiyin.

The eight extra channels are the Du, Ren, Chong, Dai, Yangqiao, Yinqiao, Yangwei and Yinwei Channels. Their courses of distribution are different from those of the twelve regular channels and they do not pertain to or connect with the *zang-fu* organs.

Each of the names of the eight extra channels conveys a special meaning: *Du* means governing; that is to say, the Du Channel has the function of governing all the *yang* channels. *Ren* means responsibility; that is, the Ren Channel is responsible to all the *yin* channels. *Chong* means vital; that is, the Chong Channel is a vital channel communicating with all the channels. *Dai* is a girdle; it implies that the Dai Channel has the function of binding up all the channels. *Qiao* is the heel. It means that the Yinqiao and Yangqiao Channels start from the foot, giving agile motility. *Wei* denotes connection; it means that the Yinwei and Yangwei Channels connect respectively with all the *yin* and *yang* channels.

Each of the twelve regular channels possesses a collateral. These added to the two collaterals of the Du and Ren Channels and the major collateral of the spleen form the fifteen collaterals.

Table 2 classifies the channels and collaterals.

The twelve regular channels are distributed interiorly and exteriorly over the body. The *qi* and blood circulate in the channels in a definite order, starting from the Lung Channel of Hand-Taiyin, flowing to other channels in an arranged pattern, completing a cycle when the Liver Channel of Foot-Jueyin is reached and then flowing again to the Lung Channel of Hand-Taiyin to start another cycle. The following table shows the order of circulation. (Tab. 3.)

Tab. 3. The order of circulation of the *qi* and blood in the twelve regular channels.

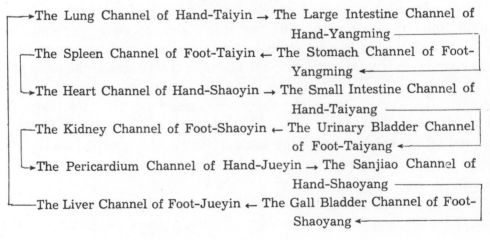

The Lung Channel of Hand-Taiyin → The Large Intestine Channel of Hand-Yangming

The Spleen Channel of Foot-Taiyin ← The Stomach Channel of Foot-Yangming ←

The Heart Channel of Hand-Shaoyin → The Small Intestine Channel of Hand-Taiyang

The Kidney Channel of Foot-Shaoyin ← The Urinary Bladder Channel of Foot-Taiyang ←

The Pericardium Channel of Hand-Jueyin → The Sanjiao Channel of Hand-Shaoyang

The Liver Channel of Foot-Jueyin ← The Gall Bladder Channel of Foot-Shaoyang ←

Tab. 2. Classification of channels and collaterals.

The system of channels & collaterals

- The twelve regular channels
  - The Lung Channel of Hand-Taiyin
  - The Large Intestine Channel of Hand-Yangming
  - The Stomach Channel of Foot-Yangming
  - The Spleen Channel of Foot-Taiyin
  - The Heart Channel of Hand-Shaoyin
  - The Small Intestine Channel of Hand-Taiyang
  - The Urinary Bladder Channel of Foot-Taiyang
  - The Kidney Channel of Foot-Shaoyin
  - The Pericardium Channel of Hand-Jueyin
  - The Sanjiao Channel of Hand-Shaoyang
  - The Gall Bladder Channel of Foot-Shaoyang
  - The Liver Channel of Foot-Jueyin
- The eight extra channels
  - The Du Channel
  - The Ren Channel
  - The Chong Channel
  - The Dai Channel
  - The Yangqiao Channel
  - The Yinqiao Channel
  - The Yangwei Channel
  - The Yinwei Channel
- The fifteen collaterals — The collaterals of the fourteen channels plus the major collateral of the spleen.

II. FUNCTIONS OF CHANNELS AND COLLATERALS

The functions of channels and collaterals consist of circulating *qi* and blood, warming and nourishing the tissues and linking up the whole body so as to keep the *zang-fu* organs, four limbs, skin, muscles, tendons and bones intact in structure and functioning synergically and make the body an organic integrity. These functions of the channels and collaterals play an important role in clinical work.

Pathologically, channels and collaterals are responsible for the occurrence and transmission of disease. When the function of the channels and collaterals is impaired, the organism is open to exogenous pathogenic factors. After the organism has been attacked, the pathogenic factors are often transmitted deep inside the body through the channels and collaterals. When exogenous pathogenic factors invade the superficial portion of the body, for instance, chills, fever and headache may be present. When these factors are transmitted to the lung through the relevant channel, there may appear symptoms and signs of the lung, such as cough, asthmatic breathing and chest pain.

Channels and collaterals are not only the entrances inward for exogenous pathogenic factors, they are also important passages through which disorders impart their influence among the *zang-fu* organs or between the *zang-fu* organs and the tissues and peripheral organs of the body. For example, dysfunction of the liver in promoting unrestraint and patency of *qi* may result in failure of the *qi* of the stomach to descend, causing nausea and vomiting. Another example is ulceration and burning pain of the tongue caused by a flare-up of the fire of the heart.

As each of the channels takes its course in a definite part of the body and each of the twelve regular channels pertains to and connects with a particular *zang* or a particular *fu* organ, the symptoms and signs manifest in a disease together with the area where they appear can serve as a guide to clinical diagnosis. For example, the liver's function of promoting unrestraint and patency of *qi* facilitates the secretion and excretion of bile. Its channel is distributed in the hypochondriac region. Yellow sclera and hypochondriac pain suggest disorder of the liver. Another example is cough and chest pain indicating disorders of the lung, which performs the function of respiration, its channel originating in the chest. Furthermore, tenderness or other abnormal reaction along the areas traversed by the channels or at certain points also aids correct diagnosis. For instance, in a case of appendicitis, there may be tenderness at point Lanwei (Appendix, Extra.); in a disease of the lung tenderness may be present at point Feishu (U.B. 13).

The theory of channels and collaterals is extensively used as a guide to treatment of diseases in the various clinical specialities, especially acupuncture and moxibustion. In acupuncture and moxibustion therapy the affected channels or *zang-fu* organs are first detected. Points are then selected from adjacent areas or from the corresponding channels in distant areas. Therapeutic results may be obtained through regulating the circulation of *qi* and blood of the channels and collaterals.

CHAPTER IV

QI, BLOOD AND BODY FLUID

Qi, blood and body fluid are fundamental substances in the human body to sustain normal vital activities. Their existence and function, especially those of qi, are generally manifest in the functional activities of various tissues and organs. Qi, blood and body fluid, together with the zang-fu organs and the channels and collaterals, constitute the theoretical basis of human physiology in traditional Chinese medicine.

I. QI

Qi is involved in various aspects in physiology, pathology and clinical treatment. Generally speaking, the word qi connotes both substance and function. For instance, clean qi, waste qi and qi from essence of food are material qi; the qi of the heart, liver, spleen, kidney and stomach and the qi of channels and collaterals are functional qi. Substance and function are two different concepts, but they are closely related and cannot be entirely separated. This is because each function must be based on a certain substance, while a certain form of substance is bound to demonstrate a corresponding function.

Qualifiers of the substance qi in the human body vary with its distribution, source and function.

Source qi (元气 yuanqi) known as the qi of the kidney, being inherited from the parents and related to reproductive function, is referred to as congenital qi. See Chapter II.

Clean qi (清气 qingqi) and qi from essence of food, obtained respectively from the atmosphere and food after birth, are known as acquired qi. The two kinds of qi meet in the chest forming essential qi (宗气 zongqi) whose main function is to nourish the heart and lung and promote their functions of dominating blood and vessels and performing respiration. Both nutrient qi (营气 yingqi) and defensive qi (卫气 weiqi) are formed from essential substances in food. The former circulates in the vessels and supplies mainly the viscera. The latter circulates outside the vessels and is mainly distributed in the muscles and skin to warm and nourish the subcutaneous tissues, control the opening and closing of the pores and defend the body against exogenous etiological factors. Hence the name.

Zang-fu and channels and collaterals, acted upon by both congenital and acquired qi, function in a way known as the qi of zang-fu and channels and collaterals. Examples are the qi of the heart, lung, spleen, kidney, stomach, channels and collaterals. The so-called "arrival of qi" in acupuncture therapy means that the needling has produced its effect with the calling into function of the channels and collaterals.

II. BLOOD

The essence of food derived by digestion and absorption of the spleen and stomach is transported to the heart and lung and transformed into red blood by the two organs. The kidney stores essence. The essence of the kidney produces bone marrow, which in turn produces blood. Blood, therefore, is formed from essence, including the essence of food and essence of the kidney. Besides, the qi of the kidney promotes transportation and transformation by the spleen and stomach and strengthens the transforming function of the heart and lung, a process that promotes blood formation. Blood is thus constituted of nutrient qi, body fluid and essence of the kidney, the material base for the functioning of blood, i.e. to circulate in the vessels nourishing the body and promote the functional activities of various tissues and organs.

Blood and qi are closely related, the formation and circulation of blood depending upon qi, while the formation and distribution of qi relate to blood. Clinically, xu (deficiency) of qi often leads to xu (deficiency) of blood, and xu (deficiency) of blood, in turn, often results in xu (deficiency) of qi. Stagnation of qi often causes stagnation of blood, and stagnation of blood, in turn, often causes stagnation of qi.

III. BODY FLUID

Food and drink, especially the latter, after absorption become body fluid, which exists in the blood and the interstices of the tissues. Body fluid is of two types. The lucid and the thin type permeates the muscles and skin to warm and nourish the muscles and to moisten the skin. The turbid and viscous type supplies the joint cavities, brain and body orifices, lubricating the joints, toning the brain and moistening the orifices.

Sweat, urine and saliva are all formed from body fluid. Blood, too, contains a large amount of body fluid. This being so, the physiology and pathology of sweat, urine, saliva and blood are closely related to the metabolism of body fluid.

CHAPTER V

ETIOLOGY

The human body is endowed with the ability to resist the invasion of various kinds of pathogenic factors so as to keep a relative balance in the interior of the body as well as between the human body and the environmental conditions. This ability is called anti-pathogenic qi (factor). The various pathogenic factors that can break either of the two states of relative balance are called pathogenic qi (factors). The occurrence of a disease is the outcome of a losing struggle by the anti-pathogenic factor against the pathogenic factor. The normal co-ordination of yin and $yang$ in the body is destroyed and an abnormal change of preponderance or discomfiture of either yin or $yang$ results.

Both the anti-pathogenic factor and its pathogenic counterpart are important in the occurrence of a disease. However, traditional Chinese medicine attaches the greater importance to the anti-pathogenic factor. Explained by the relation between the internal and the external cause, the anti-pathogenic factor is the internal cause and the leading factor in the occurrence or non-occurrence of a disease, while the pathogenic factor is the external cause and the conditional factor, the latter becoming operative through the former. When the anti-pathogenic factor is vigorous, the invasion of the pathogenic factor is hindered. If the pathogenic factor invades, it means an insufficiency of the anti-pathogenic factor. In prophylaxis and treatment of disease, therefore, traditional Chinese medicine stresses especially the protection of the anti-pathogenic factor. The efficacy of acupuncture and moxibustion in prevention and treatment of disease is due mainly to their regulating and strengthening the defensive function of the anti-pathogenic factor, and their helping to restore the relative balance within the body as well as that between the human body and its environment.

The etiology of traditional Chinese medicine has its own marked characteristics. Firstly, variations in weather which go beyond the adaptability of individuals, such as wind, cold, summer heat, dampness, dryness and heat, are directly related with disease and are considered as the pathogenic factors of many diseases. That is to say, environmental factors are not considered as mere inducing factors but as causative factors which may directly injure the human body and cause disease. Fairly radical or abnormal changes in weather are referred to as pathogenic factors, e.g., pathogenic wind, pathogenic cold, etc. Diseases are even named after these factors. For instance, pathogenic wind may cause *shangfeng*, a common cold, or injured (*shang*) by wind (*feng*); pathogenic summer heat may cause *zhongshu*, sunstroke, or hit (*zhong*) by summer heat (*shu*).

Pathogenic factors generalize the characteristics of the clinical manifestations including symptoms and signs, reflecting the preponderance or discomfiture of the anti-pathogenic and pathogenic factors when they are contesting for the upper hand. Pathogenic factors also imply pathology in traditional Chinese medicine.

Nor are pathogenic factors investigated in isolation, but attention is paid to the recognition of their nature and practical significance in disease by research into their relationship to various dysfunctions in the human body. This method of investigation, i.e., analysis of pathogenic factors on the basis of clinical manifestation, is highly significant in guiding clinical treatment.

When pathogenic factors of varying nature act upon different parts of the body, the functional disturbances and diseases that occur will be different in nature and different clinical symptoms and signs will appear, showing an objective internal relationship between pathogenic factors and the symptoms and signs caused by them. Careful differentiation of symptoms and signs enables not only the identification of pathogenic factors but, more important, it may also be learned whether the anti-pathogenic or the pathogenic factor is in preponderance, whether the *zang-fu* organs are in good order and whether the *qi* and blood are sufficient to ensure a tendency of transmission and change in a disease. This information is necessary in determining the principles of treatment. The procedure is known in traditional Chinese medicine as "tracing the causes of a disease by differentiation of symptoms and signs" and "giving treatment on the basis of investigation into the causes of a disease", or, in other words, "determining treatment on the basis of differentiation of the syndrome". This is the main traditional Chinese procedure in treating disease.

Pathogenic factors are divided into three groups, namely, the six exogenous factors, the seven emotional factors and miscellaneous pathogenic factors. There are also phlegm and stagnant blood, which are pathological products. Once these form, further pathological changes will ensue and so phlegm and non-circulating blood are referred to as secondary pathogenic factors.

Next we discuss the characteristics of the clinical symptoms and signs caused by the various pathogenic factors.

I. SIX EXOGENOUS FACTORS

The normal variations in the weather of the four seasons are generalized into wind, cold, summer heat, dampness, dryness, and heat (fire, mild heat). These are known as the six factors of the natural environment. The vital activities of the human being are closely related to changes in weather. The body has constantly to adjust its internal function so as to adapt to the variations in the six factors of the natural environment. If these factors change abnormally or over-tax the adaptability of the human body, or the body's anti-pathogenic factor is weak and vital function is impaired beyond its ability to adapt itself to the changes in weather, the occurrence of disease may depend on such factors as wind, cold, etc., which are considered as pathogenic factors and referred to as the six exogenous factors.

These pathogenic factors invade the human body from the exterior via the mouth, nose or body surface and the resultant diseases are called exogenous diseases.

1. Wind

Pathogenic wind prevails in spring, as do "wind" diseases. Exposure to the wind after sweating, or sleeping in a draught, are important inducing factors in being affected by pathogenic wind.

(1) Wind, characterized by upward and outgoing dispersion, is a *yang* pathogenic factor. When it invades the human body from outside, it often attacks the upper portion of the body, weakening the defensive *qi* and causing derangement in the opening and closing of pores over the body surface. Clinical symptoms are headache, nasal obstruction, soreness or itching of the throat, facial puffiness, aversion to wind, and sweating.

— 41 —

(2) Wind occurs in gusts and is characterized by rapid change, pathogenic wind being especially so. Diseases caused by wind are marked by migrating pain, their symptoms and signs appearing and disappearing. Onset is abrupt and disappearance sudden, e.g. the migratory joint pain of rheumatic arthritis and urticaria.

(3) Wind is characterized by constant movement.

Pathogenic wind tends to move constantly, causing abnormal motion or rigidity of the trunk or limbs; clinical manifestations are convulsion, spasm and tremor of the four limbs and stiffness of the neck. Opisthotonos in tetanus and deviation of the eyes and mouth in facial paralysis are both related to this characteristic of pathogenic wind.

(4) Wind is apt to associate itself with other pathogenic factors.

Pathogenic wind is apt to associate itself with cold, damp, dryness or heat and form complex pathogenic factors of wind-cold, wind-damp, wind-dryness or wind-heat. Wind may also be associated with phlegm, producing a wind-phlegm syndrome.

2. Cold

Pathogenic cold is prevalent in winter, as are diseases of cold. In the cold season, too little clothing, exposure to cold after sweating, and being caught in wind and rain provide chances for the development of pathogenic cold.

(1) Cold is a *yin* pathogenic factor and is likely to consume *yang qi*.

Cold is a manifestation caused by excess *yin* and therefore is a *yin* pathogenic factor. When the *yang qi* of the body is consumed by cold, it will lose its normal function of promoting body warmth, and clinical manifestations of cold will appear, such as chills, shivering, cold limbs, pallor, diarrhea with undigested food in the stool and clear urine in increased volume.

(2) Cold is characterized by contraction and stagnation.

Invasion by pathogenic cold may cause contraction of channels and collaterals and retardation of circulation of *qi* and blood. Symptoms are pain of a cold nature and numbness of extremities. Cold may also cause closing of pores with manifestations of chills and anhidrosis.

3. Summer heat

Diseases caused by pathogenic summer heat occur only in summer. Onset is often due to prolonged exposure to blazing sun on hot days, or staying in a hot room with poor ventilation.

(1) Summer heat consumes *qi* and *yin* and may disturb the mind.

Summer heat is a *yang* pathogenic factor. Its features are upward direction and dispersion. Invasion of summer heat may cause excessive sweating, thirst, shortness of breath, lassitude, and concentrated urine. In severe cases, there may be high fever, restlessness, red dry skin, and such mental symptoms as abrupt onset of delirium or coma.

(2) Summer heat often combines with damp to cause disease, as rain often accompanies the heat of summer. Manifestations are dizziness, a heavy sensation of the head, suffocating feeling in the chest, nausea, poor appetite, diarrhea, and general sluggishness.

4. Damp

Pathogenic damp occurs mainly in the late summer rainy season. Such diseases usually follow the wearing of clothing wet with rain or sweat, dwelling in a low-lying and damp place, or being in frequent contact with water during work.

(1) Damp is characterized by heaviness and turbidity.

Damp is a substantial pathogenic factor which is weighty in nature. Its invasion of the body often gives rise to such symptoms as heaviness and a sensation of distension in the head, as though it were tightly bandaged. There is also dizziness, general lassitude, fullness in the chest and epigastrium, nausea, vomiting, and a stickiness and sweetish taste in the mouth.

Pathogenic damp is foul in nature. Its invasion often causes skin diseases, abscesses and oozing ulcers, massive leukorrhea of purulent nature with foul odour, turbid urine, etc.

(2) Damp is characterized by viscosity and stagnation.

Diseases caused by pathogenic damp are often lingering. Fixed *bi* syndrome (included is rheumatoid arthritis, see p. 339) and epidemic encephalitis are examples.

5. Dryness

Invasion of pathogenic dryness often occurs in late autumn when moisture is lacking in the atmosphere.

Pathogenic dryness is apt to consume *yin* fluid, especially the *yin* of the lung. Clinical manifestations are dry, rough and chapped skin, dryness of the mouth and nose, dryness and soreness of the throat, dry cough with little sputum, etc.

6. Heat (fire, mild heat)

Heat, fire and mild heat are all *yang* pathogenic factors. They are of the same nature but different in intensity. Among them, fire is the most severe and mild heat the least severe.

Heat, like summer heat, is also characterized by dispersion, damaging *yin* with a tendency to go inward to disturb the mind. The following are some special features related to pathogenic heat:

(1) Invasion by heat is apt to stir up wind and cause disturbance of blood.

Excess of pathogenic heat exhausts the *yin* of the liver and causes malnutrition of the tendons and channels. Manifestations are high fever accompanied by coma and delirium, convulsion, stiffness of the neck, opisthotonos, and ·eyes staring upward. This is known as "extreme heat stirring up the wind". Pathogenic heat may cause extravasation by disturbing the blood. Manifestations of hemorrhage may appear, such as hematemesis, epistaxis and skin eruptions. This is called "excessive heat disturbing the blood".

(2) Invasion by heat tends to cause skin infection.

Surgical cases, such as carbuncle, furuncle, boil and ulcer with local redness, swelling, hotness and pain are caused mainly by pathogenic heat.

In addition to the six factors mentioned above, there is another known as the pestilential factor, which causes epidemic diseases. It is quite similar to pathogenic heat in nature, but more pernicious and more fierce in pathogenicity as it is usually complicated with contagious toxic pathogenic damp. Pestilential diseases are often mortal, with rapid and drastic changes as seen in smallpox, plague and cholera.

In addition, there are diseases which are not caused by exogenous pathogenic wind, cold, damp, dryness and heat (fire) but whose clinical manifestations are similar to diseases caused by them. In order not to confuse the two categories of diseases, the pathological changes of such cases are referred to as endogenous wind, cold, damp, dryness and heat (fire). As they are not within the realm of exogenous diseases, they are to be discussed in the section "Differentiation of Syndromes According to the Theory of *Zang-Fu*" in Chapter VII.

II. SEVEN EMOTIONAL FACTORS

Mental activities relating to emotion are classified in traditional Chinese medicine under joy, anger, melancholy, meditation, grief, fear and fright — known as the seven emotional factors. They are the main pathogenic factors of endogenous diseases.

The seven emotions are reflections of man's mental state as induced by various stimulations in his environment. They are physiological phenomena and will not cause disease under normal conditions. However, if the emotions are very intense and persistent or the individual is hypersensitive to the stimulations, they may result in drastic and long-standing change in emotion which leads to disease.

Diseases caused by the seven emotional factors often show dysfunction of *zang-fu* organs and disturbance in circulation of *qi* and blood. Different emotional changes selectively injure different *zang-fu* organs; e.g. anger injures the liver, fright and excessive joy injure the heart, grief and melancholy injure the lung, meditation injures the spleen, and fear injures the kidney. Clinically, disorders caused by the seven emotional factors are seen mainly in the heart, liver and spleen. The following are examples:

Excessive joy or fear and fright may cause mental restlessness and give rise to palpitation, insomnia, irritability, anxiety, and even mental disorders.

Excessive anger may cause dysfunction of the liver in promoting unrestraint and patency of vital energy and give rise to pain and distension in the costal and hypochondriac region, irregular menstruation, mental depression and irascibility. If the function of storing blood is impaired, hemorrhage may result.

Excessive grief, melancholy and meditation may cause dysfunction of the spleen and stomach in transportation and transformation, and cause anorexia and abdominal fullness and distension after meals.

III. MISCELLANEOUS PATHOGENIC FACTORS

Included are irregular food intake, over-strain and stress or lack of physical exertion, traumatic injuries, stagnant blood and phlegm.

1. Irregular food intake

(1) Voracious eating, or over-eating of raw or cold food.

These may impair the function of the spleen and stomach in transportation, transformation, reception and digestion of food and cause nausea, vomiting, belching of foul air, acid regurgitation, epigastric and abdominal pain with distension, borborygmus and diarrhea.

(2) Indulgence in alcoholic drink or greasy, highly flavoured food.

These may produce damp-heat or phlegm-heat which first injures the spleen and stomach. Dysfunction of vital organs may result from aggravation of the situation.

(3) Too little nourishment intake.

Too little nourishment intake may by due to lack of food, weakness of the spleen and stomach which hinders nourishment intake by affecting digestion and absorption, or limited variety of food owing to personal preference. Prolonged under-supply of food results in malnutrition and insufficiency of qi and blood, with resulting emaciation, lassitude, dizziness, blurring of vision, palpitation and even syncope.

(4) Intake of insanitary food.

Intake of food contaminated by poisonous materials or of stale food may impair the function of the spleen and stomach or cause intestinal parasitic diseases.

2. Over-strain and stress or lack of physical exertion

There is an old saying in China: "Running water does not go stale and door-hinges do not become worm-eaten." In other words, constant motion may prevent things from rotting, and physical exertion is important to life. However, prolonged over straining may lead to illness due to consumption of the anti-pathogenic factor and give rise to signs of feebleness such as emaciation, lassitude, excessive sweating, palpitation, dizziness and blurring of vision.

Lack of physical exercise or necessary physical exertion may cause retardation of circulation of qi and blood, general weakness, lassitude, obesity and shortness of breath after exertion. It may also lower the general resistance of the body.

Excessive sexual activity injures the qi of the kidney and causes manifestations of poor health. Backache, weakness of the limbs, dizziness, tinnitus, impotence, prospermia, lassitude and listlessness are some of these.

3. Traumatic injuries

Included are incisions, gunshot injuries, contusions, sprains, scalds and burns, and insect or animal stings and bites.

4. Stagnant blood and phlegm

Both stagnant blood and phlegm involve the following two aspects:

Substantial: Stagnant blood and phlegm may refer to pathological products, e.g. extravasated blood clot and sputum. They are secondary pathological factors which will lead to further pathological changes if not eliminated in time.

Non-substantial: Stagnant blood and phlegm are sometimes pathological concepts generalizing the characteristics of the clinical symptoms and signs. For example, a case of epilepsy with coma and rattle in the throat can be diagnosed from the characteristics of the clinical manifestations as "the heart being misted by the phlegm".

(1) Stagnant blood

Local stagnation of blood due to circulatory retardation from various causes and extravasated blood held in spaces between tissues or in cavities or tracts are substantial stagnant blood. It may remain stagnant in different parts of the body and cause different functional disturbances. Disorders caused by stagnant blood are characterized by:

a. Pain This may be stabbing or boring, or at times it is severe colicky pain. The painful area is fixed.

b. Hemorrhage The blood is often deep or dark purplish, or it has dark purple clots.

c. Ecchymoses or petechiae These take the form of purplish spots on the skin or the tongue.

d. Mass tumor, or enlargement of the internal organs in the abdomen.

(2) Phlegm

Functional disorders of the lung, spleen and kidney may cause derangement of water metabolism, eliciting abnormal distribution of body fluid, a part of which is condensed into phlegm. When phlegm is formed, it may stay in different parts of the body and result in different syndromes:

a. Phlegm-damp affecting the lung: cough, asthma and expectoration of excessive sputum.

b. Phlegm misting the heart: coma and rattle in the throat.

c. Phlegm blocking channels and collaterals: hemiplegia, deviation of the eyes and mouth and numbness of limbs.

d. Phlegm retained subcutaneously: This takes the form of soft, movable nodules.

CHAPTER VI

METHODS OF DIAGNOSIS

Inspection, auscultation and olfaction, inquiring, and palpation are known as the four diagnostic methods in traditional Chinese medicine. The case history and clinical symptoms and signs gained through the four diagnostic methods are the basis for further differentiation of the syndrome.

Each of the four diagnostic methods plays a specific role in diagnosing a disease. Only by combining the four can a comprehensive and systematic understanding of the situation of the disease be gained and a correct diagnosis made.

I. INSPECTION

Inspection is a method of diagnosis in which examination is made by observation with the eye. Included are observations of the expression, colour, appearance and tongue.

1. Observation of the expression

Expression is the outward manifestation of the vital activities. Generally speaking, if the patient is in fairly good spirits, behaves normally with a sparkle in the eyes and keen response, and if he co-operates with the doctor during examination, the disease is mild. If the patient is spiritless, indifferent in expression, with dull eyes and sluggish response or even mental disturbance, and does not co-operate during examination, the disease is serious.

2. Observation of the colour

People of different races have different skin colours, and there is wide variation among people of the same race. However, a lustrous skin with natural colour is considered normal. For instance, the complexion of a healthy Chinese is slightly dark, but shining and ruddy. Morbid complexions are: red, which denotes existence of heat; pallor, which indicates existence of cold or *xu* (deficiency) of blood; bright yellow, which suggests jaundice; and bluish purple, which is often due to stagnation of blood or severe pain.

As to the clinical significance of the colour of excretions, such as nasal discharge, sputum, stool, urine and vaginal discharge, those clear and white in colour generally denote *xu* and cold, while those turbid and yellow in colour indicate *shi* and heat.

It is advisable to observe colours in daylight, because the true colour is often not revealed under lamplight, especially if the lamp has a coloured tinge.

3. Observation of the appearance

Observations are made to see whether the body build of the patient is obese or thin, whether there is abnormality in the gait and the posture of standing, sitting and lying, and whether there is any abnormal movement of the trunk and limbs. For example, in an obese person, there is often *xu* (deficiency) of *qi* and much phlegm-damp; while in an emaciated person there is often hyperactivity of fire of the *xu* type. Paralysis of limbs usually indicates insufficiency of *qi* and blood and obstruction of channels. Convulsion, opisthotonos, deviation of the eyes and mouth and twitching of muscles are usually due to *xu* (deficiency) of *yin* and blood, which results in malnutrition of tendons and vessels. These symptoms may also be due to invasion of collaterals by pathogenic wind.

4. Observation of the tongue

Observation of the tongue including the tongue proper and its coating is an important procedure in diagnosis by inspection. There is a close connection between the tongue and the *zang-fu* organs, channels, collaterals, *qi*, blood and body fluid. Any disorder of these may result in a corresponding manifestation on the tongue. Indications of the nature of the disease can be learned by observing the colour, form and condition of dryness or moisture of both the tongue proper and its coating, and the motility of the tongue.

A normal tongue is of proper size, light red in colour, free in motion and with a thin layer of white coating over the surface which is neither dry nor over moist.

Below we describe the main manifestations of abnormal tongue proper and of its coating, and their clinical significance:

(1) Tongue proper

a. Pale tongue. A less than normally red tongue indicates syndromes of the *xu* or cold type caused by weakness of *yang qi* and insufficiency of *qi* and blood or due to invasion by exogenous pathogenic cold.

b. Red tongue. An abnormally bright red tongue indicates various heat syndromes of the *shi* type due to invasion by pathogenic heat and various heat syndromes of the *xu* type resulting from consumption of *yin* fluid.

c. Deep red tongue. A deep red colour of the tongue occurs in the severe stage of a febrile disease in which pathogenic heat has been transmitted from the exterior to the interior of the body. It can also be seen in those patients suffering from prolonged illness in which *yin* fluid has been exhausted and endogenous fire, which is of the *xu* type, is hyperactive.

d. Purplish tongue. A tongue purplish in colour, or with purple spots indicates stagnation of *qi* and blood. It also indicates preponderance of endogenous cold due to *xu* (deficiency) of *yang*.

e. Flabby tongue. A tongue larger than normal, flabby, and whitish in colour, sometimes with teeth prints on the border, indicates *xu* (deficiency) of both *qi* and *yang* and retention of phlegm-damp in the interior. Flabby tongue deep red in colour indicates preponderance of pathogenic heat in the interior and hyperactivity of the fire of the heart.

f. Cracked tongue. Irregular streaks or cracks on the tongue indicate consumption of body fluid by excessive heat, loss of the essence of the kidney and hyperactivity of fire due to *xu* (deficiency) of *yin*.

Congenital cracked tongue and cracked tongue without any morbid signs are considered normal.

g. Thorny tongue. The papillary buds over the surface of the tongue swelling up like thorns, and usually red in colour, indicates hyperactivity of pathogenic heat.

h. Rigid and tremulous tongue. A tongue that is rigid and difficult to protrude, retract or roll leads to stuttering and indicates invasion of exogenous heat and disturbance of the mind by phlegm-heat. It also indicates damage of the *yin* of the liver by strong heat which stirs up the wind, or obstruction of collaterals by wind-phlegm. The tremulous tongue seen in protracted illness often indicates *xu* (deficiency) of both *qi* and *yin*.

i. Deviated tongue. This indicates obstruction of collaterals by wind-phlegm.

(2) Tongue coating

a. White coating. The tongue's whitish coating may be thin or thick, sticky or dry. A thin white coating is normal, but when it is seen in an exogenous disease, it usually indicates invasion of the lung by wind-cold. Thick white coating usually indicates retention of food. White sticky coating usually indicates invasion by the exogenous cold-damp or retention of phlegm-damp in the interior. Dry white coating usually indicates invasion by the pestilential factor.

b. Yellow coating. A yellow coating on the tongue may be thin or thick, sticky or dry. A thin yellow coating usually indicates invasion of the lung by wind-heat, while a thick yellow coating usually indicates persistent accumulation of food in the stomach and intestines. Yellow sticky coating usually denotes accumulation of damp-heat in the interior or blockage of the lung by phlegm-heat. Dry yellow coating usually indicates accumulation of heat in the stomach and intestines which results in damage to the *yin*.

c. Greyish black coating. A greyish black coating on the tongue may be moist or dry. Greyish black moist coating usually denotes retention of cold-damp in the interior or too much endogenous cold due to *xu* (deficiency) of *yang*. Greyish black dry coating usually indicates consumption of body fluid by excessive heat or hyperactivity of fire due to *xu* (deficiency) of *yin*.

d. Peeled coating. The tongue with its coating peeling off is known as "geographic tongue". If the entire coating peels off leaving the surface mirror smooth, the condition is known as glossy tongue. Both manifestations indicate the crisis in a long illness in which the anti-pathogenic factor is severely damaged and the *yin* is grossly deficient.

The abnormal changes of the tongue proper and coating suggest the nature and changes of disease from different aspects. Generally speaking, observation of the changes in the tongue proper is mainly to differentiate whether the condition of the *zang-fu* organs, *qi*, blood and body fluid is in a *xu* or *shi* state, while observation of the tongue coating is for judging the condition of pathogenic factors. Comprehensive analysis of the changes in both the tongue proper and its coating is therefore necessary when diagnosis is made by observation of the tongue.

Attention should be paid to the exclusion of false phenomena such as the tongue proper becoming redder and the coating thinner after eating or drinking hot beverage. Some foods and drugs colour the tongue coating, e.g., olive, mulberry or plum may give it a greyish black hue; loquat, orange, coptis or riboflavin may make it yellow. Those who smoke or drink alcohol or tea often have a thick yellow or greyish yellow tongue coating. As observation of the colour of both the tongue proper and its coating is an important procedure in diagnosis, it is desirable that it be done in daylight.

II. AUSCULTATION AND OLFACTION

1. Listening

(1) Listening to the speech. In general, speaking feebly and in low tones indicates syndromes of the *xu* type, while speaking lustily indicates those of the *shi* type. Delirium means blurring of the heart by phlegm-heat. Muttering to oneself or extreme verbosity means derangement of the mind. Stuttering suggests obstruction of collaterals by wind-phlegm.

(2) Listening to the respiration. Feeble breathing accompanied by shortness of breath and sweating after slight exertion usually indicates *xu* (deficiency) of *qi* of the heart and lung; coarse breathing accompanied by asthma and rattling of sputum indicates syndromes of phlegm-heat or phlegm-damp in the lung pertaining to the *shi* type.

(3) Listening to the cough. Cough in a coarse voice usually indicates invasion of the lung by wind-cold or accumulation of cold-phlegm in the lung; cough in clear voice indicates invasion of the lung by wind-heat or accumulation of phlegm-heat in the lung. Dry cough with little sputum is often due to injury of the lung by pathogenic dryness or a long-standing *xu* (deficiency) of *yin* of the lung.

2. Smelling

Offensive smell of a discharge or excretion usually indicates heat syndromes of the *shi* type, while insipid odour indicates cold syndromes of the *xu* type. For instance:

Thick sputum with foul smell indicates phlegm-heat in the lung, while dilute and clear, odourless sputum indicates cold-phlegm in the lung.

Scanty deep yellow urine with an offensive smell indicates damp-heat in the urinary bladder, while clear, odourless and profuse urine indicates cold in the urinary bladder relating to the *xu* type.

Foul breath indicates heat in the stomach.

III. INQUIRING

Inquiry is asking the patient or the patient's companion about the disease condition in order to understand the pathological process.

It is necessary, first, to listen attentively to the chief complaint of the patient, and then ask about the onset and duration of the illness and the past history. Then, based on the patient's complaint and with the view of regarding the body as an integral whole, systematic inquiries are made according to the knowledge necessary in differentiating a syndrome. If treatment has been given, it is necessary to learn the effect of the medication taken.

Inquiring is an important means in grasping the condition of a disease. Among the questions to be asked, the main ones concern the following:

1. Chills and fever

Simultaneous occurrence of chills and fever at the beginning of a disease indicates invasion of the superficial portion of the body by exogenous pathogenic factors. If chill is the predominant condition, the indication is invasion by wind-cold, while if fever is predominant it means invasion by wind-heat.

Chills without fever may be due to endogenous cold resulting from weakness of *yang qi*. This may also occur when exogenous pathogenic cold directly affects a certain *zang* or *fu* organ. In such cases, manifestations of cold may appear at the diseased area, such as cold sensation, pain in the epigastric region and diarrhea with undigested food in the stool.

Fever may occur without chills. Sustained high fever indicates excess of heat in the interior due to invasion by exogenous pathogenic heat or transmission of exogenous pathogenic factors from the exterior to the interior. A slight fever occurring at a definite time of the day is known as tidal fever, the etiological factor being endogenous heat caused by *xu* (deficiency) of *yin*. The patient may have a feverish sensation conveyed to the body surface from the interior, called "tidal fever originating from bone".

Alternate chills and fever occurring once a day or every two or three days often suggests malaria.

2. Perspiration

When the superficial portion of the body has been invaded by exogenous pathogenic factors, sweating means invasion by wind-heat, while absence of sweat means invasion by wind-cold.

Frequent spontaneous sweating exacerbated by slight exertion is known as automatic sweating. It is usually due to weakness of *yang qi* and infirmity of the defensive *qi*.

Sweating that occurs during sleep and stops upon wakening is known as night sweating. It is usually a sign showing *xu* (deficiency) of *yin* and hyperactivity of *yang* and excess heat.

Profuse cold sweating during a severe illness is a critical sign showing total exhaustion of *yang qi*.

3. Food and drink, appetite and taste

Thirst with desire to take fluids is seen in interior heat syndromes, while absence of thirst, or thirst without desire to take fluids indicates cold-damp. Preference for cold food and beverages signifies heat syndromes, while preference for hot food and beverages implies cold syndromes. Poor appetite, tastelessness in mouth and fullness in the epigastrium and abdomen indicate weakness of the spleen and stomach. Foul belching, acid regurgitation and disgust at the sight or thought of food after voracious eating indicate retention of food. Stickiness and sweetish taste in the mouth show damp-heat in the spleen, while a bitter taste in the mouth points to hyperactivity of the fire of the liver and gall bladder.

4. Defecation and urination

Constipation due to dryness of stool generally indicates heat in the intestines which is related to a syndrome of the *shi* type: constipation occurs in persons of old age, women after childbirth or persons after a protracted illness. It indicates a syndrome of the *xu* type due to *xu* (deficiency) of *qi* and insufficiency of body fluid. Bloody stool with pus and tenesmus results chiefly from damp-heat in the intestines. Loose stool with undigested food indicates weakness and cold of the spleen and stomach.

Constant diarrhea before daybreak relates to *xu* (deficiency) of *yang* of the spleen and kidney.

Deep yellow urine generally indicates heat of the *shi* type, while clear and profuse urine indicates cold of the *xu* type. Frequent urination scanty in amount and deep yellow in colour denotes accumulation of damp-heat in the kidney and urinary bladder; frequent urination with clear urine indicates *xu* and cold of the kidney and urinary bladder. Retention of urine or difficult, dribbling urination is often due to retention of damp-heat in the urinary bladder, insufficiency of *yang* of the kidney or the presence of stones or stagnant blood. Scanty urine is often due to *xu* of both the spleen and kidney and accompanied by retention of water in the body.

5. Pain

Pain which is aggravated by pressure relates to the *shi* type and results mainly from invasion of exogenous pathogenic factors, obstruction of channels and collaterals, stagnation of *qi* and blood, intestinal parasites, retention of food or obstruction by phlegm. Pain which is alleviated by pressure relates to the *xu* type. It is usually caused by the malnutrition of tendons and channels due to insufficiency of *qi* and blood and loss of *yin* essence. Pain which is relieved by warmth is of cold nature; if it is relieved by cold it is of heat nature. Most migrating pain is due to invasion of collaterals by pathogenic wind; fixed pain is due to obstruction of collaterals by cold-damp.

Headache in an acute disease is likely to be caused by the invasion of exogenous pathogenic factors. Persistent headache with repeated attacks is generally due to stagnation of blood or upward disturbance of phlegm. Lingering headache with an empty sensation in the head accompanied by paroxysmal darkness before the eyes and blurred vision is due to insufficiency of *qi* and blood and loss of *yin* essence.

Headache can be differentiated according to the distribution of the channels on the head. For instance, occipital headache relates to the Taiyang Channel, unilateral headache to the Shaoyang Channel, frontal headache and supra-orbital pain to the Yangming Channel and vertical headache to the Jueyin Channel.

Pain above the diaphragm usually indicates disorders of the heart and lung; pain in the epigastric region indicates disorders of the spleen and stomach; pain in the lumbar region or around the umbilicus means disorders of the kidney and the Chong Channel; pain below the umbilicus and in the lower abdomen points to disorders of the kidney, urinary bladder or large and small intestines; pain in the costal and hypochondriac region indicates disorders of the liver and gall bladder.

6. Sleep

Insomnia means either difficulty in falling asleep, or inability to sleep soundly, waking easily and being unable to fall asleep again. Insomnia accompanied by dizziness and palpitation of the heart usually indicates failure of blood to nourish the heart due to *xu* of both the heart and spleen. Insomnia accompanied by restlessness in mind and dream-disturbed sleep indicates hyperactivity of the fire of the heart. Difficulty in falling asleep due to gastric discomfort as after a full meal indicates derangement of the *qi* of the stomach and restlessness in mind.

Uncontrollable drowsiness is known as lethargy. If it is accompanied by dizziness it indicates accumulation of phlegm-damp in the interior. A situation of being half asleep with general lassitude indicates *xu* (deficiency) of *yang* of the heart and kidney. Lethargic stupor with manifestations of heat indicates the early stage of coma caused by disturbance of the mind due to inward trapping of pathogenic heat, while lethargic stupor without manifestations of heat but with sputum rattling in the throat and a thick and sticky tongue coating indicates blurring of the mind by phlegm-damp.

7. Menses and leukorrhea

Women patients are also asked about the menses and leukorrhea, and for married women the obstetric history.

Menses of a shortened cycle, excessive in amount and deep red in colour relates mainly to the heat syndrome of the *shi* type; a prolonged cycle with scanty light-coloured discharge belongs to the cold syndrome of the *xu* type. Pre-menstrual distending pain in the lower abdomen which intensifies on pressure and a dark purplish menstrual flow with clots in it means stagnation of *qi* and blood. Post-menstrual lower abdominal pain that responds to pressure and a light reddish menstrual flow scanty in amount is caused by *xu* of blood.

Watery leukorrhea whitish in colour with little odour and accompanied by backache indicates *xu* (deficiency) of *yang* of the spleen and kidney and accumulation of endogenous cold; thick leukorrhea yellow in colour with offensive smell indicates the flowing downward of damp-heat.

Irregular uterine bleeding after menopause, or yellow and white vaginal discharge mixed with pus and blood may suggest a severe disease of toxic dampness in the uterus.

IV. PALPATION

Palpation is a method of diagnosis in which the pathological condition is detected by palpating, feeling and pressing certain areas of the body, here mainly feeling the pulse and palpation of channels and points.

1. Feeling the pulse

The location for feeling the pulse is above the wrist where the radial artery throbs. It is divided into three regions: *cun*, *guan* and *chi*. The region opposite to the styloid process of the radius is known as *guan*, that distal to *guan* (i.e., between *guan* and the wrist joint) is *cun* and that proximal to *guan* is *chi*. (Fig. 4.) The three regions of *cun*, *guan* and *chi* of the left hand reflect respectively the conditions of the heart, liver and kidney, and those of the right hand reflect conditions of the lung, spleen and kidney.

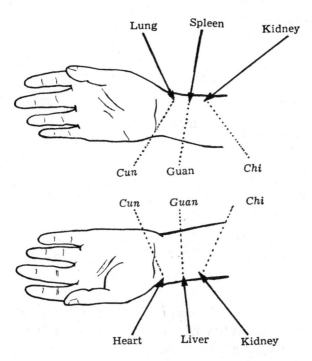

Fig. 4. The three regions for feeling pulse.

In feeling the pulse, let the patient place his hand easily on a cushion palm up. First locate the *guan* region with the middle finger, then put the index and ring fingers naturally on the *cun* and *chi* regions. Finger force is exerted first lightly, then moderately and finally heavily to get a general idea of the depth, frequency, rhythm, strength and form of the pulse. Any abnormal changes in any region of the pulse should be determined by exerting an even force on the three region, then by feeling the three regions separately and making comparisons in order to have a correct impression of the pulse as a whole.

A normal pulse is of medium frequency, i.e., 4-5 beats per breath, and regular rhythm. It is even and forceful.

Abnormal pulse readings and their clinical significance are as follows:

(1) Superficial pulse.

The pulse responds to the finger when pressed lightly and becomes weak on heavy pressure. This often occurs in the early stage of an exogenous disease, i.e., an exterior syndrome. It may also occur in patients suffering from prolonged illness and who are in a state of general weakness. In this situation, however, it is more often superficial and forceless.

(2) Deep pulse.

Superficial palpation reveals no clear pulse, which is felt only upon heavy pressure. This often occurs in interior syndromes.

(3) Slow pulse.

The rate is slow, with less than 4 beats per breath. This often occurs in cold syndromes.

(4) Rapid pulse.

The rate is quick, with more than 5 beats per breath, a situation that often occurs in heat syndromes.

(5) Pulse of the *xu* type.

The pulse is weak and forceless and disappears on heavy pressure. It often occurs in syndromes of the *xu* type.

(6) Pulse of the *shi* type.

The pulse is forceful and is felt even on deep pressure. This often occurs in syndromes of the *shi* type.

(7) Wiry pulse.

The pulse feels taut and forceful, as though pressing on the string of a drawn bow. It often occurs where there is insufficiency of the *yin* and hyperactivity of the *yang* of the liver.

(8) Rolling pulse.

The pulse feels smooth, flowing and forceful, and often occurs when there is excessive phlegm or retention of food. Rolling pulse may be observed in healthy people with ample *qi* and blood, and during pregnancy in women.

(9) Thready pulse.

The pulse is fine, as its name implies. It often occurs in the syndrome of *xu* (deficiency) of both *qi* and blood.

(10) Short pulse.

The movement is uneven and of short duration, with irregular missed beats. Short pulse of the *shi* type indicates hyperactivity of heat, excessive phlegm, stagnation of *qi* and blood and retention of food. Short pulse of the *xu* type is a sign of collapsing.

(11) Knotted pulse.

The pulse is slow and gradual with irregular missed beats, indicating endogenous cold or retention of cold-phlegm and stagnant blood in the interior.

(12) Intermittent pulse.

The pulse is slow and gradual with missed beats at regular intervals. It often occurs in patients with impairment of *qi* and blood and declining *yang qi*.

Short pulse, knotted pulse and intermittent pulse are all missed-beat pulses.

The quality of a pulse may vary according to such factors as body build, activity, and general constitution of the patient, and weather. This should be taken into consideration in making a diagnosis.

Long clinical experience is required for correctly identifying the various kinds of pulse. When two or more kinds of pulse are felt in one patient, e.g., a combination of thready and rapid, deep and thready, or thready and wiry, it is important to make a comprehensive analysis of the clinical significance of the combinations, at the same time taking into consideration the general condition of the patient.

2. Palpation of channels and points

Clinical practice demonstrates that in some diseases tenderness or other abnormal reactions may occur along the courses of the involved channels or at certain points. In disorders of the lung, for instance, there may be tenderness at point Zhongfu (Lu.1), or a nodule may be palpated at point Feishu (U.B.13); in disorders of the liver there may be tenderness at Ganshu (U.B.18) and Qimen (Liv.14), in gastralgia tenderness may occur at Weishu (U.B. 21) and Zusanli (St. 36), while in appendicitis it may occur at Lanwei (Appendix) (Extra). These signs are significant in diagnosing by palpation, and especially in giving acupuncture treatment.

Palpation of the abdomen is also an important procedure. Abdominal distention with tympanitic note on percussion but with normal urination indicates stagnation of *qi*; abdominal distention with a splashing sound and a fluctuating sensation on palpation shows accumulation of fluid. Immovable hard masses in the abdomen are stagnant blood. Unfixed soft masses may be due to stagnation of *qi*. A cluster of masses palpated in the left abdomen with constipation suggests retention of dry stool. Rebounding pain in right lower abdomen suggests appendicitis resulting from stagnation of *qi* and blood.

CHAPTER VII

DIFFERENTIATION OF SYNDROMES

Indentification of a syndrome entails making further analysis and synthesis of the clinical data obtained by applying the four diagnostic methods in order to determine the stage to which the disease has developed, its location, and the degree of opposing force between the body resistance and the pathogenic factors. Thus it can be seen that identification is made not from a simple list of symptoms and signs but from a reflection of the pathogenesis of the disease. Correct differentiation is requisite to applying correct therapeutic methods and attaining the anticipated clinical results.

There are a number of methods for differentiating syndromes of which three are introduced here briefly: 1. Differentiation of syndromes according to eight principles, 2. Differentiation of syndromes according to the theory of *zang-fu* and 3. Differentiation of syndromes according to the theory of channels and collaterals. Each of these three lays stress on a particular aspect, at the same time connecting with and supplementing one another. Differentiation of syndromes as also mentioned in preceding chapters on etiology and methods of diagnosis should be taken into consideration in clinical work.

I. DIFFERENTIATION OF SYNDROMES ACCORDING TO EIGHT PRINCIPLES

The eight principles in differentiation of syndromes are exterior and interior, cold and heat, *xu* (deficiency) and *shi* (excess), and *yin* and *yang*. This method is widely applicable clinically. Diversified as clinical manifestations and pathological changes may be, application of this method makes it possible to grasp the key link and solve the complicated problems systematically. The qualifiers exterior and interior relate to the depth of the disease, cold and heat to its nature, *xu* (deficiency) and *shi* (excess) to the opposing force in the struggle between the anti-pathogenic and the pathogenic factors, and *yin* and *yang* relate to the categories of the disease. *Yin* and *yang* are the chief principles among the eight. All the exterior syndromes, heat syndromes and syndromes of the *shi* (excess) type fall into the category of *yang*, while all the interior syndromes, cold syndromes and syndromes of the *xu* (deficiency) type fall into the category of *yin*. There may exist clinically among the syndromes those of exterior and cold, and interior and heat, which classify in the *yin* and *yang* complex. Below is given a brief description of the main clinical symptoms and signs on which differentiation of syndromes by the eight principles is based.

1. Exterior and interior

Exterior and interior form two principles relating to the depth of the diseased area and generalizing the direction of the development of the disease. Exterior syndromes refer to diseases resulting from invasion of the superficial portion of the body by exogenous pathogenic factors and are marked by sudden onset with short duration. Chief manifestations are intolerance to cold (or wind), fever, headache, nasal obstruction and superficial pulse. Interior syndromes may result from transmission of exogenous pathogenic factors to the interior if these are not eliminated in time, or they may be caused by direct attack on the *zang-fu* organs by exogenous pathogenic factors. Dysfunction of the *zang-fu* organs is also among the causes of interior syndromes. Generally speaking, the main sign in identifying exterior and interior syndromes is fever accompanied by intolerance to cold (or wind) in the former, while in the latter fever is not accompanied by intolerance to cold (or wind). Both exterior and interior syndromes may be complicated by cold, heat, *xu* (deficiency), or *shi* (excess), and their clinical manifestations vary. Care should be taken to distinguish between them. (Tab. 4.)

Exterior syndromes are usually mild and superficial as they are located on the superficial portion of the body and are the early stage of exogenous diseases. Interior syndromes are mostly severe and deep, as the pathogenic factors are in the interior of the body, damaging the *zang-fu* organs.

Tab. 4. Differentiation of cold, heat, *xu* (deficiency) and *shi* (excess) in exterior and interior syndromes.

	Exterior Syndrome	Interior Syndrome
Cold	Fever, chills, no sweat, superficial and forceful pulse, thin white tongue coating, etc.	Chills, cold limbs, pallor, absence of thirst, loose stools, clear profuse urine, deep and slow pulse, pale tongue, etc.
Heat	Fever with intolerance to wind; there may be sweating; a little thirst, superficial and rapid pulse, thin yellow tongue coating, etc.	High fever, thirst, irritability and restlessness, flushed face, red eyes, constipation, deep yellow scanty urine, rapid pulse of the *shi* type, red tongue with yellow coating, etc.
Xu (deficiency)	Sweating, intolerance to wind, superficial and slow pulse, etc.	Feeble breathing, apathy, general lassitude, palpitation, dizziness, deep pulse of the *xu* type, flabby and pale tongue with white coating, etc.
Shi (excess)	No sweat, general aching, superficial and forceful pulse, white coated tongue, etc.	Coarse breathing, sonorous voice, irritability, fullness of the chest, abdominal distention, constipation, deep pulse of the *shi* type, rough tongue with thick coating, etc.

2. Cold and heat

Cold and heat relate to two different natures of disease. Diseases caused by pathogenic heat, summer heat or dryness are mostly heat syndromes, and those caused by pathogenic cold are mostly cold syndromes. But the latter may turn into the former. Moreover, *xu* (deficiency) of *yin* or *yang* may respectively lead to heat or cold syndromes of the *xu* type. These should be distinguished from those of the *shi* type. Clinical manifestations of heat and cold syndromes of the *xu* type are to be discussed later.

Distinguishing between a cold and a heat syndrome is not difficult, as the two are opposites in nature and have markedly different manifestations.

Tab. 5. Differentiation of cold and heat syndromes of the *shi* type.

Cold syndrome of the *shi* type	Heat syndrome of the *shi* type
Chills, cold limbs, absence of thirst, pallor, excessive sputum, asthmatic breathing, abdominal pain aggravated by pressure, loose stools, clear urine of increased volume, etc.	Continuous high fever, thirst, flushed face, red eyes, fullness and distending pain in the abdomen aggravated by pressure, unconsciousness, delirium, constipation, concentrated urine, etc.
Deep slow pulse of the *shi* type.	Rapid pulse of the *shi* type.
Pale tongue with white or thick sticky coating.	Red or deep red tongue with dry yellow coating.

3. *Xu* (deficiency) and *shi* (excess)

Xu (deficiency) and *shi* (excess) are two principles used to analyze and generalize the opposing force of the anti-pathogenic and pathogenic factors during the course of the disease. Syndromes of the *xu* (deficiency) type refer to those diseases in which the function of the human body is weak, the anti-pathogenic factor insufficient and the co-ordination of *yin* and *yang* impaired, while the influence of the pathogenic factor has already become inconspicuous. Syndromes of the *shi* (excess) type refer to those diseases in which the body function is not to the point of impairment and the anti-pathogenic factor is still of sufficient strength, while the pathogenic factor is hyperactive and severe struggle proceeds between the anti-pathogenic and pathogenic factors. If the anti-pathogenic factor is weak and fails to contend with the pathogenic factor, there will result a disease complicated between *xu* (deficiency) and *shi* (excess). Syndromes of the *xu* (deficiency) type should be treated by the reinforcing method, and those of the *shi* (excess) type by the reducing method. If *xu* and *shi* contend, both reinforcing and reducing methods should be applied.

Syndromes of the *shi* (excess) type and of heat nature often intermingle, and a syndrome of the *xu* (deficiency) type often mingles with that of the cold nature. That is to say, heat syndrome is usually of the *shi* type and cold syndrome generally relates to the *xu* type. (Tab. 6.)

The main feature of syndromes of *yang xu* (deficiency of *yang*) i.e., cold syndromes of the *xu* (deficiency) type, and syndromes of *yin xu* (deficiency of *yin*) i.e., heat syndromes of the *xu* (deficiency) type are listed below. (Tab. 7.)

Tab. 6. Differentiation of syndromes of the *xu* (deficiency) and *shi* (excess) types.

Syndromes of the *xu* (deficiency) type	Syndromes of the *shi* (excess) type
Long-standing disease, listlessness, pallor, apathy, lying with the body curled up, feeble breathing, palpitation, shortness of breath, tinnitus, blurring of vision, insomnia, poor memory, spontaneous sweating, night sweating, nocturnal emission, enuresis, pain relieved by pressure, loose stools, clear urine increased in volume, etc.	Recent disease, elation, red face, restlessness, sonorous voice, coarse breathing, fullness and distension in the chest and abdomen, abdominal pain aggravated by pressure, constipation or tenesmus, painful or difficult urination, etc.
Thready pulse of the *xu* type.	Pulse of the *shi* type.
Pale tongue with thin coating.	Red tongue with thick coating.

Tab. 7. Differentiation of syndromes of *yang xu* and syndromes of *yin xu*.

Syndromes of *yin xu* (Cold syndromes of the *xu* type)	Syndromes of *yang xu* (Heat syndromes of the *xu* type)
Chills, cold limbs, sallow complexion, absence of thirst, listlessness, lassitude,. spontaneous sweating, loose stools, clear urine in large amount, etc.	Afternoon fever, malar flush, dry mouth and throat, insomnia with mental restlessness, feverish sensation in palms and soles, night sweating, constipation, concentrated urine, etc.
Deep slow pulse of the *xu* type.	Thready rapid pulse of the *xu* type.
Pale tongue with white coating.	Red tongue with little coating.

4. *Yin* and *yang*

As has been mentioned above, *yin* and *yang* are two general principles used to generalize the categories of disease. They are also used to explain some of the pathological changes of the *zang-fu* organs and tissues, e.g. syndromes of *yin xu*, syndromes of *yang xu*, syndromes of collapse of *yin*, syndromes of collapse of *yang*, etc.

So far as clinical manifestations are concerned, those characterized by hyperactivity, excitation, fidgeting and bright or red complexion come mostly within *yang* syndromes, while those characterized by hypoactivity, inhibition, quiescence and sallow or pale complexion come mainly within the *yin*. These have been shown in the descriptions of the previous six principles. The following are the main features of syndromes of collapse of *yin* and those of collapse of *yang*. (Tab. 8.)

Tab. 8. **Differentiation of syndromes of collapse of**
yin **and collapse of** *yang*.

Syndrome of collapse of *yin*	Syndrome of collapse of *yang*
Sticky sweating, shortness of breath and rapid breathing, flushed face, thirst and preference for cold drinks, hot skin, warm hands and feet, dislike of heat, restlessness.	Profuse cold sweating, feeble breathing, pallor, preference for hot drinks, cool skin, cold limbs, dislike of cold, listlessness.
Thready rapid pulse of the *xu* type.	Pulse of the *xu* type, thready and fading.
Red tongue with little saliva.	Pale and moist tongue.

II. DIFFERENTIATION OF SYNDROMES

According to the Theory of *Zang-fu*

Differentiating diseases according to the theory of *zang-fu* is to identify visceral diseases by basing on their physiological conditions, as each of them exerts different physiological functions. When disorder occurs in a *zang* or *fu* organ, it may be confined to that particular organ, or it may impart its influence to or be influenced by disorders of other organs. A brief description of the main syndromes of each of the *zang-fu* organs is given as follows for reference:

1. Syndromes of the heart

(1) Weakness of the *qi* (vital energy) of the heart

Clinical manifestations: Palpitation and shortness of breath aggravated by exertion, pale tongue, thready pulse of the *xu* type or missed-beat pulse. If there is evidence of *xu* (deficiency) of the *yang* of the heart, there may be chills, cold limbs, pallor and purplish lips. Exhaustion of the *yang* of the heart may show in profuse sweating, mental confusion and fading thready pulse.

Etiology and pathology: This syndrome is usually caused by asthenia after a long illness or mental irritation which injures the qi of the heart. When the qi of the heart is weak, it fails to pump blood normally, resulting in palpitation, shortness of breath and thready pulse of the xu type or missed-beat pulse. On the other hand, long duration of weakness of the qi of the heart may lead to weakness of the yang of the heart. When the body lacks yang, it lacks energy and heat, and manifestations such as chills, cold limbs and pallor occur. In case of exhaustion of the yang of the heart, the defensive qi of the body surface can no longer protect the essential qi and lets it dissipate. Manifestations are profuse sweating and fading thready pulse.

(2) Insufficiency of the yin of the heart.

Clinical manifestations: Palpitation, insomnia, dream-disturbed sleep, mental restlessness, with possible malar flush and low grade fever, red tongue, thready and rapid pulse.

Etiology and pathology: This syndrome is usually due to damage of yin by a febrile disease or to mental irritation which consumes the yin of the heart. Insufficiency of the yin of the heart often leads to hyperactivity of the fire (yang) of the heart, resulting in the above manifestations. Insufficiency of the yin of the heart may cause insufficiency of the blood of the heart. In that case, the yin and blood are not sufficient to nourish the heart, the heart fails in its function of housing the mind, and there appear symptoms of insomnia, poor memory, dream-disturbed sleep, etc.

(3) Stagnation of the blood of the heart.

Clinical manifestations: Palpitation, cardiac retardation and pain (paroxysms of pricking pain in mild cases and colicky pain in severe cases referring to the shoulder and back), cyanosis of lips and nails, dark purplish tongue or purple spots on the tongue, thready and missed-beat pulse.

Etiology and pathology: This syndrome is often due to mental irritation leading to stagnation of qi and, further, to stagnation of blood. Or, it may be due to insufficiency of the qi of the heart after a long illness, in which case the qi of the heart is too weak to pump the blood normally, resulting in stagnation of the blood of the heart and obstruction of the vessels. There occur palpitation, and cardiac pain which may even be colicky. Stagnation of blood often impedes the distribution of yang qi in the chest, bringing on discomfort in the chest and cyanosis of lips and nails. Dark purplish tongue or purple spots on the tongue and thready and missed-beat pulse are both manifestations of stagnation of blood and confinement of *yang qi.*

(4) Hyperactivity of the fire of the heart.

Clinical manifestations: Ulceration, swelling and pain of the mouth and tongue, insomnia accompanied with a feverish sensation, flushed face, bitter taste in mouth, hot and dark yellow urine, red tongue, rapid pulse.

Etiology and pathology: This syndrome is often due to mental irritation which causes depression of *qi.* Before long, the depressed *qi* may turn into endogenous fire to disturb the mind. So there appear insomnia accompanied with a feverish sensation. As the heart connects with the tongue and its function is reflected on the face, flare-up of the fire of the heart may cause ulceration, swelling and pain of the mouth and tongue, red tongue, bitter taste in the mouth and flushed face.

(5) Derangement of the mind.

Clinical manifestations: Mental depression, dullness, muttering to oneself, weeping and laughing without apparent reason, incoherent speech, mania, and, in severe cases, semi-consciousness and even coma.

Etiology and pathology: This syndrome is often due to mental irritation which causes depression of *qi.* The body fluid stagnates to form damp-phlegm which causes blurring of the heart and mind — the cause of the dullness and mental depression. If the depressed *qi* turns into fire and phlegm-fire disturbs the heart, mental restlessness results, with incoherent speech and mania. Blurring of the mind by phlegm-damp or phlegm-fire may be a contributing cause of coma. High fever, coma and delirium resulting from invasion of the pericardium by heat are due to pathogenic heat sinking deep in the interior of the body to disturb the mind.

2. Syndromes of the liver

(1) Depression of the *qi* of the liver.

Clinical manifestations: Hypochondriac and lower-abdominal pain and distension, distending sensation of the breasts, discomfort in the chest, belching, sighing; or there may be a sensation of a foreign body in the throat, and irregular menstruation in women.

Etiology and pathology: This syndrome is usually due to mental irritation causing depression of the *qi* of the liver and stagnation of the *qi* of the Liver Channel, which leads to hypochondriac and lower-abdominal pain and distension, distending sensation of the breasts, discomfort in the chest and sighing. Stagnation of the *qi* of the liver may affect the stomach, causing failure of the *qi* of the stomach to descend, hence the belching. The sensation of a foreign body in the throat is due to stagnation of the *qi* of the Liver Channel, which, with the phlegm, forms a lump in the throat. Depression of the *qi* of the liver and its dysfunction in promoting unrestraint and patency of *qi* may further impair its function of storing blood. Moreover, stagnation of *qi* leads to stagnation of blood — the cause of irregular menstruation.

(2) Flare-up of the fire of the liver.

Clinical manifestations: Dizziness, distending sensation in the head, headache, red eyes, bitter taste in mouth, flushed face, irascibility, sometimes even hematemesis and epistaxis, red tongue with yellow coating, wiry and rapid pulse.

Etiology and pathology: This syndrome is often due to a long-standing depression of the *qi* of the liver which later turns into fire. Or, it may be due to indulgence in drinking and smoking causing accumulation of heat which turns into fire. The upward disturbance of the fire of the liver is the cause of dizziness, distending sensation in the head, headache, red eyes, bitter taste in mouth and flushed face. Fire injures the liver, causing impairment of its function in promoting the *qi* to flow unrestrained and freely and causing irascibility. When the fire of the liver injures the blood vessels and causes extravasation of blood, hematemesis and epistaxis occur.

(3) Stagnation of cold in the channel of the liver.

Clinical manifestations: Lower-abdominal pain, swelling and distension in the testis with bearing-down pain. The scrotum may be cold and contracted, which can be alleviated by warmth. The tongue is pale with white coating, the pulse deep and wiry, or slow.

Etiology and pathology: The channel of the liver curves around the external genitalia and passes through the lower-abdominal region. When cold, which is characterized by contraction and stagnation, stays in the channel of the liver, stagnation of *qi* and blood may occur and cause lower-abdominal pain and swelling and distension of the testis with bearing-down pain. Cold and contraction of the scrotum are also due to this characteristic of pathogenic cold.

(4) Insufficiency of the blood of the liver.

Clinical manifestations: Dizziness, blurring of vision, dryness of the eyes, pallor, spasm of tendons and muscles, numbness of limbs; in women, scanty light-coloured menstrual flow with prolonged cycle.

Etiology and pathology: This syndrome often occurs after hemorrhage or other chronic diseases in which blood is consumed and that which is stored in the liver continuously decreases, failing to nourish the channels.

Moreover, *xu* (deficiency) of blood may cause rising of the wind so that spasm of tendons and muscles and numbness of limbs appear. Upward disturbance of the wind (which is of the *xu* type) is the cause of dizziness and blurring of vision. Insufficiency of the blood of the liver and disturbance in the function of storing blood result in emptiness of the Chong Channel, which is the cause of the above-mentioned menstrual abnormality.

(5) Stirring of the wind of the liver by heat.

Clinical manifestations: High fever, convulsion, neck rigidity; in severe cases, opisthotonos, coma, staring of the eyes upward; deep-red tongue, wiry and rapid pulse.

Etiology and pathology: This syndrome is due to transmission of pathogenic heat from the exterior to the interior, which burns the *yin* of the liver and deprives tendons and vessels of nourishment. Furthermore, pathogenic heat in the interior stirs up endogenous wind (which is of *xu* type), eliciting high fever, convulsion, neck rigidity and in severe cases opisthotonos. Coma is due to pathogenic heat affecting the pericardium and disturbing the mind.

3. Syndromes of the spleen

(1) Weakness of the *qi* (vital energy) of the spleen.

Clinical manifestations: Sallow complexion, anorexia, loose stools, edema, lassitude. There may be distension and a bearing-down sensation of the abdomen and prolapse of the rectum and uterus, or chronic hemorrhage such as purpura, bloody stools and uterine bleeding; pale tongue, thready pulse of the *xu* type. If there is evidence of *xu* (deficiency) of the *yang* of the spleen, there may appear cold manifestations such as chilliness and cold limbs in addition to the symptoms and signs mentioned above.

Etiology and pathology: This syndrome is often caused by irregular food intake, excessive mental strain or protracted chronic disease, which results in weakness of the *qi* of the spleen and impairs its function of transportation and transformation, with consequent poor appetite and loose stools. Accumulation of fluid in the interior is the cause of edema. Sallowness and lassitude are due to lack of essence of food, providing no source for blood formation. When the *qi* of the spleen is weak, it loses its ability to uplift the tissue, so that there is distension and a bearing-down sensation in the abdomen, and prolapse of the rectum and uterus. Weakness of the *qi* of the spleen, which controls blood, is also the cause of various kinds of chronic hemorrhage. *Xu* (deficiency) of the *yang* of the spleen is the cause for chilliness and cold limbs, as *yang* is warmth-producing.

(2) Invasion of the spleen by cold-damp.

Clinical manifestations: Fullness and distension in the chest and epigastrium, poor appetite, heaviness of the head, general lassitude, borborygmus, abdominal pain, loose stools, white sticky tongue coating, thready pulse.

Etiology and pathology: This syndrome usually occurs after chilling by rain, or it may be due to over-eating of raw or cold food. In either case, pathogenic cold-damp injures the spleen, impairing its function of transportation and transformation and resulting in poor appetite, borborygmus, abdominal pain and loose stools. As pathogenic damp is sticky and stagnant in nature, it is liable to block the passage of *qi*, causing epigastric fullness and distension, heaviness of the head and lassitude.

4. Syndromes of the lung

(1) Invasion of the lung by pathogenic wind.

Clinical manifestations: Itchy throat and cough with possible fever and chills. If wind is accompanied by cold (i.e., invasion of the lung by wind-cold), chilliness is accented, with nasal obstruction, watery nasal discharge, expectoration of mucoid sputum, and thin white tongue coating. If wind is accompanied with heat (i.e., invasion of the lung by wind-heat), fever is prominent, with redness, swelling and soreness of the throat, purulent nasal discharge, expectoration of purulent sputum and yellow tongue coating.

Etiology and pathology: Invasion of the lung by exogenous pathogenic wind disturbs its dispersing and descending function. Normal respiration of the lung is affected, producing cough and nasal obstruction. Cold, as a *yin* pathogenic factor, is liable to damage *yang qi*. So, when wind is accompanied with cold, chilliness will be more severe than fever, and there will be watery nasal discharge and white sputum. Heat as a *yang* pathogenic factor is liable to consume *yin* fluid. In the case of wind accompanied by heat, fever becomes the more prominent symptom, with thick nasal discharge and purulent sputum.

(2) Retention of damp-phlegm in the lung.

Clinical manifestations: Cough, shortness of breath, and expectoration of much dilute, white frothy sputum. Onset is generally elicited by cold. The tongue coating is white and sometimes sticky.

Etiology and pathology: This syndrome is usually due to disturbance in the normal dissemination of body fluid, the accumulation of which causes formation of damp-phlegm. When damp-phlegm stays in the lung and blocks the passage of *qi*, the function of dispersion and descending will be impaired, followed by the occurrence of the above-mentioned symptoms.

(3) Retention of phlegm-heat in the lung.

Clinical manifestations: Cough, shortness of breath or asthmatic breathing, expectoration of much thick purulent yellowish-green sputum, or even bloody foul-smelling pus. There may be chills and fever, red tongue with yellow coating and rapid pulse.

Etiology and pathology: This syndrome is usually caused by invasion of exogenous wind-heat or wind-cold which later develops into heat. The heat mixes with phlegm in the body which remains in the lung blocking the passage of *qi*, disturbing the lung's dispersing and descending function, and causing cough and shortness of breath or asthmatic breathing. Heat exhausts body fluid, causing expectoration of purulent sputum. When phlegm-heat blocks the vessels of the lung, there will be blood stagnation or ulceration leading to expectoration of foul purulent sputum specked with blood.

(4) Insufficiency of the *yin* of the lung.

Clinical manifestations: Dry unproductive cough or cough with sticky sputum scanty in amount or blood-tinged, afternoon fever, malar flush, feverish sensation in palms and soles, dry mouth, night sweating, red tongue, thready and rapid pulse.

Etiology and pathology: This syndrome is usually due to chronic lung disease which consumes the *yin* of the lung and results in insufficiency of body fluid. The lung is deprived of nourishment resulting in dysfunction in dispersing and descending, and producing dry mouth. *Xu* (deficiency) of *yin* causes endogenous heat, which squeezes out body fluid and injures the vessels. Afternoon fever, malar flush, feverish sensation in palms and soles, night sweating and expectoration of bloody sputum result.

5. Syndromes of the kidney

(1) Weakness of the *qi* (vital energy) of the kidney.

Clinical manifestations: Soreness and weakness of the lumbar region and knee joints, frequent urination, polyuria, dribbling of urine after urination, enuresis, incontinence of urine, nocturnal emission and even infertility, shortness of breath, asthmatic breathing, and thready pulse.

Etiology and pathology: This syndrome is usually due to asthenia after a long illness, senile feebleness or congenital deficiency. Weakness of the *qi* of the kidney causes inability of the urinary bladder to control urination, hence the enuresis, incontinence of urine and frequency and urgency of urination. The kidney stores essence. But when the *qi* of the kidney is weak, it fails in this function, and nocturnal emission, prospermia and even infertility result. When the *qi* of the kidney, which organ controls the reception of *qi*, is weak, it fails to help the lung perform its function of descending. Subsequent upward attack of the *qi* of the lung results in shortness of breath and asthmatic breathing.

(2) Insufficiency of the *yang* of the kidney.

Clinical manifestations: There may occur the same manifestations as in the syndrome of weakness of *qi* of the kidney, chiefly aching and coldness of the lumbar region and knee joints, chilliness, pallor, impotence, oliguria, edema of the lower limbs, pale tongue, deep and thready pulse.

Etiology and pathology: This syndrome usually occurs after a prolonged illness in which the *yang* of the kidney is injured. Or, it may be due to excess sexual activity, which injures the *yang* of the kidney. In either case, the *yang* of the kidney fails to warm the body, which explains the chilliness, aching and coldness in the lumbar region and knee joints, and impotence. Kidney presides over water metabolism, and insufficiency of the *yang* of the kidney results in its failing to divide the clear fluid from the turbid, which in turn results in oliguria. Excess fluid retained in the body is edema.

(3) Insufficiency of the *yin* of the kidney.

Clinical manifestations: Manifestations may be similar to those in the syndrome of weakness of the *qi* of the kidney; i.e., dizziness, blurring of vision, tinnitus, poor memory, feverish sensation in palms and soles, malar flush, night sweating, hot deep-yellow urine, constipation, red tongue, thready and rapid pulse.

Etiology and pathology: This syndrome usually occurs after a long illness in which the *yin* of the kidney is impaired. Or, it may be due to over-indulgence in sex, which consumes the essence of the kidney. For whichever cause the *yin* of the kidney fails in its function of producing marrow and with it filling out the brain. The result is dizziness, blurring of vision, poor memory and tinnitus. *Xu* (deficiency) of *yin* causes endogenous heat which consumes body fluid, the result being a feverish sensation in palms and soles, malar flush, night sweating, hot deep-yellow urine and constipation.

6. Syndromes of the pericardium

The syndromes of the pericardium seen clinically are invasion of the pericardium by heat. Their main manifestations are high fever, coma and delirium due to the sinking of pathogenic heat deep into the interior which disturbs the mind. For details, refer to the syndromes of the heart on "derangement of the mind".

7. Syndromes of the small intestine

Disturbance of the function of the small intestine in digestion and absorption is usually included in dysfunction of the spleen in transportation and transformation. Besides, there is a syndrome known as "heat in the heart shifting to the small intestine". Its clinical manifestations are the same as those in the syndrome of hyperactivity of the fire of the heart.

8. Syndromes of the gall bladder

Damp-heat in the gall bladder.

Clinical manifestations: The sclera and skin are bright yellow. The patient may complain of pain in the costal and hypochondriac region or severe pain in the right upper abdomen with bitter taste in the mouth. Some patients may vomit sour and bitter fluid. The tongue coating is yellow and sticky.

Etiology and pathology: The function of the gall bladder to store and excrete bile depends upon the normal function of the liver in promoting the free passage of qi. Exogenous pathogenic damp-heat, heat caused by depression of the liver, or endogenous damp-heat caused by long indulgence in alcohol or rich food may accumulate in the liver and gall bladder and impair their function in promoting the unhindered passage of qi so that bile cannot be secreted and excreted freely. An overflow of bile causes jaundice, bitter taste in the mouth and vomiting of sour and bitter fluid. Stagnation of the qi of the liver and gall bladder leads to stagnation of blood, causing hypochondriac pain and colicky pain in the right upper abdomen. As this syndrome is closely related to the liver, it is also known as the syndrome of damp-heat in the liver and gall bladder.

9. Syndromes of the stomach.

(1) Retention of food in the stomach.

Clinical manifestations: Distension and pain in the epigastric region, loss of appetite, foul belching and sour regurgitation. There may be vomiting and the tongue has a thick sticky coating.

Etiology and pathology: This syndrome is usually caused by overeating, which leads to the retention of undigested food in the stomach. The qi of the stomach ascends instead of descending as it should.

(2) Retention of fluid in the stomach due to cold.

Clinical manifestations: Fullness and dull pain in the epigastric region which is generally aggravated by cold and alleviated by warmth, succussion-sound in the epigastric region, vomiting of watery fluid, white sticky tongue coating, thready or slow pulse.

Etiology and pathology: This syndrome usually follows chilling after being caught in rain, or perhaps by eating too much raw or cold food. In either case, the cold is congealed in the stomach causing stagnation of its *qi* and causing pain. Prolonged illness injures the *yang qi* of the spleen and stomach so that the body fluid is retained in the stomach instead of being transported and transformed, hence the vomiting of watery fluid and succussion-sound in the epigastric region.

(3) Hyperactivity of the fire of the stomach.

Clinical manifestations: Burning pain in the epigastrium, thirst, and preference for cold drinks, vomiting undigested food or sour fluid; gingival swelling, pain, ulceration and bleeding, foul breath, red tongue with dry yellow coating.

Etiology and pathology: This syndrome is usually due to over-eating of rich food, which accumulates heat in the stomach. The heat consumes body fluid and causes the *qi* of the stomach to ascend. So there appear burning pain in the epigastrium, thirst, preference for cold drinks, and vomiting. Foul breath and gingival ulceration and bleeding are due to the fire element in the stomach.

10. Syndromes of the large intestine

(1) Damp-heat in the large intestine.

Clinical manifestations: Fever, abdominal pain, loose dark stools with offensive smell, frequency of bowel movements. There may be white and red mucus in stool, burning sensation of the anus, and tenesmus. The tongue is red with yellow coating and pulse rolling and rapid.

Etiology and pathology: This syndrome is usually caused by eating too much raw or cold food, or eating unclean or spoiled food. It may also be due to invasion by pathogenic summer heat and damp. Damp-heat accumulates in the large intestine and blocks the passage of *qi*, causing disturbance in its function of transmission and transformation, producing diarrhea, abdominal pain and dark, foul-smelling stools. Damp-heat may injure the blood vessels of the large intestine, producing the red mucus in the stool. Damp-heat presses downward, causing burning sensation in the anus, and tenesmus.

(2) Stasis of the large intestine.

Clinical manifestations: Distension and fullness in the abdomen, abdominal pain intensified upon pressure, constipation, nausea and vomiting, white sticky tongue coating, deep pulse of the *shi* type.

Etiology and pathology: This syndrome is usually due to retention of food, parasites or blood stagnation causing obstruction of *qi* and functional derangement of the large intestine, causing the constipation, abdominal distension and pain. The nausea and vomiting result from the *qi* of the large intestine impeding the descending of the *qi* of the stomach.

(3) Stagnation of blood and heat in the large intestine.

Clinical manifestations: Severe or drilling fixed pain in the lower abdomen which the patient is reluctant to have pressed, constipation or mild diarrhea. There may be fever and vomiting, red tongue with yellow sticky coating.

Etiology and pathology: This syndrome is usually due to inadaptability of the individual to weather changes, over-eating, or vigorous walking which causes stagnation of heat and blood and retardation of *qi*. Heat injures the vessels of the large intestine, causing local inflammation or abscess formation — the cause of the drilling pain in the lower abdomen. If the stomach is affected by failure of its *qi* to pass downward, there may be nausea and vomiting.

11. Syndromes of the urinary bladder

(1) Damp-heat in the urinary bladder.

Clinical manifestations: Frequency and urgency of urination, difficult urination scanty in amount and with reddish tinge, burning pain in the urethra. There may be blood clots or stones in the urine, red tongue with yellow coating, fairly rapid pulse.

Etiology and pathology: Damp-heat injures the urinary bladder, causing disturbance in its function of storing and discharging urine, and producing the frequency and urgency of urination. When damp-heat injures the blood vessels of the urinary bladder there may appear stagnation of blood and heat, leading to hematuria or blood clots in the urine. Prolonged retention of damp-heat in the bladder will result in the formation of stones.

(2) Disturbance in the function of the urinary bladder.

Clinical manifestations: Dribbling urination, weak stream, or even retention of urine, accompanied by weakness of the lumbar region and knee joints, intolerance to cold, pallor, pale tongue with white coating, deep thready pulse of the *xu* type.

Etiology and pathology: This syndrome is usually due to insufficiency of the *yang* of the kidney and impairment of its function of dividing the clear fluid from the turbid, which further causes disturbance of the urinary bladder in discharging urine and the above-mentioned symptoms. Manifestations of cold follow insufficiency of the *yang* of the kidney, such as intolerance to cold, cold extremities, weakness of the lumbar region and knee joints, and pallor.

Sanjiao syndromes are involved in syndromes of the *zang* and *fu* organs relating to the upper, middle and lower *jiao*. Obstruction of the upper *jiao*, for example, refers to confinement of the *qi* of the *lung*; insufficiency of the *qi* of the middle *jiao* refers to weakness of the spleen and stomach; damp-heat in the lower *jiao* means damp-heat in the urinary bladder. *Sanjiao* is unexplainable as a single entity.

III. DIFFERENTIATION OF SYNDROMES ACCCRDING TO THE THEORY OF CHANNELS AND COLLATERALS

This is to differentiate diseases on the basis of the physiology of channels and collaterals. It gives direct guidance to clinical therapy by acupuncture and moxibustion.

As each of the channels follows its specific course of circulation, the free flowing of the *qi* of the channel and sufficiency of the *qi* (vital energy) and blood, or their opposites, are bound to be manifested at the area supplied by the channel. The twelve regular channels respectively connect with and pertain to the *zang-fu* organs. Disorders of channels may affect the corresponding *zang-fu* organs, and disorders of the *zang-fu* organs will be reflected at the corresponding channels. It is possible, therefore, to determine which channel is affected by studying the location and characteristics of the symptoms and signs.

The main pathological manifestations of the twelve regular channels and the eight extra channels may be described as follows:

1. Pathological manifestations of the 12 regular channels

(1) The Lung Channel of Hand-Taiyin. Cough, asthma, hemoptysis, congested and sore throat, sensation of fullness in chest, pain in the supraclavicular fossa, shoulder, back and the anterior border of the medial aspect of the arm.

(2) The Large Intestine Channel of Hand-Yangming. Epistaxis, watery nasal discharge, toothache, congested and sore throat, pain in the neck, anterior part of the shoulder and anterior border of the extension aspect of the upper limb, borborygmus, abdominal pain, diarrhea, dysentery.

(3) The Stomach Channel of Foot-Yangming. Borborygmus, abdominal distension, edema, epigastric pain, vomiting, feeling of hunger, epistaxis, deviation of eyes and mouth, congested and sore throat, pain in the chest, abdomen and lateral aspect of the lower limbs, fever, mental disturbance.

(4) The Spleen Channel of Foot-Taiyin. Belching, vomiting, epigastric pain, abdominal distension, loose stools, jaundice, sluggishness and general malaise, stiffness and pain at the root of the tongue, swelling and coldness in the medial aspect of the thigh and knee.

(5) The Heart Channel of Hand-Shaoyin. Cardialgia, palpitation, hypochondriac pain, insomnia, night sweating, dryness of the throat, thirst, pain in the medial aspect of the upper arm, feverishness in palms.

(6) The Small Intestine Channel of Hand-Taiyang. Deafness, yellow sclera, sore throat, swelling of the cheek, distension and pain in the lower abdomen, frequent urination, pain along the posterior border of the lateral aspect of the shoulder and arm.

(7) The Urinary Bladder Channel of Foot-Taiyang. Retention of urine, enuresis, mental disturbance, malaria, ophthalmodynia, lacrimation when exposed to wind, nasal obstruction, rhinitis, epistaxis, headache, pain in the nape, upper and lower back, buttocks and posterior aspect of lower limbs.

(8) The Kidney Channel of Foot-Shaoyin. Enuresis, frequent urination, nocturnal emission, impotence, irregular menstruation, asthma, hemoptysis, dryness of the tongue, congested and sore throat, edema, lumbago, pain along the spinal column and the medial aspect of the thigh, weakness of the lower limbs, feverish sensation in soles.

(9) The Pericardium Channel of Hand-Jueyin. Cardialgia, palpitation, mental restlessness, stifling feeling in chest, flushed face, swelling in the axilla, mental disturbance, spasm of the upper limbs, feverishness in palms.

(10) The Sanjiao Channel of Hand-Shaoyang. Abdominal distension, edema, enuresis, dysuria, deafness, tinnitus, pain in the outer canthus, swelling of the cheeks, congested and sore throat, pain in the retroauricular region, shoulder, and lateral aspect of the arm and elbow.

(11) The Gall bladder Channel of Foot-Shaoyang. Headache, pain in the outer canthus, pain in the jaw, blurring of vision, bitter taste in mouth, swelling and pain in the supraclavicular fossa, pain in the axilla, pain along the lateral aspect of the chest, hypochondrium, thigh and lower limbs.

(12) The Liver Channel of Foot-Jueyin. Low back pain, fullness in the chest, pain in the lower abdomen, hernia, vertical headache, dryness of the throat, hiccup, enuresis, dysuria, mental disturbance.

2. Pathological manifestations of the eight extra channels

(1) The Du Channel. Stiffness and pain of the spinal column, opisthotonos, headache.

(2) The Ren Channel. Leukorrhea, irregular menstruation, hernia, enuresis, retention of urine, pain in the epigastric region and lower abdomen.

(3) The Chong Channel. Spasm and pain in the abdomen.

(4) The Dai Channel. Abdominal pain, weakness and pain of the lumbar region, leukorrhea.

(5) The Yangqiao Channel. Epilepsy, insomnia.

(6) The Yinqiao Channel. Hypersomnia.

(7) The Yangwei Channel. Chills and fever.

(8) The Yinwei Channel. Cardialgia.

PART II

Channels, Collaterals and Points

CHAPTER I

AN INTRODUCTION TO CHANNELS, COLLATERALS AND POINTS

Channels and collaterals are passages through which *qi* and blood circulate. Interiorly they connect with the *zang-fu* organs and exteriorly with the body surface where points are distributed. Points are thus the specific sites through which the *qi* of the *zang-fu* organs and channels is transported to the body surface. When the human body is affected by a disease, treatment is possible by puncturing the corresponding points on the body surface, which regulates the *qi* and blood in the channels. This chapter will describe the main feature of the channels and points.

I. DISTRIBUTION OF THE 14 CHANNELS ON THE BODY SURFACE

Each of the fourteen channels on the body surface has its own course. Generally speaking, the twelve regular channels are distributed symmetrically on the right and left sides of the body. Among them, the three *yin* channels of hand run from the chest to the hand, the three *yang* channels of hand from the hand to the head, the three *yang* channels of foot from the head to the foot, and the three *yin* channels of foot from the foot to the abdomen and chest. The Ren and Du Channels originate from the perineum and ascend along the anterior and the posterior midline of the body respectively. The distribution of the channels will be explained in three regions of the body: 1. the extremities, 2. the trunk, 3. the head, face and neck.

1. The extremities.

Both the upper and lower extremities are divided into the medial and lateral aspects. On the upper extremities, the flexor (palmar) side is the medial aspect and the extensor (dorsal) side is the lateral aspect. As to the lower extremities, the tibial side is the medial aspect and the fibular side is the lateral aspect. The *yang* channels are mainly located in the lateral aspect of the extremities, and the *yin* channels in the medial aspect. The arrangement of the three *yang* channels of hand and foot is generally in the following order: Yangming Channels are situated anteriorly, Shaoyang Channels intermediately and Taiyang Channels posteriorly. As to the distribution of the three *yin* channels of hand and foot, Taiyin Channels are located anteriorly, Jueyin Channels intermediately and Shaoyin Channels posteriorly.

2. The trunk.

The distribution of the fourteen channels in the trunk is as follows:

Channel	Area supplied
The Lung Channel of Hand-Taiyin	Upper porton of the lateral side of chest
The Pericardium Channel of Hand-Jueyin	Lateral side of the breast
The Heart Channel of Hand-Shaoyin	Axilla
The Large Intestine Channel of Hand-Yangming	Anterior aspect of the shoulder
The Sanjiao Channel of Hand-Shaoyang	Superior aspect of the shoulder
The Small Intestine Channel of Hand-Taiyang	Scapular region
The Stomach Channel of Foot-Yangming	The 2nd lateral line of chest and abdomen
The Gall bladder Channel of Foot-Shaoyang	Lateral side of the hypochondrium and lumbar region
The Urinary Bladder Channel of Foot-Taiyang	The 1st and 2nd lateral line of back
The Spleen Channel of Foot-Taiyin	The 3rd lateral line of chest and abdomen
The Liver Channel of Foot-Jueyin	External genitalia and hypochondriac region
The Kidney Channel of Foot-Shaoyin	The 1st lateral line of chest and abdomen
The Du Channel	Posterior midline
The Ren Channel	Anterior midline

3. The head, face and neck.

Channel	Area supplied
The Large Intestine Channel of Hand-Yangming	Neck, lower teeth and the lateral side of nose
The Sanjiao Channel of Hand-Shaoyang	Neck, postauricular region, and the lateral end of eyebrow
The Small Intestine Channel of Hand-Taiyang	Neck, zygomatic region and the interior of ear
The Stomach Channel of Foot-Yangming	Infraorbital region, upper teeth, face and the anterior aspect of neck
The Gall bladder Channel of Foot-Shaoyang	Outer canthus, temporal region, the 2nd lateral line of head and the posterior aspect of neck
The Urinary Bladder Channel of Foot-Taiyang	Inner canthus, 1st lateral line of head and posterior aspect of neck
The Du Channel	Midsagittal line of head, posterior midline of neck, philtrum and gums of upper teeth
The Ren Channel	Anterior midline of neck and mentolabial groove.

(See Tab. 9 and Fig. 5.)

II.   CLASSIFICATION OF POINTS

Points are classified into 3 categories: points of the 14 channels, extraordinary points and Ahshi points.

1.   Points of the 14 channels

The points of the 14 channels, which make up the majority of all the points on the human body, are 361 in number. Those of the 12 regular channels exist in pairs distributed symmetrically on the left and the right side of the body, while those of the Ren and Du Channels are single, aligning on the anterior and the posterior midline respectively.

Among the points of the 14 channels some having specific functions are classified under specific names according to their locations and indications, such as the Five Shu Points, Yuan (Source) Points, Luo (Connecting) Points, Xi (Cleft) Points, Back-Shu Points, Front-Mu Points, and Crossing Points. They are important specific points and will be discussed later.

Tab. 9 Distribution of the fourteen channels on the body surface.

Channel		Distribution		
		Extremities	Trunk	Head, Face and Neck
The Three Yin Channels of Hand	Taiyin	Anterior line of medial aspect of upper extremity	Upper portion of lateral side of chest	
	Jueyin	Intermediate line of medial aspect of upper extremity	Lateral side of breast	
	Shaoyin	Posterior line of medial aspect of upper extremity	Axilla	
The Three Yang Channels of Hand	Yangming	Anterior line of lateral aspect of upper extremity	Anterior aspect of shoulder	Neck, lower teeth, lateral side of nose
	Shaoyang	Intermediate line of lateral aspect of upper extremity	Superior aspect of shoulder	Neck, postauricular region, lateral end of eyebrow
	Taiyang	Posterior line of lateral aspect of upper extremity	Scapular region	Neck, zygomatic region, interior of ear

Group	Channel	Lower extremity	Chest / abdomen	Head / neck
The Three Yang Channels of Foot	Yangming	Anterior line of lateral aspect of lower extremity	The 2nd lateral line of chest and abdomen	Infraorbital region, upper teeth, face, anterior aspect of neck
	Shaoyang	Intermediate line of lateral aspect of lower extremity	Lateral side of hypochondrium and lumbar region	Outer canthus, temporal region, 2nd lateral line of head, posterior aspect of neck
	Taiyang	Posterior aspect of lower extremity	The 1st and 2nd lateral lines of back	Inner canthus, 1st lateral line of head, posterior aspect of neck
The Three Yin Channels of Foot	Taiyin	Intermediate and anterior line of medial aspect of lower extremity	The 3rd lateral line of chest and abdomen	
	Jueyin	Anterior and intermediate line of medial aspect of lower extremity	External genitalia, hypochondriac region	
	Shaoyin	Posterior line of medial aspect of lower extremity	The 1st lateral line of chest and abdomen	
The Du Channel			Posterior midline	Midsagittal line of head, posterior midline of neck, philtrum, gums of upper teeth
The Ren Channel			Anterior midline	Anterior midline of neck, mentolabial groove

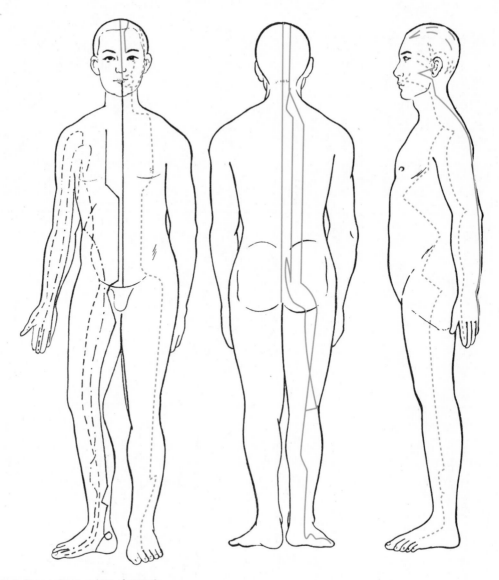

1. Red lines show *yang* channels.

   Black lines show *yin* channels.

2. — · — · — Taiyang and Shaoyin Channels of hand and foot, Ren and Du Channels

   — — — Shaoyang and Jueyin Channels of hand and foot

   ---------- Yangming and Taiyin Channels of hand and foot

Fig. 5.   Distribution of the 14 channels.

2. Extraordinary Points

These are useful in therapy, though discovered in the course of practice. They have definite locations but are not listed in the system of the 14 channels.

3. Ahshi Points

Ahshi points are tender spots or sensitive spots present in certain diseases. They have neither definite locations nor names. *Neijing* describes them: "Where there is a painful spot, there is an acupuncture point."

III. SPECIFIC POINTS

As mentioned above, among the points of the fourteen channels, a number have specific properties. They are grouped together under special names as follows:

1. Five Shu Points

Along each of the twelve regular channels, below the elbow or knee, lie five specific points, namely, Jing-Well, Ying-Spring, Shu-Stream, Jing-River and He-Sea. They are arranged in the above order from the distal ends of the limbs to the elbow or knee. These names image the flow of *qi* along the channels as the movement of water. Jing-Well is the place where the *qi* of the channel starts to bubble. Ying-Spring is where the *qi* of the channel starts to flourish. Shu-Stream is where the *qi* of the channel flourishes. Jing-River is where the *qi* of the channel increases in abundance. Finally, He-Sea represents the confluence of rivers in the sea, where the *qi* of the channel is the most flourishing.

The therapeutic properties of the Five Shu Points are as follows:

Jing-Well Points are indicated in mental illness and a stifling sensation in the chest, Ying-Spring Points in febrile diseases, Shu-Stream Points in *bi* syndrome (painful joints) caused by pathogenic wind and damp, Jing-River Points in asthma, cough and throat disorders, and He-Sea Points in disorders of the intestines, stomach and the other *fu* organs. (Each of the six *fu* organs has a He-Sea Point in the three *yang* channels of foot respectively, known as the Inferior He-Sea Point.)

2. Yuan (Source) Points

Each of the twelve regular channels has a Yuan (Source) Point in the extremities where the original *qi* is retained. In the *yin* channels, the Yuan (Source) Points coincide with the Shu-Stream Points of the Five Shu Points. The Yuan (Source) Points are of great significance in diagnosis and treatment of diseases of channels and *zang-fu* organs.

3. Luo (Connecting) Points

Each of the twelve regular channels has a collateral in the extremities connecting a definite pair of *yin* and *yang* channels which are externally-internally related. In the trunk, there are the collaterals of the Ren and Du Channels and the major collateral of the spleen distributed respectively in the posterior, anterior and lateral aspects of the body. Each of the collaterals has a Luo (Connecting) Point, making 15 in all. A Luo (Connecting) Point is used to treat diseases which involve the two externally-internally related channels and also diseases in the area supplied by the two channels.

4. Xi (Cleft) Points

The Xi (Cleft) Point is the site where the *qi* of the channel is deeply converged. There is a Xi (Cleft) Point in each of the twelve regular channels in the extremities, and one each in the four extra channels (Yinwei, Yangwei, Yinqiao, Yangqiao), — 16 in all. The Xi (Cleft) Points are used in treating acute disorders and pain in the areas supplied by their respective channels and those in their respective related organs.

5. Back-Shu Points

Back-Shu Points are Points at the back where the *qi* of the respective *zang-fu* organs is infused. They are located on either side of the vertebral column and are in close proximity to their respective related *zang-fu* organs. When any of the *zang-fu* organs malfunctions, an abnormal reaction such as tenderness will occur at the corresponding Back-Shu Point. These points play an important role in diagnosis and treatment of diseases in which their respective *zang-fu* organs are involved.

6. Front-Mu Points

Front-Mu Points are those points on the chest and abdomen where the *qi* of the respective *zang-fu* organs is infused. They are located close to their respective related *zang-fu* organs. When a *zang* or a *fu* organ is affected, an abnormal reaction such as tenderness may occur in the corresponding Front-Mu Point. These points are significant in diagnosis and treatment of diseases of their respective related *zang-fu* organs.

7. Crossing Points

Crossing Points are points at the intersection of two or more channels. They are mainly distributed on the head, face and trunk and are indicated in diseases involving several channels. The most important Crossing Points are those of the Ren and Du Channels, which have a variety of indications.

There are also Eight Influential Points dominating respectively the *zang* organs, *fu* organs, *qi*, blood, tendon, vessel, bone and marrow.

Moreover, there are Eight Confluent Points (or, the Confluent Points of the Eight Extra Channels) in the extremities where the twelve regular channels communicate with the eight extra channels.

Some points of one special group coincident with those of other special groups are of great significance in clinical practice.

IV. METHODS OF LOCATING POINTS

Each point has a definite location which must be determined accurately for effective therapeutic result. The following three methods of locating points accurately are introduced.

1. According to anatomical landmarks

Anatomical landmarks on the body surface, such as prominence or depression of the bone, joint, tendon, muscle, skin crease, hairline, border of nail, nipple, umbilicus, eye and mouth, are of specific significance in locating points. If the sites of points are in the vicinity of or on such landmarks, they can be located directly.

2. Proportional measurement

On the basis of anatomical landmarks, a measuring method has been established for locating points at a distance from anatomical landmarks — proportional measurement. The width or length of various portions of the human body are divided respectively into definite numbers of equal divisions, each division being termed one *cun*. These are taken as the unit of measurement in locating points. Obviously, the length of the *cun* depends upon the body build of the individual patient.

The following are standards for proportional measurement used in clinics.

(1) Head

Longitudinal measurement: The distance from the anterior hairline to the posterior hairline is taken as 12 *cun*. If the anterior hairline is indistinguishable, measurement can be taken from the glabella and 3 *cun* added. That is to say, the distance from the glabella to the posterior hairline is 15 *cun*. If the posterior hairline is also indistinguishable, measurement can be taken with point Dazhui (Du 14), and 3 *cun* added. The distance from the glabella to Dazhui (Du 14) then is 18 *cun*.

Transverse measurement: The distance between the two mastoid processes is 9 *cun*, as is that between points Touwei (St. 8) of both sides.

(2) Chest and abdomen

Longitudinal measurement: Measurement of the chest is based on the intercostal spaces. The distance from the end of the axillary fold on the lateral side of the chest to the tip of the 11th rib is measured as 12 *cun*. On the upper abdomen, the distance from the sternocostal angle to the centre of the umbilicus is measured as 8 *cun*. On the lower abdomen, the distance between the centre of the umbilicus and the upper border of symphysis pubis is 5 *cun*.

Transverse measurement: The distance between the two nipples or the two midclavicular lines is 8 *cun*.

(3) Back

Longitudinal measurement: This is based on the spinous processes of the vertebral column.

Transverse measurement: The distance between the medial border of the scapula and the posterior midline is 3 *cun*.

(4) Upper extremities

Upper arm: The distance between the end of the axillary fold and the transverse cubital crease is 9 *cun*.

Forearm: The distance between the transverse cubital crease and the transverse carpal crease is 12 *cun*.

The above two measurements are applicable to both the medial and the lateral aspect of the upper extremities.

(5) Lower extremities

The medial aspect of the thigh: The distance from the level of the upper border of symphysis pubis to the medial epicondyle of femur is 18 *cun*.

The lateral aspect of the thigh: The distance from the prominence of great trochanter to the middle of patella is 19 *cun*.

The medial aspect of the leg: The distance from the lower border of the medial condyle of tibia to the tip of medial malleolus is 13 *cun*.

The lateral aspect of the leg: The distance between the centre of patella and the tip of lateral malleolus is 16 *cun*.

(For proportional measurement, see Fig. 6.)

3. Finger measurement

The length and breadth of the patient's finger(s) are used as a criterion for locating points. The commonly used measuring methods are as follows:

(1) When the middle finger is flexed, the distance between the two ends of the creases of the interphalangeal joints is taken as one *cun*. (See Fig. 7.)

(2) The breadth of the four fingers (index, middle, ring and little fingers) close together at the level of the skin crease of the proximal interphalangeal joint at the dorsum of the middle finger is taken as 3 *cun*. (See Fig. 8.)

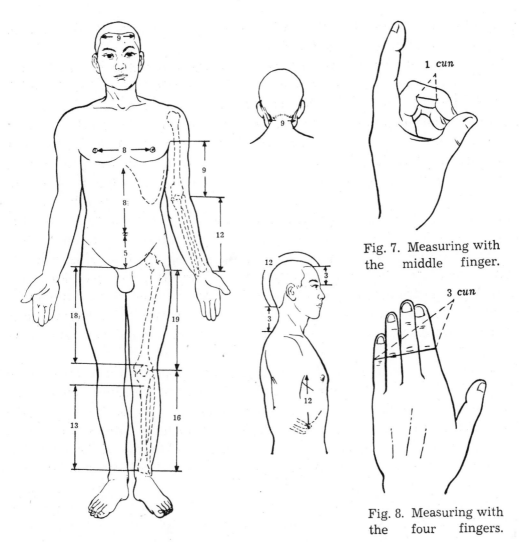

Fig. 7. Measuring with the middle finger.

Fig. 8. Measuring with the four fingers.

Fig. 6. Proportional unit.

V. AN OUTLINE OF THE THERAPEUTIC PROPERTIES OF THE POINTS OF THE 14 CHANNELS

The therapeutic properties of the points of the fourteen channels are summarized according to the principle: "The course of a channel is amenable to treatment." Points that pertain to the same channel have properties in common. For instance, all points of the Lung Channel of Hand-Taiyin can be used in treating disorders of the lung and throat, and all points of the Stomach Channel of Foot-Yangming are indicated in disorders of the gastrointestinal tract, head and face.

The therapeutic properties of the points are also based on their locations. Points located on the extremities can be used in treating disorders of both the extremities and the remote areas supplied by their pertaining channels, while points of the head, face and trunk are chiefly used in treating disorders in that area, including those of the *zang-fu* organs. For example, point Hegu (L.I. 4) of the Large Intestine Channel of Hand-Yangming, which is located on the hand, is used in treating disorders of the hand and arm and also those of the head and face where the channel passes; while point Yingxiang (L.I. 20) of the same channel, located on the face, is mainly indicated in disorders of the nose and face. Zusanli (St. 36), a point of the Stomach Channel of Foot-Yangming on the leg, is used not only to relieve disorders of the lower extremities. It is also used for disorders of the gastrointestinal tract, and the head and face at sites along the channel. Tianshu (St. 25) of the same channel on the abdomen is chiefly used to treat disorders of the abdomen, such as abdominal pain and diarrhea.

Not only do points of the same channel have therapeutic properties in common; points of the three *yin* channels or those of the three *yang* channels also have similarities in therapeutic properties. These mainly refer to the points located on the four extremities. For example, the points of the three *yin* channels of hand located on the upper extremities are indicated in disorders of the chest, and those of the three *yang* channels of hand are used in treating disorders of the head.

The therapeutic properties of the points on the trunk may be judged according to their locations and their adjacent *zang-fu* organs. In acupuncture, the human body is generally divided into the upper, middle and lower portions. Points of the chest and upper back (upper portion) are indicated in disorders of the heart and lung; those of the upper abdomen and lower back (middle portion) are indicated in disorders of the liver, gall bladder, spleen and stomach; while points of the lower abdomen and lumbosacral region (lower portion) are indicated in disorders of the kidney, intestines and urinary bladder. Owing to their specific locations, points of the head, face and neck as well as those of the Ren and Du Channels are not only indicated in diseases of the neighbouring organs, but also in constitutional symptoms.

For details, see Tab. 10, 11, and Fig. 9 — 13.

Tab. 10. Indications of points on the extremities with relation to channels.

	Channel	Indications of Individual Channel	Indications of Three Channels in Common
The Three Yin Channels of Hand	The Lung Channel of Hand-Taiyin	Disorders of lung and throat	Disorders of chest, mental illness
	The Pericardium Channel of Hand-Jueyin	Disorders of heart and stomach	
	The Heart Channel of Hand-Shaoyin	Disorders of heart	
The Three Yang Channels of Hand	The Large Intestine Channel of Hand-Yangming	Disorders of face, nose, mouth and teeth	Disorders of head, eye and throat, febrile diseases, mental illness
	The Sanjiao Channel of Hand-Shaoyang	Disorders of ear, and temporal and hypochondriac regions	
	The Small Intestine Channel of Hand-Taiyang	Disorders of neck, ear and scapular regions	

	Channel	Indications of Individual Channel	Indications of Three Channels in Common
The Three Yang Channels of Foot	The Stomach Channel of Foot-Yangming	Disorders of face, mouth, teeth, throat, stomach and intestines	
	The Gall Bladder Channel of Foot-Shaoyang	Disorders of eye, ear, and temporal and hypochondriac regions	Disorders of head, febrile diseases, mental illness
	The Urinary Bladder Channel of Foot-Taiyang	Disorders of neck, eye and dorso-lumbar region	
The Three Yin Channels of Foot	The Spleen Channel of Foot-Taiyin	Disorders of spleen, stomach and intestines	
	The Liver Channel of Foot-Jueyin	Disorders of liver and external genitalia	Disorders of abdomen and urogenital organs
	The Kidney Channel of Foot-Shaoyin	Disorders of kidney, intestines, lung and throat	

**Tab. 11. Indications of points on the head, face and trunk
with relation to locations.**

Locations of Points	Indications
Head, face, neck	Disorders of brain, eye, ear, nose, mouth, teeth and throat
Chest, upper dorsal region (corresponding to the region between the 1st and 7th thoracic vertebra)	Disorders of lung and heart
Upper abdomen, lower dorsal region (corresponding to the region between the 8th thoracic and the 1st lumbar vertebra)	Disorders of liver, gall bladder, spleen and stomach
Lower abdomen, lumbosacral region (corresponding to the region between the 2nd lumbar and the 4th sacral vertebra)	Disorders of kidney, intestines, and urinary bladder

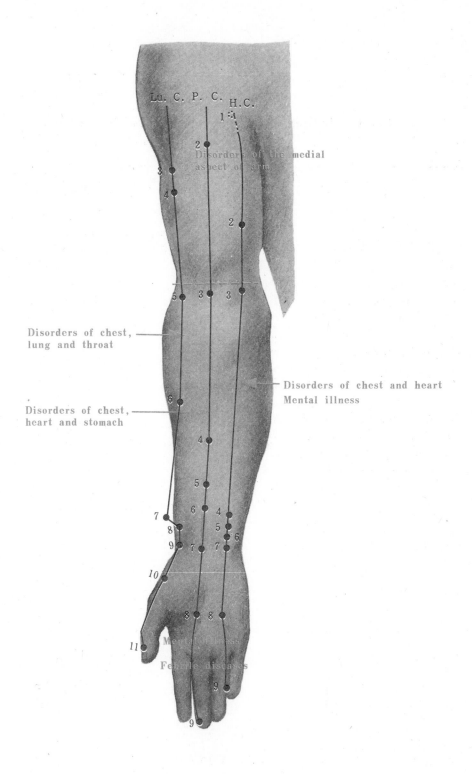

Fig. 9a. Therapeutic properties of points of
the upper extremities.

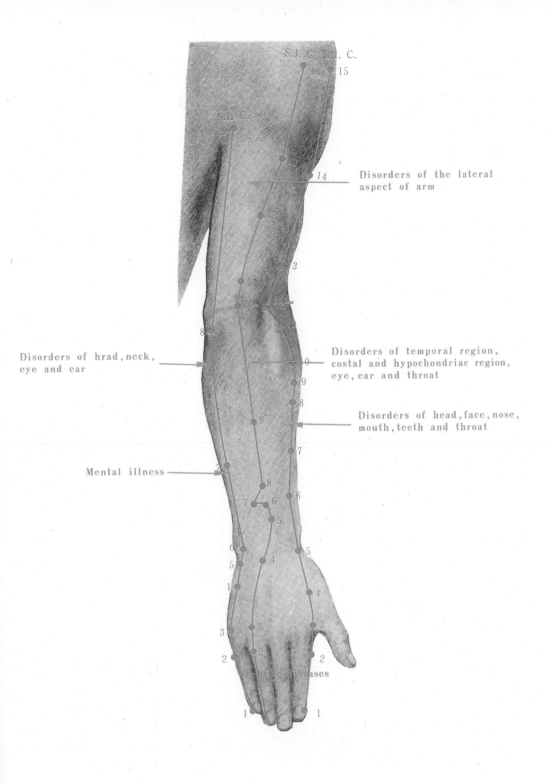

S.J. C. L.I. C.

S.I. C.

Disorders of the lateral
aspect of arm

Disorders of temporal region,
costal and hypochondriac region,
eye, ear and throat

Disorders of hrad, neck,
eye and ear

Disorders of head, face, nose,
mouth, teeth and throat

Mental illness

diseases

Fig. 9b.   Therapeutic properties of points
of the upper extremities.

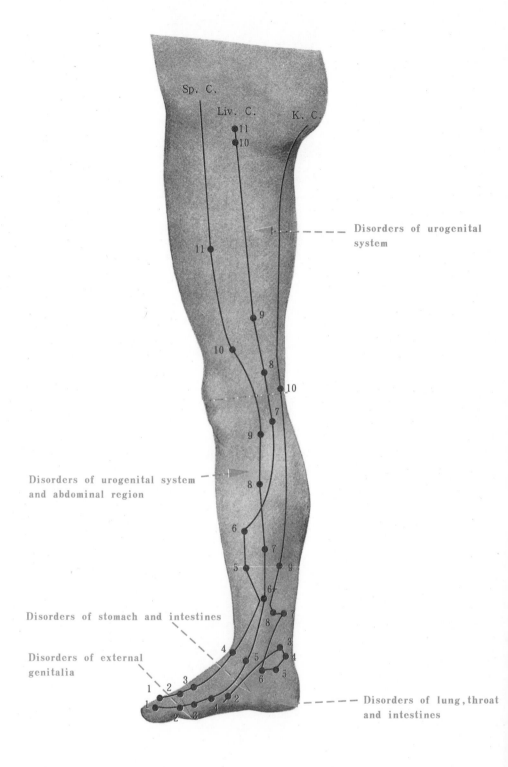

Fig. 10a. Therapeutic properties of points
of the lower extremities.

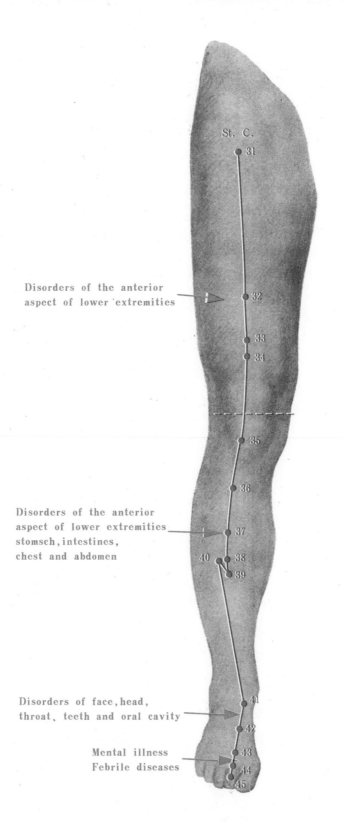

St. C.

31

Disorders of the anterior
aspect of lower extremities

32

33
34

35

36

Disorders of the anterior
aspect of lower extremities
stomsch, intestines,
chest and abdomen

37

40   38
          39

Disorders of face, head,
throat, teeth and oral cavity

41

42

Mental illness
Febrile diseases

43
44
45

Fig. 10b. Therapeutic properties of points
of the lower extremities.

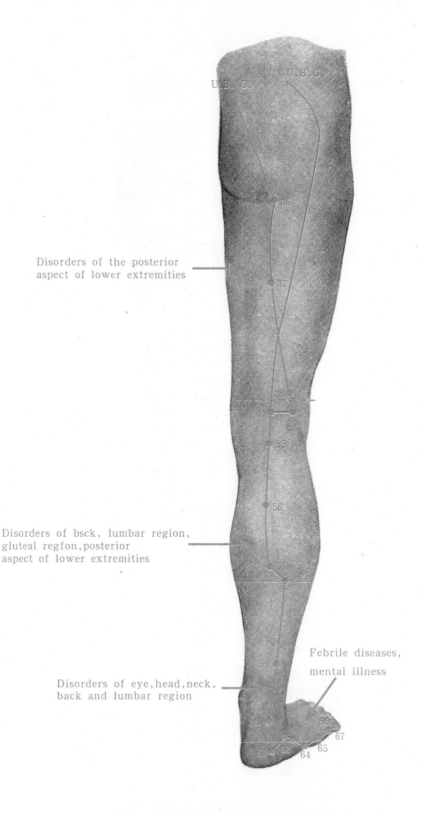

Fig. 10c. Therapeutic properties of points
of the lower extremities.

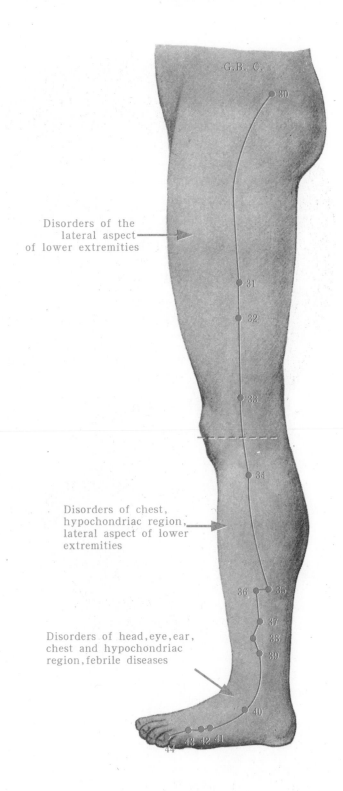

G.B. C.

80

Disorders of the
lateral aspect
of lower extremities

31

82

88

34

Disorders of chest,
hypochondriac region,
lateral aspect of lower
extremities

36   35

37
88
39

Disorders of head,eye,ear,
chest and hypochondriac
region,febrile diseases

40

43 42 41

44

Fig. 10d. Therapeutic properties of points
of the lower extremities.

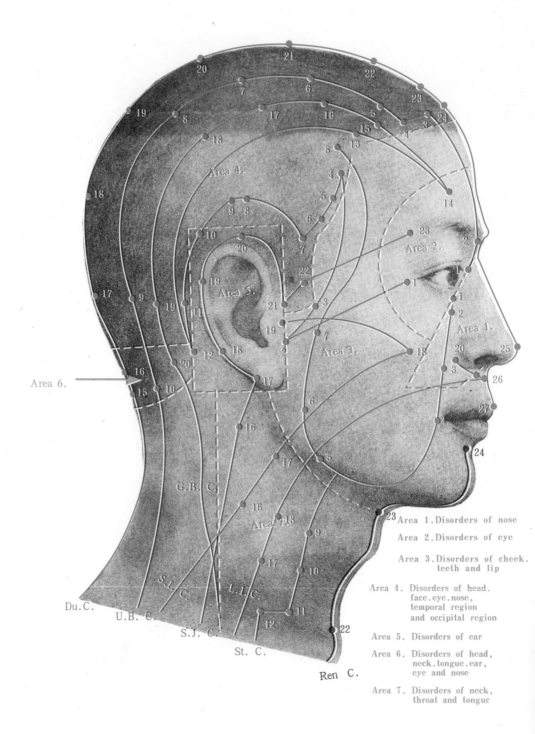

Fig. 11. Therapeutic properties of points
of the head and neck.

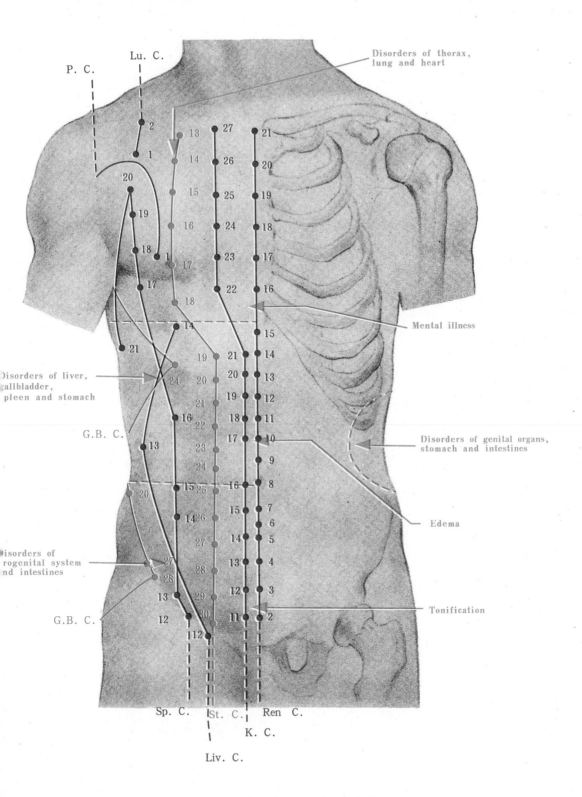

Fig. 12.   Therapeutic properties of points
of the chest and abdominal region.

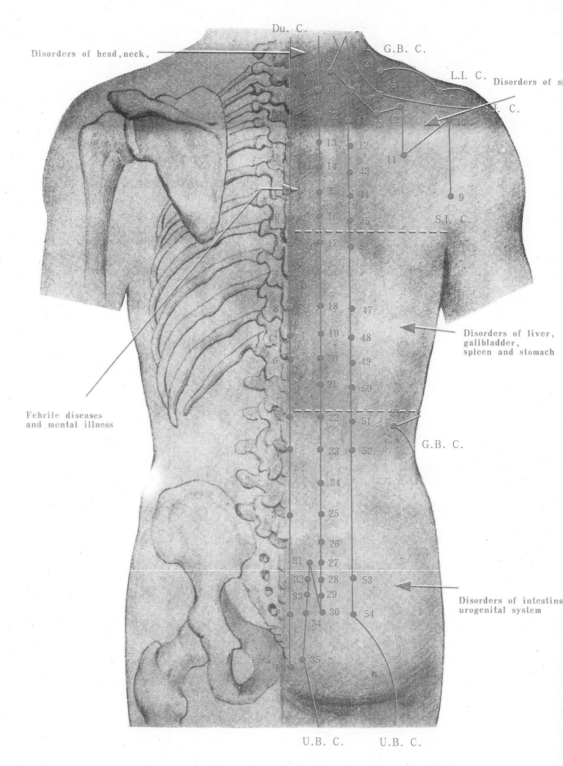

Fig. 13. Therapeutic properties of points of the back.

CHAPTER II

THE 12 REGULAR CHANNELS AND THEIR POINTS

I. THE LUNG CHANNEL OF HAND-TAIYIN

The Lung Channel of Hand-Taiyin originates from middle *jiao*, running downward to connect with the large intestine (1). Winding back, it goes along the upper orifice of the stomach (2), passes through the diaphragm (3), and enters the lung, its pertaining organ (4). From the portion of the lung communicating with the throat, it comes out transversely (Zhongfu, Lu. 1) (5). Descending along the medial aspect of the upper arm, it passes in front of the Heart Channel of Hand-Shaoyin and the Pericardium Channel of Hand-Jueyin (6) and reaches the cubital fossa (7). Then it goes continuously downward along the medial aspect of the forearm (8) and arrives at the medial side of the styloid process of the radius above the wrist, where it enters *cunkou* (the radial artery at the wrist for pulse palpation) (9). Passing the thenar eminence (10), it goes along its radial border (11), ending at the medial side of the tip of the thumb (Shaoshang, Lu. 11) (12).

The branch proximal to the wrist emerges from Lieque (Lu. 7) (13) and runs directly to the radial side of the tip of the index finger (Shangyang, L.I. 1) where it links with the Large Intestine Channel of Hand-Yangming. (See Fig. 14.)

There are altogether 11 points in this channel. They are described as follows:

1. Zhongfu (Front-Mu Point of the Lung, Lu. 1)

Location: Below the acromial extremity of the clavicle, one *cun* directly below Yunmen (Lu. 2), 6 *cun* lateral to Ren Channel. (See Fig. 15.)

Indications: Cough, asthma, pain in the chest, shoulder and back, fullness in the chest.

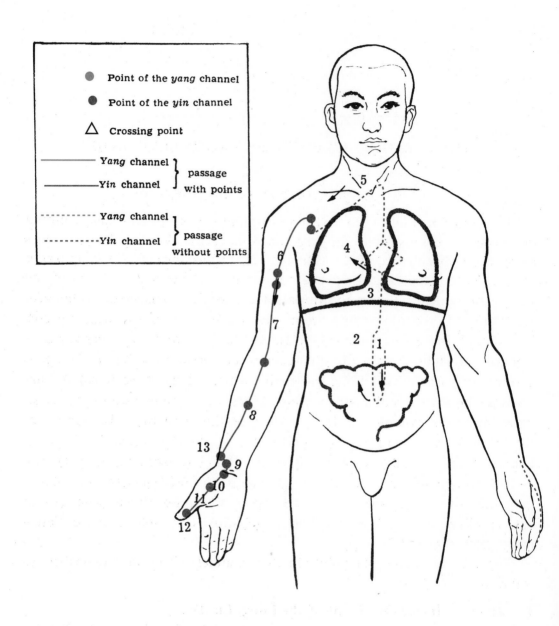

Fig. 14. The Lung Channel of Hand-Taiyin.

Method: Puncture perpendicularly 0.3-0.5 inch towards the lateral aspect of the chest. Moxibustion is applicable.

Regional anatomy

Vasculature: Superolaterally, the axillary artery and vein, the thoracoacromial artery and vein.

Innervation: The intermediate supraclavicular nerve, the branches of the anterior thoracic nerve, and the lateral cutaneous branch of the 1st intercostal nerve.

2. Yunmen (Lu. 2)

Location: In the depression below the acromial extremity of the clavicle, 6 *cun* lateral to Ren Channel. (See Fig. 15.)

Indications: Cough, asthma, pain in the chest, shoulder and arm, fullness in the chest.

Method: Puncture perpendicularly 0.5-1.0 inch. Moxibustion is applicable.

Regional anatomy

Vasculature: The cephalic vein, the thoracoacromial artery and vein; inferiorly, the axillary artery.

Innervation: The intermediate and lateral supraclavicular nerve, the branches of the anterior thoracic nerve, and the lateral cord of the brachial plexus.

3. Tianfu (Lu. 3)

Location: On the medial aspect of the upper arm, 3 *cun* below the end of the axillary fold, on the radial side of m. biceps brachii, 6 *cun* above Chize (Lu. 5).

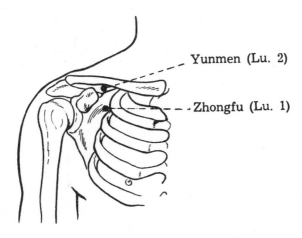

Yunmen (Lu. 2)

Zhongfu (Lu. 1)

Fig. 15. Zhongfu (Lu. 1) and Yunmen (Lu. 2).

Indications: Asthma, epistaxis, pain in the medial aspect of the arm.

Method: Puncture perpendicularly 0.3-0.5 inch.

Regional anatomy

Vasculature: The cephalic vein and muscular branches of the brachial artery and vein.

Innervation: The lateral brachial cutaneous nerve at the place where the musculocutaneous nerve passes through.

Note: The distance from the end of the axillary fold to Chize (Lu. 5) is measured as 9 *cun*.

4.   Xiabai (Lu. 4)

Location: On the medial aspect of the upper arm, 1 *cun* below Tianfu (Lu. 3), on the radial side of m. biceps brachii.

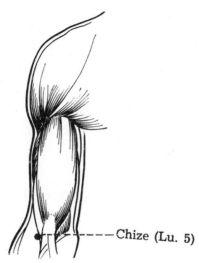

Fig. 16.   Chize (Lu. 5).

Indications: Cough, fullness in the chest, pain in the medial aspect of the arm.

Method: Puncture perpendicularly 0.3-0.5 inch. Moxibustion is applicable.

Regional anatomy See Tianfu (Lu. 3).

5.   Chize (He-Sea Point, Lu. 5)

Location: On the cubital crease, on the radial side of the tendon of m. biceps brachii. This point is located with the elbow slightly flexed. (See Fig. 16.)

Indications: Cough, hemoptysis afternoon fever, asthma, fullness in the chest, sore throat, spasmodic pain of the elbow and arm.

Method: Puncture perpendicularly 0.3-0.5 inch.

Regional anatomy

Vasculature: The branches of the radial recurrent artery and vein, the cephalic vein.

Innervation: The lateral antebrachial cutaneous nerve and the radial nerve.

6.   Kongzui (Xi-Cleft Point, Lu. 6)

Location: On the palmar aspect of the forearm, on the line joining Taiyuan (Lu. 9) and Chize (Lu. 5), 7 *cun* above Taiyuan (Lu. 9). (See Fig. 17.)

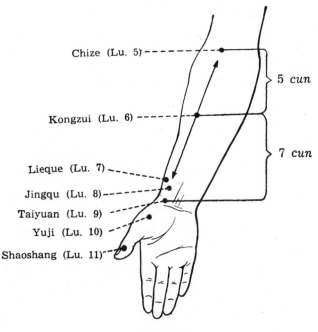

Fig. 17.

Indications: Cough, asthma, hemoptysis, sore throat, pain and motor impairment of the elbow and arm.

Method: Puncture perpendicularly 0.5-0.7 inch. Moxibustion is applicable.

Regional anatomy

Vasculature: The cephalic vein, the radial artery and vein.

Innervation: The lateral antebrachial cutaneous nerve and the superficial ramus of the radial nerve.

Note: The distance from Chize (Lu. 5) to Taiyuan (Lu. 9) is measured as 12 cun.

7. Lieque (Luo-Connecting Point, Lu. 7)

Location: Superior to the styloid process of the radius, 1.5 cun above the transverse crease of the wrist. When the index fingers and thumbs of both hands are crossed with the index finger of one hand placed on the styloid process of the radius of the other, the point is in the depression right under the tip of the index finger. (See Fig. 17 and 18.)

Indications: Headache, neck rigidity, cough, asthma, sore throat, facial paralysis, trismus, weakness of the wrist.

Method: Puncture obliquely 0.3-0.5 inch. Moxibustion is applicable.

Regional anatomy

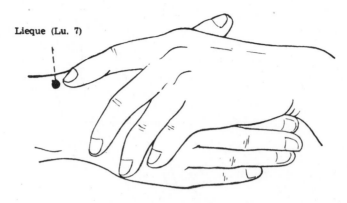

Lieque (Lu. 7)

Fig. 18. Lieque (Lu. 7).

Vasculature: The cephalic vein, branches of the radial artery and vein.

Innervation: The lateral antebrachial cutaneous nerve and the superficial ramus of the radial nerve.

Note: This point is one of the Eight Confluent Points communicating with the Ren Channel.

8. Jingqu (Jing-River Point, Lu. 8)

Location: 1 *cun* above the transverse crease of the wrist, in the depression on the radial side of the radial artery. (See Fig. 17.)

Indications: Cough, asthma, sore throat, pain in the chest and the wrist.

Method: Puncture perpendicularly 0.1-0.2 inch.

Regional anatomy

Vasculature: Laterally, the radial artery and vein.

Innervation: The lateral antebrachial cutaneous nerve and the superficial ramus of the radial nerve.

9. Taiyuan (Shu-Stream and Yuan-Source Point, Lu. 9)

Location: At the transverse crease of the wrist, in the depression on the radial side of the radial artery. (See Fig. 17.)

Indications: Asthma, cough, hemoptysis, sore throat, palpitation, pain in the chest and the medial aspect of the forearm.

Method: Puncture perpendicularly 0.2-0.3 inch. Moxibustion is applicable.

Regional anatomy

Vasculature: The radial artery and vein.

Innervation: The lateral antebrachial cutaneous nerve and the superficial ramus of the radial nerve.

Note: This point is one of the Eight Influential Points which dominates the vessels.

10. Yuji (Ying-Spring Point, Lu. 10)

Location: On the radial aspect of the midpoint of the 1st metacarpal bone, on the junction of the red and white skin (i.e., the junction of the dorsum and palm of the hand). (See Fig. 17.)

Indications: Cough, hemoptysis, sore throat, fever.

Method: Puncture perpendicularly 0.5-0.7 inch. Moxibustion is applicable.

Regional anatomy

Vasculature: Venules of the thumb draining to the cephalic vein.

Innervation: The superficial ramus of the radial nerve.

11. Shaoshang (Jing-Well Point, Lu. 11)

Location: On the radial side of the thumb, about 0.1 *cun* posterior to the corner of the nail. (See Fig. 17.)

Indications: Cough, asthma, sore throat, epistaxis, contracture and pain of fingers, febrile diseases, loss of consciousness, mental disorders.

Method: Puncture obliquely upward 0.1 inch, or prick with three-edged needle to cause bleeding.

Regional anatomy

Vasculature: The arterial and venous network formed by the palmar digital proprial artery and veins.

Innervation: The terminal nerve network formed by the mixed branches of the lateral antebrachial cutaneous nerve and the superficial ramus of the radial nerve as well as the palmar digital proprial nerve of the median nerve.

Note: In treating mental illness or epistaxis, apply moxibustion with 3-5 small moxa cones.

II. THE LARGE INTESTINE CHANNEL OF HAND-YANGMING

The Large Intestine Channel of Hand-Yangming starts from the tip of the index finger (Shangyang, L.I. 1) (1). Running upward along the radial side of the index finger and passing through the interspace of the 1st and 2nd metacarpal bones (Hegu, L.I. 4), it dips into the depression between the tendons of m. extensor pollicis longus and brevis (2). Then, following the lateral anterior aspect of the forearm (3), it reaches the lateral side of the elbow (4). From there, it ascends along the lateral anterior aspect of the upper arm (5) to the highest point of the shoulder (Jianyu, L.I. 15) (6). Then, along the anterior border of the acromion (7), it goes up to the 7th cervical vertebra (Dazhui, Du 14) (8), and descends to the supraclavicular fossa (9) to connect with the lung (10). It passes through the diaphragm (11) and enters the large intestine, its pertaining organ (12).

The branch from the supraclavicular fossa runs upward to the neck (13), passes through the cheek (14) and enters the gums of the lower teeth (15). Then it curves around the upper lip and crosses the opposite channel at the philtrum. From there, the left channel goes to the right and the right channel to the left, to both sides of the nose (Yingxiang, L.I. 20), where the Large Intestine Channel links with the Stomach Channel of Foot-Yangming (16). (See Fig. 20.)

Note: The large intestine has an Inferior He-Sea Point — Shangjuxu (St. 37). (See Fig. 21.)

The altogether 20 points in this channel are described as follows:

1. Shangyang (Jing-Well Point, L.I. 1)

Location: On the radial side of the index finger, about 0.1 *cun* posterior to the corner of the nail. (See Fig. 22.)

Indications: Toothache, sore throat, swelling of the submandibular region, numbness of fingers, febrile diseases, loss of consciousness.

Method: Puncture obliquely 0.1 inch, or prick with three-edged needle to cause bleeding.

Regional anatomy

Vasculature: The arterial and venous network formed by the dorsal digital arteries and veins.

Innervation: The palmar digital proprial nerve derived from the median nerve.

2. Erjian (Ying-Spring Point, L.I. 2)

Location: On the radial side of the index finger, distal to the metacarpophalangeal joint, at the junction of the white and red skin. The point is located with the finger slightly flexed. (See Fig. 22.)

Indications: Blurring of vision, epistaxis, toothache, sore throat, febrile diseases.

Method: Puncture perpendicularly 0.2-0.3 inch. Moxibustion is applicable.

Regional anatomy

Vasculature: The dorsal digital and palmar digital proprial arteries and veins derived from the radial artery and vein.

Innervation: The dorsal digital nerve of the radial nerve and the palmar digital proprial nerve of the median nerve.

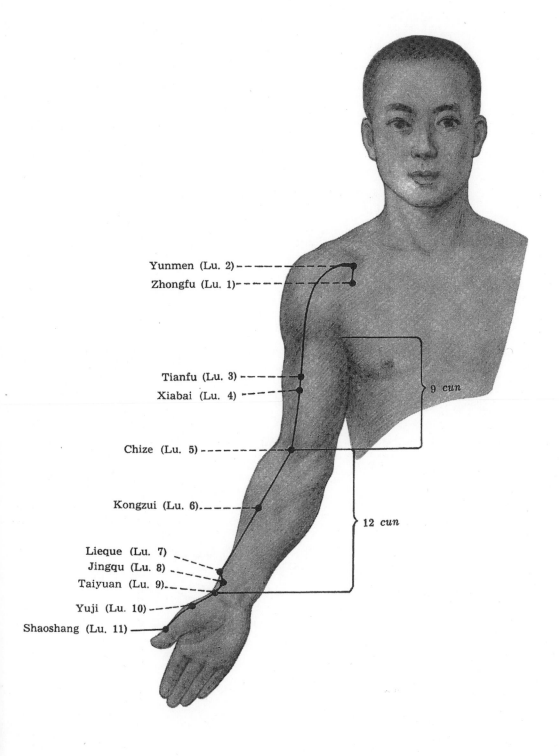

Yunmen (Lu. 2)

Zhongfu (Lu. 1)

Tianfu (Lu. 3)

Xiabai (Lu. 4)

9 *cun*

Chize (Lu. 5)

Kongzui (Lu. 6)

12 *cun*

Lieque (Lu. 7)

Jingqu (Lu. 8)

Taiyuan (Lu. 9)

Yuji (Lu. 10)

Shaoshang (Lu. 11)

Fig. 19.   The Lung Channel of Hand-Taiyin.

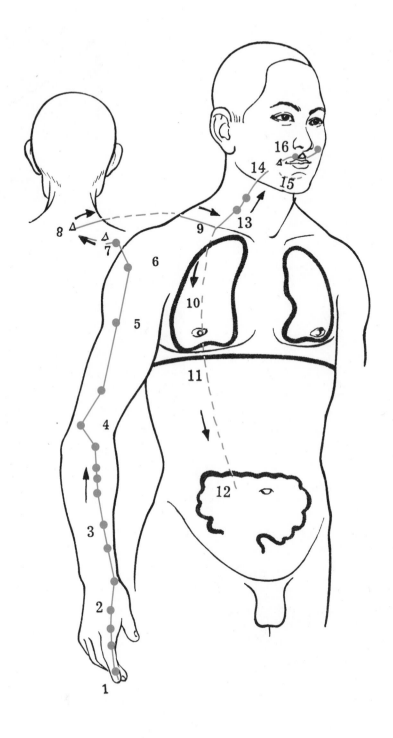

Fig. 20.　The Large Intestine Channel of Hand-Yangming.

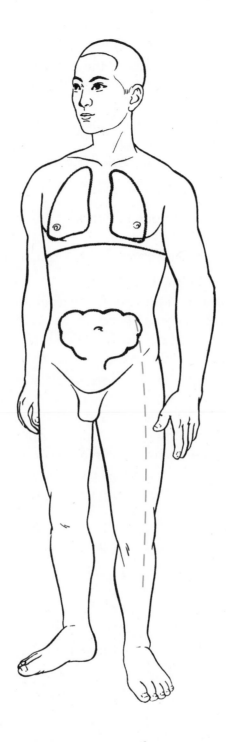

Fig. 21.   Inferior He-Sea Point of the Large Intestine Channel.
Shangjuxu (St. 37).

3. Sanjian (Shu-Stream Point, L.I. 3)

Location: When a loose fist is made, the point is on the radial side of the index finger, in the depression proximal to the head of the 2nd metacarpal bone. (See Fig. 22.)

Indications: Ophthalmalgia, toothache, sore throat, redness and swelling of fingers and the dorsum of the hand.

Method: Puncture perpendicularly 0.5-1.0 inch towards the ulnar side. Moxibustion is applicable.

Regional anatomy

Vasculature: The dorsal venous network of the hand and the branch of the 1st dorsal metacarpal artery.

Innervation: The superficial ramus of the radial nerve.

4. Hegu (Yuan-Source Point, L.I. 4)

Location: Between the 1st and 2nd metacarpal bones, approximately in the middle of the 2nd metacarpal bone on the radial side. (See Fig. 22.) Or, place in coincident position the transverse crease of the interphalangeal joint of the thumb with the margin of the web between the thumb and the index finger of the other hand. The point is where the tip of the thumb touches. (See Fig. 23.)

Indications: Headache, redness with swelling and pain of the eye, epistaxis, toothache, facial swelling, sore throat, contracture of fingers, pain of the arm, trismus, facial paralysis, febrile diseases with anhidrosis, hidrosis, amenorrhea, delayed labour, abdominal pain, constipation, dysentery.

Method: Puncture perpendicularly 0.5-0.8 inch. Moxibustion is applicable.

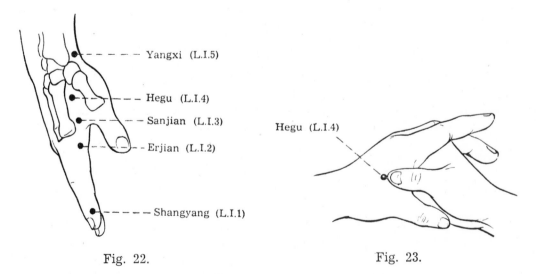

Fig. 22.   Fig. 23.

Regional anatomy

Vasculature: The venous network of the dorsum of hand; proximally, right on the radial artery piercing from the dorsum to the palm of hand.

Innervation: The superficial ramus of the radial nerve; deeper, the palmar digital proprial nerve derived from the median nerve.

Note: Acupuncture and moxibustion on this point are contraindicated during pregnancy.

5. Yangxi (Jing-River Point, L.I. 5)

Location: On the radial side of the wrist. When the thumb is tilted upward, it is in the depression between the tendons of m. extensor pollicis longus and brevis. (See Fig. 24.)

Indications: Headache, redness with swelling and pain of the eye, toothache, sore throat, pain of the wrist.

Method: Puncture perpendicularly 0.3-0.5 inch. Moxibustion is applicable.

Regional anatomy

Vasculature: The cephalic vein, the radial artery and its dorsal carpal branch.

Innervation: The superficial ramus of the radial nerve.

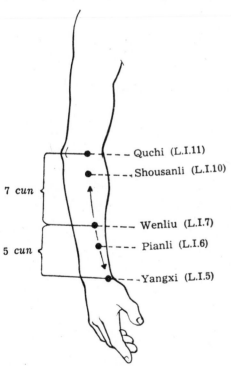

7 cun

5 cun

Quchi (L.I.11)

Shousanli (L.I.10)

Wenliu (L.I.7)

Pianli (L.I.6)

Yangxi (L.I.5)

Fig. 24.

6. Pianli (Luo-Connecting Point, L.I. 6)

Location: 3 *cun* above Yangxi (L.I. 5), on the line joining Yangxi (L.I. 5) and Quchi (L.I. 11). (See Fig. 24.)

Indications: Epistaxis, deafness, aching of the hand and arm, edema.

Method: Puncture perpendicularly 0.3-0.5 inch. Moxibustion is applicable.

Regional anatomy

Vasculature: The cephalic vein.

Innervation: On the radial side, the lateral antebrachial cutaneous nerve and the superficial ramus of the radial nerve; on the ulnar side, the posterior antebrachial cutaneous nerve and the posterior antebrachial interosseous nerve.

Note: The distance from Yangxi (L.I. 5) to Quchi (L.I. 11) is measured as 12 *cun*.

7. Wenliu (Xi-Cleft Point, L.I. 7)

Location: When a fist is made with the ulnar side downward and elbow flexed the point is 5 *cun* above Yangxi (L.I. 5). (See Fig. 24.)

Indications: Headache, facial swelling, sore throat, borborygmus, abdominal pain, aching of the shoulder and arm.

Method: Puncture perpendicularly 0.5-0.8 inch. Moxibustion is applicable.

Regional anatomy

Vasculature: The muscular branch of the radial artery, the cephalic vein.

Innervation: The posterior antebrachial cutaneous nerve and the deep ramus of the radial nerve.

8. Xialian (L.I. 8)

Location: 4 *cun* below Quchi (L.I. 11).

Indications: Pain in the elbow and arm, abdominal pain.

Method: Puncture perpendicularly 0.5-0.7 inch. Moxibustion is applicable.

Regional anatomy See Wenliu (L.I. 7).

9. Shanglian (L.I. 9)

Location: 3 *cun* below Quchi (L.I. 11).

Indications: Aching of the shoulder region, motor impairment of the upper extremities, numbness of the hand and arm, borborygmus, abdominal pain.

Method: Puncture perpendicularly 0.7-1.0 inch. Moxibustion is applicable.

Regional anatomy See Wenliu (L.I. 7).

10. Shousanli (L.I. 10)

Location: 2 *cun* below Quchi (L.I. 11). (See Fig. 24.)

Indications: Abdominal pain, vomiting and diarrhea, pain in the shoulder region, motor impairment of the upper extremities.

Method: Puncture perpendicularly 1.0-1.2 inches. Moxibustion is applicable.

Regional anatomy

Vasculature: The branches of the radial recurrent artery and vein.

Innervation: See Wenliu (L.I. 7).

11. Quchi (He-Sea Point, L.I. 11)

Location: When the elbow is flexed, the point is in the depression at the lateral end of the transverse cubital crease, midway between Chize (Lu. 5) and the lateral epicondyle of the humerus. (See Fig. 25.)

Indications: Pain of the elbow and arm, motor impairment of the upper extremities, scrofula, urticaria, abdominal pain, vomiting, diarrhea, dysentery, febrile diseases, sore throat.

Method: Puncture perpendicularly 1.0-1.5 inches. Moxibustion is applicable.

Regional anatomy

Vasculature: The branches of the radial recurrent artery and vein.

Innervation: The posterior antebrachial cutaneous nerve; deeper, on the medial side, the radial nerve.

Note: The Inferior He-Sea Point of the large intestine is Shangjuxu (St. 37), which is indicated in disorders of the large intestine.

12. Zhouliao (L.I. 12)

Location: When the elbow is flexed, the point is superior to the lateral epicondyle of the humerus, about 1 *cun* superolateral to Quchi (L.I. 11), on the medial border of the humerus.

Indications: Pain, contracture and numbness of the elbow and arm.

Method: Puncture perpendicularly 0.3-0.5 inch. Moxibustion is applicable.

Regional anatomy

Vasculature: The radial collateral artery and vein.

Innervation: The posterior antebrachial cutaneous nerve; deeper, on the medial side, the radial nerve.

Note: The distance from Quchi (L.I. 11) to the level of the end of the axillary fold is measured as 9 *cun*.

13. Hand-Wuli (L.I. 13)

Location: Superior to the lateral epicondyle of the humerus, 3 *cun* above Quchi (L.I. 11), on the line connecting Quchi (L.I. 11) and Jianyu (L.I. 15).

Indications: Contracture and pain of the elbow and arm, scrofula.

Method: Apply moxibustion with moxa stick for 5-10 minutes.

Regional anatomy

Vasculature: The radial collateral artery and vein.

Innervation: The posterior antebrachial cutaneous nerve; deeper, the radial nerve.

14. Binao (L.I. 14)

Location: On the radial side of the humerus, superior to the lower end of m. deltoideus, on the line connecting Quchi (L.I. 11) and Jianyu (L.I. 15).

Indications: Pain in the shoulder and arm, scrofula.

Method: Puncture perpendicularly or obliquely upward 0.5-0.7 inch. Moxibustion is applicable.

Regional anatomy

Vasculature: The branches of posterior circumflex humeral artery and vein, the deep brachial artery and vein.

Innervation: The posterior brachial cutaneous nerve; deeper, the radial nerve.

15. Jianyu (L.I. 15)

Location: Anteroinferior to the acromion, in the middle of the upper portion of m. deltoideus. When the arm is in full abduction, the point is in the anterior depression of the two depressions appearing at the anterior border of the acromioclavicular joint. (See Fig. 25.)

Indications: Pain of the shoulder and arm, motor impairment of the upper extremities, rubella, scrofula.

Method: Puncture obliquely downward 0.6-1.2 inches. Moxibustion is applicable.

Regional anatomy

Vasculature: The posterior circumflex artery and vein.

Innervation: The lateral supraclavicular nerve and axillary nerve.

16. Jugu (L.I. 16)

Location: In the upper aspect of the shoulder, in the depression between the acromial extremity of the clavicle and the scapular spine.

Indications: Pain in the shoulder, pain and motor impairment of the upper extremities.

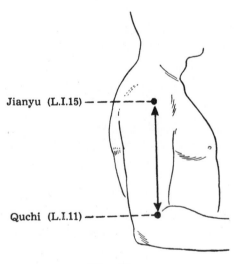

Jianyu (L.I.15)

Quchi (L.I.11)

Fig. 25.

Method: Puncture perpendicularly 0.5-0.7 inch. Moxibustion is applicable.

Regional anatomy

Vasculature: Deeper, the suprascapular artery and vein.

Innervation: Superficially, the lateral supraclavicular nerve, the branch of the accessory nerve; deeper, the suprascapular nerve.

17. Tianding (L.I. 17)

Location: On the lateral side of the neck, superior to the midpoint of the supraclavicular fossa (Quepen, St. 12), about 1 *cun* below Neck-Futu (L.I. 18), on the posterior border of m. sternocleidomastoideus.

Indications: Sore throat, hoarseness of voice, scrofula, goiter.

Method: Puncture perpendicularly 0.3-0.5 inch. Moxibustion is applicable.

Regional anatomy

Vasculature: The external jugular vein.

Innervation: Superficially, the supraclavicular nerve. It is on the posterior border of m. sternocleidomastoideus just where the cutaneous cervical nerve emerges. Deeper, the phrenic nerve.

18. Neck-Futu (L.I. 18)

Location: On the lateral side of the neck, level with the tip of Adam's apple, between the sternal head and clavicular head of m. sternocleidomastoideus.

Indications: Cough, asthma, sore throat, hoarseness of voice, scrofula, goiter.

Method: Puncture perpendicularly 0.3-0.5 inch. Moxibustion is applicable.

Regional anatomy

Vasculature: Deeper, on the medial side, the ascending cervical artery and vein.

Innervation: The great auricular nerve, cutaneous cervical nerve, lesser occipital nerve and accessory nerve.

19. Nose-Heliao (L.I. 19)

Location: Directly below the lateral margin of the nostril, level with Renzhong (Du 26.)

Indications: Epistaxis, nasal obstruction, deviation of the mouth.

Method: Puncture obliquely 0.2-0.3 inch.

Regional anatomy

Vasculature: The superior labial branches of the facial artery and vein.

Innervation: The anastomotic branch of the facial nerve and the infraorbital nerve.

20. Yingxiang (L.I. 20)

Location: In the nasolabial groove, at the level of the midpoint of the lateral border of ala nasi. (See Fig. 26.)

Indications: Nasal obstruction, epistaxis, rhinorrhea, deviation of the mouth, itching and swelling of the face.

Method: Puncture obliquely downward 0.3 inch.

Regional anatomy

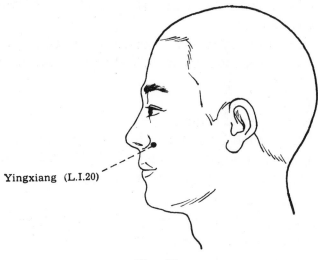

Yingxiang (L.I.20)

Fig. 26.

Vasculature: The facial artery and vein, the branches of the infraorbital artery and vein.

Innervation: The anastomotic branch of the facial and infraorbital nerves.

III. THE STOMACH CHANNEL OF FOOT-YANGMING

The Stomach Channel of Foot-Yangming starts from the lateral side of ala nasi (Yingxiang, L.I. 20) (1). It ascends to the bridge of the nose, where it meets the Urinary Bladder Channel of Foot-Taiyang (Jingming, U.B. 1) (2). Turning downward along the lateral side of the nose (Chengqi, St. 1) (3), it enters the upper gums (4). Re-emerging, it curves around the lips (5) and descends to meet the Ren Channel at the mentolabial groove (Chengjiang, Ren 24) (6). Then it runs posterolaterally across the lower portion of the cheek at Daying (St. 5) (7). Winding along the angle of the mandible (Jiache, St. 6) (8), it ascends in front of the ear and traverses Shangguan (G.B. 3) of the Gall Bladder Channel of Foot-Shaoyang (9). Then it follows the anterior hairline (10) and reaches the forehead (11).

The facial branch emerging in front of Daying (St. 5) runs downward to Renying (St. 9) (12). From there it goes along the throat and enters the supraclavicular fossa (13). Descending, it passes through the diaphragm (14), enters the stomach, its pertaining organ, and connects with the spleen (15).

The straight portion of the channel arising from the supraclavicular fossa runs downward (16), passing through the nipple. It descends by the um-

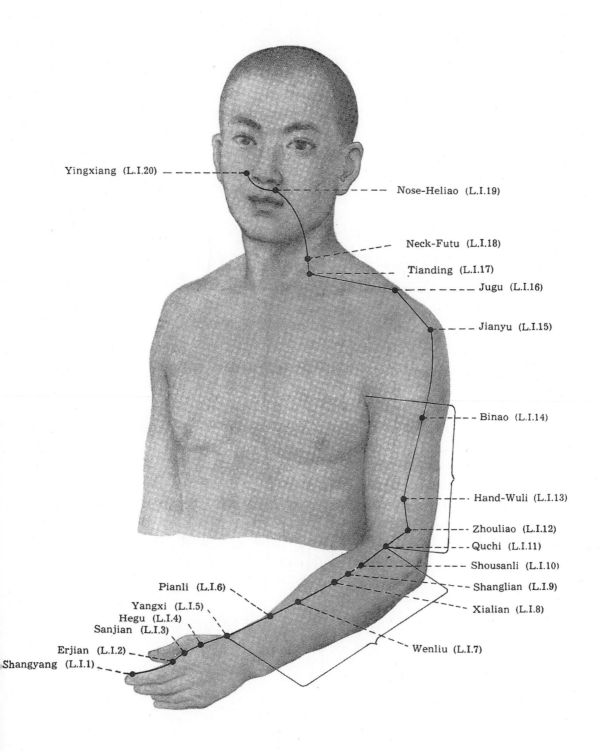

Yingxiang (L.I.20)

Nose-Heliao (L.I.19)

Neck-Futu (L.I.18)

Tianding (L.I.17)

Jugu (L.I.16)

Jianyu (L.I.15)

Binao (L.I.14)

Hand-Wuli (L.I.13)

Zhouliao (L.I.12)

Quchi (L.I.11)

Shousanli (L.I.10)

Shanglian (L.I.9)

Xialian (L.I.8)

Pianli (L.I.6)

Yangxi (L.I.5)

Hegu (L.I.4)

Sanjian (L.I.3)

Erjian (L.I.2)

Shangyang (L.I.1)

Wenliu (L.I.7)

Fig. 27. The Large Intestine Channel of Hand-Yangming.

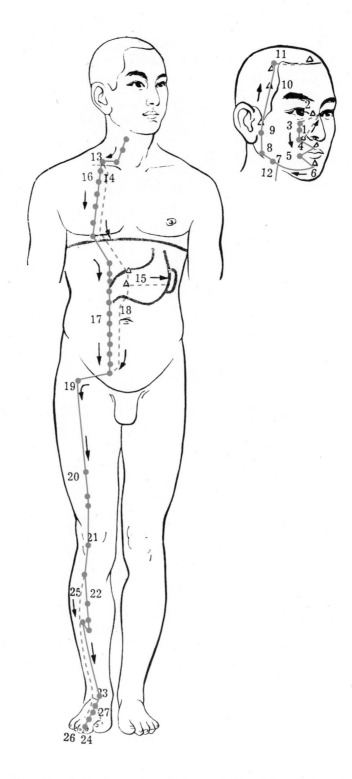

Fig. 28.　The Stomach Channel of Foot-Yangming.

bilicus and enters Qichong (St. 30) on the lateral side of the lower abdomen (17).

The branch from the lower orifice of the stomach (18) descends inside the abdomen and joins the previous portion of the channel at Qichong (St. 30). Running downward, traversing Biguan (St. 31) (19), and further through Femur-Futu (St. 32) (20), it reaches the knee (21). From there, it continues downward along the anterior border of the lateral aspect of the tibia (22), passes through the dorsum of the foot (23), and reaches the lateral side of the tip of the 2nd toe (Lidui, St. 45) (24).

The tibial branch emerges from Zusanli (St. 36), 3 *cun* below the knee (25), and enters the lateral side of the middle toe (26).

The branch from the dorsum of foot arises from Chongyang (St. 42) (27) and terminates at the medial side of the tip of the great toe (Yinbai, Sp. 1), where it links with the Spleen Channel of Foot-Taiyin. (See Fig. 28.)

The altogether 45 points in this channel are described as follows:

1. Chengqi (St. 1)

Location: Between the eyeball and the midpoint of the infraorbital ridge. (See Fig. 29.)

Indications: Redness with swelling and pain of the eye, lacrimation when attacked by wind, night blindness, facial paralysis, twitching of eyelids.

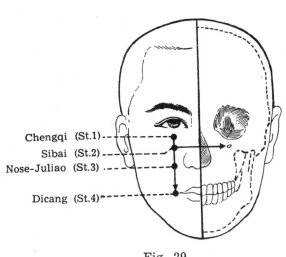

Chengqi (St.1)
Sibai (St.2)
Nose-Juliao (St.3)
Dicang (St.4)

Fig. 29.

Method: Puncture perpendicularly 0.3-0.7 inch along the infraorbital ridge. It is not advisable to manipulate the needle with large amplitude.

Regional anatomy

Vasculature: The branches of the infraorbital and ophthalmic arteries and veins.

Innervation: The branch of infraorbital nerve, the inferior branch of oculomotor nerve and the muscular branch of facial nerve.

2. Sibai (St. 2)

Location: Below Chengqi (St. 1), in the depression at the infraorbital foramen. (See Fig. 26.)

Indications: Redness and pain of the eye, facial paralysis and pain, twitching of eyelids.

Method: Puncture perpendicularly 0.2-0.3 inch. Deep puncture is contraindicated.

Regional anatomy

Vasculature: The branches of facial artery and vein, the infraorbital artery and vein.

Innervation: The branches of facial nerve. The point is precisely on the course of the infraorbital nerve.

3. Nose-Juliao (St. 3)

Location: Directly below Sibai (St. 2), at the level of the lower border of ala nasi, on the lateral side of the nasolabial groove. (See Fig. 29.)

Indications: Facial paralysis, twitching of eyelids, epistaxis, toothache, swelling of lips and cheek.

Method: Puncture perpendicularly 0.3-0.4 inch. Moxibustion is applicable.

Regional anatomy

Vasculature: The branches of the facial and infraorbital arteries and veins.

Innervation: The branches of the facial and infraorbital nerves.

4. Dicang (St. 4)

Location: Lateral to the corner of the mouth, directly below Nose-Juliao (St. 3). (See Fig. 29.)

Indications: Deviation of the mouth, salivation, twitching of eyelids.

Method: Puncture obliquely 0.5-1.0 inch with the tip of the needle directed towards Jiache (St. 6). Moxibustion is applicable.

Regional anatomy

Vasculature: The facial artery and vein.

Innervation: Superficially, the branches of the facial and infraorbital nerves; deeper, the terminal branch of buccal nerve.

5. Daying (St. 5)

Location: Anterior to the angle of mandible, on the anterior border of m. masseter, in the groove-like depression appearing when the cheek is bulged. (See Fig. 30.)

Indications: Trismus, deviation of the mouth, swelling of the cheek, toothache.

Method: Puncture obliquely 0.3 inch towards Jiache (St. 6). Avoid the artery. Moxibustion is applicable.

Regional anatomy

Vasculature: Anteriorly, the facial artery and vein.

Innervation: The facial and the buccal nerves.

6. Jiache (St. 6)

Location: One finger-breadth anterior and superior to the lower angle of the mandible where m. masseter attaches at the prominence of the muscle when the teeth are clenched. (See Fig. 30.)

Indications: Facial paralysis, swelling of the cheek, toothache, trismus, pain and stiffness of the neck, mumps.

Method: Puncture perpendicularly 0.3-0.5 inch or obliquely towards Dicang (St. 4). Moxibustion is applicable.

Regional anatomy

Vasculature: The masseteric artery.

Innervation: The great auricular nerve, facial nerve and masseteric nerve.

7. Xiaguan (St. 7)

Location: In the depression at the lower border of the zygomatic arch, anterior to the condyloid process of the mandible. This point is located with the mouth closed. (See Fig. 30.)

Indications: Deafness, tinnitus, otorrhea, facial paralysis, toothache, motor impairment of the jaw.

Method: Puncture perpendicularly 0.3-0.5 inch. Moxibustion is applicable.

Regional anatomy

Vasculature: Superficially, the transverse facial artery and vein; in the deepest layer, the maxillary artery and vein.

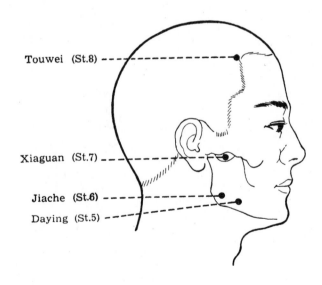

Fig. 30.

Innervation: The zygomatic branch of the facial nerve and the branches of the auriculotemporal nerve.

8. Touwei (St. 8)

Location: 0.5 *cun* within the anterior hairline at the corner of the forehead, 4.5 *cun* lateral to the Du Channel. (See Fig. 30.)

Indications: Headache, blurring of vision, ophthalmalgia, lacrimation when attacked by wind.

Method: Puncture 0.5-1.0 inch along the scalp with the tip of the needle directed horizontally upward or downward.

Regional anatomy

Vasculature: The frontal branches of the superficial temporal artery and vein.

Innervation: The branch of the auriculotemporal nerve and the temporal branch of the facial nerve.

Note: The distance between Touwei (St. 8) of both sides is 9 *cun*, equal to the distance between the two mastoid processes.

9. Renying (St. 9)

Location: Level with the tip of Adam's apple, just on the course of the common carotid artery, on the anterior border of m. sternocleidomastoideus. (See Fig. 31.)

Indications: Sore throat, asthma, dizziness, flushing of face.

Method: Puncture perpendicularly 0.3-0.5 inch. Avoid the artery.

Regional anatomy

Vasculature: The superior thyroid artery, the anterior jugular vein; laterally, the internal jugular vein; on the bifurcation of the internal and the external carotid artery.

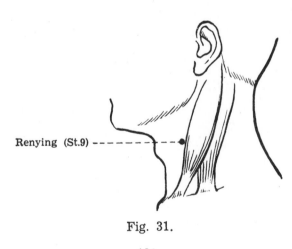

Fig. 31.

Innervation: Superficially, the cutaneous cervical nerve, the cervical branch of the facial nerve; deeper, the sympathetic trunk; laterally, the descending branch of the hypoglossal nerve and the vagus nerve.

10. Shuitu (St. 10)

Location: At the anterior border of m. sternocleidomastoideus, midway between Renying (St. 9) and Qishe (St. 11).

Indications: Sore throat, asthma.

Method: Puncture perpendicularly 0.3-0.5 inch. Moxibustion is applicable.

Regional anatomy

Vasculature: The common carotid artery.

Innervation: Superficially, the cutaneous cervical nerve; deeper, the superior cardiac nerve issued from the sympathetic nerve and the sympathetic trunk.

11. Qishe (St. 11)

Location: At the superior border of the sternal extremity of the clavicle, between the sternal head and clavicular head of m. sternocleidomastoideus.

Indications: Sore throat, asthma.

Method: Puncture perpendicularly 0.3-0.4 inch. Moxibustion is applicable.

Regional anatomy

Vasculature: Superficially, the anterior jugular vein; deeper, the common carotid artery.

Innervation: The medial supraclavicular nerve and the muscular branch of ansa hypoglossi.

12. Quepen (St. 12)

Location: In the midpoint of the supraclavicular fossa, 4 *cun* lateral to the Ren Channel.

Indications: Cough, asthma, sore throat, pain in the supraclavicular fossa.

Method: Puncture perpendicularly 0.3-0.5 inch. Avoid the artery. Deep puncture is not advisable. Moxibustion is applicable.

Regional anatomy

Vasculature: Superiorly, the transverse cervical artery.

Innervation: Superficially, the intermediate supraclavicular nerve; deeper, the supraclavicular portion of brachial plexus.

13. Qihu (St. 13)

Location: At the lower border of the middle of the clavicle, on the mammillary line.

Indications: Asthma, cough, fullness of the chest.
Method: Puncture perpendicularly 0.3 inch. Moxibustion is applicable.
Regional anatomy
Vasculature: The branches of the thoracoacromial artery and vein; superiorly, the subclavicular vein.
Innervation: The branches of the supraclavicular nerve and the anterior thoracic nerve.

14. Kufang (St. 14)

Location: In the 1st intercostal space, on the mammillary line.
Indications: Sensation of fullness and pain in the chest and hypochondriac region, cough.
Method: Puncture obliquely 0.3 inch. Moxibustion is applicable.
Regional anatomy
Vasculature: The thoracoacromial artery and vein and the branches of the lateral thoracic artery and vein.
Innervation: The branch of the anterior thoracic nerve.
Note: It is not advisable to puncture deeply on points of the chest and abdomen in order to protect the vital viscera within.

15. Wuyi (St. 15)

Location: In the 2nd intercostal space, on the mammillary line.
Indications: Cough, asthma, fullness and pain in the chest, mastitis.
Method: Puncture obliquely 0.3 inch. Moxibustion is applicable.
Regional anatomy
Vasculature: See Kufang (St. 14).
Innervation: On the course of the branch of m. pectoralis major derived from the anterior thoracic nerve.

16. Yingchuang (St. 16)

Location: In the 3rd intercostal space, on the mammillary line.
Indications: Cough, asthma, fullness and pain in the chest, mastitis.
Method: Puncture obliquely 0.3 inch. Moxibustion is applicable.
Regional anatomy
Vasculature: The lateral thoracic artery and vein.
Innervation: The branch of the anterior thoracic nerve.

17. Ruzhong (St. 17)

Location: In the centre of the nipple.
Regional anatomy
Innervation: The anterior and lateral cutaneous branches of the 4th intercostal nerve.

Note: Acupuncture and moxibustion on this point are contraindicated. This point serves only as a landmark for locating points on the chest and abdomen. The distance between the two nipples is measured as 8 *cun*.

18. Rugen (St. 18)

Location: In the intercostal space, one rib below the nipple. (See Fig. 32.)

Indications: Cough, asthma, mastitis, lactation deficiency, pain in the chest.

Method: Puncture obliquely 0.3 inch. Moxibustion is applicable.

Regional anatomy

Vasculature: The branches of the intercostal artery and vein.

Innervation: The branch of the 5th intercostal nerve.

19. Burong (St. 19)

Location: 6 *cun* above the umbilicus, 2 *cun* lateral to Juque (Ren 14).

Indications: Abdominal distension, vomiting, gastric pain, anorexia.

Method: Puncture perpendicularly 0.5-0.7 inch. Moxibustion is applicable.

Regional anatomy

Vasculature: The branches of the 7th intercostal artery and vein, the branches of the superior epigastric artery and vein.

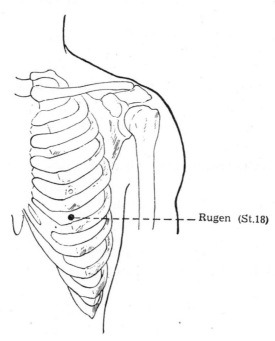

Fig. 32.

Innervation: The branch of the 7th intercostal nerve.

Note: The distance from the sternocostal angle to the centre of the umbilicus is measured as 8 *cun*. This serves as a standard for locating the points on both sides of the upper abdomen. The distance from Burong (St. 19) to Tianshu (St. 25) is measured as 6 *cun*.

20. Chengman (St. 20)

Location: 5 *cun* above the umbilicus, 2 *cun* lateral to Shangwan (Ren 13), or 1 *cun* below Burong (St. 19).

Indications: Gastric pain, abdominal distension, vomiting, anorexia.

Method: Puncture perpendicularly 0.5-1.0 inch. Moxibustion is applicable.

Regional anatomy   See Burong (St. 19).

21. Liangmen (St. 21)

Location: 4 *cun* above the umbilicus, 2 *cun* lateral to Zhongwan (Ren 12). (See Fig. 33.)

Indications: Gastric pain, vomiting, anorexia, loose stools.

Method: Puncture perpendicularly 0.7-1.0 inch. Moxibustion is applicable.

Regional anatomy

Vasculature: The branches of the 8th intercostal and superior epigastric arteries and veins.

Innervation: The branch of the 8th intercostal nerve.

22. Guanmen (St. 22)

Location: 3 *cun* above the umbilicus, 2 *cun* lateral to Jianli (Ren 11), or 1 *cun* below Liangmen (St. 21).

Indications: Abdominal distension and pain, borborygmus, diarrhea, anorexia, edema.

Method: Puncture perpendicularly 0.7-1.0 inch. Moxibustion is applicable.

Regional anatomy   See Liangmen (St. 21).

23. Taiyi (St. 23)

Location: 2 *cun* above the umbilicus, 2 *cun* lateral to Xiawan (Ren 10).

Indications: Mental disorders, irritability, restlessness, gastric pain, indigestion.

Method: Puncture perpendicularly 0.7-1.0 inch. Moxibustion is applicable.

Regional anatomy

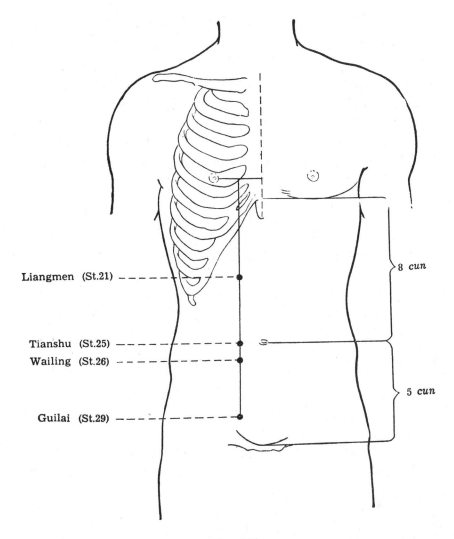

Liangmen (St.21)

Tianshu (St.25)
Wailing (St.26)

Guilai (St.29)

8 cun

5 cun

Fig. 33.

Vasculature: The branches of the 8th and 9th intercostal and inferior epigastric arteries and veins.

Innervation: The branches of the 8th and 9th intercostal nerves.

24. Huaroumen (St. 24)

Location: 1 *cun* above the umbilicus, 2 *cun* lateral to Shuifen (Ren 9).

Indications: Mental disorders, vomiting, gastric pain.

Method: Puncture perpendicularly 0.7-1.0 inch. Moxibustion is applicable.

Regional anatomy

Vasculature: The branches of the 9th intercostal and inferior epigastric arteries and veins.

Innervation: The branch of the 9th intercostal nerve.

25. Tianshu (Front-Mu Point of the large intestine, St. 25)

Location: 2 *cun* lateral to the centre of the umbilicus. (See Fig. 33.)

Indications: Abdominal pain, diarrhea, dysentery, constipati n, borborygmus, abdominal distension, edema, irregular menstruation.

Method: Puncture perpendicularly 0.7-1.2 inches. Moxibustion is applicable.

Regional anatomy

Vasculature: The branches of the 10th intercostal and inferior epigastric arteries and veins.

Innervation: The branch of the 10th intercostal nerve.

Note: The distance from the centre of the umbilicus to the upper border of symphysis pubis is measured as 5 *cun*, which serves as a criterion for measuring the points in the lower abdomen. The distance from Tianshu (St. 25) to Qichong (St. 30) is measured as 5 *cun*.

26. Wailing (St. 26)

Location: 1 *cun* below the umbilicus, 2 *cun* lateral to Abdomen-Yinjiao (Ren 7), or 1 *cun* below Tianshu (St. 25). (See Fig. 33.)

Indications: Abdominal pain, hernia.

Method: Puncture perpendicularly 0.7-1.2 inches. Moxibustion is applicable.

Regional anatomy   See Tianshu (St. 25).

27. Daju (St. 27)

Location: 2 *cun* below the umbilicus, 2 *cun* lateral to Shimen (Ren 5).

Indications: Lower abdominal distension, dysuria, hernia, seminal emission, ejaculatio praecox.

Method: Puncture perpendicularly 0.7-1.2 inches. Moxibustion is applicable.

Regional anatomy

Vasculature: The branches of the 11th intercostal artery and vein; laterally, the inferior epigastric artery and vein.

Innervation: The 11th intercostal nerve.

28. Shuidao (St. 28)

Location: 3 *cun* below the umbilicus, 2 *cun* lateral to Guanyuan (Ren 4).

Indications: Lower abdominal distension, hernia, retention of urine.

Method: Puncture perpendicularly 0.7-1.2 inches. Moxibustion is applicable.

Regional anatomy

Vasculature: The branches of the subcostal artery and vein; laterally, the inferior epigastric artery and vein.

Innervation: The branch of the subcostal nerve.

29. Guilai (St. 29)

Location: 4 *cun* below the umbilicus, 2 *cun* lateral to Zhongji (Ren 3). (See Fig. 33.)

Indications: Abdominal pain, hernia, amenorrhea, prolapse of uterus.

Method: Puncture perpendicularly 0.7-1.2 inches. Moxibustion is applicable.

Regional anatomy

Vasculature: Laterally, the inferior epigastric artery and vein.

Innervation: The iliohypogastric nerve.

30. Qichong (St. 30)

Location: 5 *cun* below the umbilicus, 2 *cun* lateral to Qugu (Ren 2), superior to the inguinal groove, on the medial side of the femoral artery.

Indications: Pain and swelling of the external genitalia, hernia, irregular menstruation.

Method: Puncture perpendicularly 0.5-1.0 inch. Moxibustion is applicable.

Regional anatomy

Vasculature: The branches of the superficial epigastric artery and vein. Laterally, the inferior epigastric artery and vein.

Innervation: The pathway of the ilioinguinal nerve.

31. Biguan (St. 31)

Location: Directly below the anterior superior iliac spine, in the depression on the lateral side of m. sartorius when the thigh is flexed. (See Fig. 34.)

Indications: Pain in the thigh, muscular atrophy, motor impairment, numbness and pain of the lower extremities.

Method: Puncture perpendicularly 1.0-1.5 inches. Moxibustion is applicable.

Regional anatomy

Vasculature: Deeper, the branches of the lateral circumflex femoral artery and vein.

Innervation: The lateral femoral cutaneous nerve.

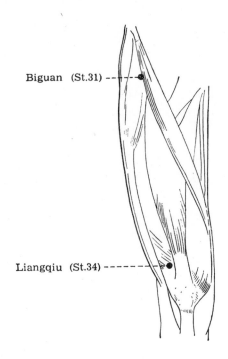

Biguan (St.31)

Liangqiu (St.34)

Fig. 34.

32. Femur-Futu (St. 32)

Location: 6 *cun* above the laterosuperior border of the patella, on the line connecting the anterior superior iliac spine and lateral border of the patella.

Indications: Pain in the lumbar and iliac region, coldness of the knee, paralysis or motor impairment and pain of the lower extremities, beriberi.

Method: Puncture perpendicularly 1.0-1.5 inches. Moxibustion is applicable.

Regional anatomy

Vasculature: The branches of the lateral circumflex femoral artery and vein.

Innervation: The anterior and lateral femoral cutaneous nerves.

33. Yinshi (St. 33)

Location: 3 *cun* above the laterosuperior border of the patella.

Indications: Numbness, soreness and motor impairment of the lower extremities.

Method: Puncture perpendicularly 0.7-1.0 inch. Moxibustion is applicable.

Regional anatomy

Vasculature: The descending branch of the lateral circumflex femoral artery.

Innervation: The anterior and lateral femoral cutaneous nerves.

34. Liangqiu (Xi-Cleft Point, St. 34)

Location: 2 *cun* above the laterosuperior border of the patella. (See Fig. 34.)

Indications: Pain and swelling of the knee, motor impairment of the lower extremities, gastric pain, mastitis.

Method: Puncture perpendicularly 0.5-1.0 inch. Moxibustion is applicable.

Regional anatomy   See Yinshi (St. 33).

35. Dubi (Also known as External Xiyan, St. 35)

Location: Ask the patient to flex the knee. The point is in the depression below the patella and lateral to the patellar ligament. (See Fig. 35.)

Indications: Pain, numbness and motor impairment of the knee, beri-beri.

Method: Puncture obliquely 0.7-1.0 inch with the needle directed slightly towards the medial side. Moxibustion is applicable.

Regional anatomy

Vasculature: The arterial and venous network around the knee joint.

Innervation: The lateral sural cutaneous nerve and the articular branch of the common peroneal nerve.

36. Zusanli (He-Sea Point, St. 36)

Location: 3 *cun* below Dubi (St. 35), one finger-breadth from the anterior crest of the tibia. (See Fig. 35.)

Indications: Gastric pain, vomiting, abdominal distension, indigestion, borborygmus, diarrhea, constipation, dysentery, mastitis, dizziness, mental disorders, hemiplegia, beriberi, aching of the knee joint and leg.

Method: Puncture perpendicularly 0.5-1.3 inches. Moxibustion is applicable.

Regional anatomy

Vasculature: The anterior tibial artery and vein.

Innervation: Superficially, the lateral sural cutaneous nerve and the cutaneous branch of the saphenous nerve; deeper, the deep peroneal nerve.

Notes:

(1) In the lateral aspect of the leg, the distance from Dubi (St. 35) to the tip of the external malleolus is measured as 16 *cun*.

(2) This is an important point for tonic purpose.

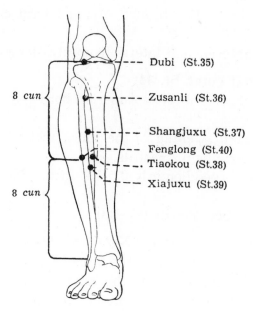

8 cun { Dubi (St.35)

Zusanli (St.36)

Shangjuxu (St.37)

Fenglong (St.40)

Tiaokou (St.38)

Xiajuxu (St.39)

8 cun {

Fig. 35.

37. Shangjuxu (St. 37)

Location: 6 *cun* below Dubi (St. 35), one finger-breadth from the anterior crest of the tibia. (See Fig. 35.)

Indications: Abdominal pain and distension, dysentery, borborygmus, diarrhea, appendicitis, hemiplegia, beriberi.

Method: Puncture perpendicularly 0.5-1.3 inches. Moxibustion is applicable.

Regional anatomy   See Zusanli (St. 36).

Note: This is the Inferior He-Sea Point of the large intestine and is indicated in disorders of the large intestine.

38. Tiaokou (St. 38)

Location: 8 *cun* below Dubi (St. 35), 2 *cun* below Shangjuxu (St. 37), midway between Dubi (St. 35) and Jiexi (St. 41). (See Fig. 35.)

Indications: Muscular atrophy, motor impairment, pain and paralysis of the leg, shoulder pain.

Method: Puncture perpendicularly 0.5-1.0 inch.   Moxibustion is applicable.

Regional anatomy   See Zusanli (St. 36).

39. Xiajuxu (St. 39)

Location: 9 *cun* below Dubi (St. 35), 3 *cun* below Shangjuxu (St. 37), about one finger-breadth from the anterior crest of the tibia. (See Fig. 35.)

Indications: Lower abdominal pain, backache referring to testis, mastitis, muscular atrophy, motor impairment, pain and paralysis of the lower extremities.

Method: Puncture perpendicularly 0.5-1.0 inch. Moxibustion is applicable.

Regional anatomy

Vasculature: The anterior tibial artery and vein.

Innervation: The branches of the superficial peroneal nerve and the deep peroneal nerve.

Note: This is the Inferior He-Sea Point of the small intestine and is indicated in disorders of the small intestine.

40. Fenglong (Luo-Connecting Point, St. 40)

Location: 8 *cun* superior and anterior to the external malleolus, about one finger-breadth posterior to Tiaokou (St. 38). (See Fig. 35.)

Indications: Chest pain, asthma, excessive sputum, sore throat, muscular atrophy, motor impairment, pain, paralysis or swelling of the lower extremities, headache, dizziness, mental disorders, epilepsy.

Method: Puncture perpendicularly 0.5-1.0 inch. Moxibustion is applicable.

Regional anatomy

Vasculature: The branches of the anterior tibial artery and vein.

Innervation: The superficial peroneal nerve.

41. Jiexi (Jing-River Point, St. 41)

Location: At the junction of the dorsum of foot and the leg, between the tendons of m. extensor digitorum longus and hallucis longus, approximately at the level of the tip of the external malleolus. (See Fig. 36.)

Indications: Edema of the head and face, headache, dizziness and vertigo, abdominal distension, constipation, muscular atrophy, motor impairment, pain and paralysis of the lower extremities, mental disorder of depressive type.

Method: Puncture perpendicularly 0.5-0.7 inch. Moxibustion is applicable.

Regional anatomy

Vasculature: The anterior tibial artery vein.

Innervation: The superficial and deep peroneal nerves.

42. Chongyang (Yuan-Source Point, St. 42)

Location: Distal to Jiexi (St. 41), at the highest point of the dorsum of foot, in the depression between the 2nd and 3rd metatarsal bones and the cuneiform bone. (See Fig. 36.)

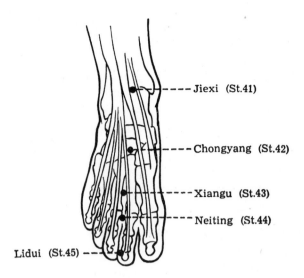

Fig. 36

Indications: Facial paralysis, muscular atrophy and motor impairment of foot, redness and swelling of the dorsum of foot.

Method: Puncture perpendicularly 0.3 inch. Avoid the artery. Moxibustion is applicable.

Regional anatomy

Vasculature: The dorsal artery and vein of foot, the dorsal venous network of foot.

Innervation: Superficially, the medial dorsal cutaneous nerve of foot derived from the superficial peroneal nerve; deeper, the deep peroneal nerve.

43. Xiangu (Shu-Stream Point, St. 43)

Location: In the depression distal to the junction of the 2nd and 3rd metatarsal bones. (See Fig. 36.)

Indications: Facial or general edema, borborygmus, abdominal pain, pain and swelling of the dorsum of foot.

Method: Puncture perpendicularly 0.5-0.7 inch. Moxibustion is applicable.

Regional anatomy

Vasculature: The dorsal venous network of foot.

Innervation: The medial dorsal cutaneous nerve of foot.

44. Neiting (Ying-Spring Point, St. 44)

Location: Proximal to the web margin between the 2nd and 3rd toes, in the depression distal and lateral to the 2nd metatarsodigital joint. (See Fig. 36.)

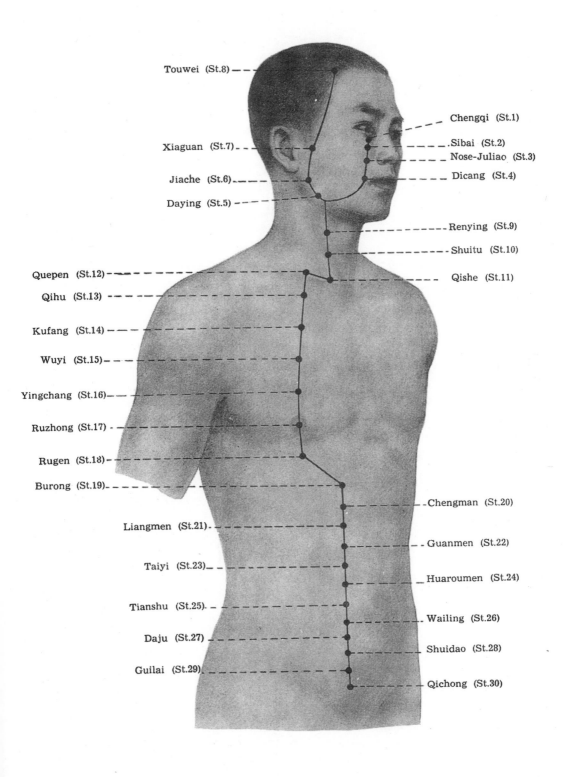

Fig. 37a. The Stomach Channel of Foot-Yangming.

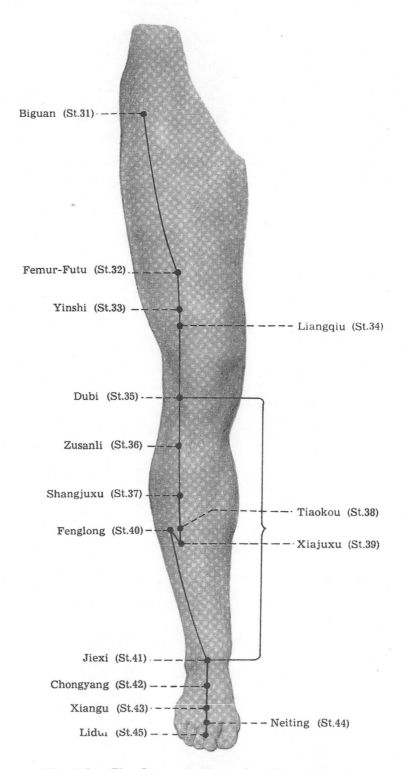

Biguan (St.31)

Femur-Futu (St.32)

Yinshi (St.33)

Liangqiu (St.34)

Dubi (St.35)

Zusanli (St.36)

Shangjuxu (St.37)

Tiaokou (St.38)

Fenglong (St.40)

Xiajuxu (St.39)

Jiexi (St.41)

Chongyang (St.42)

Xiangu (St.43)

Neiting (St.44)

Lidui (St.45)

Fig. 37b. The Stomach Channel of Foot-Yangming.

Indications: Toothache, deviation of the mouth, epistaxis, abdominal pain or distension, diarrhea, dysentery, pain and swelling of the dorsum of foot, febrile diseases.

Method: Puncture perpendicularly 0.3-0.5 inch. Moxibustion is applicable.

Regional anatomy

Vasculature: The dorsal venous network of foot.

Innervation: Just where the lateral branch of the medial dorsal cutaneous nerve divides into dorsal digital nerves.

45. Lidui (Jing-Well Point, St. 45)

Location: On the lateral side of the 2nd toe, about 0.1 *cun* posterior to the corner of nail. (See Fig. 36.)

Indications: Facial swelling, deviation of the mouth, toothache, epistaxis, distending sensation of the chest and abdomen, cold in the leg and foot, febrile diseases, dream-disturbed sleep, mental confusion.

Method: Puncture obliquely 0.1 inch. Moxibustion is applicable.

Regional anatomy

Vasculature: The arterial and venous network formed by the dorsal digital artery and vein of foot.

Innervation: The dorsal digital nerve derived from the superficial peroneal nerve.

IV. THE SPLEEN CHANNEL OF FOOT-TAIYIN

The Spleen Channel of Foot-Taiyin starts from the tip of the big toe (Yinbai, Sp. 1) (1). It runs along the medial aspect of the foot at the junction of the red and white skin (2), and ascends in front of the medial malleolus (3) up to the leg (4). It follows the posterior aspect of the tibia (5), crosses and goes in front of the Liver Channel of Foot-Jueyin (6). Passing through the anterior medial aspect of the knee and thigh (7), it enters the abdomen (8), then the spleen, its pertaining organ, and connects with the stomach (9). From there it ascends, traversing the diaphragm (10), and running alongside the esophagus (11). When it reaches the root of the tongue it spreads over its lower surface (12).

The branch from the stomach goes upward through the diaphragm (13), and flows into the heart to link with the Heart Channel of Hand-Shaoyin (14). (See Fig. 38.)

There are altogether 21 points in this channel, which may be described as follows:

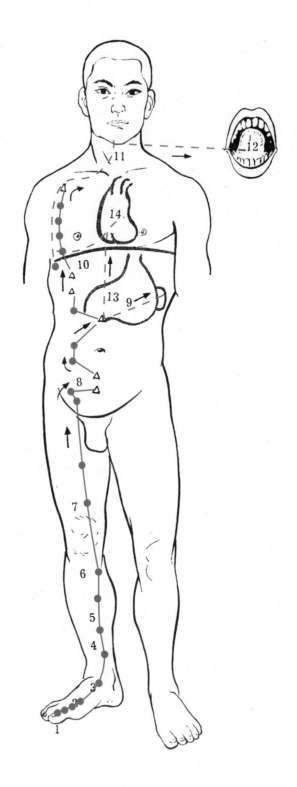

Fig. 38.　The Spleen Channel of Foot-Taiyin.

1. Yinbai (Jing-Well Point, Sp. 1)

Location: On the medial side of the big toe, about 0.1 *cun* posterior to the corner of the nail. (See Fig. 39.)

Indications: Abdominal distension, uterine bleeding, mental disorders, dream-disturbed sleep, convulsion.

Method: Puncture obliquely 0.1 inch. Moxibustion is applicable.

Regional anatomy

Vasculature: The dorsal digital artery.

Innervation: On the anastomosis of the dorsal digital nerve derived from the superficial peroneal nerve and the plantar digital proprial nerve.

2. Dadu (Ying-Spring Point, Sp. 2)

Location: On the medial side of the big toe, distal and inferior to the 1st metatarsodigital joint, at the junction of the red and white skin. (See Fig. 39.)

Indications: Abdominal distension, gastric pain, febrile diseases with anhidrosis.

Method: Puncture perpendicularly 0.1-0.2 inch. Moxibustion is applicable.

Regional anatomy

Vasculature: The branches of the medial plantar artery and vein.

Innervation: The plantar digital proprial nerve derived from the medial plantar nerve.

3. Taibai (Shu-Stream and Yuan-Source Point, Sp. 3)

Location: Proximal and inferior to the head of the 1st metatarsal bone, at the junction of the red and white skin. (See Fig. 39.)

Indications: Gastric pain, abdominal distension, sluggishness, dysentery, constipation, vomiting, diarrhea, beriberi.

Method: Puncture perpendicularly 0.3 inch. Moxibustion is applicable.

Regional anatomy

Vasculature: The dorsal venous network of foot, the medial plantar artery and the branches of the medial tarsal artery.

Innervation: The branches of the saphenous nerve and superficial peroneal nerve.

4. Gongsun (Luo-Connecting Point, Sp. 4)

Location: In the depression distal and inferior to the base of the 1st metatarsal bone, at the junction of the red and white skin. (See Fig. 39.)

Indications: Gastric pain, vomiting, borborygmus, abdominal pain, diarrhea, dysentery.

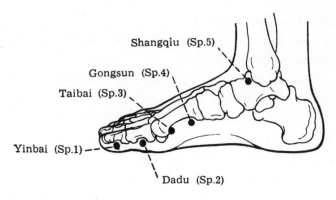

Fig. 39.

Method: Puncture perpendicularly 0.5-1.0 inch. Moxibustion is applicable.

Regional anatomy

Vasculature: The medial tarsal artery and the dorsal venous network of foot.

Innervation: The saphenous nerve and the branch of the superficial peroneal nerve.

Note: This is one of the Eight Confluent Points communicating with the Chong Channel.

5. Shangqiu (Jing-River Point, Sp. 5)

Location: In the depression distal and inferior to the medial malleolus, midway between the tuberosity of the navicular bone and the tip of the medial malleolus. (See Fig. 39.)

Indications: Borborygmus, abdominal distension, stiffness and pain of the tongue, constipation, diarrhea, pain in the foot and ankle joint.

Method: Puncture perpendicularly 0.2-0.3 inch. Moxibustion is applicable.

Regional anatomy

Vasculature: The medial tarsal artery and the great saphenous vein.

Innervation: The medial crural cutaneous nerve and the branch of the superficial peroneal nerve.

6. Sanyinjiao (Sp. 6)

Location: 3 *cun* directly above the tip of the medial malleolus, on the posterior border of the tibia, on the line drawn from the medial malleolus to Yinlingquan (Sp. 9). (See Fig. 40.)

Indications: Borborygmus, abdominal distension, loose stools with undigested food, irregular menstruation, uterine bleeding, leukorrhea, prolapse of uterus, amenorrhea, sterility, difficult labour, seminal emission, pain of the external genitalia, hernia, dysuria, enuresis, muscular atrophy, motor impairment and paralysis and pain of the lower extremities, insomnia.

Method: Puncture perpendicularly 0.5-1.0 inch. Moxibustion is applicable.

Regional anatomy

Vasculature: The great saphenous vein, the posterior tibial artery and vein.

Innervation: Superficially, the medial crural cutaneous nerve; deeper, in the posterior aspect, the tibial nerve.

Notes:

(1) Sanyinjiao (Sp. 6) is the meeting point of the three *yin* channels of foot (the Spleen Channel of Foot-Taiyin, the Kidney Channel of Foot-Shaoying and the Liver Channel of Foot-Jueyin).

(2) Acupuncture is contraindicated during pregnancy.

(3) In the medial aspect of the leg, the distance from the tip of the medial malleolus to the lower border of the medial condyle of the tibia (Yinlingquan, Sp. 9) is measured as 13 *cun*.

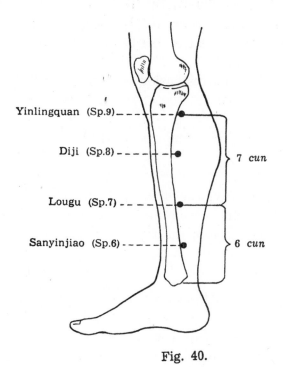

Fig. 40.

7. Lougu (Sp. 7)

Location: 6 *cun* above the tip of the medial malleolus, 3 *cun* above Sanyinjiao (Sp. 6). (See Fig. 40.)

Indications: Abdominal distension, borborygmus, cold, numbness and paralysis of the knee and leg.

Method: Puncture perpendicularly 0.5-1.0 inch. Moxibustion is applicable.

Regional anatomy   See Sanyinjiao (Sp. 6).

8. Diji (Xi-Cleft Point, Sp. 8)

Location: 3 *cun* below the medial condyle of the tibia, on the line connecting Yinlingquan (Sp. 9) and the medial malleolus. (See Fig. 40.)

Indications: Abdominal distension, anorexia, dysentery, irregular menstruation, dysuria, seminal emission, edema.

Method: Puncture perpendicularly 0.5-1.0 inch. Moxibustion is applicable.

Regional anatomy

Vasculature: Anteriorly, the great saphenous vein and the branch of the genu suprema artery; deeper, the posterior tibial artery and vein.

Innervation: See Sanyinjiao (Sp. 6).

9. Yinlingquan (He-Sea Point, Sp. 9)

Location: On the lower border of the medial condyle of the tibia, in the depression between the posterior border of the tibia and m. gastrocnemius. (See Fig. 40.)

Indications: Abdominal distension, edema, jaundice, diarrhea, dysuria, incontinence of urine, pain of the external genitalia, seminal emission, pain in the knee.

Method: Puncture perpendicularly 0.5-1.0 inch. Moxibustion is applicable.

Regional anatomy

Vasculature: Anteriorly, the great saphenous vein, the genu suprema artery; deeper, the posterior tibial artery and vein.

Innervation: Superficially, the medial crural cutaneous nerve; deeper, the tibial nerve.

10. Xuehai (Sp. 10)

Location: When knee is flexed, the point is 2 *cun* above the mediosuperior border of the patella, on the bulge of the medial portion of m. quadriceps femoris. Another way to locate this point is to cup your right palm to the patient's left knee, with the thumb on its medial side and the other four

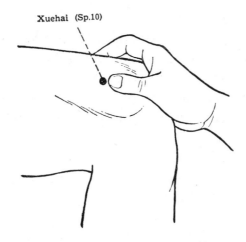

Xuehai (Sp.10)

Fig. 41.

fingers directed proximally. The point is where the tip of your thumb rests. (See Fig. 41.)

Indications: Irregular menstruation, dysmenorrhea, amenorrhea, uterine bleeding, pain in the medial aspect of the thigh, eczema, urticaria.

Method: Puncture perpendicularly 0.7-1.2 inches. Moxibustion is applicable.

Regional anatomy

Vasculature: The muscular branches of the femoral artery and vein.

Innervation: The anterior femoral cutaneous nerve and the muscular branch of the femoral nerve.

Note: In the medial aspect of the thigh, the distance from the level of the upper border of symphysis pubis to the medial epicondyle of femur is measured as 18 *cun*.

11.   Jimen (Sp. 11)

Location: 6 *cun* above Xuehai (Sp. 10), on the line drawn from Xuehai (Sp. 10) to Chongmen (Sp. 12).

Indications: Retention of urine, enuresis, pain and swelling in the inguinal region.

Method: Puncture perpendicularly 0.3-0.5 inch. Deep puncture is contraindicated. Moxibustion is applicable.

Regional anatomy

Vasculature: Superficially, the great saphenous vein; deeper on the lateral side, the femoral artery and vein.

Innervation: The anterior femoral cutaneous nerve; deeper, the saphenous nerve.

12. Chongmen (Sp. 12)

Location: Superior to the lateral end of the inguinal groove, on the lateral side of the femoral artery, at the level of the upper border of symphysis pubis, 3.5 *cun* lateral to Qugu (Ren 2).

Indications: Abdominal pain, hernia, retention of urine.

Method: Puncture perpendicularly 0.5-1.0 inch. Moxibustion is applicable.

Regional anatomy

Vasculature: On the medial side, the femoral artery.

Innervation: Just where the femoral nerve traverses.

13. Fushe (Sp. 13)

Location: 0.7 *cun* above Chongmen (Sp. 12), 4 *cun* lateral to the Ren Channel.

Indications: Abdominal pain, hernia, mass in the abdomen.

Method: Puncture perpendicularly 0.7-1.0 inch. Moxibustion is applicable.

Regional anatomy

Innervation: The ilioinguinal nerve.

14. Fujie (Sp. 14)

Location: 3 *cun* above Fushe (Sp. 13), 1.3 *cun* below Daheng (Sp. 15), on the lateral side of m. rectus abdominis.

Indications: Abdominal pain around the umbilical region, hernia, diarrhea.

Method: Puncture perpendicularly 0.5-1.0 inch. Moxibustion is applicable.

Regional anatomy

Vasculature: The 11th intercostal artery and vein.

Innervation: The 11th intercostal nerve.

15. Daheng (Sp. 15)

Location: 4 *cun* lateral to the centre of the umbilicus, on the mammillary line, lateral to m. rectus abdominis. (See Fig. 42.)

Indications: Dysentery, constipation, pain in the lower abdomen.

Method: Puncture perpendicularly 0.5-1.0 inch. Moxibustion is applicable.

Regional anatomy

Vasculature: The 10th intercostal artery and vein.

Innervation: The 10th intercostal nerve.

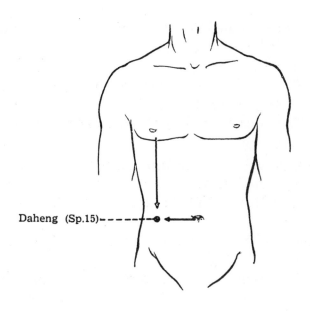

Daheng (Sp.15)

Fig. 42.

16. Fuai (Sp. 16)

Location: 3 *cun* above Daheng (Sp. 15).

Indications: Abdominal pain, indigestion, constipation, dysentery.

Method: Puncture perpendicularly 0.5-1.0 inch. Moxibustion is applicable.

Regional anatomy

Vasculature: The 8th intercostal artery and vein.

Innervation: The 8th intercostal nerve.

17. Shidou (Sp. 17)

Location: 6 *cun* lateral to the Ren Channel, or 2 *cun* lateral to the mammillary line, in the 5th intercostal space.

Indications: Sensation of fullness and pain in the chest and hypochondriac region.

Method: Puncture obliquely 0.3-0.5 inch. Moxibustion is applicable.

Regional anatomy

Vasculature: The thoracoepigastric vein.

Innervation: The lateral cutaneous branch of the 5th intercostal nerve.

18. Tianxi (Sp. 18)

Location: 2 *cun* lateral to the nipple, in the 4th intercostal space.

Indications: Sensation of fullness and pain in the chest, cough, mastitis, lactation deficiency.

Method: Puncture obliquely 0.4-0.5 inch, or apply moxa stick for 5-10 minutes.

Regional anatomy

Vasculature: The branches of the lateral thoracic artery and vein, the thoracoepigastric artery and vein, the 4th intercostal artery and vein.

Innervation: The lateral cutaneous branch of the 4th intercostal nerve.

19. Xiongxiang (Sp. 19)

Location: One rib above Tianxi (Sp. 18), in the 3rd intercostal space, 6 *cun* lateral to the Ren Channel.

Indications: Sensation of fullness and pain in the chest and hypochondriac region.

Method: Puncture obliquely 0.4-0.5 inch. Moxibustion is applicable.

Regional anatomy

Vasculature: The lateral thoracic artery and vein, the 3rd intercostal artery and vein.

Innervation: The lateral cutaneous branch of the 3rd intercostal nerve.

20. Zhourong (Sp. 20)

Location: One rib above Xiongxiang (Sp. 19), directly below Zhongfu (Lu. 1) and Yunmen (Lu. 2), in the 2nd intercostal space, 6 *cun* lateral to the Ren Channel.

Indications: Sensation of fullness in the chest and hypochondriac region, cough.

Method: Puncture obliquely 0.4-0.5 inch. Moxibustion is applicable.

Regional anatomy

Vasculature: The lateral thoracic artery and vein, the 2nd intercostal artery and vein.

Innervation: The muscular branch of the anterior thoracic nerve, the lateral cutaneous branch of the 2nd intercostal nerve.

21. Dabao (Major Luo-Connecting Point of the spleen, Sp. 21)

Location: On the mid-axillary line, 6 *cun* below the axilla, midway between the axilla and the free end of the 11th rib.

Indications: Pain in the chest and hypochondriac region, asthma, general aching and weakness.

Method: Puncture obliquely 0.3-0.5 inch. Moxibustion is applicable.

Regional anatomy

Vasculature: The thoracodorsal artery and vein, the 7th intercostal artery and vein.

Innervation: The 7th intercostal nerve and the terminal branch of the long thoracic nerve.

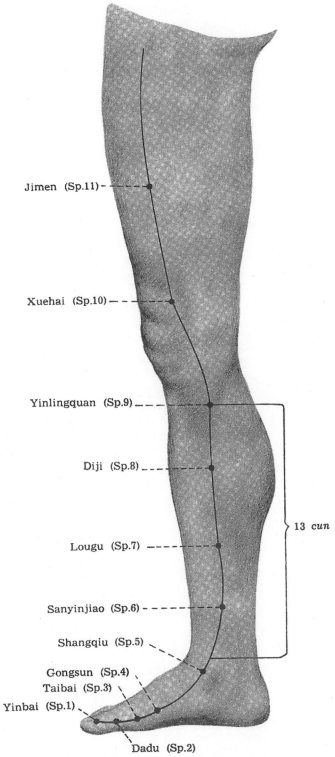

Jimen (Sp.11)

Xuehai (Sp.10)

Yinlingquan (Sp.9)

Diji (Sp.8)

13 *cun*

Lougu (Sp.7)

Sanyinjiao (Sp.6)

Shangqiu (Sp.5)

Gongsun (Sp.4)
Taibai (Sp.3)
Yinbai (Sp.1)

Dadu (Sp.2)

Fig. 43a.   The Spleen Channel of Foot-Taiyin.

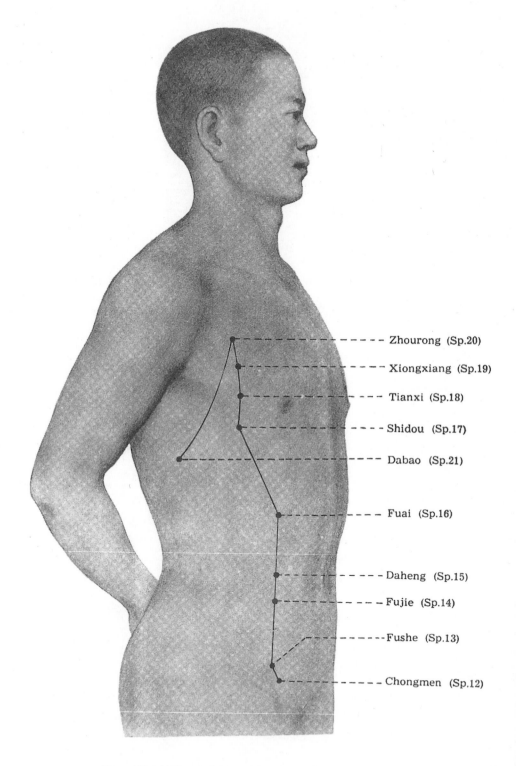

Zhourong (Sp.20)

Xiongxiang (Sp.19)

Tianxi (Sp.18)

Shidou (Sp.17)

Dabao (Sp.21)

Fuai (Sp.16)

Daheng (Sp.15)

Fujie (Sp.14)

Fushe (Sp.13)

Chongmen (Sp.12)

Fig. 43b. The Spleen Channel of Foot-Taiyin.

V. THE HEART CHANNEL OF HAND-SHAOYIN

The Heart Channel of Hand-Shaoyin originates from the heart. Emerging, it spreads over the "heart system" (i.e., the vessels connecting the heart with the other *zang-fu* organs) (1). It passes through the diaphragm to connect with the small intestine (2).

The ascending portion of the channel from the "heart system" (3) runs alongside the esophagus (4) to connect with the "eye system" (i.e., the tissues connecting the eyeball) (5).

The straight portion of the channel from the "heart system" goes upward to the lung (6). Then it turns downward and emerges from the axilla (Jiquan, H. 1). From there it goes along the posterior border of the medial aspect of the upper arm behind the Lung Channel of Hand-Taiyin and the Pericardium Channel of Hand-Jueyin (7) down to the cubital fossa (8). From there it descends along the posterior border of the medial aspect of the forearm to the pisiform region proximal to the palm (9) and enters the palm (10). Then it follows the medial aspect of the little finger to its tip (Shaochong, H. 9) (11) and links with the Small Intestine Channel of Hand-Taiyang. (See Fig. 44.)

There are altogether 9 points in this channel. They are described as follows:

1. Jiquan (H. 1)

Location: In the centre of the axilla, on the medial side of the axillary artery.

Indications: Pain in the costal and cardiac regions, scrofula, cold and pain of the elbow and arm.

Method: Puncture perpendicularly 0.5-1.0 inch. Avoid the artery. Moxibustion is applicable.

Regional anatomy

Vasculature: Laterally, the axillary artery.

Innervation: The ulnar nerve, median nerve and medial brachial cutaneous nerve.

2. Qingling (H. 2)

Location: When the elbow is flexed, the point is 3 *cun* above the medial end of the transverse cubital crease (Shaohai, H. 3), in the groove medial to m. biceps brachii.

Indications: Yellowish sclera, pain in the hypochondriac region, shoulder and arm.

Method: Puncture perpendicularly 0.3-0.5 inch. Moxibustion is applicable.

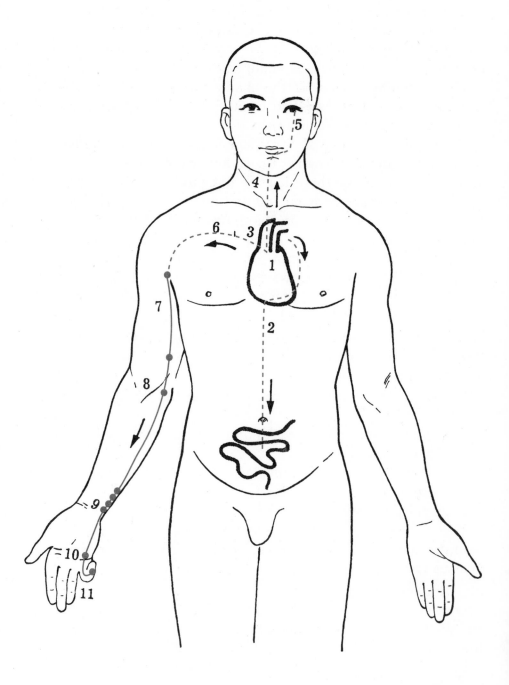

Fig. 44. The Heart Channel of Hand-Shaoyin.

Regional anatomy

Vasculature: The basilic vein, the superior ulnar collateral artery.

Innervation: The medial antebrachial cutaneous nerve, the medial brachial cutaneous nerve and the ulnar nerve.

Note: On the upper arm, the distance from the end of the axillary fold to the transverse cubital crease (Shaohai, H. 3) is measured as 9 *cun*.

3. Shaohai (He-Sea Point, H. 3)

Location: When the elbow is flexed, the point is at the medial end of the transverse cubital crease, in the depression anterior to the medial epicondyle of the humerus. (See Fig. 45.)

Indications: Cardiac pain, numbness of the arm, hand tremor, contracture of the elbow, pain in the axilla and hypochondriac region, scrofula.

Method: Puncture perpendicularly 0.3-0.5 inch. Moxibustion is applicable.

Regional anatomy

Vasculature: The basilic vein, the inferior ulnar collateral artery, the ulnar recurrent artery and vein.

Innervation: The medial antebrachial cutaneous nerve.

4. Lingdao (Jing-River Point, H. 4)

Location: On the radial side of the tendon of m. flexor carpi ulnaris, 1.5 *cun* above the transverse crease of the wrist when the palm faces upward. (See Fig. 45.)

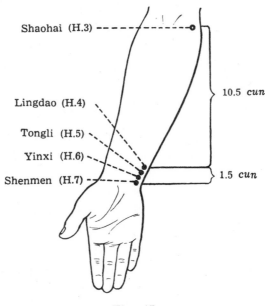

Fig. 45.

Indications: Cardiac pain, sudden hoarseness of voice, contracture of the elbow and arm, convulsion.

Method: Puncture perpendicularly 0.3-0.5 inch. Moxibustion is applicable.

Regional anatomy

Vasculature: The ulnar artery.

Innervation: The medial antebrachial cutaneous nerve; on the ulnar side, the ulnar nerve.

Note: The distance from Shaohai (H. 3) to Shenmen (H. 7) is measured as 12 *cun*.

5. Tongli (Luo-Connecting Point, H. 5)

Location: When the palm faces upward, the point is on the radial side of the tendon of m. flexor carpi ulnaris, 1 *cun* above the transverse crease of the wrist. (See Fig. 45.)

Indications: Palpitation, dizziness, blurring of vision, sore throat, sudden hoarseness of voice, aphasia with stiffness of the tongue, pain in the wrist and arm.

Method: Puncture perpendicularly 0.3-0.5 inch. Moxibustion is applicable.

Regional anatomy   See Lingdao (H. 4).

6. Yinxi (Xi-Cleft Point, H. 6)

Location: On the radial side of the tendon of m. flexor carpi ulnaris, 0.5 *cun* above the transverse crease of the wrist. (See Fig. 45.)

Indications: Cardiac pain, hysteria, night sweating.

Method: Puncture perpendicularly 0.3-0.5 inch. Moxibustion is applicable.

Regional anatomy   See Lingdao (H. 4).

7. Shenmen (Shu-Stream and Yuan-Source Point, H. 7)

Location: On the transverse crease of the wrist, in the articular region between the pisiform bone and the ulna, in the depression on the radial side of the tendon of m. flexor carpi ulnaris. (See Fig. 45.)

Indications: Cardiac pain, irritability, mental disorders, epilepsy, poor memory, palpitation, hysteria, insomnia, yellowish sclera, pain in the hypochondriac region, feverish sensation in the palm.

Method: Puncture perpendicularly 0.3-0.5 inch. Moxibustion is applicable.

Regional anatomy   See Lingdao (H. 4).

8. Shaofu (Ying-Spring Point, H. 8)

Location: On the palmar surface, between the 4th and 5th metacarpal bones. When a fist is made, the point is where the tip of the little finger rests. (See Fig. 46.)

Indications: Palpitation, pain in the chest, twitching and contracture of the little finger, feverish sensation in the palm, skin pruritus, dysuria, enuresis.

Method: Puncture perpendicularly 0.3-0.5 inch. Moxibustion is applicable.

Regional anatomy

Vasculature: The common palmar digital artery and vein.

Innervation: The 4th common palmar digital nerve derived from the ulnar nerve.

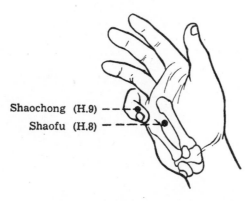

Shaochong (H.9)
Shaofu (H.8)

Fig. 46.

9. Shaochong (Jing-Well Point, H. 9)

Location: On the radial side of the little finger, about 0.1 *cun* posterior to the corner of the nail. (See Fig. 46.)

Indications: Palpitation, cardiac pain, pain in the chest and hypochondriac region, mental disorders, febrile diseases, loss of consciousness.

Method: Puncture obliquely 0.1 inch, or prick with three-edged needle to cause bleeding. Moxibustion is applicable.

Regional anatomy

Vasculature: The arterial and venous network formed by the palmar digital proprial artery and vein.

Innervation: The palmar digital proprial nerve derived from the ulnar nerve.

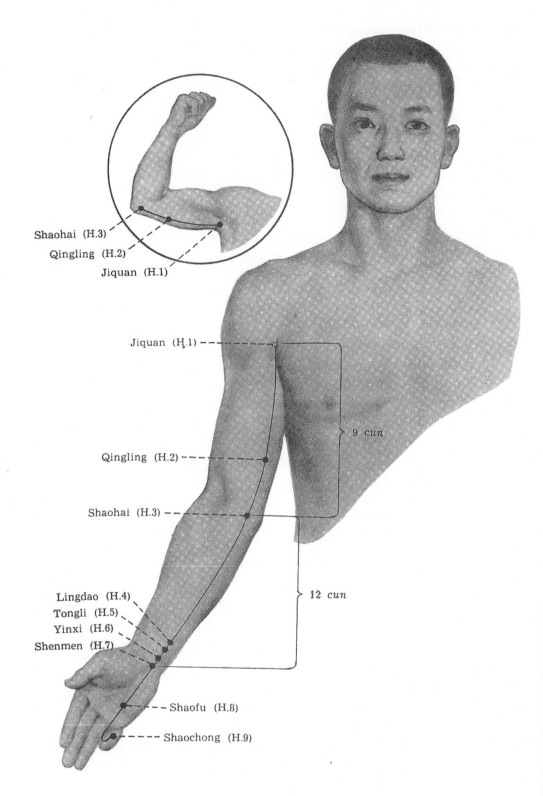

Shaohai (H.3)
Qingling (H.2)
Jiquan (H.1)

Jiquan (H.1)

9 cun

Qingling (H.2)

Shaohai (H.3)

Lingdao (H.4)
Tongli (H.5)
Yinxi (H.6)
Shenmen (H.7)

12 cun

Shaofu (H.8)

Shaochong (H.9)

Fig. 47. The Heart Channel of Hand-Shaoyin. 9 *cun* and 12 *cun*.

VI. THE SMALL INTESTINE CHANNEL OF HAND-TAIYANG

The Small Intestine Channel of Hand-Taiyang starts from the ulnar side of the tip of the little finger (Shaoze, S.I. 1) (1). Following the ulnar side of the dorsum of hand it reaches the wrist where it emerges from the styloid process of the ulna (2). From there it ascends along the posterior aspect of the forearm (3), passes between the olecranon of the ulna and the medial epicondyle of the humerus, and runs along the posterior border of the lateral aspect of the upper arm (4) to the shoulder joint (5). Circling around the scapular region (6), it meets the Du Channel on the superior aspect of the shoulder at Dazhui (Du 14) (7). Then, turning downward to the supraclavicular fossa (8), it connects with the heart (9). From there it descends along the esophagus (10), passes through the diaphragm (11), reaches the stomach (12), and finally enters the small intestine, its pertaining organ (13).

The branch from the supraclavicular fossa (14) ascends to the neck (15), and further to the cheek (16). Via the outer canthus (17), it enters the ear (Tinggong, S.I. 19) (18).

The branch from the cheek (19) runs upward to the infraorbital region (Quanliao, S.I. 18) and further to the lateral side of the nose. Then it reaches the inner canthus (Jingming, U.B. 1) to link with the Urinary Bladder Channel of Foot-Taiyang (20). (See Fig. 48.)

Note: The small intestine has an Inferior He-Sea Point — Xiajuxu (St. 39). (See Fig. 49.)

There are 19 points in this channel. They are described as follows:

1. Shaoze (Jing-Well Point, S.I. 1)

Location: On the ulnar side of the little finger, about 0.1 *cun* posterior to the corner of the nail. (See Fig. 50.)

Indications: Febrile diseases, loss of consciousness, lactation deficiency, sore throat, cloudiness of cornea.

Method: Puncture obliquely 0.1 inch. Moxibustion is applicable.

Regional anatomy

Vasculature: The arterial and venous network formed by the palmar digital proprial artery and vein and the dorsal digital artery and vein.

Innervation: The palmar digital proprial nerve and the dorsal digital nerve derived from the ulnar nerve.

2. Qiangu (Ying-Spring Point, S.I. 2)

Location: When a loose fist is made, the point is distal to the metacarpophalangeal joint, at the junction of the red and white skin. (See Fig. 50.)

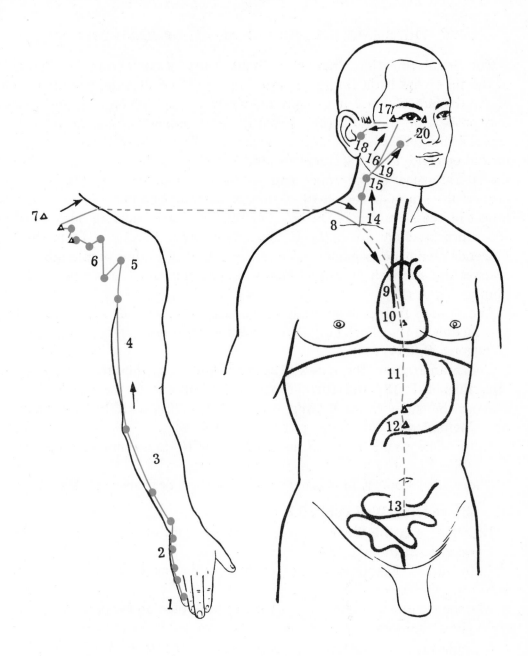

Fig. 48. The Small Intestine Channel of Hand-Taiyang.

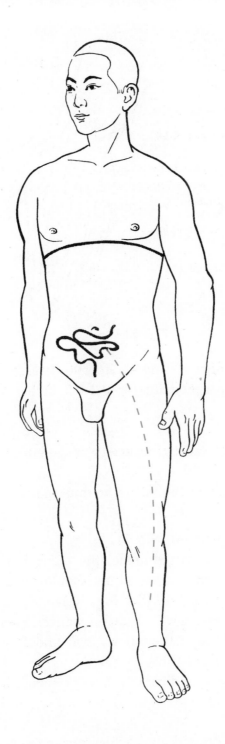

Fig. 49. Inferior He-Sea Point of the Small Intestine Channel.
Xiajuxu (St. 39).

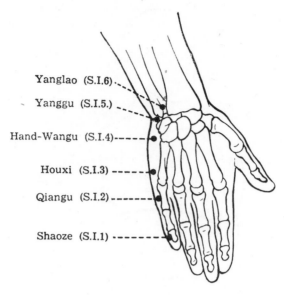

Yanglao (S.I.6).

Yanggu (S.I.5.)

Hand-Wangu (S.I.4)

Houxi (S.I.3)

Qiangu (S.I.2)

Shaoze (S.I.1)

Fig. 50.

Indications: Numbness of fingers, febrile diseases.

Method: Puncture perpendicularly 0.2-0.3 inch. Moxibustion is applicable.

Regional anatomy

Vasculature: The dorsal digital artery and vein arising from the ulnar artery and vein.

Innervation: The dorsal digital nerve and palmar digital proprial nerve derived from the ulnar nerve.

3. Houxi (Shu-Stream Point, S.I. 3)

Location: When a loose fist is made, the point is proximal to the head of the 5th metacarpal bone on the ulnar side, in the depression at the junction of the red and white skin. (See Fig. 50.)

Indications: Headache, neck rigidity, congestion of the eye, deafness, contracture and twitching of the elbow, arm and fingers, febrile diseases, epilepsy, malaria, night sweating.

Method: Puncture perpendicularly 0.5-0.7 inch. Moxibustion is applicable.

Regional anatomy

Vasculature: The dorsal digital artery and vein, the dorsal venous network of the hand.

Innervation: The dorsal branch derived from the ulnar nerve.

Note: This is one of the Eight Confluent Points communicating with the Du Channel.

4. Hand-Wangu (Yuan-Source Point, S.I. 4)

Location: On the ulnar side of the palm, in the depression betweem the base of the 5th metacarpal bone and the triquetral bone. (See Fig. 50.)

Indications: Headache, neck rigidity, cloudiness of cornea, pain in the hypochondriac region, jaundice, febrile diseases.

Method: Puncture perpendicularly 0.3-0.5 inch. Moxibustion is applicable.

Regional anatomy

Vasculature: The posterior carpal artery (the branch of the ulnar artery), the dorsal venous network of the hand.

Innervation: The dorsal branch of the ulnar nerve.

5. Yanggu (Jing-River Point, S.I. 5)

Location: On the ulnar side of the wrist, in the depression between the styloid process of the ulna and the triquetral bone. (See Fig. 50.)

Indications: Swelling of the neck and submandibular region, pain in the wrist and the lateral aspect of the arm, febrile diseases.

Method: Puncture perpendicularly 0.3-0.4 inch. Moxibustion is applicable.

Regional anatomy

Vasculature: The posterior carpal artery.

Innervation: The dorsal branch of the ulnar nerve.

6. Yanglao (Xi-Cleft Point, S.I. 6)

Location: Dorsal to the head of the ulna. When the palm faces the chest, the point is in the bony cleft on the radial side of the styloid process of the ulna. (See Fig. 51, 52.)

Indications: Blurring of vision, aching of the shoulder, back, elbow and arm.

Method: Puncture perpendicularly 0.3-0.5 inch. Moxibustion is applicable.

Regional anatomy

Vasculature: The terminal branches of the posterior interosseous artery and vein, the dorsal venous network of the wrist.

Innervation: The anastomotic branches of the posterior antebrachial cutaneous nerve and the dorsal branch of the ulnar nerve.

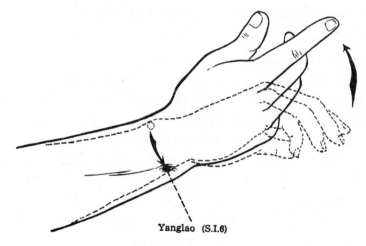

Yanglao (S.I.6)

Fig. 51.

7. Zhizheng (Luo-Connecting Point, S.I. 7)

Location: 5 *cun* proximal to the wrist, on the line joining Yanggu (S.I. 5) and Xiaohai (S.I. 8). (See Fig. 52.)

Indications: Neck rigidity, contracture and twitching of elbow, pain in fingers, febrile diseases, mental disorders.

Method: Puncture perpendicularly 0.3-0.5 inch. Moxibustion is applicable.

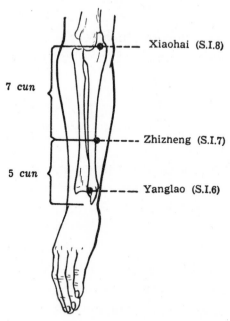

Xiaohai (S.I.8)

7 *cun*

Zhizneng (S.I.7)

5 *cun*

Yanglao (S.I.6)

Fig. 52.

Regional anatomy

Vasculature: The terminal branches of the posterior interosseous artery and vein.

Innervation: Superficially, the branch of the medial antebrachial cutaneous nerve; deeper, on the radial side, the posterior interosseous nerve.

Note: The distance from Yanggu (S.I. 5) to Xiaohai (S.I. 8) is measured as 12 *cun*.

8. Xiaohai (He-Sea Point, S.I. 8)

Location: Between the olecranon of the ulna and the medial epicondyle of the humerus. The point is located with the elbow flexed. (See Fig. 52, 53.)

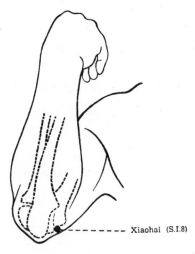

Fig. 53.

Indications: Swelling of the cheek, pain in the nape and the lateroposterior aspect of the shoulder and arm, epilepsy.

Method: Puncture perpendicularly 0.3-0.7 inch. Moxibustion is applicable.

Regional anatomy

Vasculature: The superior and inferior ulnar collateral arteries and veins, the ulnar recurrent artery and vein.

Innervation: The branches of the medial antebrachial cutaneous nerve, the ulnar nerve.

Note: The Inferior He-Sea Point of the small intestine is Xiajuxu (St. 39), which is indicated in disorders of the small intestine.

9. Jianzhen (S.I. 9)

Location: Posterior and inferior to the shoulder joint. When the arm is adducted, the point is 1 *cun* above the posterior end of the axillary fold. (See Fig. 54.)

Indications: Pain in the scapular region, pain and motor impairment of the hand and arm.

Method: Puncture perpendicularly 0.5-1.0 inch. Moxibustion is applicable.

Regional anatomy

Vasculature: The circumflex scapular artery and vein.

Innervation: The branch of the axillary nerve; deeper in the superior aspect, the radial nerve.

10. Naoshu (S.I. 10)

Location: When the arm is adducted, the point is directly above Jianzhen (S.I. 9), in the depression inferior and lateral to the scapular spine. (See Fig. 54.)

Indications: Aching and weakness of the shoulder and arm.

Method: Puncture perpendicularly 0.8-1.0 inch. Moxibustion is applicable.

Regional anatomy

Vasculature: The posterior circumflex humeral artery and vein; deeper, the suprascapular artery and vein.

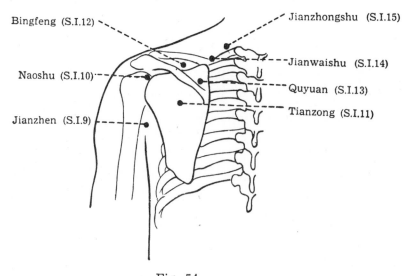

Fig. 54.

Innervation: The posterior cutaneous nerve of arm, the axillary nerve; deeper, the suprascapular nerve.

11. Tianzong (S.I. 11)

Location: In the infrascapular fossa, at the junction of the upper and middle third of the distance between the lower border of the scapular spine and the inferior angle of the scapula. (See Fig. 54.)

Indications: Pain in the scapular region, pain in the lateroposterior aspect of the elbow and arm.

Method: Puncture obliquely 0.5-1.0 inch. Moxibustion is applicable.

Regional anatomy

Vasculature: The muscular branches of the circumflex scapular artery and vein.

Innervation: The suprascapular nerve.

12. Bingfeng (S.I. 12)

Location: In the centre of the suprascapular fossa, directly above Tianzong (S.I. 11). When the arm is lifted, the point is at the site of the depression. (See Fig. 54.)

Indications: Pain in the scapular region, numbness and aching of the upper extremities.

Method: Puncture perpendicularly 0.5-0.7 inch. Moxibustion is applicable.

Regional anatomy

Vasculature: The suprascapular artery and vein.

Innervation: The lateral suprascapular nerve and accessory nerve; deeper, the suprascapular nerve.

13. Quyuan (S.I. 13)

Location: On the medial extremity of the suprascapular fossa, about midway between Naoshu (S.I. 10) and the spinous process of the 2nd thoracic vertebra. (See Fig. 54.)

Indications: Pain and stiffness of the scapular region.

Method: Puncture perpendicularly 0.3-0.5 inch. Moxibustion is applicable.

Regional anatomy

Vasculature: Superficially, the descending branches of the transverse cervical artery and vein; deeper, the muscular branch of the suprascapular artery and vein.

Innervation: Superficially, the lateral branch of the posterior ramus of the 2nd thoracic nerve, the accessory nerve; deeper, the muscular branch of the suprascapular nerve.

14. Jianwaishu (S.I. 14)

Location: 3 *cun* lateral to the lower border of the spinous process of tne 1st thoracic vertebra (Taodao, Du 13), on the vertical line drawn from the vertebral border of the scapula. (See Fig. 54.)

Indications: Aching of the shoulder and back, rigidity of neck.

Method: Puncture obliquely 0.3-0.6 inch. Moxibustion is applicable.

Regional anatomy

Vasculature: Deeper, the transverse cervical artery and vein.

Innervation: Superficially, the medial cutaneous branches of the posterior rami of the 1st and 2nd thoracic nerves, the accessory nerve; deeper, the dorsal scapular nerve.

15. Jianzhongshu (S.I. 15)

Location: 2 *cun* lateral to the lower border of the spinous process of the 7th cervical vertebra (Dazhui, Du 14). (See Fig. 54.)

Indications: Cough, asthma, pain in the shoulder and back.

Method: Puncture obliquely 0.3-0.6 inch. Moxibustion is applicable.

Regional anatomy   See Jianwaishu (S.I. 14).

16. Tianchuang (S.I. 16)

Location: In the lateral aspect of the neck, on the posterior border of m. sternocleidomastoideus, posterosuperior to Neck-Futu (L.I. 18).

Indications: Deafness, tinnitus, sore throat, stiffness and pain of neck.

Method: Puncture perpendicularly 0.5-0.8 inch. Moxibustion is applicable.

Regional anatomy

Vasculature: The ascending cervical artery.

Innervation: The cutaneous cervical nerve, the emerging portion of the great auricular nerve.

17. Tianrong (S.I. 17)

Location: Posterior to the angle of mandible, in the depression on the anterior border of m. sternocleidomastoideus. (See Fig. 55.)

Indications: Deafness, tinnitus, sore throat, foreign body sensation in throat, swelling of cheek.

Method: Puncture perpendicularly 0.5-0.8 inch. Moxibustion is applicable.

Regional anatomy

Vasculature: Anteriorly, the external jugular vein; deeper, the internal carotid artery and internal jugular vein.

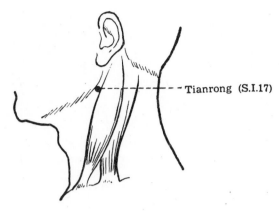

Fig. 55.

Innervation: Superficially, the anterior branch of the great auricular nerve, the cervical branch of the facial nerve; deeper, the superior cervical ganglion of the sympathetic trunk.

18. Quanliao (S.I. 18)

Location: Directly below the outer canthus, in the depression on the lower border of zygoma. (See Fig. 56.)

Indications: Facial paralysis, twitching of eyelids, toothache, yellowish sclera.

Method: Puncture perpendicularly 0.5-0.8 inch.

Regional anatomy

Vasculature: The branches of the transverse facial artery and vein.

Innervation: The facial and infraorbital nerves.

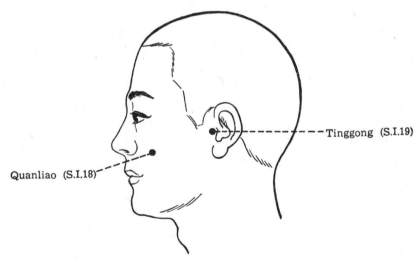

Fig. 56.

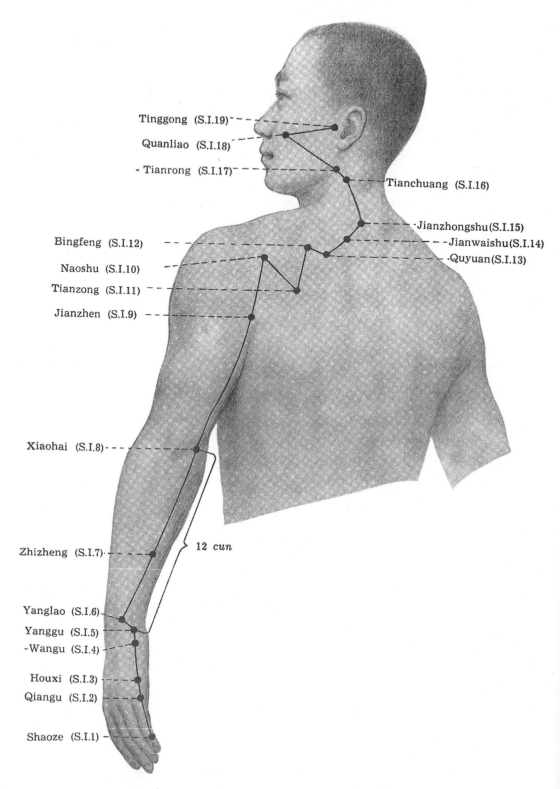

Fig. 57. The Small Intestine Channel of Hand-Taiyang.

19. Tinggong (S.I. 19)

Location: Between the tragus and the mandibular joint, where a depression is formed when the mouth is slightly open. (See Fig. 56.)

Indications: Deafness, tinnitus, otorrhea.

Method: Puncture perpendicularly 0.3-1.0 inch. Moxibustion is applicable.

Regional anatomy

Vasculature: The auricular branches of the superficial temporal artery and vein.

Innervation: The branch of the facial nerve, the auriculotemporal nerve.

VII. THE URINARY BLADDER CHANNEL OF FOOT-TAIYANG

The Urinary Bladder Channel of Foot-Taiyang starts from the inner canthus (Jingming, U.B. 1) (1). Ascending to the forehead (2) it joins the Du Channel at the vertex (Baihui, Du 20) (3), where a branch arises running to the temple (4).

The straight portion of the channel enters and communicates with the brain from the vertex (5). It then emerges and bifurcates into two lines, descending along the posterior aspect of the neck (6). Running downward alongside the medial aspect of the scapula and parallel to the vertebral column (7), it reaches the lumbar region (8), where it enters the body cavity via the paravertebral muscle (9) to connect with the kidney (10) and join its pertaining organ, the urinary bladder (11).

The branch of the lumbar region descends through the gluteal region (12) and ends in the popliteal fossa (13).

The branch from the posterior aspect of the neck runs straight downward along the medial border of the scapula (14). Passing through the gluteal region (Huantiao, G.B. 30) (15) downward along the posterior aspect of the thigh on the lateral side (16), it meets the preceding branch descending from the lumbar region in the popliteal fossa (17). From there it descends to the leg (18) and further to the posterior aspect of the external malleolus (19). Then, running along the tuberosity of the 5th metatarsal bone (20), it reaches the lateral side of the tip of the little toe (Zhiyin, U.B. 67), where it links with the Kidney Channel of Foot-Shaoyin (21). (See Fig. 58.)

There are altogether 67 points in this channel, described as follows:

1. Jingming (U.B. 1)

Location: 0.1 *cun* superior to the inner canthus. Ask the patient to close the eyes when locating the point. (See Fig. 59.)

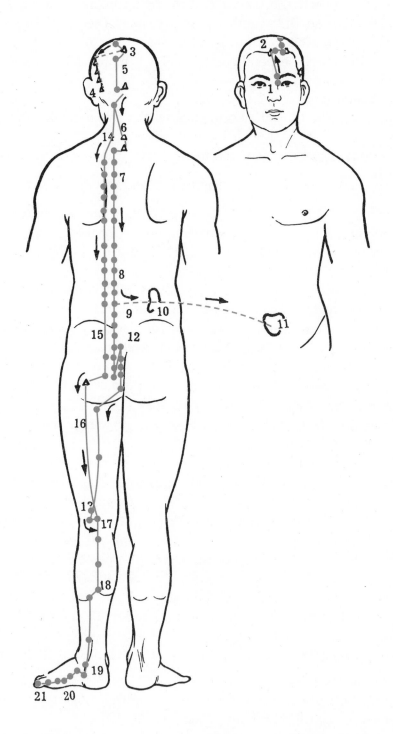

Fig. 58. The Urinary Bladder Cnannel of Foot-Taiyang.

Indications: Redness, swelling and pain of the eye, lacrimation when attacked by wind, itching of the canthus, night blindness, colour blindness.

Method: Puncture perpendicularly 0.3 inch along the orbital wall. It is not advisable to twist or lift and thrust the needle vigorously.

Regional anatomy

Vasculature: The angular artery and vein; deeper, superiorly, the ophthalmic artery and vein.

Innervation: Superficially, the supratrochlear and infratrochlear nerves; deeper, the branches of the oculomotor nerve, the ophthalmic nerve.

2. Zanzhu (U.B. 2)

Location: On the medial extremity of the eyebrow, or on the supraorbital notch. (See Fig. 59.)

Indications: Headache, blurring and failing of vision, pain in the supraorbital region, lacrimation in face of wind, redness, swelling and pain of the eye, twitching of eyelids.

Method: Puncture 0.3-0.5 inch horizontally along the skin with the needle directed inferiorly or laterally, or prick with three-edged needle to cause bleeding.

Regional anatomy

Vasculature: The frontal artery and vein.

Innervation: The medial branch of the frontal nerve.

3. Meichong (U.B. 3)

Location: Directly above the medial extremity of the eyebrow, 0.5 *cun* within the anterior hairline, between Shenting (Du 24) and Quchai (U.B. 4).

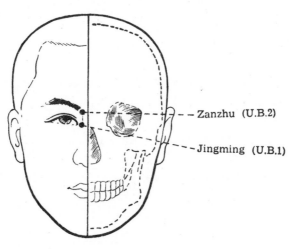

Fig. 59.

Indications: Headache, giddiness, epilepsy.

Method: Puncture 0.3-0.5 inch horizontally along the skin with the needle directed upward.

Regional anatomy   See Zanzhu (U.B. 2).

4. Quchai (U.B. 4)

Location: 1.5 *cun* lateral to Shenting (Du 24), at the junction of the medial third and lateral two-thirds of the distance from Shenting (Du 24) to Touwei (St. 8).

Indications: Frontal vertical headache, blurring of vision, ophthalmalgia, nasal obstruction, epistaxis.

Method: Puncture 0.3-0.5 inch horizontally along the skin with the needle directed upward.

Regional anatomy

Vasculature: The frontal artery and vein.

Innervation: The lateral branch of the frontal nerve.

Note: The distance from the midpoint of the anterior hairline to the midpoint of the posterior hairline is measured as 12 *cun*. If the anterior hairline is indistinguishable, it may be measured from the glabella (Yingtang, Extra.) with 3 *cun* added.

5. Wuchu (U.B. 5)

Location: Directly above Quchai (U.B. 4), 1 *cun* inside the anterior hairline.

Indications: Headache, blurring of vision, epilepsy.

Method: Puncture 0.3-0.5 inch horizontally along the skin.

Regional anatomy   See Quchai (U.B. 4).

6. Chengguang (U.B. 6)

Location: 1.5 *cun* posterior to Wuchu (U.B. 5), 1.5 *cun* lateral to the Du Channel.

Indications: Headache, blurring of vision, nasal obstruction.

Method: Puncture 0.3-0.5 inch horizontally along the skin.

Regional anatomy

Vasculature: The anastomotic network of the frontal artery and vein, the superficial temporal artery and vein and the occipital artery and vein.

Innervation: The anastomotic branch of the lateral branch of the frontal nerve and the great occipital nerve.

7. Tongtian (U.B. 7)

Location: 1.5 *cun* posterior to Chengguang (U.B. 6), 1.5 *cun* lateral to the Du Channel.

Indications: Headache, dizziness, nasal obstruction, epistaxis, rhinorrhea.
Method: Puncture 0.3-0.5 inch horizontally along the skin.
Regional anatomy
Vasculature: The anastomotic network of the superficial temporal artery and vein and the occipital artery and vein.
Innervation: The branch of the great occipital nerve.

8. Luoque (U.B. 8)

Location: 1.5 *cun* posterior to Tongtian (U.B. 7), 1.5 *cun* lateral to the Du Channel.
Indications: Dizziness, tinnitus, mental confusion.
Method: Puncture 0.3-0.5 inch horizontally along the skin.
Regional anatomy
Vasculature: The branches of the occipital artery and vein.
Innervation: The branch of the great occipital nerve.

9. Yuzhen (U.B. 9)

Location: 1.3 *cun* lateral to Naohu (Du 17), on the lateral side of the superior border of the external occipital protuberance.
Indications: Headache, ophthalmalgia, nasal obstruction.
Method: Puncture 0.3-0.5 inch horizontally along the skin with the needle directed downward.
Regional anatomy
Vasculature: The occipital artery and vein.
Innervation: The branch of the great occipital nerve.

10. Tianzhu (U.B. 10)

Location: 1.3 *cun* lateral to Yamen (Du 15), within the posterior hairline, on the lateral side of m. trapezius.
Indications: Headache, neck rigidity, nasal obstruction, pain in the shoulder and back.
Method: Puncture perpendicularly 0.5 inch.
Regional anatomy
Vasculature: The occipital artery and vein.
Innervation: The great occipital nerve.

11. Dashu (U.B. 11)

Location: 1.5 *cun* lateral to the lower border of the spinous process of the 1st thoracic vertebra, about 2 finger-breadths from the Du Channel. (See Fig. 60.)
Indications: Cough, fever, headache, aching of the scapular region, stiffness and rigidity of the neck.

Method: Puncture obliquely 0.5 inch. Moxibustion is applicable.

Regional anatomy

Vasculature: The medial cutaneous branches of the posterior branches of the intercostal artery and vein.

Innervation: The medial cutaneous branches of the posterior rami of the 1st and 2nd thoracic nerves; deeper, their lateral cutaneous branches.

Notes:

(1) This is one of the Eight Influential Points dominating the bone.

(2) The distance from the midpoint of the vertebral column (Du Channel) to the vertical line from the vertebral border of the scapula is measured as 3 *cun*. This serves as a criterion for locating points transversely on the back. All points on the line from Dashu (U.B. 11) to Baihuanshu (U.B. 30) are 1.5 *cun* lateral to the Du Channel.

12. Fengmen (U.B. 12)

Location: 1.5 *cun* lateral to the lower border of the spinous process of the 2nd thoracic vertebra. (See Fig. 60.)

Indications: Common cold, cough, fever and headache, neck rigidity, backache.

Method: Puncture obliquely 0.5 inch. Moxibustion is applicable.

Regional anatomy

Vasculature: The medial cutaneous branches of the posterior branches of the intercostal artery and vein.

Innervation: Superficially, the medial cutaneous branches of the posterior rami of the 2nd and 3rd thoracic nerves; deeper, their lateral cutaneous branches.

13. Feishu (Back-Shu Point of the lung, U.B. 13)

Location: 1.5 *cun* lateral to the lower border of the spinous process of the 3rd thoracic vertebra. (See Fig. 60.)

Indications: Cough, asthma, hemoptysis, afternoon fever, night sweating.

Method: Puncture obliquely 0.5 inch. Moxibustion is applicable.

Regional anatomy

Vasculature: The medial cutaneous branches of the posterior branches of the intercostal artery and vein.

Innervation: The medial cutaneous branches of the posterior rami of the 3rd and 4th thoracic nerves; deeper, their lateral branches.

14. Jueyinshu (Back-Shu Point of the Pericardium, U.B. 14)

Location: 1.5 *cun* lateral to the lower border of the spinous process of the 4th thoracic vertebra.

Regional anatomy

Vasculature: The medial cutaneous branches of the posterior branches of the intercostal artery and vein.

Innervation: The medial cutaneous branches of the posterior rami of the 4th and 5th thoracic nerves; deeper, their lateral branches.

15. Xinshu (Back-Shu Point of the Heart, U.B. 15)

Location: 1.5 *cun* lateral to the lower border of the spinous process of the 5th thoracic vertebra. (See Fig. 60.)

Indications: Epilepsy, panic, palpitation, forgetfulness, irritability, cough, hemoptysis.

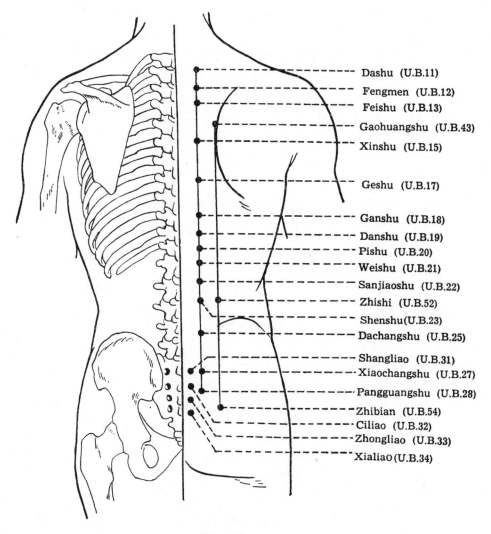

Dashu (U.B.11)
Fengmen (U.B.12)
Feishu (U.B.13)
Gaohuangshu (U.B.43)
Xinshu (U.B.15)

Geshu (U.B.17)

Ganshu (U.B.18)
Danshu (U.B.19)
Pishu (U.B.20)
Weishu (U.B.21)
Sanjiaoshu (U.B.22)
Zhishi (U.B.52)
Shenshu(U.B.23)
Dachangshu (U.B.25)

Shangliao (U.B.31)
Xiaochangshu (U.B.27)
Pangguangshu (U.B.28)
Zhibian (U.B.54)
Ciliao (U.B.32)
Zhongliao (U.B.33)
Xialiao(U.B.34)

Fig. 60.

Method: Puncture obliquely 0.5 inch. Moxibustion is applicable.

Regional anatomy

Vasculature: The medial cutaneous branches of the posterior branches of the intercostal artery and vein.

Innervation: The medial cutaneous branches of the posterior rami of the 5th and 6th thoracic nerves; deeper, their lateral branches.

16. Dushu (U.B. 16)

Location: 1.5 *cun* lateral to the lower border of the spinous process of the 6th thoracic vertebra.

Indications: Cardiac pain, abdominal pain.

Method: Puncture obliquely 0.5 inch. Moxibustion is applicable.

Regional anatomy

Vasculature: The medial branches of the posterior branches of the intercostal artery and vein, the descending branch of the transverse cervical artery.

Innervation: The dorsal scapular nerve, the medial cutaneous branches of the posterior rami of the 6th and 7th thoracic nerves; deeper, their lateral branches.

17. Geshu (U.B. 17)

Location: 1.5 *cun* lateral to the lower border of the spinous process of the 7th thoracic vertebra. (See Fig. 60.)

Indications: Vomiting, hiccup, difficulty in swallowing, asthma, cough, hemoptysis, afternoon fever, night sweating.

Method: Puncture obliquely 0.5 inch. Moxibustion is applicable.

Regional anatomy

Vasculature: The medial branches of the posterior branches of the intercostal artery and vein.

Innervation: The medial branches of the posterior rami of the 7th and 8th thoracic nerves; deeper, their lateral branches.

Note: This is one of the Eight Influential Points dominating blood.

18. Ganshu (Back-Shu Point of the Liver, U.B. 18)

Location: 1.5 *cun* lateral to the lower border of the spinous process of the 9th thoracic vertebra. (See Fig. 60.)

Indications: Jaundice, pain in the hypochondriac region, hematemesis, epistaxis, redness of the eye, blurring of vision, night blindness, pain in the back, mental confusion, epilepsy.

Method: Puncture obliquely 0.5 inch. Moxibustion is applicable.

Regional anatomy

Vasculature: The medial branches of the posterior branches of the intercostal artery and vein.

Innervation: The medial cutaneous branches of the posterior rami of the 9th and 10th thoracic nerves; deeper, their lateral branches.

19. Danshu (Back-Shu Point of the Gall Bladder, U.B. 19)

Location: 1.5 *cun* lateral to the lower border of the spinous process of the 10th thoracic vertebra. (See Fig. 60.)

Indications: Jaundice, bitter taste in mouth, pain in the chest and hypochondriac region, pulmonary tuberculosis, afternoon fever.

Method: Puncture obliquely 0.5 inch. Moxibustion is applicable.

Regional anatomy

Vasculature: The medial branches of the posterior branches of the intercostal artery and vein.

Innervation: The medial cutaneous branches of the posterior rami of the 10th and 11th thoracic nerves; deeper, their lateral branches.

20. Pishu (Back-Shu Point of the Spleen, U.B. 20)

Location: 1.5 *cun* lateral to the lower border of the spinous process of the 11th thoracic vertebra. (See Fig. 60.)

Indications: Abdominal distension, jaundice, vomiting, diarrhea, dysentery, indigestion, edema, pain in the back.

Method: Puncture obliquely 0.5 inch. Moxibustion is applicable.

Regional anatomy

Vasculature: The medial branches of the posterior branches of the intercostal artery and vein.

Innervation: The medial cutaneous branches of the posterior rami of the 11th and 12th thoracic nerves; deeper, their lateral branches.

21. Weishu (Back-Shu Point of the Stomach, U.B. 21)

Location: 1.5 *cun* lateral to the lower border of the spinous process of the 12th thoracic vertebra. (See Fig. 60.)

Indications: Pain in the chest, hypochondriac and epigastric region, abdominal distension, nausea, vomiting, borborygmus, indigestion.

Method: Puncture obliquely 0.5 inch. Moxibustion is applicable.

Regional anatomy

Vasculature: The medial branches of the posterior branches of the subcostal artery and vein.

Innervation: The medial cutaneous branch of the posterior ramus of the 12th thoracic nerve; deeper, its lateral branch.

22. Sanjiaoshu (Back-Shu Point of *Sanjiao,* U.B. 22)

Location: 1.5 *cun* lateral to the lower border of the spinous process of the 1st lumbar vertebra. (See Fig. 60.)

Indications: Abdominal distension, borborygmus, indigestion, vomiting, diarrhea, dysentery, edema, pain and stiffness of the lower back.

Method: Puncture perpendicularly 1.0–1.5 inches. Moxibustion is applicable.

Regional anatomy

Vasculature: The posterior rami of the 1st lumbar artery and vein.

Innervation: The lateral cutaneous branch of the posterior ramus of the 10th thoracic nerve; deeper, the lateral branch of the posterior ramus of the 1st lumbar nerve.

23. Shenshu (Back-Shu Point of the Kidney, U.B. 23)

Location: 1.5 *cun* lateral to the lower border of the spinous process of the 2nd lumbar vertebra. (See Fig. 60.)

Indications: Seminal emission, impotence, enuresis, irregular menstruation, leukorrhea, backache, weakness of the knee, blurring of vision, tinnitus, deafness, edema.

Method: Puncture perpendicularly 0.1–1.5 inches. Moxibustion is applicable.

Regional anatomy

Vasculature: The posterior rami of the 2nd lumbar artery and vein.

Innervation: The lateral cutaneous branch of the posterior ramus of the 1st lumbar nerve; deeper, its lateral branch.

24. Qihaishu (U.B. 24)

Location: 1.5 *cun* lateral to the lower border of the spinous process of the 3rd lumbar vertebra.

Indication: Low back pain.

Method: Puncture perpendicularly 1.0–1.5 inches. Moxibustion is applicable.

Regional anatomy

Vasculature: The posterior rami of the 3rd lumbar artery and vein.

Innervation: The lateral cutaneous branch of the posterior ramus of the 2nd lumbar nerve.

25. Dachangshu (Back-Shu Point of the Large intestine, U.B. 25)

Location: 1.5 *cun* lateral to the lower border of the spinous process of the 4th lumbar vertebra, approximately at the level of the upper border of the iliac crest. (See Fig. 60.)

Indications: Abdominal pain and distension, borborygmus, diarrhea, constipation, low back pain.

Method: Puncture perpendicularly 1.0-1.5 inches. Moxibustion is applicable.

Regional anatomy

Vasculature: The posterior rami of the 4th lumbar artery and vein.

Innervation: The posterior ramus of the 3rd lumbar nerve.

26. Guanyuanshu (U.B. 26)

Location: 1.5 *cun* lateral to the lower border of the spinous process of the 5th lumbar vertebra.

Indications: Abdominal distension, diarrhea, low back pain.

Method: Puncture perpendicularly 0.7-1.0 inch. Moxibustion is applicable.

Regional anatomy

Vasculature: The posterior branches of the lowest lumbar artery and vein.

Innervation: The posterior ramus of the 5th lumbar nerve.

27. Xiaochangshu (Back-Shu Point of the Small intestine, U.B. 27)

Location: At the level of the 1st posterior sacral foramen, 1.5 *cun* lateral to the Du Channel. (See Fig. 60.)

Indications: Seminal emission, hematuria, enuresis, lower abdominal pain and distension, dysentery.

Method: Puncture perpendicularly 0.5-1.0 inch. Moxibustion is applicable.

Regional anatomy

Vasculature: The posterior branches of the lateral sacral artery and vein.

Innervation: The lateral branch of the posterior ramus of the 1st sacral nerve.

28. Pangguangshu (Back-Shu Point of the Urinary Bladder, U.B. 28)

Location: At the level of the 2nd posterior sacral foramen, 1.5 *cun* lateral to the Du Channel, in the depression between the medial border of the posterior superior iliac spine and the sacrum. (See Fig. 60.)

Indications: Retention of urine, enuresis, diarrhea, constipation, pain and stiffness of lower back.

Method: Puncture perpendicularly 0.5-1.0 inch. Moxibustion is applicable.

Regional anatomy

Vasculature: The posterior branches of the lateral sacral artery and vein.

Innervation: The lateral branches of the posterior rami of the 1st and 2nd sacral nerves.

29. Zhonglüshu (U.B. 29)

Location: At the level of the 3rd posterior sacral foramen, 1.5 *cun* lateral to the Du Channel.

Indications: Dysentery, hernia, pain and stiffness of lower back.

Method: Puncture perpendicularly 0.7-1.0 inch. Moxibustion is applicable.

Regional anatomy

Vasculature: The posterior branches of the lateral sacral artery and vein, the branches of the inferior gluteal artery and vein.

Innervation: The lateral branches of the posterior rami of the 3rd and 4th sacral nerves.

30. Baihuanshu (U.B. 30)

Location: At the level of the 4th posterior sacral foramen, 1.5 *cun* lateral to the Du Channel.

Indications: Seminal emission, irregular menstruation, leukorrhea, hernia, pain in the lower back and hip joint.

Method: Puncture perpendicularly 0.7-1.0 inch.

Regional anatomy

Vasculature: The inferior gluteal artery and vein; deeper, the internal pudendal artery and vein.

Innervation: The lateral branches of the posterior rami of the 3rd and 4th sacral nerves, the inferior gluteal nerve.

31. Shangliao (U.B. 31)

Location: In the 1st posterior sacral foramen, about midway between the posterior superior iliac spine and the Du Channel. (See Fig. 60.)

Indications: Low back pain, irregular menstruation, prolapse of uterus, leukorrhea, scanty urine, constipation.

Method: Puncture perpendicularly 0.7-1.0 inch. Moxibustion is applicable.

Regional anatomy

Vasculature: The posterior branches of the lateral sacral artery and vein.

Innervation: At the site where the posterior ramus of the 1st sacral nerve passes.

Note: The eight sacral foramina are acupuncture points, known as Baliao (eight *liao*), namely, Shangliao (both sides, U.B. 31), Ciliao (both sides, U.B. 32), Zhongliao (both sides, U.B. 33) and Xialiao (both sides, U.B. 34).

32. Ciliao (U.B. 32)

Location: In the 2nd posterior sacral foramen, about midway between the lower border of the posterior superior iliac spine and the Du Channel. (See Fig. 60.)

Indications: Low back pain, irregular menstruation, leukorrhea, hernia, muscular atrophy, motor impairment and *bi* syndrome (rheumatic pain) of the lower extremities.

Method: Puncture perpendicularly 0.7-1.0 inch. Moxibustion is applicable.

Regional anatomy

Vasculature: The posterior branches of the lateral sacral artery and vein.

Innervation: On the course of the posterior ramus of the 2nd sacral nerve.

33. Zhongliao (U.B. 33)

Location: In the 3rd posterior sacral foramen, between Zhonglüshu (U.B. 29) and the Du Channel. (See Fig. 60.)

Indications: Irregular menstruation, leukorrhea, low back pain, dysuria, constipation.

Method: Puncture perpendicularly 0.7-1.0 inch. Moxibustion is applicable.

Regional anatomy

Vasculature: The posterior branches of the lateral sacral artery and vein.

Innervation: On the course of the posterior ramus of the 3rd sacral nerve.

34. Xialiao (U.B. 34)

Location: In the 4th posterior sacral foramen, between Baihuanshu (U.B. 30) and the Du Channel. (See Fig. 60.)

Indications: Lower abdominal pain, constipation, dysuria, low back pain.

Method: Puncture perpendicularly 0.5-1.0 inch. Moxibustion is applicable.

Regional anatomy

Vasculature: The branches of the inferior gluteal artery and vein.

Innervation: On the course of the posterior ramus of the 4th sacral nerve.

35. Huiyang (U.B. 35)

Location: On either side of the tip of the coccyx, 0.5 *cun* lateral to the Du Channel.

Indications: Leukorrhea, impotence, dysentery, hemafecia, hemorrhoids, diarrhea.

Method: Puncture perpendicularly 0.5-1.0 inch. Moxibustion is applicable.

Regional anatomy

Vasculature: The branches of the inferior gluteal artery and vein.

Innervation: The coccygeal nerve.

36. Chengfu (U.B. 36)

Location: In the middle of the transverse gluteal fold. Locate the point in prone position.

Indications: Hemorrhoids, pain in the lumbar, sacral, gluteal and femoral regions.

Method: Puncture perpendicularly 0.7-1.5 inches. Moxibustion is applicable.

Regional anatomy

Vasculature: The artery and vein running alongside the sciatic nerve.

Innervation: Superficially, the posterior femoral cutaneous nerve; deeper, the sciatic nerve.

37. Yinmen (U.B. 37)

Location: 6 *cun* below Chengfu (U.B. 36), on the line joining Chengfu (U.B. 36) and Weizhong (U.B. 40).

Indications: Pain in the lower back and thigh.

Method: Puncture perpendicularly 0.7-1.5 inches. Moxibustion is applicable.

Regional anatomy

Vasculature: Laterally, the 3rd perforating branches of the deep femoral artery and vein.

Innervation: The posterior femoral cutaneous nerve; deeper, the sciatic nerve.

38. Fuxi (U.B. 38)

Location: 1 *cun* above Weiyang (U.B. 39), on the medial side of the tendon of m. biceps femoris. The point is located with the knee slightly flexed.

Indications: Numbness of the gluteal and femoral region, contracture of the tendons in the popliteal fossa.

Method: Puncture perpendicularly 0.5-1.0 inch. Moxibustion is applicable.

Regional anatomy

Vasculature: The superolateral genicular artery and vein.

Innervation: The posterior femoral cutaneous nerve and the common peroneal nerve.

39. Weiyang (U.B. 39)

Location: Lateral to Weizhong (U.B. 40), on the medial border of the tendon of m. biceps femoris. (See Fig. 61.)

Indications: Pain and stiffness of the lower back, lower abdominal distension, dysuria, cramp of the leg and foot.

Method: Puncture perpendicularly 0.5-1.0 inch. Moxibustion is applicable.

Regional anatomy   See Fuxi (U.B. 38).

Note: This is the Inferior He-Sea Point of *sanjiao* and is indicated in disorders of *sanjiao*.

40. Weizhong (He-Sea Point, U.B. 40)

Location: Midpoint of the transverse crease of the popliteal fossa, between the tendons of m. biceps femoris and m. semitendinosus. Locate the point in prone position or with flexed knee. (See Fig. 61.)

Indications: Low back pain, motor impairment of the hip joint, contracture of the tendons in the popliteal fossa, muscular atrophy, motor impairment and pain of the lower extremities, hemiplegia, abdominal pain, vomiting and diarrhea.

Method: Puncture perpendicularly 0.5-1.5 inches, or prick with three-edged needle to cause bleeding.

Regional anatomy

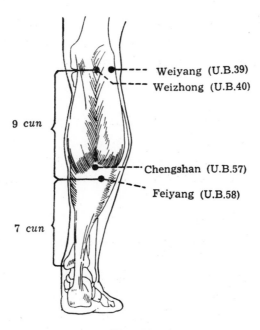

Fig. 61.

Vasculature: Superficially, the femoropopliteal vein; deeper and medially, the popliteal vein; deepest, the popliteal artery.

Innervation: The posterior femoral cutaneous nerve, the tibial nerve.

41. Fufen (U.B. 41)

Location: 3 *cun* lateral to the lower border of the spinous process of the 2nd thoracic vertebra, about 4 finger-breadths lateral to the midline of the vertebral column.

Indications: Stiffness and pain of the shoulder, back, and neck, numbness of the elbow and arm.

Method: Puncture obliquely downward 0.3-0.5 inch. Moxibustion is applicable.

Regional anatomy

Vasculature: The descending branch of the transverse cervical artery, the lateral branches of the posterior branches of the intercostal artery and vein.

Innervation: The lateral cutaneous branches of the posterior rami of the 1st and 2nd thoracic nerves; deeper, the dorsal scapular nerve.

Note: All the points located on the line from Fufen (U.B. 41) to Zhibian (U.B. 54) are 3 *cun* lateral to the Du Channel.

42. Pohu (U.B. 42)

Location: 3 *cun* lateral to the lower border of the spinous process of the 3rd thoracic vertebra.

Indications: Pulmonary tuberculosis, cough, asthma, neck rigidity, pain in the shoulder and back.

Method: Puncture obliquely downward 0.3-0.5 inch. Moxibustion is applicable.

Regional anatomy

Vasculature: The posterior branch of the intercostal artery, the descending branch of the transverse cervical artery.

Innervation: The medial cutaneous branches of the posterior rami of the 2nd and 3rd thoracic nerve; deeper, their lateral branches and the dorsal scapular nerve.

43. Gaohuangshu (U.B. 43)

Location: 3 *cun* lateral to the lower border of the spinous process of the 4th thoracic vertebra. (See Fig. 60.)

Indications: Pulmonary tuberculosis, cough, asthma, hemoptysis, night sweating, poor memory, seminal emission, indigestion.

Method: Puncture obliquely 0.3-0.5 towards the scapula. Frequent or prolonged moxibustion is desirable.

Regional anatomy

Vasculature: The posterior branch of the intercostal artery and the descending branch of the transverse cervical artery.

Innervation: The medial cutaneous branches of the posterior rami of the 2nd and 3rd thoracic nerves; deeper, their lateral branches and the dorsoscapular nerve.

44.   Shentang (U.B. 44)

Location: 3 *cun* lateral to the lower border of the spinous process of the 5th thoracic vertebra.

Indications: Asthma, cough, pain and stiffness of the back.

Method: Puncture obliquely 0.5 inch. Moxibustion is applicable.

Regional anatomy

Vasculature: The posterior branches of the intercostal artery and vein, the descending branch of the transverse cervical artery.

Innervation: The medial cutaneous branches of the posterior rami of the 4th and 5th thoracic nerves; deeper, their lateral branches and the dorsal scapular nerve.

45.   Yixi (U.B. 45)

Location: 3 *cun* lateral to the lower border of the spinous process of the 6th thoracic vertebra.

Indications: Cough, asthma, pain in the shoulder and back.

Method: Puncture obliquely downward 0.5 inch. Moxibustion is applicable.

Regional anatomy

Vasculature: The posterior branches of the intercostal artery and vein.

Innervation: The medial cutaneous branches of the posterior rami of the 5th and 6th thoracic nerves; deeper, their lateral branches.

46.   Geguan (U.B. 46)

Location: 3 *cun* lateral to the lower border of the spinous process of the 7th thoracic vertebra, approximately at the level of the inferior angle of the scapula.

Indications: Difficulty in swallowing, vomiting, belching, pain and stiffness of the back.

Method: Puncture obliquely downward 0.5 inch. Moxibustion is applicable.

Regional anatomy

Vasculature: The posterior branches of the intercostal artery and vein.

Innervation: The medial cutaneous branches of the posterior rami of the 6th and 7th thoracic nerves; deeper, their lateral branches.

47. Hunmen (U.B. 47)

Location: 3 *cun* lateral to the lower border of the spinous process of the 9th thoracic vertebra.

Indications: Pain in the chest, back and hypochondriac region, vomiting, diarrhea.

Method: Puncture obliquely downward 0.5 inch. Moxibustion is applicable.

Regional anatomy

Vasculature: The posterior branches of the intercostal artery and vein.

Innervation: The lateral branches of the posterior rami of the 7th and 8th thoracic nerves.

48. Yanggang (U.B. 48)

Location: 3 *cun* lateral to the lower border of the spinous process of the 10th thoracic vertebra.

Indications: Borborygmus, abdominal pain, diarrhea, jaundice.

Method: Puncture obliquely downward 0.5 inch. Moxibustion is applicable.

Regional anatomy

Vasculature: The posterior branches of the intercostal artery and vein.

Innervation: The lateral branches of the posterior rami of the 8th and 9th thoracic nerves.

49. Yishe (U.B. 49)

Location: 3 *cun* lateral to the lower border of the spinous process of the 11th thoracic vertebra.

Indications: Abdominal distension, borborygmus, diarrhea, vomiting, difficulty in swallowing.

Method: Puncture obliquely downward 0.5 inch. Moxibustion is applicable.

Regional anatomy

Vasculature: The posterior branches of the intercostal artery and vein.

Innervation: The lateral branches of the posterior rami of the 10th and 11th thoracic nerves.

50. Weicang (U.B. 50)

Location: 3 *cun* lateral to the lower border of the process of the 12th thoracic vertebra.

Indications: Abdominal distension, pain in the epigastric region and the back.

Method: Puncture obliquely downward 0.5 inch. Moxibustion is applicable.

Regional anatomy

Vasculature: The posterior branches of the subcostal artery and vein.

Innervation: The lateral branch of the posterior ramus of the 11th thoracic nerve.

51. Huangmen (U.B. 51)

Location: 3 *cun* lateral to the lower border of the spinous process of the 1st lumbar vertebra.

Indications: Pain in the epigastric region, abdominal mass, constipation.

Method: Puncture perpendicularly 0.5-1.0 inch. Moxibustion is applicable.

Regional anatomy

Vasculature: The posterior branches of the 1st lumbar artery and vein.

Innervation: The lateral branch of the posterior ramus of the 12th thoracic nerve.

52. Zhishi (U.B. 52)

Location: 3 *cun* lateral to the lower border of the spinous process of the 2nd lumbar vertebra. (See Fig. 60.)

Indications: Seminal emission, impotence, dysuria, edema, pain and stiffness of the lower back.

Method: Puncture perpendicularly 0.7-1.0 inch. Moxibustion is applicable.

Regional anatomy

Vasculature: The posterior branches of the 2nd lumbar artery and vein.

Innervation: The lateral branch of the posterior ramus of the 12th thoracic nerve and the lateral branch of the 1st lumbar nerve.

53. Baohuang (U.B. 53)

Location: 3 *cun* lateral to the lower border of the spinous process of the 2nd sacral vertebra, level with Ciliao (U.B. 32).

Indications: Borborygmus, abdominal distension, pain in the lower back.

Method: Puncture perpendicularly 0.7-1.3 inches. Moxibustion is applicable.

Regional anatomy

Vasculature: The superior gluteal artery and vein.

Innervation: The superior cluneal nerves; deeper, the superior gluteal nerve.

54. Zhibian (U.B. 54)

Location: Directly below Baohuang (U.B. 53), 3 *cun* lateral to Du Channel, about 4 finger-breadths lateral to the hiatus of the sacrum. (See Fig. 60.)

Indications: Pain in the lumbosacral region, hemorrhoids, muscular atrophy, motor impairment and motor impairment and pain of the lower extremities.

Method: Puncture perpendicularly 1.0-1.5 inches. Moxibustion is applicable.

Regional anatomy

Vasculature: The inferior gluteal artery and vein.

Innervation: The inferior gluteal nerve, the posterior femoral cutaneous nerve and the sciatic nerve.

55. Heyang (U.B. 55)

Location: 2 *cun* directly below Weizhong (U.B. 40), between the medial and lateral heads of m. gastrocnemius, on the line joining Weizhong (U.B. 40) and Chengshan (U.B. 57).

Indications: Backache, aching, numbness and paralysis of the lower extremities.

Method: Puncture perpendicularly 0.7-1.0 inch. Moxibustion is applicable.

Regional anatomy

Vasculature: The small saphenous vein; deeper, the popliteal artery and vein.

Innervation: The medial sural cutaneous nerve; deeper, the tibial nerve.

Note: The distance from Weizhong (U.B. 40) to the level of the tip of the external malleolus is measured as 16 *cun*.

56. Chengjin (U.B. 56)

Location: Midway between Heyang (U.B. 55) and Chengshan (U.B. 57), in the centre of the belly of m. gastrocnemius.

Indications: Pain in the leg, hemorrhoids, acute lower back pain.

Method: Puncture perpendicularly 0.5-1.5 inches. Moxibustion is applicable.

Regional anatomy

Vasculature: The small saphenous vein; deeper, the posterior tibial artery and vein.

Innervation: The medial sural cutaneous nerve; deeper, the tibial nerve.

57. Chengshan (U.B. 57)

Location: Directly below the belly of m. gastrocnemius, on the line connecting Weizhong (U.B. 40) and tendo calcaneus, about 8 *cun* below Weizhong (U.B. 40). (See Fig. 61.)

Indications: Low back pain, spasm of the gastrocnemius, hemorrhoids, constipation.

Method: Puncture perpendicularly 0.5-1.0 inch. Moxibustion is applicable.

Regional anatomy   See Chengjin (U.B. 56).

58.   Feiyang (Luo-Connecting Point, U.B. 58)

Location: 7 *cun* directly above Kunlun (U.B. 60), on the posterior border of fibula, about 1 *cun* inferior and lateral to Chengshan (U.B. 57). (See Fig. 61.)

Indications: Headache, blurring of vision, nasal obstruction, epistaxis, lumbago, weakness of the leg.

Method: Puncture perpendicularly 0.7-1.0 inch. Moxibustion is applicable.

Regional anatomy

Innervation: The lateral sural cutaneous nerve.

59.   Fuyang (U.B. 59)

Location: 3 *cun* directly above Kunlun (U.B. 60). (See Fig. 62.)

Indications: Heavy feeling in the head, headache, low back pain, redness and swelling of the external malleolus, paralysis of the lower extremities.

Method: Puncture perpendicularly 0.5-1.0 inch. Moxibustion is applicable.

Regional anatomy

Vasculature: The small saphenous vein; deeper, the terminal branch of the peroneal artery.

Innervation: The sural nerve.

·Note: Fuyang (U.B. 59) is the Xi-Cleft Point of the Yangqiao Channel.

60.   Kunlun (Jing-River Point, U.B. 60)

Location: In the depression between the external malleolus and tendo calcaneus. (See Fig. 62.)

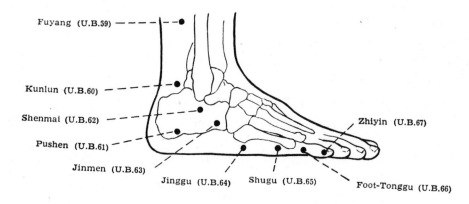

Fig. 62.

Indications: Headache, neck rigidity, blurring of vision, epistaxis, spasm and pain of the shoulder and arm, backache, pain in the heel, epilepsy in children, difficult labour.

Method: Puncture perpendicularly 0.5 inch. Moxibustion is applicable.

Regional anatomy

Vasculature: The small saphenous vein, the posteroexternal malleolar artery and vein.

Innervation: The sural nerve.

Note: Acupuncture is contraindicated during pregnancy.

61. Pushen (U.B. 61)

Location: Posterior and inferior to the external malleolus, directly below Kunlun (U.B. 60), in the depression of the calcaneum at the junction of the red and white skin. (See Fig. 62.)

Indications: Muscular atrophy and weakness of the lower extremities, pain in the heel.

Method: Puncture perpendicularly 0.3-0.5 inch. Moxibustion is applicable.

Regional anatomy

Vasculature: The external calcaneal branches of the peroneal artery and vein.

Innervation: The external calcaneal branch of the sural nerve.

62. Shenmai (U.B. 62)

Location: In the depression directly below the external malleolus. (See Fig. 62.)

Indications: Epilepsy, mental confusion, headache, dizziness, insomnia, backache, aching of the lower extremities.

Method: Puncture perpendicularly 0.3 inch. Moxibustion is applicable.

Regional anatomy

Vasculature: The external malleolar arterial network.

Innervation: The sural nerve.

Note: This is one of the Eight Confluent Points communicating with the Yangqiao Channel.

63. Jinmen (Xi-Cleft Point, U.B. 63)

Location: Anterior and inferior to Shenmai (U.B. 62), in the depression lateral to the cuboid bone. (See Fig. 62.)

Indications: Epilepsy, infantile convulsion, backache, pain in the external malleolus, motor impairment and pain of the lower extremities.

Method: Puncture perpendicularly 0.5 inch. Moxibustion is applicable.

Regional anatomy

Vasculature: The lateral plantar artery and vein.

Innervation: The lateral dorsal cutaneous nerve of foot; deeper, the lateral plantar nerve.

64.   Jinggu (Yuan-Source Point, U.B. 64)

Location: On the lateral side of the dorsum of foot, below the tuberosity of the 5th metatarsal bone, at the junction of the red and white skin. (See Fig. 62.)

Indications: Epilepsy, headache, neck rigidity, pain in the lower back and legs.

Method: Puncture perpendicularly 0.3-0.5 inch. Moxibustion is applicable.

Regional anatomy   See Jinmen (U.B. 63).

65.   Shugu (Shu-Stream Point, U.B. 65)

Location: On the lateral side of the dorsum of foot, posterior and inferior to the head of the 5th metatarsal bone, at the junction of the red and white skin. (See Fig. 62.)

Indications: Mental confusion, headache, neck rigidity, blurring of vision, backache, pain in the posterior aspect of the lower extremities.

Method: Puncture perpendicularly 0.3 inch. Moxibustion is applicable.

Regional anatomy

Vasculature: The 4th common plantar digital artery and vein.

Innervation: The 4th common plantar digital nerve and the lateral dorsal cutaneous nerve of foot.

66.   Foot-Tonggu (Ying-Spring Point, U.B. 66)

Location: In the depression anterior and inferior to the 5th metatarsophalangeal joint. (See Fig. 62.)

Indications: Headache, neck rigidity, blurring of vision, epistaxis.

Method: Puncture perpendicularly 0.2 inch. Moxibustion is applicable.

Regional anatomy

Vasculature: The plantar digital artery and vein.

Innervation: The plantar digital proprial nerve and the lateral dorsal cutaneous nerve of foot.

67.   Zhiyin (Jing-Well Point, U.B. 67)

Location: On the lateral side of the small toe, about 0.1 *cun* posterior to the corner of the nail. (See Fig. 62.)

Indications: Headache, nasal obstruction, epistaxis, ophthalmalgia, feverish sensation in sole, difficult labour.

Method: Puncture obliquely 0.1 inch. Moxibustion is applicable.

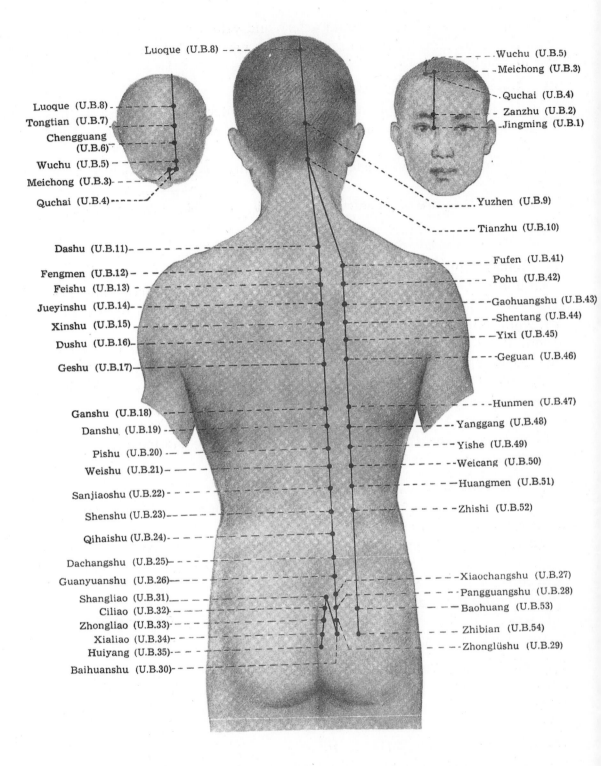

Fig. 63a. The Urinary Bladder Channel of Foot-Taiyang.

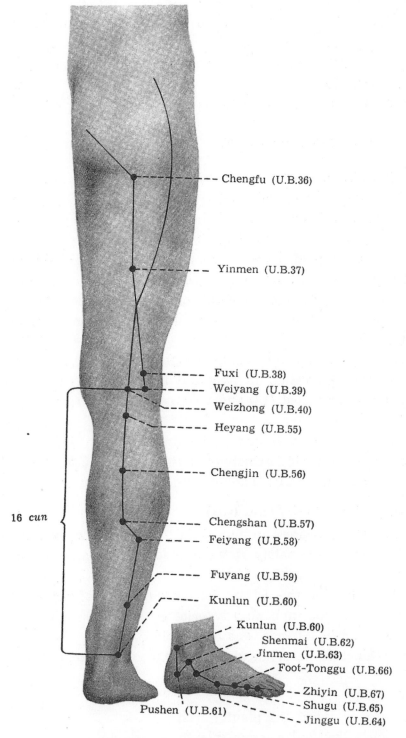

16 cun

Chengfu (U.B.36)

Yinmen (U.B.37)

Fuxi (U.B.38)
Weiyang (U.B.39)
Weizhong (U.B.40)
Heyang (U.B.55)

Chengjin (U.B.56)

Chengshan (U.B.57)
Feiyang (U.B.58)

Fuyang (U.B.59)
Kunlun (U.B.60)

Kunlun (U.B.60)
Shenmai (U.B.62)
Jinmen (U.B.63)
Foot-Tonggu (U.B.66)
Zhiyin (U.B.67)
Shugu (U.B.65)
Jinggu (U.B.64)
Pushen (U.B.61)

Fig. 63b. The Urinary Bladder Channel of Foot-Taiyang.

Regional anatomy

Vasculature: The network formed by the dorsal digital artery and plantar digital proprial artery.

Innervation: The plantar digital proprial nerve and the lateral dorsal cutaneous nerve of foot.

Note: Acupuncture on this point is contraindicated during pregnancy.

VIII. THE KIDNEY CHANNEL OF FOOT-SHAOYIN

The Kidney Channel of Foot-Shaoyin starts from the inferior aspect of the small toe (1) and runs obliquely towards the sole (Yongquan, K. 1). Emerging from the lower aspect of the tuberosity of the navicular bone (2) and running behind the medial malleolus (3), it enters the heel (4). Then it ascends along the medial side of the leg (5) to the medial side of the popliteal fossa (6) and goes further upward along the postero-medial aspect of the thigh (7) towards the vertebral column (Changqiang, Du 1), where it enters the kidney, its pertaining organ (8), and connects with the urinary bladder (9).

The straight portion of the channel re-emerges from the kidney (10). Ascending and passing through the liver and diaphragm (11), it enters the lung (12), runs along the throat (13) and terminates at the root of the tongue (14).

A branch springs from the lung, joins the heart and flows into the chest to link with the Pericardium Channel of Hand-Jueyin (15). (See Fig. 64.)

There are 27 points in this channel, described as follows:

1. Yongquan (Jing-Well Point, K. 1)

Location: In the depression appearing on the sole when the foot is in plantar flexion, approximately at the junction of the anterior and middle third of the sole. (See Fig. 65.)

Indications: Pain in the vertex, dizziness, blurring of vision, sore throat, dryness of the tongue, aphonia, dysuria, dyschesia, infantile convulsion, feverish sensation in the sole, loss of consciousness.

Method: Puncture perpendicularly 0.3-0.5 inch. Moxibustion is applicable.

Regional anatomy

Vasculature: Deeper, the plantar arch.

Innervation: The 2nd common plantar digital nerve.

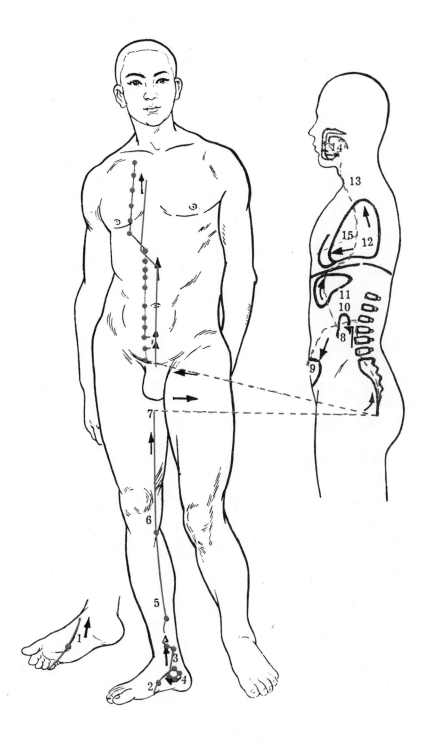

Fig. 64.   The Kidney Channel of Foot-Shaoyin.

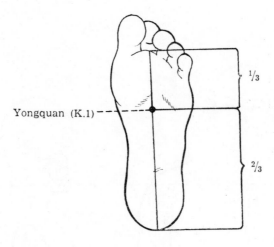

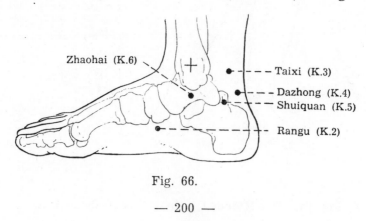

Fig. 65.

2. Rangu (Ying-Spring Point, K. 2)

Location: Anterior and inferior to the medial malleolus, in the depression on the lower border of the tuberosity of the navicular bone. (See Fig. 66.)

Indications: Pruritus vulvae, prolapse of uterus, irregular menstruation, seminal emission, hemoptysis, diarrhea, swelling and pain of the dorsum of foot.

Method: Puncture perpendicularly 0.3 inch. Moxibustion is applicable.
Regional anatomy

Vasculature: The branches of the medial plantar and medial tarsal arteries.

Innervation: The terminal branch of the medial crural cutaneous nerve, the medial plantar nerve.

3. Taixi (Shu-Stream and Yuan-Source Point, K. 3)

Location: In the depression between the medial malleolus and tendo calcaneus, level with the tip of the medial malleolus. (See Fig. 66.)

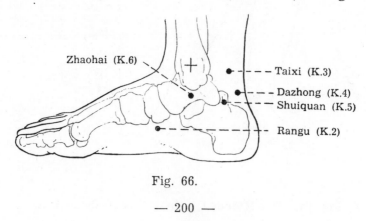

Fig. 66.

Indications: Sore throat, toothache, deafness, hemoptysis, asthma, irregular menstruation, insomnia, seminal emission, impotence, frequency of micturition, pain in the lower back.

Method: Puncture perpendicularly 0.3 inch. Moxibustion is applicable.

Regional anatomy

Vasculature: Anteriorly, the posterior tibial artery and vein.

Innervation: The medial crural cutaneous nerve, on the course of the tibial nerve.

4. Dazhong (Luo-Connecting Point, K. 4)

Location: Posterior and inferior to the medial malleolus, in the depression medial to the attachment of tendo calcaneus. (See Fig. 66.)

Indications: Hemoptysis, asthma, pain and stiffness of the lumbosacral region, dysuria, pain in the heel.

Method: Puncture perpendicularly 0.3 inch. Moxibustion is applicable.

Regional anatomy

Vasculature: The medial calcaneal branch of the posterior tibial artery.

Innervation: The medial crural cutaneous nerve, on the course of the medial calcaneal ramus derived from the tibial nerve.

5. Shuiquan (Xi-Cleft Point, K. 5)

Location: 1 *cun* directly below Taixi (K. 3), in the depression anterior and superior to the medial side of the tuberosity of the calcaneum. (See Fig. 66.)

Indications: Irregular menstruation, dysmenorrhea, prolapse of uterus, dysuria, blurring of vision.

Method: Puncture perpendicularly 0.4 inch. Moxibustion is applicable.

Regional anatomy   See Dazhong (K. 4).

6. Zhaohai (K. 6)

Location: 1 *cun* below the medial malleolus. (See Fig. 66.)

Indications: Irregular menstruation, prolapse of uterus, pruritus vulvae, hernia, frequency of micturition, epilepsy, sore throat, insomnia.

Method: Puncture perpendicularly 0.3-0.5 inch. Moxibustion is applicable.

Regional anatomy

Vasculature: Posteroinferiorly, the posterior tibial artery and vein.

Innervation: The medial crural cutaneous nerve; deeper, the tibial nerve.

Note: Zhaohai (K. 6) is one of the Eight Confluent Points communicating with the Yinqiao Channel.

7. Fuliu (Jing-River Point, K. 7)

Location: 2 *cun* directly above Taixi (K. 3), on the anterior border of tendo calcaneus. (See Fig. 67.)

Indications: Diarrhea, borborygmus, edema, abdominal distension, swelling of leg, muscular atrophy, weakness and paralysis of foot, night sweating, spontaneous sweating.

Method: Puncture perpendicularly 0.3-0.5 inch. Moxibustion is applicable.

Regional anatomy

Vasculature: Deeper, anteriorly, the posterior tibial artery and vein.

Innervation: The medial sural and medial crural cutaneous nerves; deeper, the tibial nerve.

Note: In the medial aspect of the leg, the distance from the tip of the medial malleolus to the level of Yinlingquan (Sp. 9) is measured as 13 *cun*.

8. Jiaoxin (K. 8)

Location: 2 *cun* above Taixi (K. 3), 0.5 *cun* anterior to Fuliu (K. 7), posterior to the medial border of tibia. (See Fig. 67.)

Indications: Irregular menstruation, uterine bleeding, prolapse of uterus, diarrhea, constipation, pain and swelling of testis.

Method: Puncture perpendicularly 0.4 inch. Moxibustion is applicable.

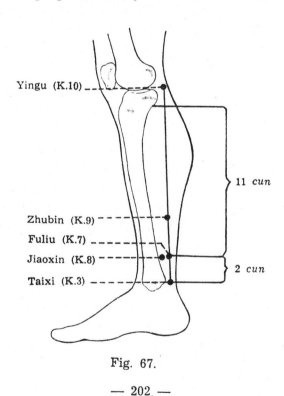

Fig. 67.

Regional anatomy

Vasculature: Deeper, the posterior tibial artery and vein.

Innervation: The medial crural cutaneous nerve; deeper, the tibial nerve.

Note: Jiaoxin (K. 8) is the Xi-Cleft Point of the Yinqiao Channel.

9. Zhubin (K. 9)

Location: On the line drawn from Taixi (K. 3) to Yingu (K. 10), at the lower end of the belly of m. gastrocnemius in the medial aspect, about 5 *cun* above Taixi (K. 3). (See Fig. 67.)

Indications: Mental disorders, pain in the medial aspect of the leg.

Method: Puncture perpendicularly 0.5-0.8 inch. Moxibustion is applicable.

Regional anatomy

Vasculature: Deeper, the posterior tibial artery and vein.

Innervation: The medial sural cutaneous nerve and medial crural cutaneous nerve; deeper, the tibial nerve.

Note: Zhubin (K. 9) is the Xi-Cleft Point of the Yinwei Channel.

10. Yingu (He-Sea Point, K. 10)

Location: On the medial side of the popliteal fossa, level with Weizhong (U.B. 40), between the tendons of m. semitendinosus and semimembranosus when the knee is flexed. (See Fig. 67.)

Indications: Impotence, hernia, uterine bleeding, pain in the medial aspect of the thigh and knee.

Method: Puncture perpendicularly 0.8-1.0 inch. Moxibustion is applicable.

Regional anatomy

Vasculature: The medial superior genicular artery and vein.

Innervation: The medial femoral cutaneous nerve.

11. Henggu (K. 11)

Location: 5 *cun* below the umbilicus, on the superior border of symphysis pubis, 0.5 *cun* lateral to Qugu (Ren 2).

Indications: Pain in the external genitalia, seminal emission, impotence, retention of urine.

Method: Puncture perpendicularly 0.5-0.8 inch. Moxibustion is applicable.

Regional anatomy

Vasculature: The inferior epigastric artery and external pudendal artery.

Innervation: The branch of the iliohypogastric nerve.

Notes:

(1)   On the lower abdomen, the distance from Henggu (K. 11) to Huangshu (K. 16) is measured as 5 *cun*. All the points on the line joining these points are 0.5 *cun* lateral to the Ren Channel.

(2)   The distance between the two nipples is measured as 8 *cun*, which serves as a standard for transverse measurement on the abdomen.

12.   Dahe (K. 12)

Location: 4 *cun* below the umbilicus, 0.5 *cun* lateral to Zhongji (Ren 3). (See Fig. 68.)

Indications: Pain in the external genitalia, seminal emission, leukorrhea.

Method: Puncture perpendicularly 0.5-1.0 inch. Moxibustion is applicable.

Regional anatomy

Vasculature: The muscular branches of the inferior epigastric artery and vein.

Innervation: The branches of the subcostal nerve and the iliohypogastric nerve.

13.   Qixue (K. 13)

Location: 3 *cun* below the umbilicus, 0.5 *cun* lateral to Guanyuan (Ren 4).

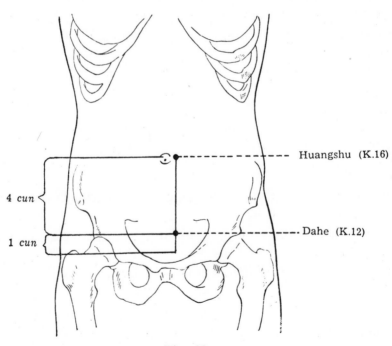

Fig. 68.

Indications: Irregular menstruation, diarrhea.

Method: Puncture perpendicularly 0.5-1.0 inch. Moxibustion is applicable.

Regional anatomy

Vasculature: See Dahe (K. 12).

Innervation: The subcostal nerve.

14. Siman (K. 14)

Location: 2 *cun* below the umbilicus, 0.5 *cun* lateral to Shimen (Ren 5).

Indications: Uterine bleeding, irregular menstruation, postpartum abdominal pain, diarrhea.

Method: Puncture perpendicularly 0.5-1.0 inch. Moxibustion is applicable.

Regional anatomy

Vasculature: See Dahe (K. 12).

Innervation: The 11th intercostal nerve.

15. Abdomen-Zhongzhu (K. 15)

Location: 1 *cun* below the umbilicus, 0.5 *cun* lateral to Abdomen-Yinjiao (Ren 7).

Indications: Irregular menstruation, lower abdominal pain, constipation.

Method: Puncture perpendicularly 0.5-1.0 inch. Moxibustion is applicable.

Regional anatomy

Vasculature: See Dahe (K. 12).

Innervation: The 10th intercostal nerve.

16. Huangshu (K. 16)

Location: 0.5 *cun* lateral to the centre of the umbilicus. (See Fig. 68.)

Indications: Abdominal pain, vomiting, abdominal distension, constipation.

Method: Puncture perpendicularly 0.5-1.0 inch. Moxibustion is applicable.

Regional anatomy

Vasculature: See Dahe (K. 12).

Innervation: The 10th intercostal nerve.

17. Shangqu (K. 17)

Location: 2 *cun* above the umbilicus, 0.5 *cun* lateral to Xiawan (Ren 10).

Indications: Fullness of abdomen, diarrhea, constipation.

Method: Puncture perpendicularly 0.5-1.0 inch. Moxibustion is applicable.

Regional anatomy

Vasculature: The branches of the superior and inferior epigastric arteries and veins.

Innervation: The 9th intercostal nerve.

Note: On the upper abdomen, all the points within the line from Huang-shu (K. 16) to Youmen (K. 21) are 0.5 *cun* lateral to the Ren Channel. The distance between the two points is 6 *cun*.

18. Shiguan (K. 18)

Location: 3 *cun* above the umbilicus, 0.5 *cun* lateral to Jianli (Ren 11).

Indications: Vomiting, abdominal pain, constipation, postpartum abdominal pain.

Method: Puncture perpendicularly 0.5-1.0 inch. Moxibustion is applicable.

Regional anatomy

Vasculature: The branches of the superior epigastric artery and vein.

Innervation: The 8th intercostal nerve.

19. Yindu (K. 19)

Location: 4 *cun* above the umbilicus, 0.5 *cun* lateral to Zhongwan (Ren 12).

Indications: Borborygmus, abdominal distension and pain.

Method: Puncture perpendicularly 0.5-1.0 inch. Moxibustion is applicable.

Regional anatomy   See Shiguan (K. 18).

20. Abdomen-Tonggu (K. 20)

Location: 5 *cun* above the umbilicus, 0.5 *cun* lateral to Shangwan (Ren 13).

Indications: Abdominal pain and distension, vomiting, indigestion.

Method: Puncture perpendicularly 0.5-1.0 inch. Moxibustion is applicable.

Regional anatomy   See Shiguan (K. 18).

21. Youmen (K. 21)

Location: 6 *cun* above the umbilicus, 0.5 *cun* lateral to Juque (Ren 14).

Indications: Abdominal pain, vomiting, diarrhea.

Method: Puncture perpendicularly 0.3-0.7 inch. Moxibustion is applicable.

Regional anatomy

Vasculature: See Shiguan (K. 18).

Innervation: The 7th intercostal nerve.

22. Bulang (K. 22)

Location: In the 5th intercostal space, 2 *cun* lateral to the Ren Channel.
Indications: Cough, asthma.
Method: Puncture obliquely 0.3-0.5 inch. Moxibustion is applicable.
Regional anatomy
Vasculature: The 5th intercostal artery and vein.
Innervation: The anterior cutaneous branch of the 5th intercostal nerve; deeper, the 5th intercostal nerve.
Note: The distance between the midsternal line (Ren Channel) and the mammillary line is measured as 4 *cun*.

23. Shenfeng (K. 23)

Location: In the 4th intercostal space, 2 *cun* lateral to the Ren Channel.
Indications: Cough, asthma, sensation of fullness in the chest and hypochondriac region, mastitis.
Method: Puncture obliquely 0.3-0.5 inch. Moxibustion is applicable.
Regional anatomy
Vasculature: The 4th intercostal artery and vein.
Innervation: The anterior cutaneous branch of the 4th intercostal nerve; deeper, the 4th intercostal nerve.

24. Lingxu (K. 24)

Location: In the 3rd intercostal space, 2 *cun* lateral to the Ren Channel.
Indications: Cough, asthma, pain and fullness of the chest and hypochondriac region, mastitis.
Method: Puncture obliquely 0.3-0.5 inch. Moxibustion is applicable.
Regional anatomy
Vasculature: The 3rd intercostal artery and vein.
Innervation: The anterior cutaneous branch of the 3rd intercostal nerve; deeper, the 3rd intercostal nerve.

25. Shencang (K. 25)

Location: In the 2nd intercostal space, 2 *cun* lateral to the Ren Channel.
Indications: Cough, asthma, chest pain.
Method: Puncture obliquely 0.3-0.5 inch. Moxibustion is applicable.
Regional anatomy
Vasculature: The 2nd intercostal artery and vein.
Innervation: The anterior cutaneous branch of the 2nd intercostal nerve; deeper, the 2nd intercostal nerve.

26. Yuzhong (K. 26)

Location: In the 1st intercostal space, 2 *cun* lateral to the Ren Channel.

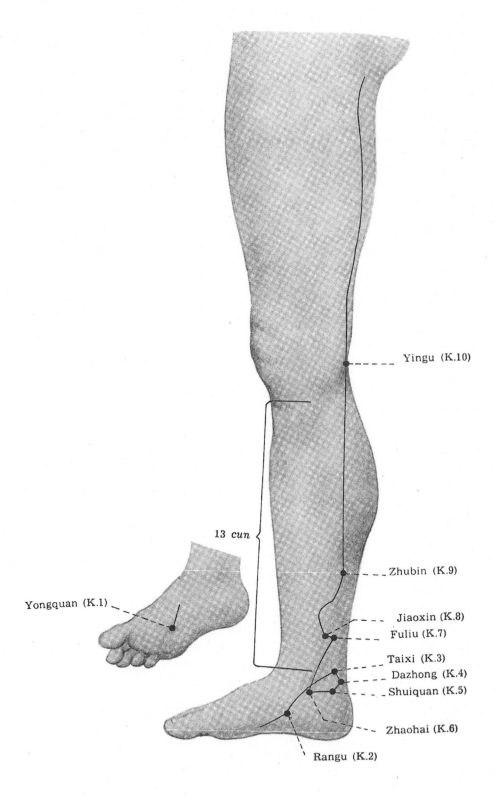

Yingu (K.10)

13 cun

Zhubin (K.9)

Yongquan (K.1)

Jiaoxin (K.8)
Fuliu (K.7)

Taixi (K.3)
Dazhong (K.4)
Shuiquan (K.5)

Zhaohai (K.6)

Rangu (K.2)

Fig. 69a.   The Kidney Channel of Foot-Shaoyin.

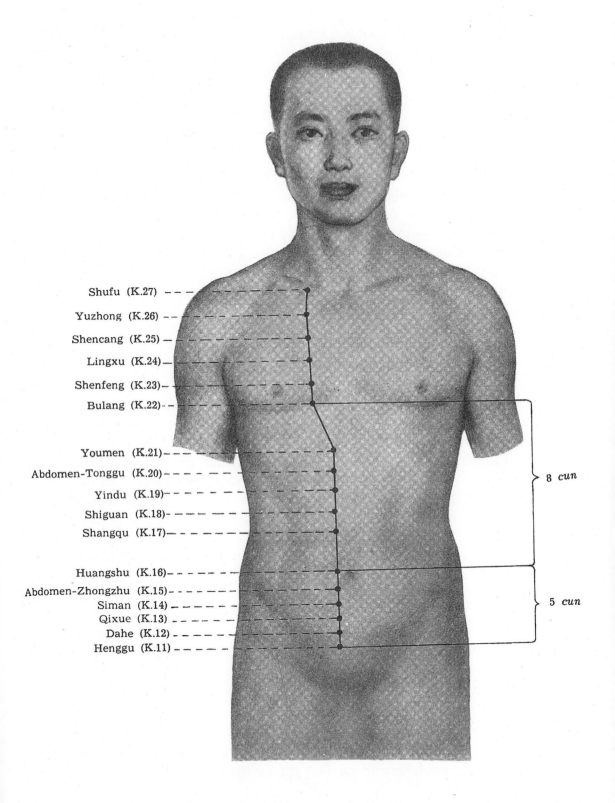

Shufu (K.27)

Yuzhong (K.26)

Shencang (K.25)

Lingxu (K.24)

Shenfeng (K.23)

Bulang (K.22)

Youmen (K.21)

Abdomen-Tonggu (K.20)

Yindu (K.19)

Shiguan (K.18)

Shangqu (K.17)

Huangshu (K.16)

Abdomen-Zhongzhu (K.15)

Siman (K.14)

Qixue (K.13)

Dahe (K.12)

Henggu (K.11)

8 cun

5 cun

Fig. 69b. The Kidney Channel of Foot-Shaoyin.

Indications: Cough, asthma, sensation of fullness in the chest and hypo-chondriac region.

Method: Puncture obliquely 0.3-0.5 inch. Moxibustion is applicable.

Regional anatomy

Vasculature: The 1st intercostal artery and vein.

Innervation: The anterior cutaneous branch of the 1st intercostal nerve, the medial supraclavicular nerve; deeper, the 1st intercostal nerve.

27. Shufu (K. 27)

Location: In the depression on the lower border of the clavicle, 2 *cun* lateral to the Ren Channel.

Indications: Cough, asthma, chest pain.

Method: Puncture perpendicularly 0.3 inch. Moxibustion is applicable.

Regional anatomy

Vasculature: The anterior perforating branches of the internal mammary artery and vein.

Innervation: The medial supraclavicular nerve.

IX.   THE PERICARDIUM CHANNEL OF HAND-JUEYIN

The Pericardium Channel of Hand-Jueyin originates from the chest. Emerging, it enters its pertaining organ, the pericardium (1). Then, it descends through the diaphragm (2) to the abdomen, connecting succes-sively with the upper, middle and lower *jiao* (i.e., *sanjiao*) (3).

A branch arising from the chest runs inside the chest (4), emerges from the costal region at a point 3 *cun* below the anterior axillary fold (Tianchi, P. 1) (5) and ascends to the axilla (6). Following the medial as-pect of the upper arm, it runs downward between the Lung Channel of Hand-Taiyin and the Heart Channel of Hand-Shaoyin (7) to the cubital fossa (8), further downward to the forearm between the tendons of m. palmaris longus and m. flexor carpi radialis (9), ending in the palm (10). From there it passes along the middle finger right down to its tip Zhong-chong (P. 9) (11).

Another branch arises from the palm at Laogong (P. 8) (12), runs along the ring finger to its tip (Guanchong, S.J. 1) and links with the Sanjiao Channel of Hand-Shaoyang. (See Fig. 70.)

There are 9 points in this channel, described as follows:

1.   Tianchi (P. 1)

Location: 1 *cun* lateral to the nipple, in the 4th intercostal space.

Indications: Suffocating sensation in the chest, pain in the hypochon-driac region, swelling and pain of the axillary region.

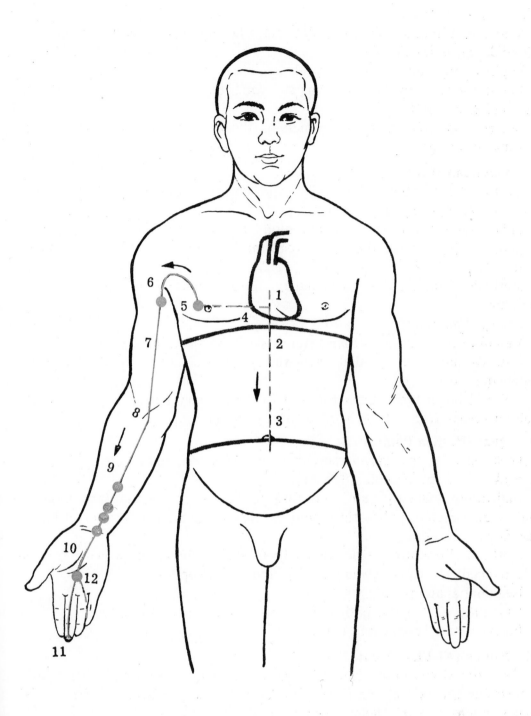

Fig. 70. The Pericardium Channel of Hand-Jueyin.

Method: Puncture obliquely 0.2 inch. Deep puncture is not advisable. Moxibustion is applicable.

Regional anatomy

Vasculature: The thoracoepigastric vein, the branches of the lateral thoracic artery and vein.

Innervation: The muscular branch of the anterior thoracic nerve, the 4th intercostal nerve.

2. Tianquan (P. 2)

Location: 2 *cun* below the end of the anterior axillary fold, between the two heads of m. biceps brachii.

Indications: Pain in the cardiac region, distension of the hypochondriac region, cough, pain in the chest, back and medial aspect of the upper arm.

Method: Puncture perpendicularly 0.5-0.7 inch. Moxibustion is applicable.

Regional anatomy

Vasculature: The muscular branches of the brachial artery and vein.

Innervation: The medial brachial cutaneous nerve and musculocutaneous nerve.

Note: The distance from the end of the axillary fold to the transverse cubital crease (Quze, P. 3) is measured as 9 *cun*.

3. Quze (He-Sea Point, P. 3)

Location: On the transverse cubital crease, at the ulnar side of the tendon of m. biceps brachii. (See Fig. 71.)

Indications: Gastric pain, vomiting, febrile diseases, irritability, pain in the cardiac region, palpitation, pain in the elbow and arm, tremor of hand and arm.

Method: Puncture perpendicularly 0.5-0.8 inch, or prick with three-edged needle to cause bleeding. Moxibusion is applicable.

Regional anatomy

Vasculature: On the pathway of the brachial artery and vein.

Innervation: The median nerve.

4. Ximen (Xi-Cleft Point, P. 4)

Location: 5 *cun* above the transverse crease of the wrist, on the line connecting Quze (P. 3) and Daling (P. 7), between the tendons of m. palmaris longus and m. flexor carpi radialis. (See Fig. 72.)

Indications: Cardiac pain, palpitation, hematemesis, epistaxis, furuncles.

Method: Puncture perpendicularly 0.5-0.8 inch. Moxibustion is applicable.

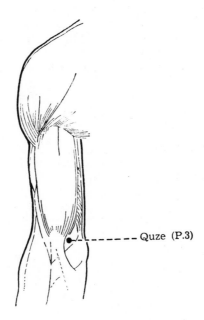

Fig. 71. Quze (P. 3).

Regional anatomy

Vasculature: The median artery and vein; deeper, the anterior interosseous artery and vein.

Innervation: The medial antebrachial cutaneous nerve; deeper, the median nerve; deepest, the anterior interosseous nerve.

Note: On the forearm, the distance from Quze (P. 3) to Daling (P. 7) is measured as 12 *cun*.

5.   Jianshi (Jing-River Point, P. 5)

Location: 3 *cun* above the transverse crease of the wrist, between the tendons of m. palmaris longus and m. flexor carpi radialis. (See Fig. 72.)

Indications: Cardiac pain, palpitation, gastric pain, vomiting, febrile diseases, irritability, malaria, mental disorders, epilepsy, swelling of the axilla, twitching or contracture of the elbow, pain of the arm.

Method: Puncture perpendicularly 0.5-1.0 inch. Moxibustion is applicable.

Regional anatomy

Vasculature: The median artery and vein; deeper, the anterior interosseous artery and vein.

Innervation: The medial and lateral antebrachial cutaneous nerves, the palmar cutaneous branch of the median nerve; deepest, the anterior interosseous nerve.

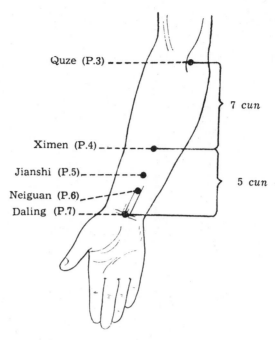

Fig. 72.

6. Neiguan (Luo-Connecting Point, P. 6)

Location: 2 *cun* above the transverse crease of the wrist, between the tendons of m. palmaris longus and m. flexor carpi radialis. (See Fig. 72.)

Indications: Cardiac pain, palpitation, gastric pain, vomiting, mental disorders, epilepsy, contracture and pain of the elbow and arm, febrile diseases, malaria.

Method: Puncture perpendicularly 0.5-1.0 inch. Moxibustion is applicable.

Regional anatomy See Jianshi (P. 5)

Note: This is one of the Eight Confluent Points communicating with the Yinwei Channel.

7. Daling (Shu-Stream and Yuan-Source Point, P. 7)

Location: In the depression in the middle of the transverse crease of the wrist, between the tendons of m. palmaris longus and m. flexor carpi radialis. (See Fig. 72.)

Indications: Cardiac pain, palpitation, gastric pain, vomiting, panic, mental disorders, epilepsy, pain in the chest and hypochondriac region.

Method: Puncture perpendicularly 0.3-0.5 inch. Moxibustion is applicable.

Regional anatomy

Vasculature: The palmar arterial and venous network of the wrist.

Innervation: Deeper, the median nerve.

8. Laogong (Ying-Spring Point, P. 8)

Location: When the hand is placed with the palm upward, the point is between the 2nd and 3rd metacarpal bones, proximal to the metacarpophalangeal joint, on the radial side of the 3rd metacarpal bone. (See Fig. 73.)

Indications: Cardiac pain, mental disorders, epilepsy, vomiting, stomatitis, foul breath, fungus infection of hand and foot.

Method: Puncture perpendicularly 0.3-0.5 inch. Moxibustion is applicable.

Regional anatomy

Vasculature: The common palmar digital artery.

Innervation: The 2nd common palmar digital nerve of the median nerve.

9. Zhongchong (Jing-Well Point, P. 9)

Location: In the centre of the tip of the middle finger. (See Fig. 73.)

Indications: Cardiac pain, irritability, loss of consciousness, aphasia with stiffness of the tongue, febrile diseases, heat stroke, infantile convulsion, feverish sensation in the palm.

Method: Puncture obliquely 0.1 inch, or prick with three-edged needle to cause bleeding. Moxibustion is applicable.

Regional anatomy

Vasculature: The arterial and venous network formed by the palmar digital proprial artery and vein.

Innervation: The palmar digital proprial nerve of the median nerve.

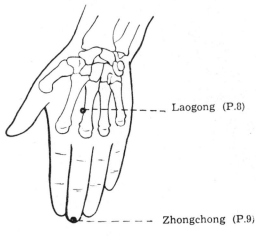

Laogong (P.8)

Zhongchong (P.9)

Fig. 73.

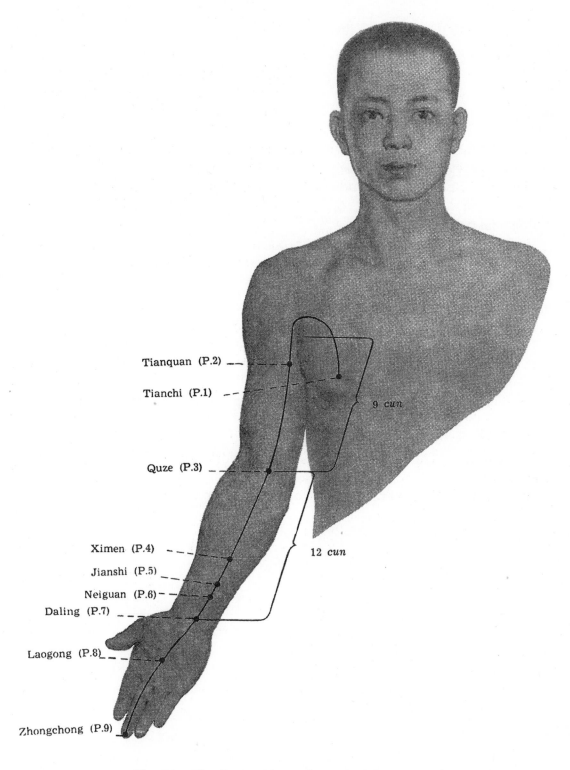

Tianquan (P.2)

Tianchi (P.1)

9 *cun*

Quze (P.3)

Ximen (P.4)

Jianshi (P.5)

Neiguan (P.6)

Daling (P.7)

12 *cun*

Laogong (P.8)

Zhongchong (P.9)

Fig. 74. The Pericardium Channel of Hand-Jueyin.

Note: It is also considered that Zhongchong (P. 9) is located 0.1 *cun* posterior to the corner of the nail of the middle finger on the radial side.

X. THE SANJIAO CHANNEL OF HAND-SHAOYANG

The Sanjiao Channel of Hand-Shaoyang originates from the tip of the ring finger (Guanchong S.J. 1) (1), running upward between the 4th and 5th metacarpal bones (2) along the dorsal aspect of the wrist (3) to the lateral aspect of the forearm between the radius and ulna (4). Passing through the olecranon (5) and along the lateral aspect of the upper arm (6), it reaches the shoulder region (7), where it goes across and passes behind the Gall Bladder Channel of Foot-Shaoyang (8). Winding over to the supraclavicular fossa (9), it spreads in the chest to connect with the pericardium (10). It then descends through the diaphragm down to the abdomen, and joins its pertaining organ, the upper, middle and lower *jiao* (i.e., *sanjiao*) (11).

A branch originates from the chest (12). Running upward, it emerges from the supraclavicular fossa (13). From there it ascends to the neck (14), running along the posterior border of the ear (15), and further to the superior aspect of the ear (16). Then it turns downward to the cheek and terminates in the infraorbital region (17).

The auricular branch arises from the retroauricular region and enters the ear (18). Then it emerges in front of the ear, crosses the previous branch at the cheek and reaches the outer canthus (Sizhukong, S.J. 23) to link with the Gall Bladder Channel of Foot-Shaoyang (19). (See Fig. 75.)

Note: *Sanjiao* has an Inferior He-Sea Point which is Weiyang (U.B. 39). (See Fig. 76.)

There are 23 points in this channel, which are described as follows:

1. Guanchong (Jing-Well Point, S.J. 1)

Location: On the lateral side of the ring finger, about 0.1 *cun* posterior to the corner of the nail. (See Fig. 77.)

Indications: Headache, redness of the eyes, sore throat, stiffness of the tongue, febrile diseases, irritability.

Method: Puncture obliquely 0.1 inch, or prick with three-edged needle to cause bleeding. Moxibustion is applicable.

Regional anatomy

Vasculature: The arterial and venous network formed by the palmar digital proprial artery and vein.

Innervation: The palmar digital proprial nerve derived from the ulnar nerve.

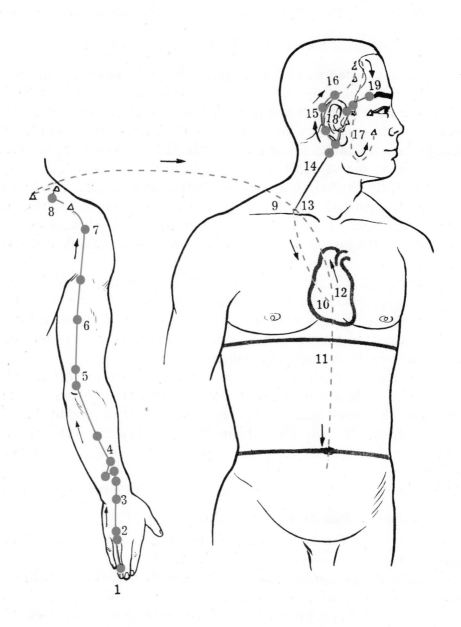

Fig. 75.   The Sanjiao Channel of Hand-Shaoyang.

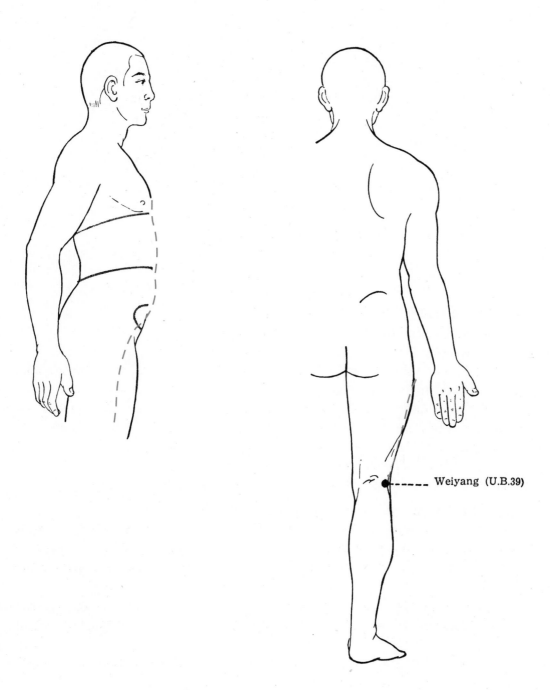

Weiyang (U.B.39)

Fig. 76.   Inferior He-Sea Point of the Sanjiao Channel. Weiyang (U.B. 39).

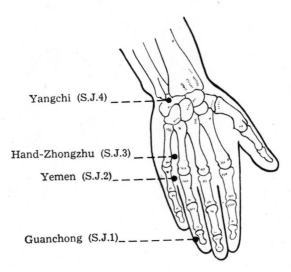

Fig. 77.

2. Yemen (Ying-Spring Point, S.J. 2)

Location: Proximal to the margin of the web between the ring and small fingers. The point is located with clenched fist. (See Fig. 77.)

Indications: Headache, redness of the eyes, deafness, sore throat, pain in the hand and arm, malaria.

Method: Puncture obliquely 0.3-0.5 inch towards the interspace of the metacarpal bones. Moxibustion is applicable.

Regional anatomy

Vasculature: The dorsal digital artery of the ulnar artery.

Innervation: The dorsal branch of the ulnar nerve.

3. Hand-Zhongzhu (Shu-Stream Point, S.J. 3)

Location: When the hand is placed with the palm facing downward, the point is on the dorsum of hand between the 4th and 5th metacarpal bones, in the depression proximal to the metacarpophalangeal joint. (See Fig. 77.)

Indications: Headache, redness of the eyes, deafness, tinnitus, sore throat, pain in the elbow and arm, motor impairment of fingers, febrile diseases.

Method: Puncture perpendicularly 0.3-0.5 inch. Moxibustion is applicable.

Regional anatomy

Vasculature: The dorsal venous network of hand and the 4th dorsal metacarpal artery.

Innervation: The dorsal branch of the ulnar nerve.

4. Yangchi (Yuan-Source Point, S.J. 4)

Location: At the junction of the ulna and carpal bones, in the depression lateral to the tendon of m. extensor digitorum communis. (See Fig. 77.)

Indications: Pain in the wrist, shoulder and arm, malaria, deafness.

Method: Puncture perpendicularly 0.3 inch. Moxibustion is applicable.

Regional anatomy

Vasculature: Inferiorly, the dorsal venous network of the wrist and the posterior carpal artery.

Innervation: The dorsal branch of the ulnar nerve and the terminal branch of the posterior antebrachial cutaneous nerve.

5. Waiguan (Luo-Connecting Point, S. J. 5)

Location: 2 *cun* above Yangchi (S.J. 4), between the radius and ulna. (See Fig. 78.)

Indications: Febrile diseases, headache, pain in the cheek and the hypochondriac region, deafness, tinnitus, motor impairment of the elbow and arm, pain of fingers, hand tremor.

Method: Puncture perpendicularly 0.7-1.0 inch. Moxibustion is applicable.

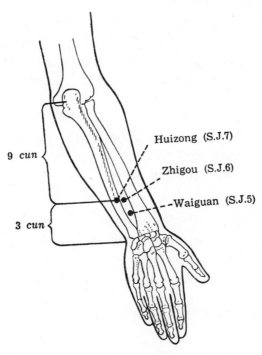

Fig. 78.

Regional anatomy

Vasculature: Deeper, the posterior and anterior interosseous arteries and veins.

Innervation: The posterior antebrachial cutaneous nerve; deeper, the posterior interosseous nerve of the radial nerve and the anterior interosseous nerve of the median nerve.

Notes:

(1) This is one of the Eight Confluent Points communicating with the Yangwei Channel.

(2) On the forearm, the distance from Yangchi (S.J. 4) to the olecranon is measured as 12 *cun*.

6. Zhigou (Jing-River Point, S. J. 6)

Location: 3 *cun* above Yangchi (S.J. 4), between the ulna and radius. (See Fig. 78.)

Indications: Sudden hoarseness of voice, tinnitus, deafness, aching and heavy sensation of the shoulder and back, vomiting, constipation.

Method: Puncture perpendicularly 0.7-1.0 inch. Moxibustion is applicable.

Regional anatomy See Waiguan (S.J. 5).

7. Huizong (Xi-Cleft Point, S. J. 7)

Location: 3 *cun* proximal to the wrist, about one finger-breadth lateral to Zingou (S.J. 6), on the radial side of the ulna. (See Fig. 78.)

Indications: Deafness, pain of the upper extremities, epilepsy.

Method: Puncture perpendicularly 0.5-1.0 inch. Moxibustion is applicable.

Regional anatomy

Vasculature: The posterior interosseous artery and vein.

Innervation: The posterior and medial antebrachial cutaneous nerves; deeper, the posterior and anterior interossous nerves.

8. Sanyangluo (S. J. 8)

Location: 4 *cun* above Yangchi (S.J. 4), between the radius and ulna.

Indications: Sudden hoarseness of voice, deafness, pain in the hand and arm.

Method: Puncture perpendicularly 0.5-1.0 inch. Moxibustion is applicable.

Regional anatomy   See Huizong (S.J. 7).

9. Sidu (S. J. 9)

Location: 5 *cun* below the olecranon, between the radius and ulna.

Indications: Sudden hoarseness of voice, deafness, toothache, pain in the forearm.

Method: Puncture perpendicularly 0.5-1.0 inch. Moxibustion is applicable.

Regional anatomy   See Huizong (S.J. 7).

10.   Tianjing (He-Sea Point, S. J. 10)

Location: When the elbow is flexed, the point is in the depression about 1 *cun* superior to the olecranon. (See Fig. 79.)

Indications: Unilateral headache, pain in the costal and hypochondriac region, neck, shoulder and arm, scrofula, epilepsy.

Method: Puncture perpendicularly 0.3-0.5 inch. Moxibustion is applicable.

Regional anatomy

Vasculature: The arterial and venous network of the elbow.

Innervation: The posterior brachial cutaneous nerve and the muscular branch of the radial nerve.

Note: The Inferior He-Sea Point of *sanjiao* is Weiyang (U.B. 39), which is indicated in disorders of *sanjiao*.

11.   Qinglengyuan (S. J. 11)

Location: 1 *cun* above Tianjing (S.J. 10).

Indications: Pain in the shoulder and arm.

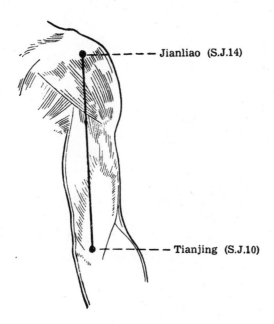

Fig. 79.

Method: Puncture perpendicularly 0.3 inch. Moxibustion is applicable.

Regional anatomy

Vasculature: The terminal branches of the median collateral artery and vein.

Innervation: The posterior brachial cutaneous nerve and the muscular branch of the radial nerve.

Note: On the upper arm, the distance from the olecranon to the level of the end of the posterior axillary fold is measured as 9 *cun*.

12. Xiaoluo (S. J. 12)

Location: On the line joining the olecranon and Jianliao (S.J. 14), midway between Qinglengyuan (S.J. 11) and Naohui (S.J. 13). It is just on the lower end of the bulge of the lateral head of m. triceps brachii when the forearm is in pronation.

Indications: Headache, stiffness and pain of the neck, pain in the arm.

Method: Puncture perpendicularly 0.5-0.7 inch. Moxibustion is applicable.

Regional anatomy

Vasculature: The median collateral artery and vein.

Innervation: The posterior brachial cutaneous nerve and the muscular branch of the radial nerve.

13. Naohui (S. J. 13)

Location: On the line joining Jianliao (S.J. 14) and the olecranon, 3 *cun* below Jianliao (S.J. 14), on the posterior border of m. deltoideus.

Indications: Pain in the shoulder and arm, goiter.

Method: Puncture perpendicularly 0.5-0.8 inch. Moxibustion is applicable.

Regional anatomy

Vasculature: The median collateral artery and vein.

Innervation: The posterior brachial cutaneous nerve, the muscular branch of the radial nerve; deeper, the radial nerve.

14. Jianliao (S. J. 14)

Location: Posterior and inferior to the acromion, in the depression about 1 *cun* posterior to Jianyu (L.I. 15). (See Fig. 79.)

Indications: Heavy sensation of the shoulder, pain in the arm.

Method: Puncture perpendicularly or obliquely downward 0.7-1.0 inch. Moxibustion is applicable.

Regional anatomy

Vasculature: The muscular branch of the posterior circumflex humeral artery.

Inntervation: The muscular branch of the axillary nerve.

15. Tianliao (S. J. 15)

Location: Midway between Jianjing (G.B. 21) and Quyuan (S.I. 13), on the superior angle of the scapula.

Indications: Pain in the shoulder and arm, pain and stiffness of the neck.

Method: Puncture perpendicularly 0.3-0.5 inch. Moxibustion is applicable.

Regional anatomy

Vasculature: The descending branch of the transverse cervical artery; deeper, the muscular branch of the suprascapular artery.

Innervation: The accessory nerve and the branch of the suprascapular nerve.

16. Tianyou (S. J. 16)

Location: Posterior and inferior to the mastoid process, on the posterior border of m. sternocleidomastoideus, level with Tianrong (S.I. 17) and Tianzhu (U.B. 10).

Indications: Dizziness, facial swelling, sudden deafness, blurring of vision, neck rigidity.

Method: Puncture perpendicularly 0.3-0.5 inch. Moxibustion is applicable.

Regional anatomy

Vasculature: The posterior auricular artery.

Innervation: The lesser occipital nerve.

17. Yifeng (S. J. 17)

Location: Posterior to the lobule of the ear, in the depression between the mandible and mastoid process. (See Fig. 80.)

Indications: Tinnitus, deafness, facial paralysis, trismus, swelling of the cheek.

Method: Puncture perpendicularly 0.5-1.0 inch. Moxibustion is applicable.

Regional anatomy

Vasculature: The posterior auricular artery and vein, the external jugular vein.

Innervation: The great auricular nerve; deeper, the site where the facial nerve perforates out of the stylomastoid foramen.

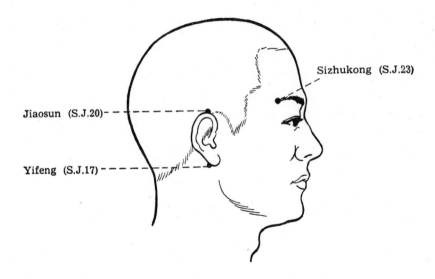

Fig. 80.

18. Qimai (S. J. 18)

Location: In the centre of the mastoid process, at the junction of the middle and lower third of the curve formed by Yifeng (S.J. 17) and Jiaosun (S.J. 20) posterior to the helix.

Indications: Headache, tinnitus, deafness.

Method: Puncture obliquely 0.1 inch, or prick to cause bleeding. Moxibustion is applicable.

Regional anatomy

Vasculature: The posterior auricular artery and vein.

Innervation: The posterior auricular branch of the great auricular nerve.

19. Luxi (S. J. 19)

Location: Posterior to the ear, at the junction of the upper and middle third of the curve formed by Yifeng (S.J. 17) and Jiaosun (S.J. 20) behind the helix.

Indications: Headache, tinnitus, earache.

Method: Puncture obliquely 0.1 inch. Moxibustion is applicable.

Regional anatomy

Vasculature: The posterior auricular artery and vein.

Innervation: The anastomotic branch of the great auricular nerve and the lesser occipital nerve.

20. Jiaosun (S. J. 20)

Location: Directly above the ear apex, within the hairline of the temple. (See Fig. 80.)

Indications: Redness and swelling of the ear, redness, swelling and pain of the eye, toothache.

Method: Puncture obliquely downward 0.1 inch. Moxibustion is applicable.

Regional anatomy

Vasculature: The branches of the superficial temporal artery and vein.

Innervation: The branches of the auriculotemporal nerve.

21. Ermen (S. J. 21)

Location: In the depression anterior to the supratragic notch and slightly superior to the condyloid process of the mandible. The point is located with the mouth open.

Indications: Deafness, tinnitus, otorrhea, toothache.

Method: Puncture perpendicularly 0.3-0.5 inch. Moxibustion is applicable.

Regional anatomy

Vasculature: The superficial temporal artery and vein.

Innervation: The branches of the auriculotemporal nerve and facial nerve.

22. Ear-Heliao (S. J. 22)

Location: Anterior and superior to Ermen (S.J. 21), level with the root of the auricle, on the posterior border of the hairline of the temple where the superficial temporal artery passes.

Indications: Tinnitus, headache, heavy sensation of the head, lockjaw.

Method: Puncture obliquely 0.1-0.3 inch. Avoid the artery. Moxibustion is applicable.

Regional anatomy

Vasculature: The superficial temporal artery and vein.

Innervation: The branch of the auriculotemporal nerve, on the course of the temporal branch of the facial nerve.

23. Sizhukong (S. J. 23)

Location: In the depression at the lateral end of the eyebrow. (See Fig. 80.)

Indications: Headache, blurring of vision, redness and pain of the eye, twitching of the eyelid.

Method: Puncture posteriorly 0.3 inch horizontally along the skin.

Regional anatomy

Vasculature: The frontal branches of the superficial temporal artery and vein.

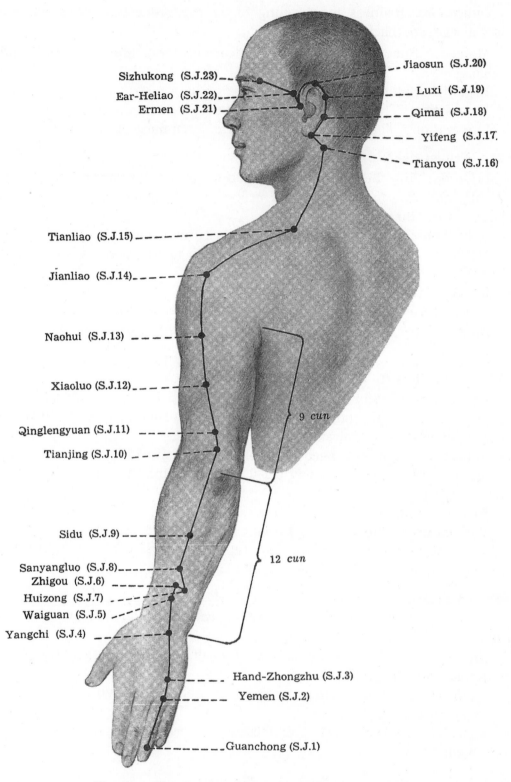

Sizhukong (S.J.23)

Ear-Heliao (S.J.22)

Ermen (S.J.21)

Jiaosun (S.J.20)

Luxi (S.J.19)

Qimai (S.J.18)

Yifeng (S.J.17)

Tianyou (S.J.16)

Tianliao (S.J.15)

Jianliao (S.J.14)

Naohui (S.J.13)

Xiaoluo (S.J.12)

Qinglengyuan (S.J.11)

Tianjing (S.J.10)

9 cun

Sidu (S.J.9)

Sanyangluo (S.J.8)

Zhigou (S.J.6)

Huizong (S.J.7)

Waiguan (S.J.5)

Yangchi (S.J.4)

12 cun

Hand-Zhongzhu (S.J.3)

Yemen (S.J.2)

Guanchong (S.J.1)

Fig. 81. The Sanjiao Channel of Hand-Shaoyang.

Innervation: The zygomatic branch of the facial nerve and the branch of the auriculotemporal nerve.

XI. THE GALL BLADDER CHANNEL OF FOOT-SHAOYANG

The Gall bladder Channel of Foot-Shaoyang originates from the outer canthus (Tongziliao, G.B. 1) (1), ascends to the corner of the forehead (Hanyan, G.B. 4) (2), then curves downward to the retroauricular region (Fengchi, G.B. 20) (3) and runs along the side of the neck in front of the Sanjiao Channel of Hand-Shaoyang to the shoulder (4). Turning back, it traverses and passes behind the Sanjiao Channel of Hand-Shaoyang down to the supraclavicular fossa (5).

The retroauricular branch arises from the retroauricular region (6) and enters the ear. It then comes out and passes the preauricular region (7) to the posterior aspect of the outer canthus (8).

The branch arising from the outer canthus (9) runs downward to Daying (St. 5) (10) and meets the Sanjiao Channel of Hand-Shaoyang in the infraorbital region (11). Then, passing through Jiache (St. 6) (12), it descends to the neck and enters the supraclavicular fossa where it meets the main channel (13). From there it further descends into the chest (14), passes through the diaphragm to connect with the liver (15) and enters its pertaining organ, the gall bladder (16). Then it runs inside the hypochondriac region (17), comes out from the lateral side of the lower abdomen near the femoral artery at the inguinal region (18). From there it runs superficially along the margin of the pubic hair (19) and goes traversely into the hip region (Huantiao, G.B. 30) (20).

The straight portion of the channel runs downward from the supraclavicular fossa (21), passes in front of the axilla (22) along the lateral aspect of the chest (23) and through the free ends of the floating ribs (24) to the hip region where it meets the previous branch (25). Then it descends along the lateral aspect of the thigh (26) to the lateral side of the knee (27). Going further downward along the anterior aspect of the fibula (28) all the way to its lower end (Xuanzhong, G.B. 39) (29), it reaches the anterior aspect of the external malleolus (30). It then follows the dorsum of the foot to the lateral side of the tip of the 4th toe (Foot-Qiaoyin, G.B. 44) (31).

The branch of the dorsum of the foot springs from Foot-Linqi (G.B. 41), runs between the 1st and 2nd metatarsal bones to the distal portion of the great toe and terminates at its hairy region (Dadun, Liv. 1), where it links with the Liver Channel of Foot-Jueyin (32). (See Fig. 82.)

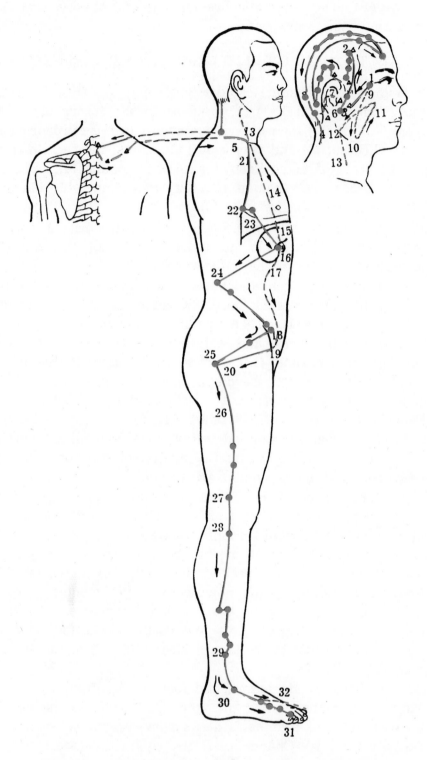

Fig. 82.   The Gall Bladder Channel of Foot-Shaoyang.

The points of this channel are 44 in number and are described as follows:

1. Tongziliao (G. B. 1)

Location: Lateral to the outer canthus, in the depression on the lateral side of the orbit. (See Fig. 83.)

Indications: Headache, ophthalmalgia, failing of vision, redness of the eye and lacrimation.

Method: Puncture laterally 0.2-0.3 inch horizontally along the skin. Moxibustion is applicable.

Regional anatomy

Vasculature: The zygomaticoorbital artery and vein.

Innervation: The zygomaticofacial and zygomaticotemporal nerves, the temporal branch of the facial nerve.

2. Tinghui (G. B. 2)

Location: Anterior to the intertragic notch, directly below Tinggong (S.I. 19), at the posterior border of the condyloid process of the mandible. The point is located with the mouth open. (See Fig. 83.)

Indications: Tinnitus, deafness, toothache.

Method: Puncture perpendicularly 0.5-0.7 inch. Moxibustion is applicable.

Regional anatomy

Vasculature: The superficial temporal artery.

Innervation: The great auricular nerve and facial nerve.

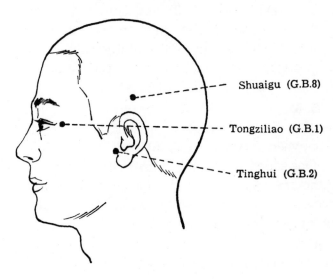

Shuaigu (G.B.8)

Tongziliao (G.B.1)

Tinghui (G.B.2)

Fig. 83.

3. Shangguan (G. B. 3)

Location: In front of the ear, on the upper border of the zygomatic arch, in the depression directly above Xiaguan (St. 7).

Indications: Headache, deafness, tinnitus, toothache, facial paralysis.

Method: Puncture perpendicularly 0.3 inch. Deep puncture is not advisable. Moxibustion is applicable.

Regional anatomy

Vasculature: The zygomaticoorbital artery and vein.

Innervation: The zygomatic branch of the facial nerve and the zygomaticofacial nerve.

4. Hanyan (G. B. 4)

Location: Within the hairline of the temporal region, midway of the upper half of the distance between Touwei (St. 8) and Qubin (G.B. 7).

Indications: One-sided headache, blurring of vision, pain in the outer canthus, tinnitus.

Method: Puncture 0.3-0.5 inch horizontally along the skin with the needle directed posteriorly. Moxibustion is applicable.

Regional anatomy

Vasculature: The parietal branches of the superficial temporal artery and vein.

Innervation: Just on the temporal branch of the auriculotemporal nerve.

5. Xuanlu (G. B. 5)

Location: Within the hairline of the temporal region, midway of the border line connecting Touwei (St. 8) and Qubin (G.B. 7).

Indications: One-sided headache, pain in the outer canthus.

Method: Puncture 0.3-0.5 inch horizontally along the skin with the needle directed posteriorly. Moxibustion is applicable.

Regional anatomy   See Hanyan (G.B. 4).

6. Xuanli (G. B. 6)

Location: Within the hairline inferior to the corner of the temporal region, midway between Xuanlu (G.B. 5) and Qubin (G.B. 7).

Indications: One-sided headache, pain in the outer canthus.

Method: Puncture 0.2-0.3 inch horizontally along the skin with the needle directed posteriorly. Moxibustion is applicable.

Regional anatomy   See Hanyan (G.B. 4).

7. Qubin (G. B. 7)

Location: Within the hairline anterior and superior to the auricle, about 1 finger-breadth anterior to Jiaosun (S.J. 20).

Indications: Pain in the temporal region, swelling of the cheek and submandibular region, lockjaw.

Method: Puncture 0.2-0.3 inch horizontally along the skin with the needle directed posteriorly. Moxibustion is applicable.

Regional anatomy   See Hanyan (G.B. 4).

8.　Shuaigu (G. B. 8)

Location: Superior to the apex of the auricle, 1.5 *cun* within the hairline. (See Fig. 83.)

Indication: One-sided headache.

Method: Puncture 0.3-0.5 inch horizontally along the skin. Moxibustion is applicable.

Regional anatomy

Vasculature: The parietal branches of the superficial temporal artery and vein.

Innervation: The anastomotic branch of the auriculotemporal nerve and great occipital nerve.

9.　Tianchong (G. B. 9)

Location: Posterior and superior to the auricle, 2 *cun* within the hairline, about 0.5 *cun* posterior to Shuaigu (G.B. 8).

Indications: Headache,　swelling of the gums, mental disturbance of depressive type.

Method: Puncture 0.3 inch horizontally along the skin.

Regional anatomy

Vasculature: The posterior auricular artery and vein.

Innervation: The branch of the great occipital nerve.

10.　Fubai (G. B. 10)

Location: Posterior and superior to the mastoid process, in the middle of the curve line drawn from Tianchong (G.B. 9) to Head-Qiaoyin (G.B. 11).

Indications: Headache, tinnitus, deafness.

Method: Puncture 0.3 inch horizontally along the skin. Moxibustion is applicable.

Regional anatomy   See Tianchong (G.B. 9).

11.　Head-Qiaoyin (G. B. 11)

Location: Posterior and superior to the mastoid process, on the line connecting Fubai (G.B. 10) and Head-Wangu (G.B. 12).

Indications: Headache, pain in the neck, earache, deafness, tinnitus.

Method: Puncture 0.3 inch horizontally along the skin. Moxibustion is applicable.

Regional anatomy

Vasculature: The branches of the posterior auricular artery and vein.

Innervation: The anastomotic branch of the great and lesser occipital nerves.

12. Head-Wangu (G. B. 12)

Location: In the depression posterior and inferior to the mastoid process.

Indications: Headache, insomnia, pain and stiffness of the neck, swelling of the cheek, toothache, facial paralysis.

Method: Puncture obliquely downward 0.3-0.5 inch. Moxibustion is applicable.

Regional anatomy

Vasculature: The posterior auricular artery and vein.

Innervation: The lesser occipital nerve.

13. Benshen (G. B. 13)

Location: 0.5 *cun* within the hairline of the forehead, at the junction of the medial two-thirds and lateral third of the distance from Shenting (Du 24) to Touwei (St. 8).

Indications: Headache, blurring of vision, epilepsy.

Method: Puncture 0.3-0.5 inch horizontally along the skin with the needle directed posteriorly. Moxibustion is applicable.

Regional anatomy

Vasculature: The frontal branches of the superficial temporal artery and vein, the lateral branches of the frontal artery and vein.

Innervation: The lateral branch of the frontal nerve.

Note: The distance between Shenting (Du 24) and Touwei (St. 8) is measured as 4.5 *cun*.

14. Yangbai (G. B. 14)

Location: On the forehead, 1 *cun* above the midpoint of the eyebrow, approximately at the junction of the upper two-thirds and lower third of the vertical line drawn from the anterior hairline to the eyebrow. (See Fig. 84.)

Indications: Frontal headache, blurring of vision, lacrimation on exposure to wind, pain in the outer canthus, twitching of eyelids.

Method: Puncture 0.3-0.5 inch horizontally along the skin with the needle directed downward. Moxibustion is applicable.

Regional anatomy

Vasculature: The lateral branches of the frontal artery and vein.

Innervation: On the lateral branch of the frontal nerve.

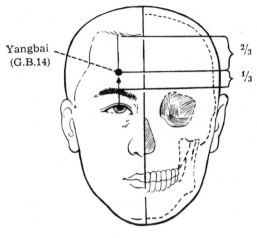

Fig. 84.

15. Head-Linqi (G. B. 15)

Location: Directly above Yangbai (G.B. 14), 0.5 *cun* within the hairline, midway between Shenting (Du 24) and Touwei (St. 8).

Indications: Headache, blurring of vision, lacrimation on exposure to wind, pain in the outer canthus, nasal obstruction.

Method: Puncture 0.3-0.5 inch horizontally along the skin with the needle directed upward. Moxibustion is applicable.

Regional anatomy

Vasculature: The frontal artery and vein.

Innervation: The anastomotic branch of the medial and lateral branches of the frontal nerve.

Note: The distance between the anterior and posterior hairline is measured as 12 *cun*.

16. Muchuang (G. B. 16)

Location: 1.5 *cun* posterior to Head-Linqi (G.B. 15), on the line connecting Head-Linqi (G.B. 15) and Fengchi (G.B. 20).

Indications: Headache, blurring of vision, red and painful eyes.

Method: Puncture 0.3-0.5 inch horizontally along the skin with the needle directed posteriorly. Moxibustion is applicable.

Regional anatomy

Vasculature: The frontal branches of the superficial temporal artery and vein.

Innervation: The anastomotic branch of the medial and lateral branches of the frontal nerve.

17. Zhengying (G. B. 17)

Location: 1.5 *cun* posterior to Muchuang (G.B. 16), on the line joining Head-Linqi (G.B. 15) and Fengchi (G.B. 20).

Indications: One-sided headache. blurring of vision.

Method: Puncture 0.3-0.5 inch horizontally along the skin with the needle directed posteriorly. Moxibustion is applicable.

Regional anatomy

Vasculature: The anastomotic plexus formed by the parietal branches of the superficial temporal artery and vein and the occipital artery and vein.

Innervation: The anastomotic branch of the frontal and great occipital nerves.

18. Chengling (G. B. 18)

Location: 1.5 *cun* posterior to Zhengying (G.B. 17), on the line connecting Head-Linqi (G.B. 15) and Fengchi (G.B. 20).

Indications: Headache, rhinorrhea, epistaxis.

Method: Puncture 0.3-0.5 inch horizontally along the skin with the needle directed posteriorly. Moxibustion is applicable.

Regional anatomy

Vasculature: The branches of the occipital artery and vein.

Innervation: The branch of the great occipital nerve.

19. Naokong (G. B. 19)

Location: Directly above Fengchi (G.B. 20), level with Naohu (Du 17), on the lateral side of the external occipital protuberance.

Indications: Headache, pain and stiffness of the neck.

Method: Puncture downward 0.3-0.5 inch horizontally along the skin. Moxibustion is applicable.

Regional anatomy   See Chengling (G.B. 18).

20. Fengchi (G. B. 20)

Location: In the posterior aspect of the neck, below the occipital bone, in the depression between the upper portion of m. sternocleidomastoideus and m. trapezius. (See Fig. 85.)

Indications: Headache, dizziness, pain and stiffness of the neck, red and painful eyes, rhinorrhea, pain in the shoulder and back, febrile diseases, common cold.

Method: Puncture perpendicularly 0.5-1.0 inch towards the tip of the nose. Moxibustion is applicable.

Regional anatomy

Vasculature: The branches of the occipital artery and vein.

Innervation: The branch of the lesser occipital nerve.

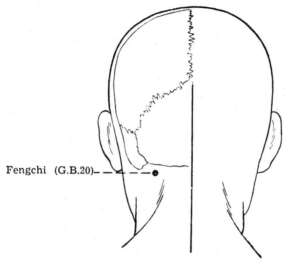

Fengchi (G.B.20)

Fig. 85.

21. Jianjing (G. B. 21)

Location: Midway between Dazhui (Du 14) and the acromion, at the highest point of the shoulder. (See Fig. 86.)

Indications: Neck rigidity, pain in the shoulder and back, motor impairment of the hand and arm, mastitis, apoplexy, difficult labour.

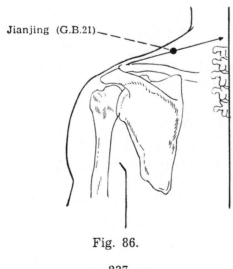

Jianjing (G.B.21)

Fig. 86.

Method: Puncture perpendicularly 0.5 inch. Moxibustion is applicable.
Regional anatomy
Vasculature: The transverse cervical artery and vein.
Innervation: The lateral branch of the subraclavicular nerve, the accessory nerve.

22. Yuanye (G. B. 22)
Location: On the midaxillary line, 3 *cun* below the axilla.
Indications: Pain in the hypochondriac region, swelling of the axillary region.
Method: Puncture obliquely 0.3-0.5 inch. Moxibustion is applicable.
Regional anatomy
Vasculature: The thoracoepigastric vein, the lateral thoracic artery and vein, the 5th intercostal artery and vein.
Innervation: The lateral cutaneous branch of the 5th intercostal nerve, the branch of the long thoracic nerve.
Note: In the lateral aspect of the chest, the distance from the axilla to the free end of the 11th rib is measured as 12 *cun*.

23. Zhejin (G. B. 23)
Location: 1 *cun* anterior to Yuanye (G.B. 22), approximately level with the nipple.
Indications: Fullness of the chest, asthma.
Method: Puncture obliquely 0.3-0.5 inch. Moxibustion is applicable.
Regional anatomy
Vasculature: The lateral thoracic artery and vein, the 5th intercostal artery and vein.
Innervation: The lateral cutaneous branch of the 5th intercostal nerve.

24. Riyue (Front-Mu Point of the gall bladder, G. B. 24)
Location: Inferior to the nipple, between the cartilages of the 7th and 8th ribs, one rib below Qimen (Liv. 14). (See Fig. 87.)
Indications: Vomiting, regurgitation, jaundice, hiccup.
Method: Puncture obliquely 0.3-0.5 inch. Moxibustion is applicable.
Regional anatomy
Vasculature: The 7th intercostal artery and vein.
Innervation: The 7th intercostal nerve.

25. Jingmen (Front-Mu Point of the kidney, G. B. 25)
Location: On the lateral side of the abdomen, on the lower border of the free end of the 12th rib. (See Fig. 88.)
Indications: Borborygmus, diarrhea, abdominal distension, pain in the lower back and hypochondriac region.

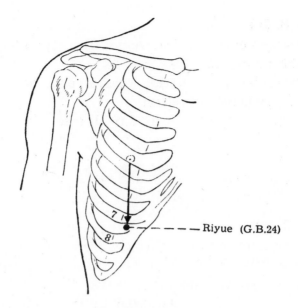

Fig. 87.

Method: Puncture perpendicularly 0.3-0.5 inch. Moxibustion is applicable.

Regional anatomy

Vasculature: The 11th intercostal artery and vein.

Innervation: The 11th intercostal nerve.

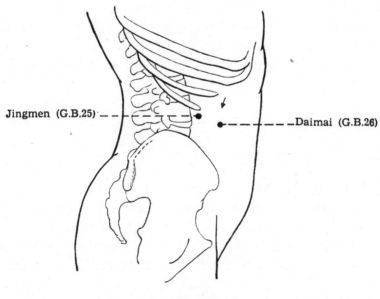

Fig. 88.

26. Daimai (G. B. 26)

Location: Directly below the free end of the 11th rib (Zhangmen, Liv. 13), level with the umbilicus. (See Fig. 88.)

Indications: Irregular menstruation, leukorrhea, hernia, pain in the lower back and hypochondriac region.

Method: Puncture perpendicularly 0.5-1.0 inch. Moxibustion is applicable.

Regional anatomy

Vasculature: The subcostal artery and vein.

Innervation: The subcostal nerve.

27. Wushu (G. B. 27)

Location: In the lateral side of the abdomen, in front of the anterior superior iliac spine, 3 *cun* below the level of the umbilicus.

Indications: Leukorrhea, pain in the lower back and hip joint, hernia.

Method: Puncture perpendicularly 0.5-1.0 inch. Moxibustion is applicable.

Regional anatomy

Vasculature: The superficial and deep circumflex iliac arteries and veins.

Innervation: The iliohypogastric nerve.

28. Weidao (G. B. 28)

Location: Anterior and inferior to the anterior superior iliac spine, 0.5 *cun* anterior and inferior to Wushu (G.B. 27).

Indications: Pain in the lower back and hip joint, leukorrhea, lower abdominal pain, prolapse of uterus.

Method: Puncture perpendicularly 0.5-1.0 inch. Moxibustion is applicable.

Regional anatomy

Vasculature: The superficial and deep circumflex iliac arteries and veins.

Innervation: The ilioinguinal nerve.

29. Femur-Juliao (G. B. 29)

Location: Midway between the anterosuperior iliac spine and the great trochanter. Locate this point in lateral recumbent position.

Indications: Pain in the back and lower extremities, paralysis.

Method: Puncture perpendicularly 0.5-1.0 inch. Moxibustion is applicable.

Regional anatomy

Vasculature: The branches of the superficial circumflex iliac artery and vein, the ascending branches of the lateral circumflex femoral artery and vein.

Innervation: The lateral femoral cutaneous nerve.

30. Huantiao (G. B. 30)

Location: At the junction of the middle and lateral third of the distance between the great trochanter and the hiatus of the sacrum (Yaoshu, Du 2). When locating the point, put the patient in lateral recumbent position with the thigh flexed. (See Fig. 89.)

Indications: Pain in the lower back and hip region, muscular atrophy, motor impairment, pain and weakness of the lower extremities, hemiplegia.

Method: Puncture perpendicularly 1.5-2.5 inches. Moxibustion is applicable.

Regional anatomy

Vasculature: Medially, the inferior gluteal artery and vein.

Innervation: The inferior cluneal cutaneous nerve, the inferior gluteal nerve; deeper, the sciatic nerve.

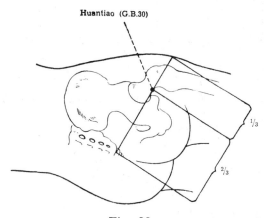

Huantiao (G.B.30)

Fig. 89.

31. Fengshi (G. B. 31)

Location: On the midline of the lateral aspect of the thigh, 7 *cun* above the transverse politeal crease. When the patient is standing erect with the hands close to the sides, the point is where the tip of the middle finger touches. (See Fig. 90.)

Indications: Hemiplegia, muscular atrophy, motor impairment and pain of the lower extremities, general pruritus.

Method: Puncture perpendicularly 0.7-1.2 inches. Moxibustion is applicable.

Regional anatomy

Vasculature: The muscular branches of the lateral circumflex femoral artery and vein.

Innervation: The lateral femoral cutaneous nerve, the muscular branch of the femoral nerve.

Note: In the lateral aspect of the thigh, the distance from the great trochanter to the level of the transverse popliteal crease is measured as 19 *cun*.

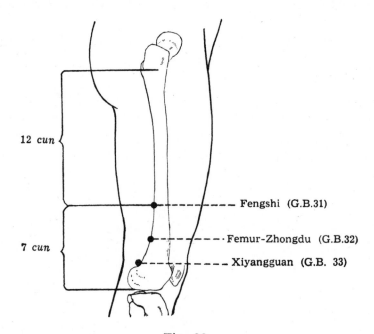

Fig. 90.

32. Femur-Zhongdu (G. B. 32)

Location: In the lateral aspect of the thigh, 5 *cun* above the transverse popliteal crease, between m. vastus lateralis and m. biceps femoris. (See Fig. 90.)

Indications: Muscular atrophy, motor impairment, numbness and pain and weakness of the lower extremities, hemiplegia.

Method: Puncture perpendicularly 0.5-0.8 inch. Moxibustion is applicable.

Regional anatomy   See Fengshi (G.B. 31).

33. Xiyangguan (G. B. 33)

Location: When the knee is flexed, the point is 3 *cun* above Yanglingquan (G.B. 34), lateral to the knee joint, in the depression between the tendon of m. biceps femoris and the femur. (See Fig. 90.)

Indications: Pain and swelling of the knee, contracture of the tendons in popliteal fossa, numbness of the leg.

Method: Puncture perpendicularly 0.5 inch.

Regional anatomy

Vasculature: The superior lateral genicular artery and vein.

Innervation: The terminal branch of the lateral femoral cutaneous nerve.

34. Yanglingquan (He-Sea Point, G. B. 34)

Location: In the depression anterior and inferior to the head of the fibula. (See Fig. 91.)

Indications: Hemiplegia, muscular atrophy, motor impairment, numbness and pain of the lower extremities, pain and swelling of the knee, pain in the hypochondriac and costal region, bitter taste in mouth, vomiting.

Method: Puncture perpendicularly 0.8-1.2 inches. Moxibustion is applicable.

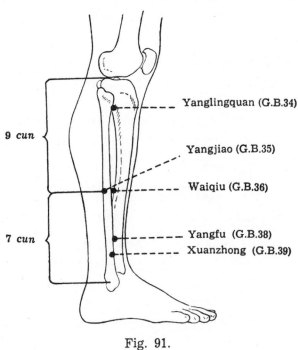

Fig. 91.

Regional anatomy

Vasculature: The inferior lateral genicular artery and vein.

Innervation: Just where the common peroneal nerve bifurcates into the superficial and deep peroneal nerves.

Note: This is one of the Eight Influential Points dominating the tendons.

35. Yangjiao (G. B. 35)

Location: 7 *cun* above the tip of the external malleolus, on the posterior border of the fibula, within the distance between the tip of the external malleolus and Yanglingquan (G.B. 34), level with Waiqiu (G.B. 36) and Feiyang (U.B. 58). (See Fig. 91.)

Indications: Fullness of the chest and hypochondriac region, knee pain, muscular atrophy and weakness of the foot.

Method: Puncture perpendicularly 0.5-0.8 inch. Moxibustion is applicable.

Regional anatomy

Vasculature: The branches of the peroneal artery and vein.

Innervation: The lateral sural cutaneous nerve.

Notes:

(1) This is the Xi-Cleft Point of the Yangwei Channel.

(2) In the lateral aspect of the leg, the distance from the midpoint of the knee to the level of the tip of the external malleolus is measured as 16 *cun*.

36. Waiqiu (Xi-Cleft Point, G. B. 36)

Location: 7 *cun* above the tip of the external malleolus, on the anterior border of the fibula. (See Fig. 91.)

Indications: Pain in the neck, chest and hypochondriac region.

Method: Puncture perpendicularly 0.5-0.8 inch. Moxibustion is applicable.

Regional anatomy

Vasculature: The branches of the anterior tibial artery and vein.

Innervation: The superficial peroneal nerve.

37. Guangming (Luo-Connecting Point, G. B. 37)

Location: 5 *cun* directly above the tip of the external malleolus, on the anterior border of the fibula.

Indications: Pain in the knee, muscular atrophy, motor impairment and pain of the lower extremities, ophthalmalgia, night blindness, distending pain of the breast.

Method: Puncture perpendicularly 0.7-1.0 inch. Moxibustion is applicable.

Regional anatomy

Vasculature: The branches of the anterior tibial artery and vein.

Innervation: The superficial peroneal nerve.

38. Yangfu (Jing-River Point, G. B. 38)

Location: 4 *cun* above and slightly anterior to the tip of the external malleolus, on the anterior border of the fibula, between m. extensor digitorum longus and m. peronaeus brevis. (See Fig. 91.)

Indications: One-sided headache, pain in the outer canthus, supraclavicular fossa and axillary region, scrofula, pain in the chest, hypochondriac region and lateral aspect of the lower extremities, malaria.

Method: Puncture perpendicularly 0.5-0.7 inch. Moxibustion is applicable.

Regional anatomy   See Guangming (G.B. 37).

39. Xuanzhong (Also known as Juegu, G.B. 39)

Location: 3 *cun* above the tip of the external malleolus, in the depression between the posterior border of the fibula and the tendons of m. peronaeus longus and brevis. (See Fig. 91.)

Indications: Hemiplegia, neck rigidity, fullness of the chest, distension of the abdomen, pain in the hypochondriac region, knee and leg, beriberi.

Method: Puncture perpendicularly 0.4-0.5 inch. Moxibustion is applicable.

Regional anatomy   See Guangming (G.B. 37).

Note: This is one of the Eight Influential Points dominating the marrow.

40. Qiuxu (Yuan-Source Point, G.B. 40)

Location: Anterior and inferior to the external malleolus, in the depression on the lateral side of the tendon of m. extensor digitorum longus. (See Fig. 92.)

Indications: Pain in the neck, chest and hypochondriac region, swelling of the axillary region, vomiting, acid regurgitation, muscular atrophy, motor impairment, weakness and pain of the lower extremities, pain and swelling in the lateral aspect of the ankle joint, malaria.

Method: Puncture perpendicularly 0.3-0.5 inch. Moxibustion is applicable.

Regional anatomy

Vasculature: The branch of the anterolateral malleolar artery.

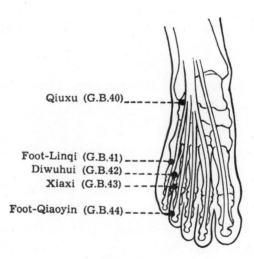

Qiuxu (G.B.40)

Foot-Linqi (G.B.41)
Diwuhui (G.B.42)
Xiaxi (G.B.43)

Foot-Qiaoyin (G.B.44)

Fig. 92.

Innervation: The branches of the intermediate dorsal cutaneous nerve and superficial peroneal nerve.

41. Foot-Linqi (Shu-Stream Point, G. B. 41)

Location: In the depression distal to the junction of the 4th and 5th metatarsal bones, on the lateral side of the tendon of m. extensor digiti minimi of foot. (See Fig. 92.)

Indications: Pain in the outer canthus, blurring of vision, pain in the costal and hypochondriac region, pain and swelling of the dorsum of foot, distending pain of the breast, malaria.

Method: Puncture perpendicularly 0.3-0.5 inch. Moxibustion is applicable.

Regional anatomy

Vasculature: The dorsal arterial and venous network of foot, the 4th dorsal metatarsal artery and vein.

Innervation: The branch of the intermediate dorsal cutaneous nerve of the foot.

Note: This is one of the Eight Confluent Points communicating with the Dai Channel.

42. Diwuhui (G. B. 42)

Location: Between the 4th and 5th metatarsal bones, on the medial side of the tendon of m. extensor digiti minimi of foot. (See Fig. 92.)

Indications: Red and painful eyes, swelling of the axillary region, redness and swelling of the dorsum of foot, distending pain of the breast.

Method: Puncture perpendicularly 0.3-0.4 inch.

Regional anatomy See Foot-Linqi (G.B. 41).

43. Xiaxi (Ying-Spring Point, G. B. 43)

Location: Between the 4th and 5th toes, proximal to the margin of the web. (See Fig. 92.)

Indications: Pain in the outer canthus, blurring of vision, tinnitus, pain in the cheek, submandibular region and costal and hypochondriac region, febrile diseases.

Method: Puncture obliquely upward 0.2-0.3 inch. Moxibustion is applicable.

Regional anatomy

Vasculature: The dorsal digital artery and vein.

. Innervation: The dorsal digital nerve.

44. Foot-Qiaoyin (Jing-Well Point, G. B. 44)

Location: On the lateral side of the 4th toe, about 0.1 *cun* posterior to the corner of the nail. (See Fig. 92.)

Indications: One-sided headache, ophthalmalgia, deafness, pain in the hypochondriac region, dream-disturbed sleep, febrile diseases.

Method: Puncture obliquely 0.1-0.2 inch. Moxibustion is applicable.

Regional anatomy

Vasculature: The arterial and venous network formed by the dorsal digital artery and vein and plantar digital artery and vein.

Innervation: The dorsal digital nerve.

XII. THE LIVER CHANNEL OF FOOT-JUEYIN

The Liver Channel of Foot-Jueyin starts from the dorsal hairy region of the great toe (Dadun, Liv. 1) (1). Running upward along the dorsum of foot (2), passing through Zhongfeng (Liv. 4), 1 *cun* in front of the medial malleolus (3), it ascends to an area 8 *cun* above the medial malleolus, where it runs across and behind the Spleen Channel of Foot-Taiyin (4). Then it runs further upward to the medial side of the knee (5) along the medial aspect of the thigh (6) to the pubic hairy region (7), where it curves around the external genitalia (8) and goes up to the lower abdomen (9). It then runs upward and curves round the stomach to enter the liver, its pertaining organ, and connect with the gall bladder (10). From there it continues to ascend, passing through the diaphragm (11), and branching out in the costal and hypochondriac region (12). Then it ascends along the posterior aspect of the throat (13) to the nasopharynx (14) and connects with the "eye system" (15). Running further upward, it emerges from the forehead (16) and meets the Du Channel at the vertex (17).

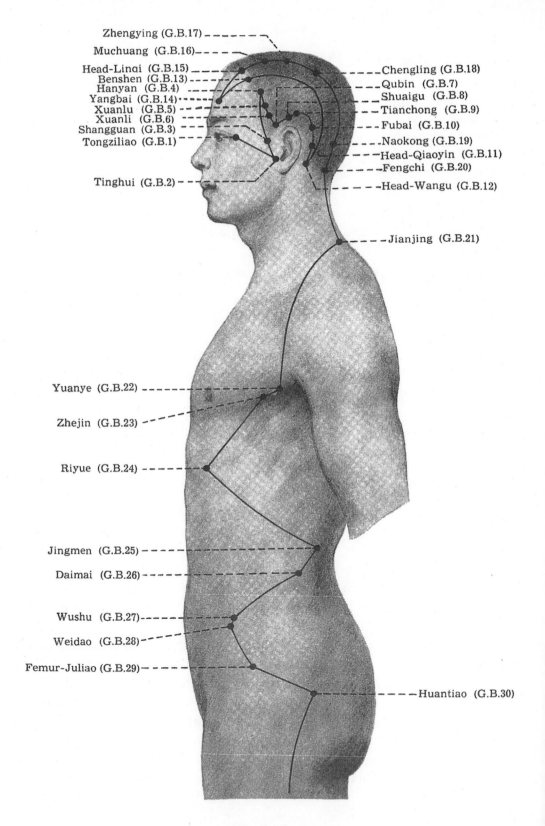

Zhengying (G.B.17)

Muchuang (G.B.16)

Head-Linai (G.B.15)
Benshen (G.B.13)
Hanyan (G.B.4)
Yangbai (G.B.14)
Xuanlu (G.B.5)
Xuanli (G.B.6)
Shangguan (G.B.3)
Tongziliao (G.B.1)

Tinghui (G.B.2)

Chengling (G.B.18)
Qubin (G.B.7)
Shuaigu (G.B.8)
Tianchong (G.B.9)
Fubai (G.B.10)
Naokong (G.B.19)
Head-Qiaoyin (G.B.11)
Fengchi (G.B.20)
Head-Wangu (G.B.12)

Jianjing (G.B.21)

Yuanye (G.B.22)

Zhejin (G.B.23)

Riyue (G.B.24)

Jingmen (G.B.25)

Daimai (G.B.26)

Wushu (G.B.27)

Weidao (G.B.28)

Femur-Juliao (G.B.29)

Huantiao (G.B.30)

Fig. 93a. The Gall bladder Channel of Foot-Shaoyang.

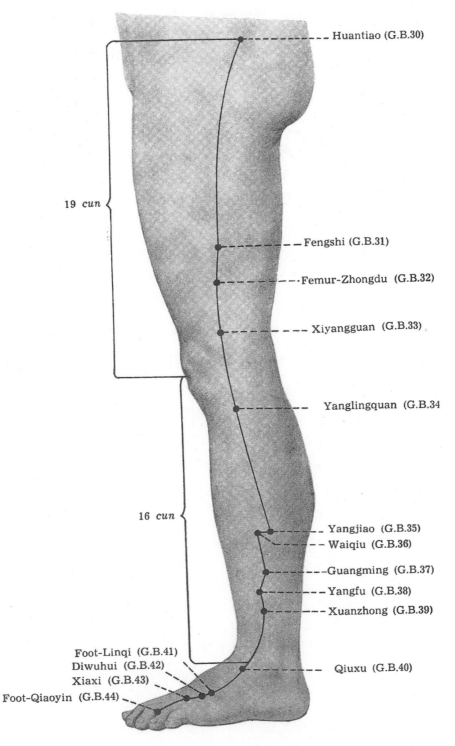

Huantiao (G.B.30)

19 *cun*

Fengshi (G.B.31)

Femur-Zhongdu (G.B.32)

Xiyangguan (G.B.33)

Yanglingquan (G.B.34

16 *cun*

Yangjiao (G.B.35)

Waiqiu (G.B.36)

Guangming (G.B.37)

Yangfu (G.B.38)

Xuanzhong (G.B.39)

Foot-Linqi (G.B.41)

Diwuhui (G.B.42)

Xiaxi (G.B.43)

Foot-Qiaoyin (G.B.44)

Qiuxu (G.B.40)

Fig. 93b. The Gall bladder Channel of Foot-Shaoyang.

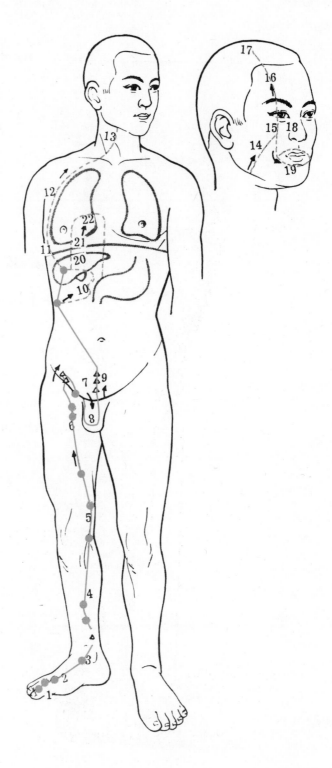

Fig. 94.   The Liver Channel of Foot-Jueyin.

The branch which arises from the "eye system" runs downward into the cheek (18) and curves around the inner surface of the lips (19).

The branch arising from the liver (20) passes through the diaphragm (21), flows into the lung and links with the Lung Channel of Hand-Taiyin (22). (See Fig. 94.)

The points of this channel are 14 in number and are described as follows:

1. Dadun (Jing-Well Point, Liv. 1)

Location: On the lateral side of the dorsum of the terminal phalanx of the great toe, between the lateral corner of the nail and interphalangeal joint. (See Fig. 95.)

Indications: Prolapse of uterus, hernia, uterine bleeding, enuresis.

Method: Puncture obliquely 0.1-0.2 inch. Moxibustion is applicable.

Regional anatomy

Vasculature: The dorsal digital artery and vein.

Innervation: The dorsal digital nerve derived from the deep peroneal nerve.

2. Xingjian (Ying-Spring Point, Liv. 2)

Location: Between the 1st and 2nd toe, proximal to the margin of the web. (See Fig. 95.)

Indications: Menorrhagia, urethralgia, enuresis, retention of urine, hernia, deviation of mouth, redness, swelling and pain of the eye, pain in the hypochondriac region, headache, blurring of vision, epilepsy, convulsion, insomnia.

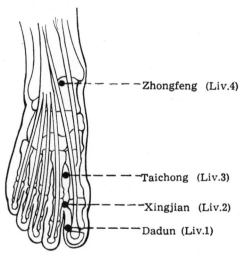

Zhongfeng (Liv.4)

Taichong (Liv.3)

Xingjian (Liv.2)

Dadun (Liv.1)

Fig. 95.

Method: Puncture obliquely 0.5 inch. Moxibustion is applicable.
Regional anatomy

Vasculature: The dorsal venous network of the foot and the 1st dorsal digital artery and vein.

Innervation: The site where the dorsal digital nerves split from the deep peroneal nerve.

3.　Taichong (Shu-Stream and Yuan-Source Point, Liv. 3)

Location: In the depression distal to the junction of the 1st and 2nd metatarsal bones. (See Fig. 95.)

Indications: Uterine bleeding, hernia, enuresis, retention of urine, pain in the anterior aspect of the medial malleolus, fullness in the hypochondriac region, deviation of mouth, infantile convulsion, epilepsy, headache, vertigo, insomnia.

Method: Puncture perpendicularly 0.5 inch. Moxibustion is applicable.
Regional anatomy

Vasculature: The dorsal venous network of the foot, the 1st dorsal metatarsal artery.

Innervation: The branch of the deep peroneal nerve.

4.　Zhongfeng (Jing-River Point, Liv. 4)

Location: 1 *cun* anterior to the medial malleolus, midway between Shangqiu (Sp. 5) and Jiexi (St. 41), in the depression on the medial side of the tendon of m. tibialis anterior. (See Fig. 95.)

Indications: Pain in the external genitalia, seminal emission, retention of urine, hernia.

Method: Puncture perpendicularly 0.3-0.5 inch. Moxibustion is applicable.

Regional anatomy

Vasculature: The dorsal venous network of foot and the anterior medial malleolar artery.

Innervation: The branch of the medial dorsal cutaneous nerve of the foot and the saphenous nerve.

5.　Ligou (Luo Connecting Point, Liv. 5)

Location: 5 *cun* above the tip of the medial malleolus, on the medial aspect and near the medial border of the tibia. (See Fig. 96.)

Indications: Irregular menstruation, dysuria, hernia, leg pain.

Method: Puncture 0.3-0.5 inch posteriorly horizontally along the skin. Moxibustion is applicable.

Regional anatomy

Vasculature: Posteriorly, the great saphenous vein.

Innervation: The branch of the saphenous nerve.

Note: In the medial aspect of the leg, the distance from the tip of the medial malleolus to Yinlingquan (Sp. 9) is measured as 13 *cun*.

6. Foot-Zhongdu (Xi-Cleft Point, Liv. 6)

Location: 7 *cun* above the tip of the medial malleolus, or 2 *cun* above Ligou (Liv. 5), on the medial aspect and near the medial border of the tibia. (See Fig. 96.)

Indications: Uterine bleeding, hernia.

Method: Puncture 0.3-0.5 inch horizontally along the skin. Moxibustion is applicable.

Regional anatomy

Vasculature: The great saphenous vein.

Innervation: The branch of the saphenous nerve.

7. Xiguan (Liv. 7)

Location: Posterior and inferior to the medial condyle of the tibia, in the upper portion of the medial head of m. gastrocnemius, 1 *cun* posterior to Yinlingquan (Sp. 9). (See Fig. 96.)

Indication: Pain in the medial aspect of the knee.

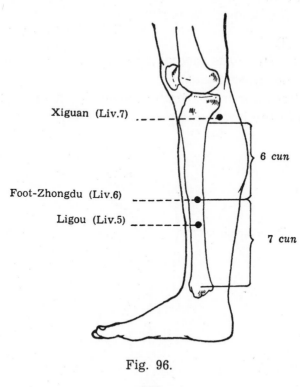

Fig. 96.

Method: Puncture perpendicularly 0.4-0.6 inch. Moxibustion is applicable.

Regional anatomy

Vasculature: Deeper, the posterior tibial artery.

Innervation: The branch of the medial sural cutaneous nerve; deeper, the tibial nerve.

8. Ququan (He-Sea Point, Liv. 8)

Location: On the medial side of the knee joint. When the knee is flexed, the point is above the medial end of the transverse popliteal crease, posterior to the medial condyle of the tibia, on the anterior border of the insertion of m. semimembranosus and m. semitendinosus. (See Fig. 97.)

Indications: Prolapse of uterus, lower abdominal pain, dysuria, pruritus vulvae, mania, seminal emission, pain in the external genitalia, knee and medial aspect of the thigh.

Method: Puncture perpendicularly 0.5-0.8 inch. Moxibustion is applicable.

Regional anatomy

Vasculature: Anteriorly, the great saphenous vein, on the pathway of the genu suprema artery.

Innervation: The saphenous nerve.

9. Yinbao (Liv. 9)

Location: 4 *cun* above the medial epicondyle of the femur, between m. vastus medialis and m. sartorius.

Indications: Irregular menstruation, dysuria, pain in the lumbosacral region referring to the lower abdomen.

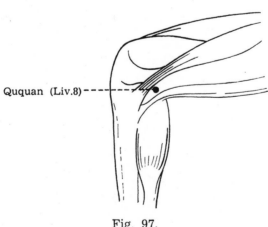

Fig. 97.

Method: Puncture perpendicularly 0.6-0.7 inch. Moxibustions is applicable.

Regional anatomy

Vasculature: Deeper, on the lateral side, the femoral artery and vein, the superficial branch of the medial circumflex femoral artery.

Innervation: The anterior femoral cutaneous nerve, on the pathway of the anterior branch of the obturator nerve.

Note: In the medial aspect of the thigh, the distance from the medial epicondyle of the femur to the level of the upper border of symphysis pubis is measured as 18 *cun*.

10. Femur-Wuli (Liv. 10)

Location: 3 *cun* below Qichong (St. 30), on the lateral border of m. abductor longus.

Indications: Lower abdominal distension, retention of urine.

Method: Puncture perpendicularly 0.5-1.0 inch. Moxibustion is applicable.

Regional anatomy

Vasculature: The superficial branches of the medial circumflex femoral artery and vein.

Innervation: The genitofemoral nerve, the anterior femoral cutaneous nerve; deeper, the anterior branch of the obturator· nerve.

11. Yinlian (Liv. 11)

Location: 2 cun below Qichong (St. 30), on the lateral border of m. abductor longus.

Indications: Irregular menstruation, pain in the thigh and leg.

Method: Puncture perpendicularly 0.5-1.0 inch. Moxibustion is applicable.

Regional anatomy

Vasculature: The branches of the medial circumflex femoral artery and vein.

Innervation: The genitofemoral nerve, the branch of the medial femoral cutaneous nerve; deeper, the anterior branch of the obturator nerve.

12. Jimai (Liv. 12)

Location: Inferior and lateral to the pubic spine, 2.5 *cun* lateral to the Ren Channel, at the inguinal groove lateral and inferior to Qichong (St. 30).

Indications: Pain in the external genitalia, hernia.

Method: Apply a moxa stick for 3-5 minutes.

Regional anatomy

Vasculature: The branches of the external pudendal artery and vein, the pubic branches of the inferior epigastric artery and vein; laterally, the femoral vein.

Innervation: The ilioinguinal nerve; deeper, in the inferior aspect, the anterior branch of the obturator nerve.

13. Zhangmen (Front-Mu Point of the spleen, Liv. 13)

Location: On the lateral side of the abdomen, below the free end of the 11th floating rib. (See Fig. 98.)

Indications: Vomiting, abdominal distension, diarrhea, indigestion, pain in the dorso-lumbar, hypochondriac and costal regions.

Method: Puncture perpendicularly 0.8-1.0 inch. Moxibustion is applicable.

Regional anatomy

Vasculature: The terminal branch of the 10th intercostal artery.

Innervation: Slightly inferiorly, the 10th intercostal nerve.

Note: This is one of the Eight Influential Points dominating the *zang* organs.

14. Qimen (Front-Mu Point of the liver, Liv. 14)

Location: On the mammillary line, two ribs below the nipple, in the 6th intercostal space. (See Fig. 98.)

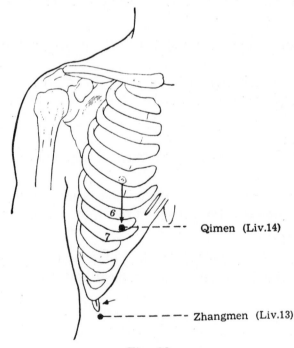

Fig. 98.

Indications: Pain in the chest and hypochondriac region, abdominal distension, fullness of the chest, vomiting, hiccup.

Method: Puncture obliquely 0.3 inch. Moxibustion is applicable.

Regional anatomy

Vasculature: The 6th intercostal artery and vein.

Innervation: The 6th intercostal nerve.

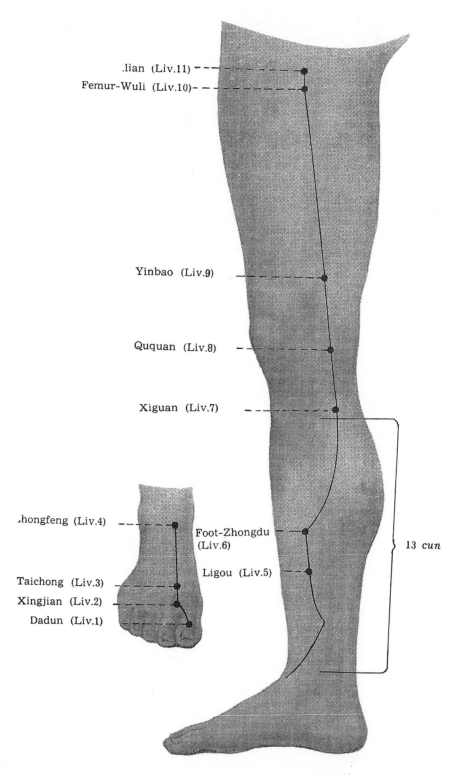

.lian (Liv.11)

Femur-Wuli (Liv.10)

Yinbao (Liv.9)

Ququan (Liv.8)

Xiguan (Liv.7)

.hongfeng (Liv.4)

Foot-Zhongdu (Liv.6)

Ligou (Liv.5)

Taichong (Liv.3)

Xingjian (Liv.2)

Dadun (Liv.1)

13 *cun*

Fig. 99a. The Liver Channel of Foot-Jueyin.

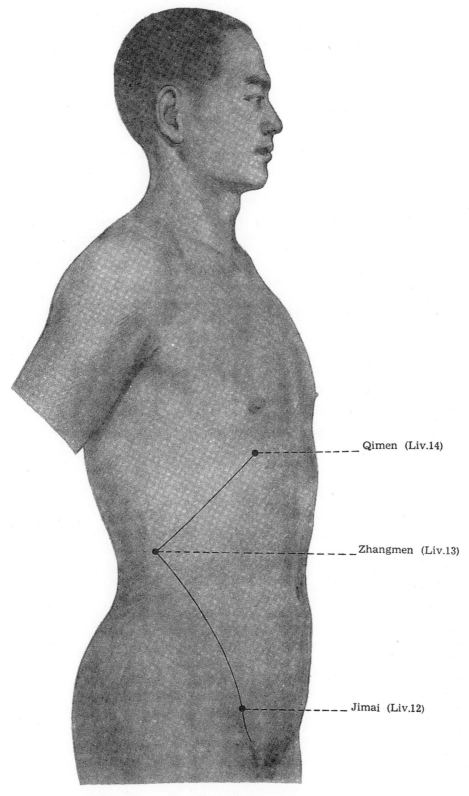

Qimen (Liv.14)

Zhangmen (Liv.13)

Jimai (Liv.12)

Fig. 99b. The Liver Channel of Foot-Jueyin.

CHAPTER III

THE EIGHT EXTRA CHANNELS AND THEIR POINTS
(APPENDIX: EXTRAORDINARY POINTS)

I. THE DU CHANNEL

The Du Channel originates from the inside of the lower abdomen. Descending, it emerges at the perineum (1). Then it ascends posteriorly along the interior of the spinal column (2) to Fengfu (Du 16) at the nape, where it enters the brain (3). It further ascends to the vertex (4) and winds along the forehead to the columella of the nose (5). (See Fig. 100.)

There are 28 points in this channel, described as follows:

1. Changqiang (Luo-Connecting Poin, Du 1)

Location: Midway between the tip of the coccyx and the anus. Locate the point in prone position. (See Fig. 101, 102.)

Indications: Hemafecia, diarrhea, constipation, hemorrhoids, prolapse of rectum, pain in the lower back.

Method: Puncture perpendicularly 0.5-1.0 inch. Moxibustion is applicable.

Regional anatomy

Vasculature: The branches of the inferior hemorrhoid artery and vein.

Innervation: The posterior ramus of the coccygeal nerve, the hemorrhoid nerve.

2. Yaoshu (Du 2)

Location: In the hiatus of the sacrum.

Indications: Irregular menstruation, pain and stiffness of the lower back, epilepsy, hemorrhoids, muscular atrophy, motor impairment and numbness and pain of the lower extremities.

Method: Puncture obliquely upward 0.5 inch. Moxibustion is applicable.

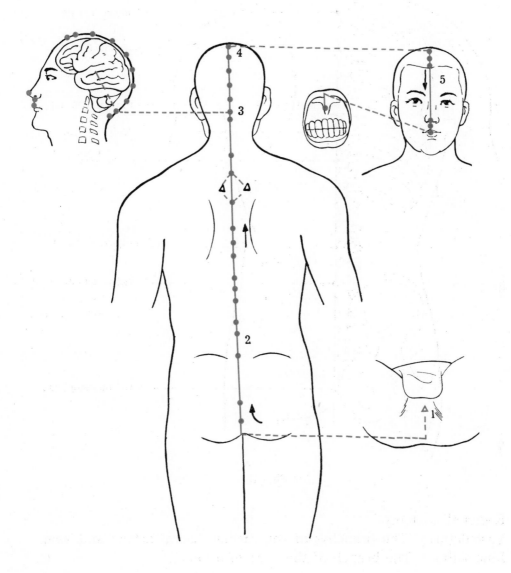

Fig. 100. The Du Channel.

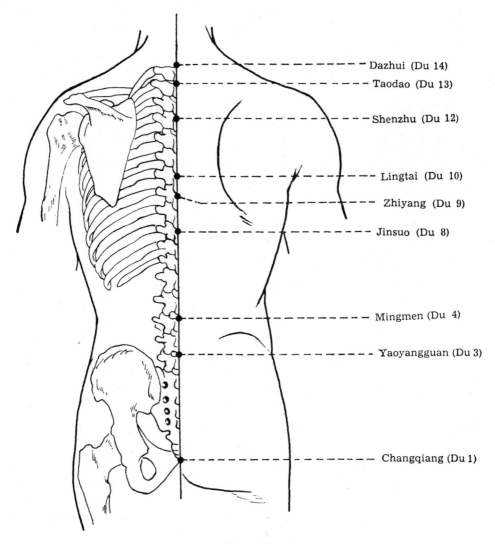

Fig. 101.

Regional anatomy

Vasculature: The branches of the median sacral artery and vein.

Innervation: The branch of the coccygeal nerve.

3. Yaoyangguan (Du 3)

Location: Below the spinous process of the 4th lumbar vertebra. (See Fig. 101, 102.)

Indications: Pain in the lumbosacral region, muscular atrophy, motor impairment and numbness and pain of the lower extremities, irregular menstruation, seminal emission, impotence.

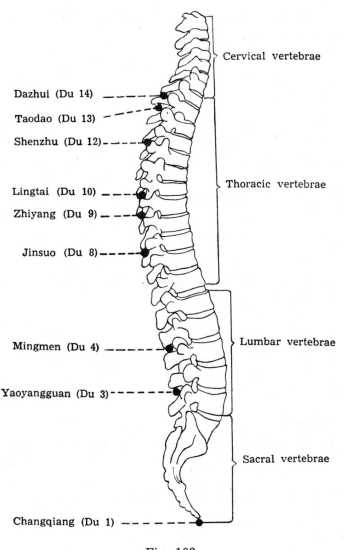

Dazhui (Du 14)

Taodao (Du 13)

Shenzhu (Du 12)

Lingtai (Du 10)

Zhiyang (Du 9)

Jinsuo (Du 8)

Mingmen (Du 4)

Yaoyangguan (Du 3)

Changqiang (Du 1)

Cervical vertebrae

Thoracic vertebrae

Lumbar vertebrae

Sacral vertebrae

Fig. 102.

Method: Puncture perpendicularly 0.5-1.0 inch. Moxibustion is applicable.

Regional anatomy

Vasculature: The posterior branch of the lumbar artery.

Innervation: The medial branch of the posterior ramus of the lumbar nerve.

4. Mingmen (Du 4)

Location: Below the spinous process of the 2nd lumbar vertebra. (See Fig. 101, 102.)

Indications: Stiffness of the back, lumbago, leukorrhea, impotence, seminal emission, diarrhea.

Method: Puncture perpendicularly 0.5-1.0 inch. Moxibustion is applicable.

Regional anatomy   See Yaoyangguan (Du 3).

5. Xuanshu (Du 5)

Location: Below the spinous process of the 1st lumbar vertebra.

Indications: Diarrhea with undigested food, pain and stiffness of the lower back.

Method: Puncture the point perpendicularly 0.5-1.0 inch. Moxibustion is applicable.

Regional anatomy   See Yaoyangguan (Du 3).

6. Jizhong (Du 6)

Location: Below the spinous process of the 11th thoracic vertebra.

Indications: Jaundice, diarrhea, epilepsy.

Method: Puncture perpendicularly 0.5-1.0 inch.

Regional anatomy

Vasculature: The posterior branch of the 11th intercostal artery.

Innervation: The medial branch of the posterior ramus of the 11th thoracic nerve.

7. Zhongshu (Du 7)

Location: Below the spinous process of the 10th thoracic vertebra.

Indications: Pain in the epigastric region, low back pain, stiffness of the back.

Method: Puncture perpendicularly 0.5-1.0 inch. Moxibustion is applicable.

Regional anatomy

Vasculature: The posterior branch of the 10th intercostal artery.

Innervation: The medial branch of the posterior ramus of the 10th thoracic nerve.

8. Jinsuo (Du 8)

Location: Below the spinous process of the 9th thoracic vertebra. (See Fig. 101, 102.)

Indications: Epilepsy, stiffness of the back, gastric pain.

Method: Puncture perpendicularly 0.5-1.0 inch. Moxibustion is applicable.

Regional anatomy

Vasculature: The posterior branch of the 9th intercostal artery.

Innervation: The medial branch of the posterior ramus of the 9th thoracic nerve.

9. Zhiyang (Du 9)

Location: Below the spinous process of the 7th thoracic vertebra, approximately at the level of the inferior angle of the scapula. (See Fig. 101, 102.)

Indications: Cough, asthma, jaundice, pain in the chest and back, stiffness of the spinal column.

Method: Puncture obliquely upward 0.5-1.0 inch. Moxibustion is applicable.

Regional anatomy

Vasculature: The posterior branch of the 7th intercostal artery.

Innervation: The medial branch of the posterior ramus of the 7th thoracic nerve.

10. Lingtai (Du 10)

Location: Below the spinous process of the 6th thoracic vertebra. (See Fig. 101, 102.)

Indications: Cough, asthma, back pain, neck rigidity, furuncles.

Method: Puncture perpendicularly 0.5-1.0 inch. Moxibustion is applicable.

Regional anatomy

Vasculature: The posterior branch of the 6th intercostal artery.

Innervation: The medial branch of the posterior ramus of the 6th thoracic nerve.

11. Shendao (Du 11)

Location: Below the spinous process of the 5th thoracic vertebra.

Indications: Poor memory, anxiety, palpitation, cardiac pain, pain and stiffness of the back, cough.

Method: Puncture perpendicularly 0.5-1.0 inch. Moxibustion is applicable.

Regional anatomy

Vasculature: The posterior branch of the 5th intercostal artery.

Innervation: The medial branch of the posterior ramus of the 5th thoracic nerve.

12. Shenzhu (Du 12)

Location: Below the spinous process of the 3rd thoracic vertebra. (See Fig. 101, 102.)

Indications: Cough, asthma, epilepsy, pain and stiffness of the lower back, furuncles.

Method: Puncture perpendicularly 0.5-1.0 inch. Moxibustion is applicable.

Regional anatomy

Vasculature: The posterior branch of the 3rd intercostal artery.

Innervation: The medial branch of the posterior ramus of the 3rd thoracic nerve.

13. Taodao (Du 13)

Location: Below the spinous process of the 1st thoracic vertebra. (See Fig. 101, 102.)

Indications: Stiffness of the back, headache, malaria, febrile diseases.

Method: Puncture perpendicularly 0.5-1.0 inch. Moxibustion is applicable.

Regional anatomy

Vasculature: The posterior branch of the 1st intercostal artery.

Innervation: The medial branch of the posterior ramus of the 1st thoracic nerve.

14. Dazhui (Du 14)

Location: Between the spinous processes of the 7th cervical vertebra and the 1st thoracic vertebra, approximately at the level of the shoulder. (See Fig. 101, 102.)

Indications: Febrile diseases, malaria, common cold, afternoon fever, cough, asthma, neck rigidity, stiffness of the back, epilepsy.

Method: Puncture perpendicularly 0.5-1.0 inch. Frequent moxibustion or moxibustion for a longer period is advisable.

Regional anatomy

Vasculature: The branch of the transverse cervical artery.

Innervation: The posterior ramus of the 8th cervical nerve and the medial branch of the posterior ramus of the 1st thoracic nerve.

15. Yamen (Du 15)

Location: At the midpoint of the nape, 0.5 *cun* below Fengfu (Du 16), in the depression 0.5 *cun* within the hairline. (See Fig. 103.)

Indications: Mental disorders, epilepsy, sudden hoarseness of voice, stiffness of tongue and post-apoplexy aphasia.

Method: Puncture perpendicularly 0.5-1.0 inch. Deep puncture is not advisable.

Regional anatomy

Vasculature: The branches of the occipital artery and vein.

Innervation: The 3rd occipital nerve.

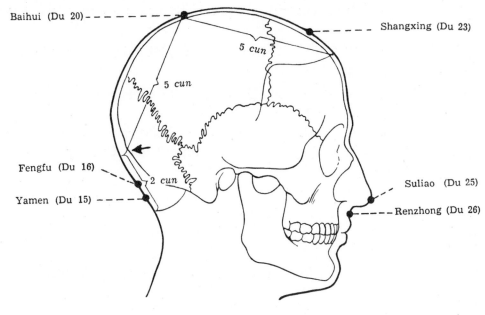

Fig. 103.

Note: The distance from the anterior hairline to the posterior hairline is measured as 12 *cun*.

16. Fengfu (Du 16)

Location: Directly below the external occipital protuberance, in the depression between m. trapezius of both sides. (See Fig. 103.)

Indications: Headache, neck rigidity, blurring of vision, epistaxis, sore throat, post-apoplexy aphasia, mental disorders, hemiplegia.

Method: Puncture perpendicularly 0.5-1.0 inch. Deep puncture is not advisable.

Regional anatomy

Vasculature: The branch of the occipital artery.

Innervation: The branches of the 3rd occipital nerve and the great occipital nerve.

17. Naohu (Du 17)

Location: 1.5 *cun* above Fengfu (Du 16), superior to the external occipital protuberance.

Indications: Epilepsy, dizziness, pain and stiffness of the neck.

Method: Puncture 0.3-0.5 inch horizontally along the skin. Moxibustion is applicable.

Regional anatomy

Vasculature: The branches of the occipital arteries and veins of both sides.

Innervation: The branch of the great occipital nerve.

18. Qiangjian (Du 18)

Location: 1.5 *cun* above Naohu (Du 17), midway between Fengfu (Du 16) and Baihui (Du 20).

Indications: Mania, headache, blurring of vision, neck rigidity.

Method: Puncture 0.3-0.5 inch horizontally along the skin. Moxibustion is applicable.

Regional anatomy See Naohu (Du 17).

19. Houding (Du 19)

Location: 1.5 *cun* above Qiangjian (Du 18).

Indications: Mania, epilepsy, headache, vertigo.

Method: Puncture 0.3-0.5 inch horizontally along the skin. Moxibustion is applicable.

Regional anatomy See Naohu (Du 17).

20. Baihui (Du 20)

Location: 7 *cun* above the posterior hairline, on the midpoint of the line connecting the apexes of the two auricles. (See Fig. 103.)

Indications: Mental disorders, apoplexy, headache, dizziness, tinnitus, blurring of vision, nasal obstruction, prolapse of rectum.

Method: Puncture 0.3-0.5 inch horizontally along the skin. Moxibustion is applicable.

Regional anatomy

Vasculature: The anastomotic network formed by the superficial temporal arteries and veins and the occipital arteries and veins of both sides.

Innervation: The branch of the great occipital nerve.

21. Qianding (Du 21)

Location: 1.5 *cun* anterior to Baihui (Du 20).

Indications: Epilepsy, dizziness, blurring of vision, vertical headache, rhinorrhea.

Method: Puncture 0.3-0.5 inch horizontally along the skin. Moxibustion is applicable.

Regional anatomy

Vasculature: The anastomotic network formed by the right and left superficial temporal arteries and veins.

Innervation: On the communicating site of the branch of the frontal nerve with the branch of the great occipital nerve.

22. Xinhui (Du 22)

Location: 3 *cun* anterior to Baihui (Du 20), 2 *cun* posterior to the anterior hairline.

Indications: Headache, blurring of vision, rhinorrhea.

Method: Puncture 0.3-0.5 inch horizontally along the skin. Moxibustion is applicable.

Regional anatomy

Vasculature: The anastomotic network formed by the superficial temporal artery and vein and the frontal artery and vein.

Innervation: The branch of the frontal nerve.

23. Shangxing (Du 23)

Location: 1 *cun* within the anterior hairline, 4 *cun* anterior to Baihui (Du 20). (See Fig. 103.)

Indications: Headache, ophthalmalgia, rhinorrhea, epistaxis, mental disorders.

Method: Puncture 0.3-0.5 inch posteriorly horizontally along the skin, or prick with three-edged needle to cause bleeding. Moxibustion may be applied.

Regional anatomy

Vasculature: The branches of the frontal artery and vein, the branches of the superficial temporal artery and vein.

Innervation: The branch of the frontal nerve.

24. Shenting (Du 24)

Location: On the midsagittal line of the head, 0.5 *cun* within the anterior hairline.

Indications: Epilepsy, anxiety, palpitation, insomnia, headache, vertigo, rhinorrhea.

Method: Puncture 0.3-0.5 inch horizontally along the skin with the needle directed upward. Moxibustion is applicable.

Regional anatomy

Vasculature: The branches of the frontal artery and vein.

Innervation: The branch of the frontal nerve.

Note: The distance from the anterior hairline to glabella (Yintang, Extra.) is measured as 3 *cun*.

25. Suliao (Du 25)

Location: On the tip of the nose. (See Fig. 103.)

Indications: Loss of consciousness, nasal obstruction, epistaxis, rosacea.

Method: Puncture perpendicularly 0.2-0.3 inch.

Regional anatomy

Vasculature: The lateral nasal branches of the facial artery and vein.
Innervation: The external nasal branch of the anterior ethmoid nerve.

26. Renzhong (Also known as Shuigou, Du 26)

Location: Below the nose, a little above the midpoint of the philtrum. (See Fig. 103.)

Indications: Mental disorders, epilepsy, infantile convulsion, coma, trismus, facial paralysis, swelling of the face, pain and stiffness of the lower back.

Method: Puncture obliquely upward 0.2-0.3 inch.

Regional anatomy

Vasculature: The superior labial artery and vein.

Innervation: The buccal branch of the facial nerve, the branch of the infraorbital nerve.

27. Duiduan (Du 27)

Location: On the median tubercle of the upper lip, at the junction of the philtrum and the upper lip.

Indications: Mental disorders, stiffness of the lip, pain in the gums.

Method: Puncture perpendicularly 0.2-0.3 inch.

Regional anatomy

Vasculature: The superior labial artery and vein.

Innervation: The buccal branch of the facial nerve and the branch of the infraorbital nerve.

28. Mouth-Yinjiao (Du 28)

Location: Between the upper lip and the upper labial gingiva, in the frenulum of the upper lip.

Indications: Mental disorders, rhinorrhea, pain and swelling of the gums.

Method: Puncture obliquely upward 0.1-0.2 inch, or prick with three-edged needle to cause bleeding.

Regional anatomy

Vasculature: The superior labial artery and vein.

Innervation: The branch of the superior alveolar nerve.

II. THE REN CHANNEL

The Ren Channel arises from the lower abdomen and emerges from the perineum (1). It runs anteriorly to the pubic region (2) and ascends along the interior of the abdomen, passing through Guanyuan (Ren 4) and the other points along the front midline (3) to the throat (4). Run-

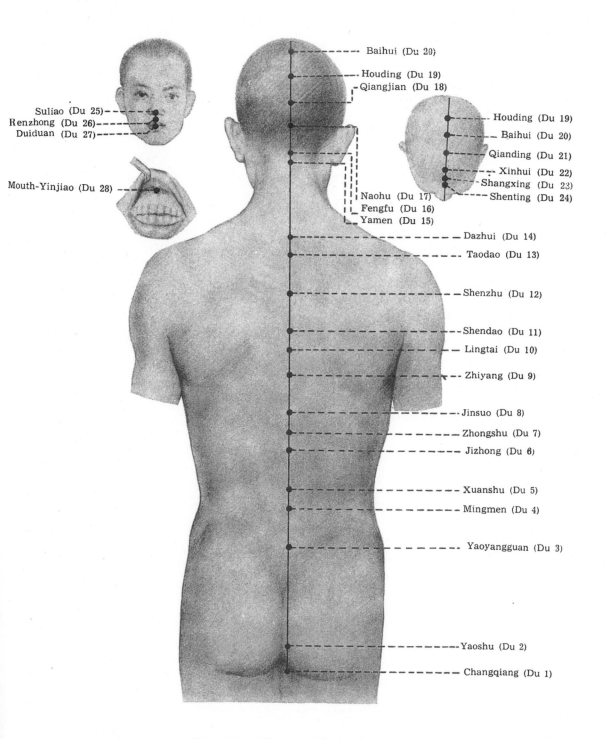

Suliao (Du 25)
Renzhong (Du 26)
Duiduan (Du 27)

Mouth-Yinjiao (Du 28)

Baihui (Du 20)
Houding (Du 19)
Qiangjian (Du 18)

Houding (Du 19)
Baihui (Du 20)
Qianding (Du 21)
Xinhui (Du 22)
Shangxing (Du 23)
Shenting (Du 24)

Naohu (Du 17)
Fengfu (Du 16)
Yamen (Du 15)

Dazhui (Du 14)
Taodao (Du 13)

Shenzhu (Du 12)

Shendao (Du 11)
Lingtai (Du 10)
Zhiyang (Du 9)

Jinsuo (Du 8)
Zhongshu (Du 7)
Jizhong (Du 6)

Xuanshu (Du 5)
Mingmen (Du 4)

Yaoyangguan (Du 3)

Yaoshu (Du 2)
Changqiang (Du 1)

Fig. 104. The Du Channel.

ning further upward, it curves around the lips (5), passes through the cheek (6) and enters the infraorbital region (Chengqi, St. 1) (7). (See Fig. 105.)

The points of this channel are 24 in number, and are described as follows:

1. Huiyin (Ren 1)

Location: In the centre of the perineum. It is between the anus and the scrotum in males and between the anus and the posterior labial commissure in females.

Indications: Pruritus vulvae, irregular menstruation, pain and swelling of the anus, retention of urine, enuresis, seminal emission, mental disorders.

Method: Puncture perpendicularly 0.5-0.8 inch. Moxibustion is applicable.

Regional anatomy

Vasculature: The branches of the perineal artery and vein.

Innervation: The branch of the perineal nerve.

2. Qugu (Ren 2)

Location: On the midline of the abdomen, just above the symphysis pubis.

Indications: Seminal emission, impotence, leukorrhea, retention of urine, hernia.

Method: Puncture perpendicularly 0.3-1.0 inch. Moxibustion is applicable.

Regional anatomy

Vasculature: The branches of the inferior epigastric artery and the obturator artery.

Innervation: The branch of the iliohypogastric nerve.

Note: The distance from the centre of the umbilicus to the superior border of symphsis pubis is measured as 5 *cun*, which serves as a standard for longitudinal measurement on the lower abdomen.

3. Zhongji (Front-Mu Point of the urinary bladder, Ren 3)

Location: On the anterior midline, 4 *cun* below the umbilicus, 1 *cun* above the upper border of symphysis pubis. (See Fig. 106.)

Indications: Seminal emission, enuresis, retention of urine, frequency of micturition, pain in the lower abdomen, irregular menstruation, uterine bleeding, leukorrhea, prolapse of uterus, pain of the external genitalia, pruritus vulvae.

Method: Puncture perpendicularly 0.8 inch. Moxibustion is applicable.

Regional anatomy

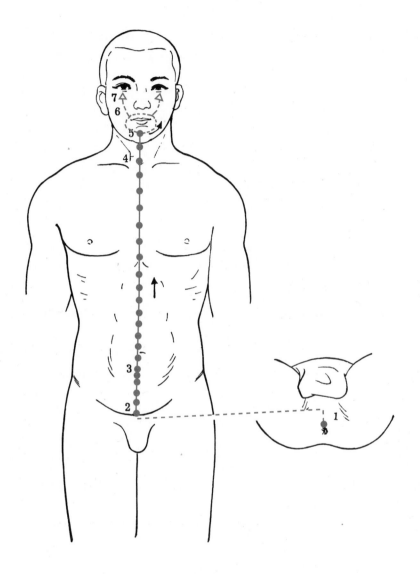

Fig. 105.　The Ren Channel.

Vasculature: The branches of the superficial epigastric and inferior epigastric arteries and veins.

Innervation: The branch of the iliohypogastric nerve.

4. Guanyuan (Front-Mu Point of the small intestine, Ren 4)

Location: On the midline of the abdomen, 3 *cun* below the umbilicus. (See Fig. 106.)

Indications: Seminal emission, enuresis, frequency of micturition, retention of urine, irregular menstruation, dysmenorrhea, amenorrhea, leukorrhea, uterine bleeding, prolapse of uterus, postpartum hemorrhage, hernia, lower abdominal pain, diarrhea, flaccid type of apoplexy.

Method:. Puncture perpendicularly 0.8-1.2 inches. Moxibustion may be applied fairly long and frequently.

Regional anatomy

Vasculature: See Zhongji (Ren 3).

Innervation: The anterior cutaneous nerve of the subcostal nerve.

Note: This is one of the important points for tonification.

5. Shimen (Front-Mu Point of *Sanjiao*, Ren 5)

Location: On the midline of the abdomen, 2 *cun* below the umbilicus. (See Fig. 106.)

Indications: Uterine bleeding, leukorrhea, amenorrhea, postpartum hemorrhage, hernia, abdominal pain, diarrhea, retention of urine, enuresis, edema.

Method: Puncture perpendicularly 0.5-1.0 inch. Moxibustion is applicable.

Regional anatomy

Vasculature: See Zhongji (Ren 3).

Innervation: The anterior cutaneous branch of the 11th intercostal nerve.

Note: Ancient literature claimed that puncturing this point may cause sterility.

6. Qihai (Ren 6)

Location: On the midline of the abdomen, 1.5 *cun* below the umbilicus. (See Fig. 106.)

Indications: Uterine bleeding, leukorrhea, irregular menstruation, postpartum hemorrhage, hernia, enuresis, abdominal pain, diarrhea, constipation, edema, flaccid type of apoplexy.

Method: Puncture perpendicularly 0.8-1.2 inches. Moxibustion may be applied often.

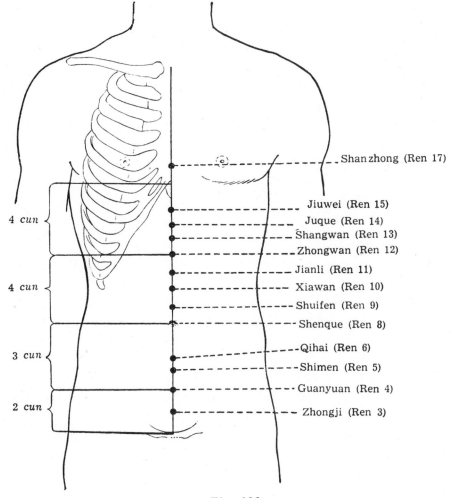

Fig. 106.

Regional anatomy   See Shimen (Ren 5).
Note: This is one of the important points for tonification.

7. Abdomen-Yinjiao (Ren 7)

Location: On the midline of the abdomen, 1 *cun* below the umbilicus.

Indications: Uterine bleeding, leukorrhea, irregular menstruation, pruritus vulvae, abdominal pain around the umbilicus, hernia, postpartum hemorrhage.

Method: Puncture perpendicularly 0.8-1.2 inches. Moxibustion is applicable.

Regional anatomy

Vasculature: See Zhongji (Ren 3).

Innervation: The anterior cutaneous branch of the 10th intercostal nerve.

8. Shenque (Ren 8)

Location: In the centre of the umbilicus. (See Fig. 106.)

Indications: Flaccid type of apoplexy, borborygmus, abdominal pain, unchecked diarrhea, prolapse of rectum.

Method: Puncture is contraindicated. Moxibustion is applied with large cones, 5-15 in number, or with moxa stick for 5-15 minutes.

Regional anatomy

Vasculature: The inferior epigastric artery and vein.

Innervation: The anterior cutaneous branch of the 10th intercostal nerve.

9. Shuifen (Ren 9)

Location: On the midline of the abdomen, 1 *cun* above the umbilicus. (See Fig. 106.)

Indications: Borborygmus, abdominal pain, edema.

Method: Puncture perpendicularly 0.5-1.0 inch. Moxibustion is applicable.

Regional anatomy

Vasculature: See Shenque (Ren 8).

Innervation: The anterior cutaneous branches of the 8th and 9th intercostal nerves.

Note: The distance between the centre of the umbilicus and the sternocostal angle is measured as 8 *cun*, which serves as a standard for longitudinal measurement on the upper abdomen.

10. Xiawan (Ren 10)

Location: On the midline of the abdomen, 2 *cun* above the umbilicus. (See Fig. 106.)

Indications: Gastric pain, abdominal distension, dysentery, borborygmus, vomiting, stool with undigested food.

Method: Puncture perpendicularly 0.8-1.2 inches. Moxibustion is applicable.

Regional anatomy

Vasculature: See Shenque (Ren 8).

Innervation: The anterior cutaneous branch of the 8th intercostal nerve.

11. Jianli (Ren 11)

Location: On the midline of the abdomen, 3 *cun* above the umbilicus. (See Fig. 106.)

Indications: Gastric pain, vomiting, anorexia, abdominal distension, edema.

Method: Puncture perpendicularly 0.8-1.2 inches. Moxibustion is applicable.

Regional anatomy

Vasculature: The branches of the superior and inferior epigastric arteries.

Innervation: The anterior cutaneous branch of the 8th intercostal nerve.

12. Zhongwan (Front-Mu Point of the stomach, Ren 12)

Location: On the midline of the abdomen, 4 *cun* above the umbilicus. (See Fig. 106.)

Indications: Gastric pain, abdominal distension, regurgitation, vomiting, diarrhea, dysentery, stool with undigested food.

Method: Puncture perpendicularly 1.0-1.5 inches. Moxibustion is applicable.

Regional anatomy

Vasculature: The superior epigastric artery and vein.

Innervation: The anterior cutaneous branch of the 7th intercostal nerve.

Note: This is one of the Eight Influential Points dominating the *fu* organs.

13. Shangwan (Ren 13)

Location: On the midline of the abdomen, 5 *cun* above the umbilicus. (See Fig. 106.)

Indications: Gastric pain, regurgitation, vomiting, epilepsy.

Method: Puncture perpendicularly 0.8-1.2 inches. Moxibustion is applicable.

Regional anatomy   See Zhongwan (Ren 12).

14. Juque (Front-Mu Point of the heart, Ren 14)

Location: On the midline of the abdomen, 6 *cun* above the umbilicus. (See Fig. 106.)

Indications: Pain in the cardiac region and the chest, regurgitation, difficulty in swallowing, nausea, vomiting, mental disorders, epilepsy, palpitation.

Method: Puncture perpendicularly 0.3-0.8 inch. Moxibustion is applicable.

Regional anatomy   See Zhongwan (Ren 12).

15. Jiuwei (Luo-Connecting Point, Ren 15)

Location: Below the xyphoid process, 7 *cun* above the umbilicus. Locate the point in supine position with arms uplifted. (See Fig. 106.)

Indications: Pain in the cardiac region and the chest, regurgitation, mental disorders, epilepsy.

Method: Puncture obliquely downward 0.5 inch.

Regional anatomy See Zhongwan (Ren 12).

Note: In case of elongated xyphoid process, puncture Juque (Ren 14) instead.

16. Zhongting (Ren 16)

Location: On the midline of the sternum, level with the 5th intercostal space.

Indications: Sensation of fullness in the chest, difficulty in swallowing.

Method: Puncture 0.3-0.5 inch horizontally along the skin. Moxibustion is applicable.

Regional anatomy

Vasculature: The perforating branches of the internal mammary artery and vein.

Innervation: The anterior cutaneous branch of the 6th intercostal nerve.

17. Shanzhong (Mu-Front Point of the pericardium, Ren 17)

Location: On the midline of the sternum, between the nipples, level with the 4th intercostal space. (See Fig. 106.)

Indications: Asthma, hiccup, pain in the chest, lactation deficiency.

Method: Puncture 0.3-0.5 inch horizontally along the skin. Moxibustion is applicable.

Regional anatomy

Vasculature: See Zhongting (Ren 16).

Innervation: The anterior cutaneous branch of the 4th intercostal nerve.

Note: This is one of the Eight Influential Points dominating *qi*.

18. Yutang (Ren 18)

Location: On the midline of the sternum, level with the 3rd intercostal space.

Indications: Cough, asthma, pain in the chest.

Method: Puncture 0.3-0.5 inch horizontally along the skin. Moxibustion is applicable.

Regional anatomy

Vasculature: See Zhongting (Ren 16).

Innervation: The anterior cutaneous branch of the 3rd intercostal nerve.

19. Chest-Zigong (Ren 19)

Location: On the midline of the sternum, level with the 2nd intercostal space.

Indications: Cough, asthma, pain in the chest.

Method: Puncture 0.3-0.5 inch horizontally along the skin. Moxibustion is applicable.

Regional anatomy

Vasculature: See Zhongting (Ren 16).

Innervation: The anterior cutaneous branch of the 2nd intercostal nerve.

20. Huagai (Ren 20)

Location: On the midline of the sternum, at the level of the 1st intercostal space.

Indications: Asthma, cough, pain in the chest.

Method: Puncture 0.3-0.5 inch horizontally along the skin. Moxibustion is applicable.

Regional anatomy

Vasculature: See Zhongting (Ren 16).

Innervation: The anterior cutaneous branch of the 1st intercostal nerve.

21. Xuanji (Ren 21)

Location: On the midline of the sternum, midway between Tiantu (Ren 22) and Huagai (Ren 20).

Indications: Cough, asthma, pain in the chest.

Method: Puncture 0.3-0.5 inch horizontally along the skin. Moxibustion is applicable.

Regional anatomy

Vasculature: See Zhongting (Ren 16).

Innervation: The medial supraclavicular nerve and the anterior cutaneous branch of the 1st intercostal nerve.

22. Tiantu (Ren 22)

Location: In the centre of the suprasternal fossa. (See Fig. 107.)

Indications: Cough, asthma, sudden hoarseness of voice, sore throat, hiccup.

Method: Puncture obliquely 0.5-0.7 inch towards the postercinferior aspect of the sternum. Deep puncture is not advisable. Moxibustion is applicable.

Regional anatomy

Vasculature: Superficially, the jugular arch and the branch of the inferior thyroid artery; deeper, the trachea; inferiorly, at the posterior aspect of the sternum, the inominate vein and aortic arch.

Innervation: The medial supraclavicular nerve.

23. Lianquan (Ren 23)

Location: Above the Adam's apple, in the depression at the upper border of the hyoid bone. (See Fig. 107.)

Indications: Swelling of the subglossal region, salivation with glossoplegia, aphasia with stiffness of tongue, sudden hoarseness of voice, difficulty in swallowing.

Method: Puncture perpendicularly 0.5-1.0 inch with the needle directed upward.

Regional anatomy

Vasculature: The anterior jugular vein.

Innervation: The branch of the cutaneous cervical nerve, the hypoglossal nerve, and the branch of the glossopharyngeal nerve.

24. Chengjiang (Ren 24)

Location: In the depression in the centre of the mentolabial groove. (See Fig. 107.)

Indications: Facial paralysis, facial swelling, swelling of the gums, toothache, salivation, mental disorders.

Method: Puncture obliquely upward 0.2-0.3 inch. Moxibustion is applicable.

Regional anatomy

Vasculature: The branches of the inferior labial artery and vein.

Innervation: The branch of the facial nerve.

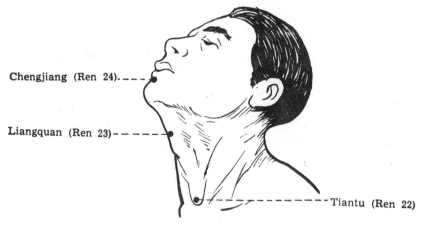

Chengjiang (Ren 24)

Liangquan (Ren 23)

Tiantu (Ren 22)

Fig. 107.

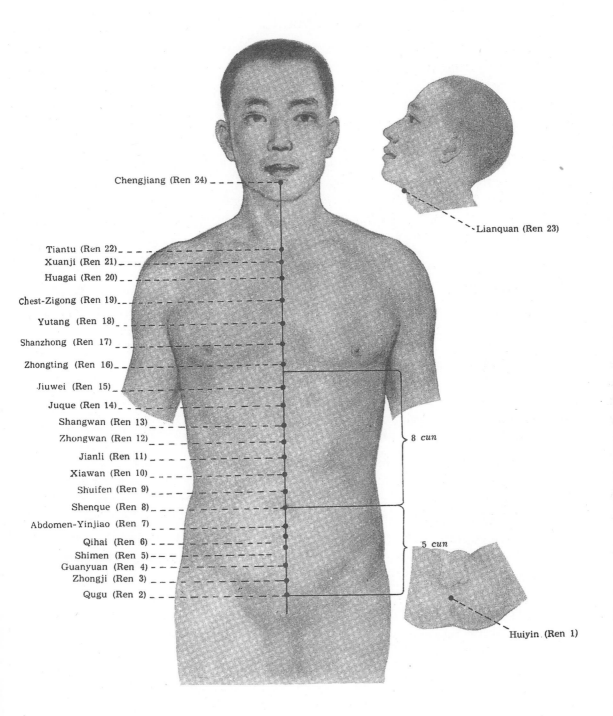

Chengjiang (Ren 24)

Lianquan (Ren 23)

Tiantu (Ren 22)
Xuanji (Ren 21)
Huagai (Ren 20)
Chest-Zigong (Ren 19)
Yutang (Ren 18)
Shanzhong (Ren 17)
Zhongting (Ren 16)
Jiuwei (Ren 15)
Juque (Ren 14)
Shangwan (Ren 13)
Zhongwan (Ren 12)
Jianli (Ren 11)
Xiawan (Ren 10)
Shuifen (Ren 9)
Shenque (Ren 8)
Abdomen-Yinjiao (Ren 7)
Qihai (Ren 6)
Shimen (Ren 5)
Guanyuan (Ren 4)
Zhongji (Ren 3)
Qugu (Ren 2)

8 *cun*

5 *cun*

Huiyin (Ren 1)

Fig. 108. The Ren Channel.

III. THE CHONG CHANNEL

The Chong Channel originates in the lower abdomen, descends and emerges from the perineum (1). It then ascends and runs inside the vertebral column (2), while its superficial portion passes through the region of Qichong where it splits into two and coincides with the Kidney Channel of Foot-Shaoyin, running along both sides of the abdomen (3) up to the throat (4), and curving around the lips (5).

The coalescent points of this channel are as follows:

Huiyin (Ren 1), Henggu (K. 11), Dahe (K. 12), Qixue (K. 13), Siman (K. 14), Abdomen-Zhongzhu (K. 15), Huangshu (K. 16), Shangqu (K. 17), Shiguan (K. 18), Yindu (K. 19), Abdomen-Tonggu (K. 20), Youmen (K. 21). (See Fig. 109.)

IV. THE DAI CHANNEL

The Dai Channel starts below the hypochondriac region (1). Running obliquely downward through Daimai (G.B. 26), Wushu (G.B. 27) and Weidao (G.B. 28), it runs transversely around the waist like a belt (2).

The coalescent points of this channel are Daimai (G.B. 26), Wushu (G.B. 27) and Weidao (G.B. 28). (See Fig. 110.)

V. THE YANGQIAO CHANNEL

The Yangqiao Channel starts from the lateral side of the heel (Shenmai, U.B. 62; Pushen, U.B. 61) (1). Ascending along the external malleolus (2) and passing the posterior border of the fibula, it goes onwards along the lateral aspect of the thigh and the posterior aspect of the hypochondrium to the posterior axillary fold. From there, it winds over to the shoulder and ascends along the neck to the corner of the mouth. Then it enters the inner canthus (Jingming, U.B. 1) to communicate with the Yinqiao Channel. It then runs further upward along the Urinary Bladder Channel of Foot-Taiyang to the forehead and meets the Gall Bladder Channel of Foot-Shaoyang at Fengchi (G.B. 20) (3).

The coalescent points of the Yangqiao Channel are as follows:

Shenmai (U.B. 62), Pushen (U.B. 61), Fuyang (U.B. 59), Femur-Juliao (G.B. 29), Naoshu (S.I. 10), Jianyu (L.I. 15), Jugu (L.I. 16), Dicang (St. 4), Nose-Juliao (St. 3), Chengqi (St. 1), Jingming (U.B. 1), Fengchi (U.B.20). (See Fig. 111.)

VI. THE YINQIAO CHANNEL

The Yinqiao Channel starts from the posterior aspect of the navicular bone (Zhaohai, K. 6) (1). It ascends to the upper portion of the medial

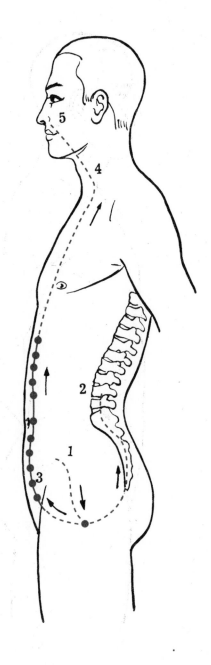

Fig. 109.   The Chong Channel.

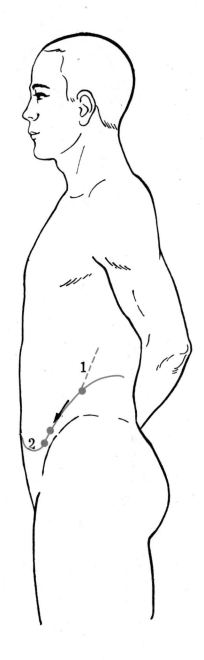

Fig. 110.　The Dai Channel.

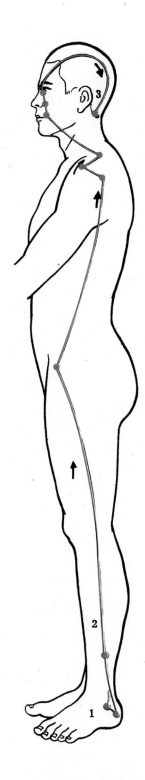

Fig. 111. The Yangqiao Channel.

malleolus (2) and runs straight upward along the posterior border of the medial aspect of the thigh (3) to the external genitalia (4). From there it ascends further along the chest (5) to the supraclavicular fossa (6). Running further upward lateral to the Adam's apple in front of Renying (St. 9) (7), and then along the zygoma (8), it reaches the inner canthus (Jingming, U.B. 1) and communicates with the Yangqiao Channel (9).

The coalescent points of this channel are Zhaohai (K. 6), Jiaoxin (K. 8). (See Fig. 112.)

VII. THE YANGWEI CHANNEL

The Yangwei Channel begins at the heel (Jinmen U.B. 63) (1). Ascending to the external malleolus (2), it runs upward along the Gall Bladder Channel of Foot-Shaoyang, passing through the hip region (3) and further upward along the posterior aspect of the hypochondriac and costal region (4) and the posterior aspect of the axilla to the shoulder (5). From there it further ascends to the forehead (6), and then turns backward to the back of the neck, where it communicates with the Du Channel (Fengfu, Du 16; Yamen, Du 15) (7).

The coalescent points of the Yangwei Channel are as follows:

Jinmen (U.B. 63), Yangjiao (G.B. 35), Naoshu (S.I. 10), Tianliao (S.J. 15), Jianjing (G.B. 21), Touwei (St. 8), Benshen (G.B. 13), Yangbai (G.B. 14), Head-Linqi (G.B. 15), Muchuang (G.B. 16), Zhengying (G.B. 17), Chengling (G.B. 18), Naokong (G.B. 19), Fengchi (G.B. 20), Fengfu (Du 16), Yamen (Du 15). (See Fig. 113.)

VIII. THE YINWEI CHANNEL

The Yinwei Channel starts from the medial side of the leg (Zhubin, K. 9) (1), and ascends along the medial aspect of the thigh to the abdomen (2) to communicate with the Spleen Channel of Foot-Taiyin (3). Then it runs along the chest (4) and communicates with the Ren Channel at the neck (Tiantu, Ren 22; Lianquan, Ren 23) (5).

The coalescent points of the Yinwei Channel are: Zhubin (K. 9), Fushe (Sp. 13), Daheng (Sp. 15), Fuai (Sp. 16), Qimen (Liv. 14), Tiantu (Ren 22), Lianquan (Ren 23). (See Fig. 114.)

APPENDIX: EXTRAORDINARY POINTS

1. Yintang

Location: Midway between the medial ends of the two eyebrows (the glabella). (See Fig. 115.)

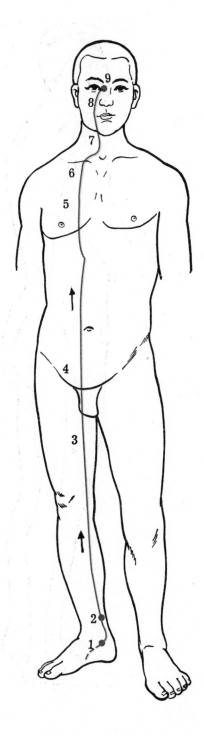

Fig. 112. The Yinqiao Channel.

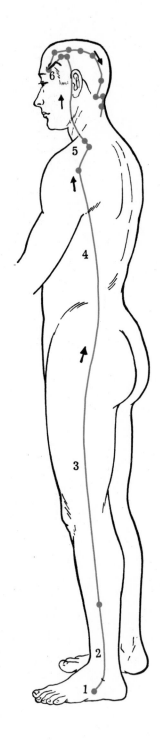

Fig. 113. The Yangwei Channel.

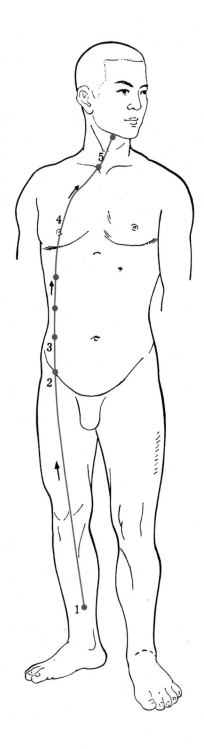

Fig. 114. The Yinwei Channel.

Indications: Infantile convulsion, frontal headache, rhinorrhea.

Method: Puncture 0.3-0.5 inch downward horizontally along the skin, or prick to cause bleeding.

2. Taiyang

Location: In the depression about 1 *cun* posterior to the midpoint between the lateral end of the eyebrow and the outer canthus. (See Fig. 115.)

Indications: Headache, redness, swelling and pain of the eye.

Method: Puncture perpendicularly or obliquely and posteriorly 0.3-0.4 inch, or prick with three-edged needle to cause bleeding.

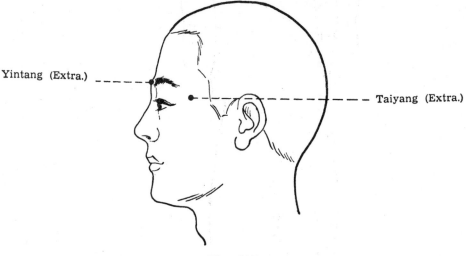

Fig. 115.

3. Yuyao

Location: In the middle of the eyebrow. When one is looking straight forward, the point is directly above the pupil. (See Fig. 116.)

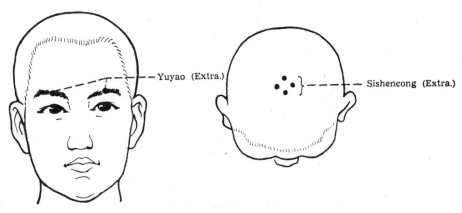

Fig. 116.

Indications: Pain in the supraorbital region, twitching of eyelids, cloudiness of the cornea, redness, swelling and pain of the eye.

Method: Puncture 0.2-0.3 inch horizontally along the skin.

4. Sishencong

Location: A group of 4 points at the vertex, 1 *cun* respectively posterior, anterior, and lateral to Baihui (Du 20). (See Fig. 116.)

Indications: Headache, dizziness, insomnia, poor memory, epilepsy.

Method: Puncture obliquely 0.5-1.0 inch.

5. Jinjin, Yuye

Location: On the veins on both sides of the frenulum of the tongue. (See Fig. 117.)

Indications: Continual vomiting, aphasia with stiffness of tongue.

Method: Ask the patient to place the tip of the tongue on the hard palate. Prick the veins with three-edged needle to cause bleeding.

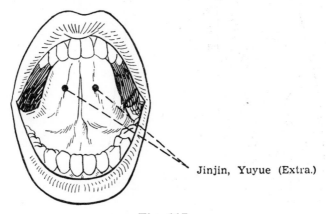

Jinjin, Yuyue (Extra.)

Fig. 117.

6. Dingchuan (Asthma Relief)

Location: 0.5 *cun* lateral to Dazhui (Du 14). (See Fig. 118.)

Indications: Asthma, cough, neck rigidity, pain in the shoulder and back.

Method: Puncture obliquely 0.5-1.0 inch towards the vertebral body. Moxibustion is applicable.

7. Huatuo Jiaji

Location: A group of points on both sides of the spinal column at the lateral borders of each spinous process from the 1st thoracic vertebra to the 5th lumbar vertebra. It is believed that these points were used as Back-Shu Points by the ancient famous doctor Huatou. Below the Hua-

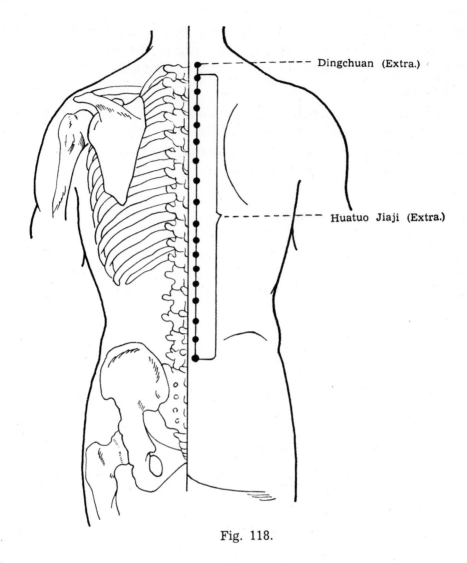

Dingchuan (Extra.)

Huatuo Jiaji (Extra.)

Fig. 118.

tuo Jiaji Points are the Baliao Points, i.e., Shangliao (U.B. 31), Ciliao (U.B. 32), Zhongliao (U.B. 33) and Xialiao (U.B. 34). (See Fig. 118.)

Indications: Similar to those of the Back-Shu Points. The Jiaji Points on the upper back are indicated in disorders of the chest, heart and lung; those on the lower back are indicated in disorders of the upper abdomen, liver, gall bladder, spleen and stomach; and those in the lumbar region are used in disorders of the lower abdomen, kidney, intestines, urinary bladder and lower extremities.

Method: Puncture perpendicularly along the lateral side of the spinous process, 0.5-1.0 inch for points along the thoracic vertebrae and 1.5-2.0 inches for those along the lumbar vertebrae. Moxibustion is applicable.

8. Weiguanxiashu

Location: 1.5 *cun* lateral to the lower border of the spinous process of the 8th thoracic vertebra. (See Fig. 119.)

Indications: Vomiting, abdominal pain.

Method: Puncture obliquely 0.5-0.7 inch. Moxibustion is applicable.

9. Yaoyan

Location: In the depression lateral to the interspace between the spinous processes of the 4th and 5th lumbar vertebrae. The point is located in prone position. (See Fig. 119.)

Indications: Pulmonary tuberculosis, irregular menstruation, backache.

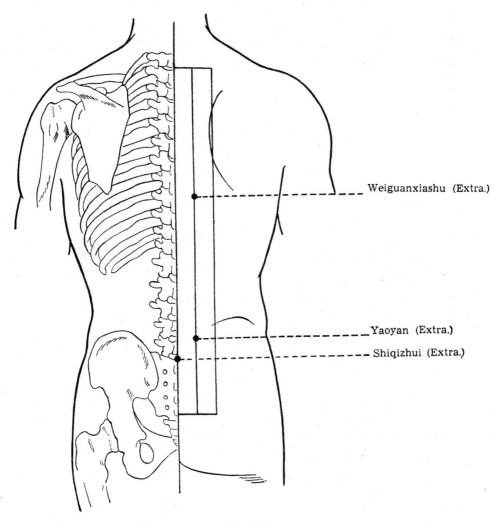

Weiguanxiashu (Extra.)

Yaoyan (Extra.)

Shiqizhui (Extra.)

Fig. 119.

Method: Puncture perpendicularly 0.5-1.5 inches. Moxibustion is applicable.

10. Shiqizhui (17th Vertebra)

Location: In the depression below the spinous process of the 5th lumbar vertebra. (See Fig. 119.)

Indication: Backache.

Method: Puncture perpendicularly 0.5-1.0 inch. Moxibustion is applicable.

11. Abdomen-Zigong

Location: 4 *cun* below the umbilicus, 3 *cun* lateral to Zhongji (Ren 3). (See Fig. 120.)

Indications: Prolapse of uterus, irregular menstruation.

Method: Puncture perpendicularly 1.0-1.5 inches. Moxibustion is applicable.

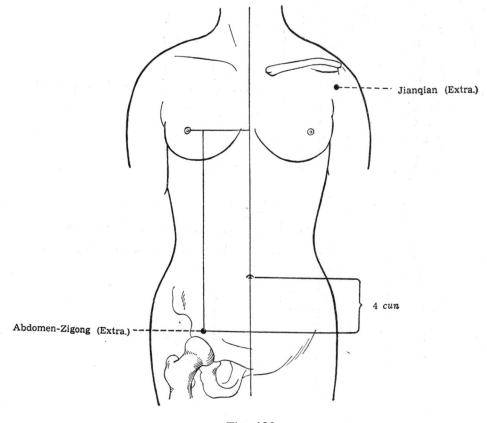

Fig. 120.

12. Jianqian (Also known as Jianneiling)

Location: When the arm is adducted, the point is midway between the end of the anterior axillary fold and Jianyu (L.I. 15). (See Fig. 120.)

Indications: Pain in the shoulder and arm, paralysis of the upper extremities.

Method: Puncture perpendicularly 0.6-1.0 inch. Moxibustion is applicable.

13. Zhongquan

Location: On the dorsum of the wrist, radial to the tendon of m. extensor digitorum communis, in the depression between Yangchi (S.J. 4) and Yangxi (L.I. 5). (See Fig. 121.)

Indications: Stifling feeling in the chest, hematemesis, gastric pain.

Method: Puncture perpendicularly 0.3-0.5 inch. Moxibustion is applicable.

14. Sifeng

Location: On the palmar surface, in the transverse creases of the proximal interphalangeal joints of the index, middle, ring and little fingers. (See Fig. 121.)

Indication: Malnutrition and indigestion syndrome in children.

Method: Prick with three-edged needle and squeeze out a small amount of yellowish viscous fluid.

15. Shixuan

Location: On the tips of the ten fingers, about 0.1 *cun* distal to the nails. (See Fig. 121.)

Indications: Apoplexy, febrile diseases, coma, sore throat, numbness of finger tips.

Method: Prick with three-edged needle to cause bleeding.

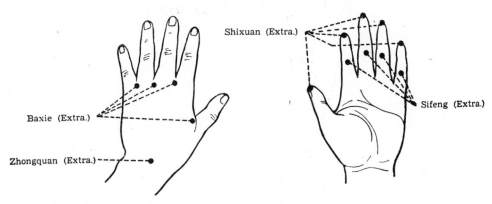

Fig. 121.

16. Baxie

Location: On the dorsum of the hand, on the webs between the five fingers of both hands, 8 in all. Make a loose fist to locate the points. (See Fig. 121.)

Indications: Redness and swelling of the dorsum of the hand, spasm and contracture of fingers.

Method: Puncture obliquely 0.3-0.5 inch towards the interspaces of metacarpal bones.

17. Xiyan

Location: A pair of points in two depressions medial and lateral to the patellar ligament, named medial and lateral Xiyan respectively, located with the knee flexed. (See Fig. 122.)

Indications: Pain and coldness of the knee, weakness of the lower extremities.

Method: Puncture obliquely 0.5-1.0 inch towards the middle of the patella. Moxibustion is applicable.

18. Lanwei (Appendix)

Location: About 2 *cun* below Zusanli (St. 36). (See Fig. 122.)

Indications: Appendicitis, muscular atrophy, motor impairment and *bi* syndrome of the lower extremities.

Method: Puncture perpendicularly 0.5-1.3 inches.

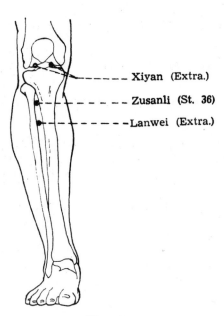

Fig. 122.

19. Dannang (Gallbladder)

Location: About 1 *cun* below Yanglingquan (G.B. 34). (See Fig. 123.)

Indications: Pain in the hypochonodriac region, muscular atrophy, motor impairment, pain and weakness of the lower extremities.

Method: Puncture perpendicularly 0.5-1.3 inches.

20. Bafeng

Location: On the dorsum of foot, on the webs between the five toes, proximal to the margins of the webs, 8 points in all. (See Fig. 124.)

Indications: Beriberi, redness and swelling of the dorsum of foot.

Method: Puncture obliquely upward 0.5 inch. (Fig. 124)

Fig. 124

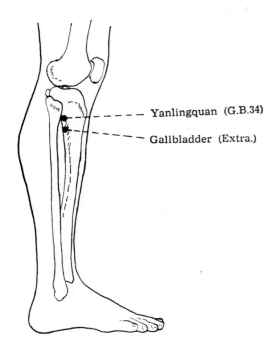

Yanlingquan (G.B.34)

Gallbladder (Extra.)

Fig. 123.

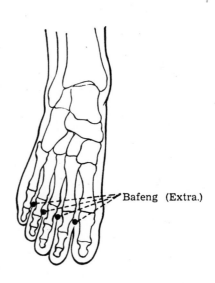

Bafeng (Extra.)

Fig. 124.

PART III

Acupuncture and Moxibustion Therapy
(APPENDIX: CUPPING)

CHAPTER I

TECHNIQUE OF ACUPUNCTURE AND MOXIBUSTION

Acupuncture and moxibustion are two distinct therapeutic methods frequently used in conjunction in the clinic. Acupuncture treats disease by puncturing certain points of the human body with metal needles, while moxibustion is applying heat produced by ignited moxa-wool over the points of the skin surface. Though equipment or material used in the two methods are different, the therapeutic and preventive results in both are achieved through promoting smooth circulation of the channels and adjusting qi and blood by stimulating the points and channels. In this chapter, some of the commonly used methods of acupuncture and moxibustion are introduced. As the filiform needle is the instrument most frequently used in acupuncture, stress is placed on its manipulation.

I. MANIPULATION OF THE FILIFORM NEEDLE

1. The Needles and How to Use Them

(1) The Needle: The needles may be of gold, silver or alloy. The needles in most common use today are made of high quality stainless steel. On the basis of structure, the filiform needle may be divided into four parts — the handle, the root, the body and the tip. (Fig. 125)

The size and length of the needles most commonly used are as follows (Tab. 12, 13):

Length

Tab. 12

Inch	0.5	1.0	1.5	2.0	2.5	3.0	4.0	5.0
MM.	12.7	25.4	38.1	50.8	63.5	76.2	101.6	127

Calibre

Tạb. 13

Gauge	26	28	30	32
Diameter (mm.)	0.46	0.38	0.32	0.26

A good needle is one that is strong and flexible and has a round, smooth body and tip shaped like a pine-needle.

(2) How to practise needling.

The filiform needle is very fine and flexible, and so demands precise finger force to insert it into the skin skillfully and manipulate it freely. In order to minimize possible pain to the patient, appropriate finger force must be mastered through practice, and it is advisable to start practising with a shorter and thicker needle, progressing to a finer and longer one.

(a) Practise with sheets of paper. Fold fine soft tissue into a small packet about 5 × 8 cm. in size and 1 cm. thick. Try puncturing it. Hold the paper packet in the left hand and the handle of the needle with the thumb, index and middle fingers of the right hand. Rotate the needle in and out. As your finger force grows stronger, the thickness of the packet may be increased. (See Fig. 126.)

(b) Practise with a small cotton cushion of about 5-6 cm. in diameter wrapped in gauze. Hold the cushion with the left hand and the needle with the thumb, index and middle fingers of the right hand. Insert the needle into it and practise the lift-thrust and rotation procedure. (Fig. 127)

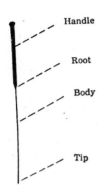

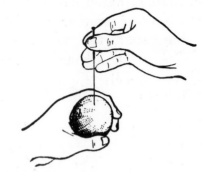

Fig. 125.
Filiform needle.

Fig. 126. Practising needling on folded paper.

Fig. 127. Practising needling on cotton cushion.

(c) Practise on your own body: This may follow the manipulation methods on paper packet and cotton cushion, so as to have personal experience of the acupuncture sensation in clinical practice.

2. Preparation for Giving Treatment

(1) Equipment: Needles of various sizes, a tray, forceps, sterilized cotton balls, 75% alcohol or 1.5% iodine, or 2% gentian violet, etc. Inspect the needles carefully for any bends or erosion. The tip of the needle should be neither too dull nor too sharp, nor should it be hooked.

(2) Sterilization: Strict sterilization of the needle is imperative. Dry or ordinary autoclave, or boiling, may be used. The area on the body surface selected for puncture should be sterilized with 75% alcohol and 1.5% iodine. The operator's fingers should be sterilized routinely.

(3) Posture of the patient: Full exposure of the points selected determines the patient's position. The operator must be able to work without hindrance, while the patient is relaxed and comfortable. Clinically, there are the following postures of the patient according to the points selected.

Sitting position with forearms resting on table; sitting erect with both elbows flexed and resting on table; and lying in lateral recumbent, supine, or prone position. (Fig. 128-132.)

3. Insertion and Withdrawal of the Needle

(1) Insertion:

Generally, the needle is held with the right hand, known clinically as the puncturing hand, with the thumb and index fingers holding the handle

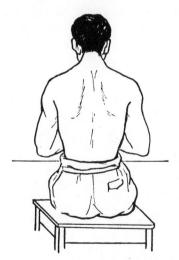

Fig. 128.
Sitting, slightly bending.

Fig. 129. Sitting erect with elbows flexed on table.

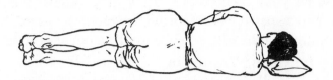

Fig. 130.   Recumbent position.

Fig. 131.   Supine position.

Fig. 132.   Prone position.

of the needle and the middle finger backing the index finger near the needle root. (Fig. 133) The left hand, known as the pressing hand, presses upon the area close to the point. The co-ordination of the two hands is conducive to a swift penetration of the needle tip into the skin, which reduces pain on insertion.

According to the length of the needle and the location of the point, there are various methods of insertion.   The four main techniques are as follows:

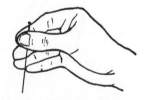

Fig. 133.   Holding the needle.

(a) Inserting the needle aided by the pressure of the finger of the pressing hand: Press beside the acupuncture point with the nail of the thumb or the index finger of the pressing hand, then insert the needle into the point against the nail. This method is suitable for puncturing with short needles such as those used for puncturing Neiguan (P. 6), Zhaohai (K. 6) etc. (Fig. 134.)

(b) Inserting the needle with the help of the puncturing and pressing hands.

Hold the tip of the needle wrapped in a cotton ball with the thumb and index fingers of the pressing hand; fix it directly over the selected point; meanwhile hold the handle of the needle with the puncturing hand. As the pressing hand pushes the needle tip into the skin, the puncturing hand presses it downward to the required depth.

This method is suitable for puncturing with long needles, such as those used in puncturing Huantiao (G.B. 30), Zhibian (U.B. 54) etc. (Fig. 135.)

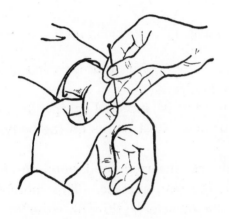

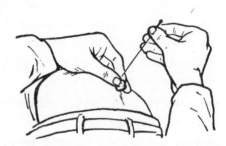

Fig. 134. Pressing with finger. Fig. 135. Co-ordination of fingers of both hands.

(c) Inserting the needle with the fingers stretching the skin: Stretch the skin where the point is located to cause tension with the thumb and the index finger of the pressing hand to facilitate the insertion of the needle. This method is indicated for points where the skin is loose such as Tianshu (St. 25), Guanyuan (Ren 4), etc. on the abdomen. (Fig. 136.)

(d) Inserting the needle by pinching up the skin: Pinch up the skin at the point with the thumb and index finger of the pressing hand, insert the needle into the skin sidewise with the right hand. This method is suitable for puncturing points of the head and face where the soft tissue is thin, such as Zanzhu (U.B. 2), Dicang (St. 4), Yintang (Extra.), etc. (Fig. 137.)

(2) The angle formed by the needle and the skin surface:

The degree of the angles formed by the needle and the skin surface in

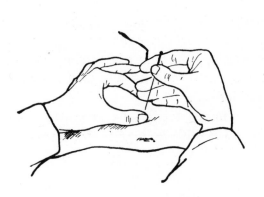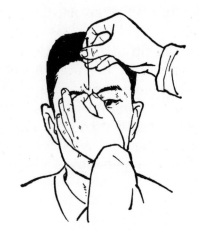

Fig. 136. Stretching the skin.   Fig. 137. Pinching up the skin.

puncturing depends upon the location of the point and the therapeutic purpose. There are the following three angles:

(a) Perpendicular, in which the needle is inserted perpendicularly forming a 90° angle with the skin surface. Most points on the body can be punctured perpendicularly.

(b) Oblique, in which the needle is inserted obliquely to form an angle of approximately 45° with the skin surface. This method is indicated for points located where the muscle is thin or close to important viscera, such as Lieque (Lu. 7) of the forearm, Jiuwei (Ren 15) of the abdominal area, Qimen (Liv. 14) of the chest, points on the back, etc.

(c) Transverse, also known as horizontal puncture when the needle enters the skin forming an angle of from 15°-25° with its surface. This method is preferred for points on the face and head where the muscle is thin, such as Baihui (Du 20) and Touwei (St. 8), of the head, Zanzhu (U.B. 2), Yangbai (G.B. 14) and Dicang (St. 4) of the face, Shanzhong (Ren 17) of the chest, etc. (Fig. 138.)

(3) Depth of needle insertion:

This depends upon the thickness of the tissue where the point is located, pathological condition, and the strength of sensation the patient experiences. As a rule, points on the extremities, abdomen and lumbo-sacral region may be punctured deep.

(4) Withdrawal of the needle: To prevent bleeding at the site of puncture and after-sensation, it is necessary to rotate the needle back and

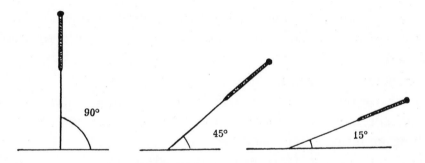

Fig. 138.   Direction of the needle.

forth gently before withdrawing it, then press the puncture site gently with a cotton ball upon withdrawal.

4. The Appearance of *Qi* (Needling Reaction) and the Method of Reinforcing and Reducing

(1) The arrival of *qi* (needling reaction) and inducing *qi* (needling reaction): When the needle is inserted to a certain depth, the patient may feel soreness, numbness or distension around the point. The operator at the same time may feel tenseness around the needle. This is what is known as "arrival of *qi*". Then according to the pathological condition, the reinforcing (*bu*) or reducing (*xie*) procedure is applied. If *qi* (needling reaction) is absent, check to see whether the point is located accurately or the direction of the needle is correct. If *qi* still does not "arrive", the needle may be retained for a short time, or manipulated gently with lift-thrust movements. The needle reaction may also be induced by such auxiliary manipulations as:

(a) Twirling the needle with the thumb and index finger of the right hand in one direction with an amplitude of 360° or more, repeating the manipulation once or twice if necessary.

(b) Scraping of the handle of the needle: When the needle is retained, steady it by placing the thumb of the right hand lightly on top of it, then scrape the handle with the nail of the index or middle finger upward from the bottom.

(c) Vibrating the needle: Hold the needle with the right hand and apply quick lift-thrust movement with small amplitude to cause vibration.

Delay in the arrival of *qi* in some patients may be due to local obstruction of the channel. In that case, cease forceful manipulation and apply mild moxibustion. Or select other points to evoke the vital energy of the channels.

There are patients, however, with weak constitution who give no response to needling by whatever method, and therapeutic results cannot be expected.

(2) Commonly used reinforcing and reducing methods:

There are various manipulation methods, but their action does not go beyond reinforcing (*bu*, supplementing or increasing) and reducing (*xie*, diminishing or decreasing). Because the nature of a disease relates either to *xu* (deficiency) or *shi* (excess), the methods used should correspond. The reinforcing procedure is to correct the deficiency of vital function and strengthen body resistance, while reducing is to eliminate the excess of pathogenic factor. Therapeutic results are generally achieved by these methods, and rich experience has been accumulated in their use by doctors of all ages. Following is a brief description of some of the frequently used methods.

(a) Lifting and thrusting the needle: The effect of reinforcing and reducing is achieved through the speed and the force in repeated lifting and thrusting of the needle.

Reinforcing: Once the needling sensation is felt, lift the needle gently and slowly, then thrust it heavily and rapidly.

Reducing: Lift the needle forcefully and rapidly then thrust it gently and slowly.

(b) Method of rotating the needle: The effect of re-enforcing and reducing depends on the amplitude and speed of the needle rotation.

Reinforcing: When the needle reaches a certain depth, rotate it back and forth continuously with small amplitude and slowly.

Reducing: Rotate the needle continuously back and forth with large amplitude and rapidly.

(c) Even movement: This method is used in treating diseases which are a typical of both the *xu* (deficiency) and *shi* (excess) nature. Application is by inserting the needle to a certain depth till sensation is felt, then rotating, lifting and thrusting the needle evenly and gently at moderate speed to cause a mild sensation. The needle is withdrawn also at moderate speed. (Tab. 14)

The lift-thrust and rotation methods can be used co-ordinately with either of the two as the main method. The application of the above manipulation methods depends upon the nature of the disease, i.e. *xu* or *shi*, and the location of the points over thin or thick muscle.

Table 14

Manipulation method after *qi* is present	Reinforcing	Reducing
Lifting and thrusting the needle	Thrust heavily and rapidly Lift gently and slowly	Lift forcefully and rapidly Thrust gently and slowly
Rotating the needle	Small amplitude with low frequency	Large amplitude with high frequency.

The effect of the reinforcing and reducing method of needling depends mainly on the general health of the patient. When the vital energy is undamaged and there is sound body resistance and prompt reponse to acupuncture, a marked therapeutic result will be obtained; otherwise the therapeutic result will be indefinite. In other words, the effect of the reinforcing and reducing procedures is closely connected with the vital function of the organism.

Moreover, the effect of reinforcing and reducing is affected by the pathological condition. That is to say, different manifestations of the effect may appear in different pathological conditions. An instance is the lowering of blood pressure in a patient with hypertension, and raising it in hypotension. Similarly, needling may have a spasmolytic effect to intestinal spasm, while promoting peristalsis in intestinal paralysis.

The effect of reinforcing and reducing manipulation is also connected with the therapeutic properties of the points. Needling points Zusanli (St. 36), Qihai (Ren 6), Guanyuan (Ren 4), Shenshu (U.B. 23) will have reinforcing effect in promoting functional activity. On the other hand, reducing effect may be obtained by pricking Shixuan (Extra), Weizhong (U.B. 40), Quze (P. 3) in order to bring down fever and expel the excess of pathogenic factor. Hence, clinically, choosing points according to the pathological condition of *xu* and *shi* nature is also an important way to obtain reinforcing and reducing effects.

5. Precautions

(1) It is advisable to apply few needles or to delay giving acupuncture treatment for patients who are either famished or over-eaten, intoxicated, over fatigued or very weak.

(2) It is contraindicated to puncture points on the lower abdomen and lumbosacral region for women pregnant under three months. After three months pregnancy it is contraindicated to puncture, in addition, points of

the upper abdomen, and those causing strong sensation such as Hegu (L.I. 4), Sanyinjiao (Sp. 6), Kunlun (U.B. 60) and Zhiyin (U.B. 67). The fontanelle of infants should not be punctured.

(3) Historic medical literature of the past contraindicates certain points on the human body for puncture or deep puncture. Most of these points are located close to vital organs or large blood vessels, such as Chengqi (St. 1) located below the pupil, Jiuwei (Ren 15) near the important viscera, Jimen (Sp. 11), the femoral artery, etc. These points should generally be punctured obliquely or horizontally to avoid accident.

6. Management of Possible Accidents in Acupuncture

(1) Fainting: This may occur due to weakness or to nervous tension on receiving acupuncture for the first time, or to too forceful manipulation. The prodromes are dizziness and vertigo, irritability, nausea, pallor, staring eyes and dull appearance. In severe cases there may be shock and unconsiousness, deep pulse. The needles should be removed at once and the patient asked to relax, the operator help him to lie down. In mild cases, offer warm drinks. The symptoms will disappear after a short rest. In severe cases, press Renzhong (Du 26) with the fingernail, or puncture Renzhong (Du 26) and Zhongchong (P. 9). Moxibustion may be applied to Baihui (Du 20) and Zusanli (St. 36). Generally the patient will respond, but if not, then other emergency measures should be taken.

(2) Stuck Needle:

After the needle is inserted, it is found at times difficult or impossible to rotate, lift and thrust. This situation, known as stuck needle, may be due to various causes. If it is due to muscle spasm, the needle should be retained for a while, and then rotated for removal. Another method is to press the area around the needle, or puncture another point nearby, to relieve the muscle tension. If the needle is entangled with fibrous tissue, rotate it gently and slowly to disentangle it. Lift and thrust slightly until the muscle is completely relaxed, then withdraw the needle.

(3) Bent Needle:

This generally happens when the needle is inserted with uneven finger force or too forcefully, or the needle strikes hard tissue. The handle of the needle may be struck accidentally, or the patient may suddenly change position while the needle is in place. If the bend is slight, the needle may be removed slowly without rotating. If pronounced, move the needle slightly and withdraw it by following the course of the bend. If the patient has changed position, move him to his original position and then withdraw the needle.

(4) Broken Needle:

Forceful manipulation of the needle, muscle spasm, the patient changing position, or poor quality of the needle or eroded base of needle all may be causes. The doctor should be calm and advise the patient not to move. If the broken needle protrudes above the skin, remove it with forceps. If not, press the tissues around the site until the broken end is exposed, then remove with forceps. If it is completely under the skin, surgery should be resorted to. To prevent accident, careful inspection of the quality of the needle should be made. The needle must be somewhat longer than the required depth of the insertion.

(5) Hematoma: After withdrawal of the needle, a pin-point red mark may remain. This is considered normal, and it will disappear of itself. If a bruise or swelling occurs due to injury to vessels, the site should be massaged and hot compresses applied to promote absorption of the hemostasis.

(6) After withdrawal of the needle, there may remain an uncomfortable feeling due to over stimulation. If the sensation is not too severe, it may be relieved by gently massaging the local area. If the discomfort persists, it may be relieved by applying moxibustion.

II. OTHER ACUPUNCTURE METHODS

1. The Three-edged Needle

(1) The needle: The head is triangular in shape, with a sharp tip. Stainless steel is the material most often used. (Fig. 139.)

Fig. 139. Three-edged needle.

(2) Indications: High fever, mental disorders, sore throat, local congestion or swelling.

(3) Manipulation: Prick superficially 0.05-0.1 inch deep at the selected point to cause bleeding.

(4) Precaution: Pricking should be light and superficial, the amount of bleeding determined by the pathological condition. Vigorous pricking is not permissible, nor is it advisable to apply this method for weak patients, expectant mothers or patients with hemorrhagic diseases.

2. The Cutaneous or Tapping Needle

(1) The needle: The cutaneous needle is used to prick the skin superficially by tapping. Two types are used:

(a) The seven-star needle, composed of seven short stainless steel needles inlaid onto a small round plate attached vertically to a handle 5-6 inches long.

(b) The plum-blossom needle, composed of 5 stainless steel needles in a bundle and attached perpendicularly to a handle one foot long. The points of the needles should be even and not too sharp so as to avoid pain and bleeding. (Fig. 140.)

(2) Indications: This superficial tapping method is particularly suitable for women, children and those who are sensitive to pain. It is indicated in headache, dizziness and vertigo, insomnia, enterogastric disorders, chronic disorders in women, and some types of skin diseases.

(3) Manipulation:

Hold the handle of the needle and tap the skin surface with flexible movement of the wrist only. Tapping may be light or heavy according to the constitution of the patient and the nature of the disease. Duration and number of taps depend on the individual patient. Bleeding does not occur in light tapping, while heavy tapping should draw very little blood. Location for tapping necessarily depends on the pathological condition, distribution of the channels and the location of points.

3. The Intradermal or Imbedding Needle

(1) The needle is short and is used for subcutaneous implantation. There are two types:

(a) The thumbtack type, which is about 0.3 cm. long with a head like a thumbtack, and

(b) The grain-like type, about 1 cm. long with a head like a grain of wheat.

Both types are usually of stainless steel or sterling silver. (Fig. 141.)

(2) Indications: Chronic diseases of the internal organs, persistent and multiple painful diseases.

(3) Manipulation: The grain-like type needle is suitable for implantation at points and tenderness on various parts of the body, while the thumbtack type is suitable for implantation in the ear.

(4) Precautions:

The duration of implantation depends on the season of the year. In summer, the duration should be limited to 1-2 days, care should be taken to prevent infection at the puncture site due to perspiration. In autumn and winter, the needles may be retained longer according to the need in specific cases.

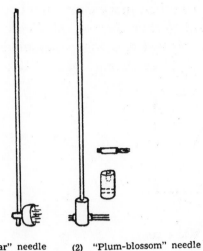

(1) "Seven-star" needle   (2) "Plum-blossom" needle

Fig. 140.   Cutaneous needle.

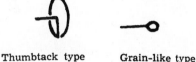

Thumbtack type   Grain-like type

Fig. 141.   Intradermal needle.

III.   MOXIBUSTION

Moxibustion treats and prevents diseases by applying heat to points or certain locations of the human body. The material used is mainly "moxa-wool" in the form of a large cigarette or small cones.

Moxa-wool is made of dry moxa, or mugwort leaves (*Artemisia vulgaris*), ground finely, with the coarse stems removed. It has the properties of warming and removing obstruction of the channels, eliminating cold and damp and thus promoting normal functioning of the organs. Burning moxa-wool has the following advantages.

Its heat is mild and at the same time penetrates deep beneath the skin, giving a sensation of comfort;

Moxa-wool can be kneaded into small cones of various sizes, is easy to ignite, aromatic and drives away damp and foul air.

Artemisia vulgaris grows extensively and profusely in China. It has been used for curative purposes in China for several thousand years.

1.   Preparation

(1) The moxibustion tray contains moxa wool, moxa sticks and matches.

(a) Making moxa cones: Place a small amount of moxa wool on a board, knead it into a cone with the thumb, index and middle fingers. Three sizes may be made: The smallest is the size of a grain of wheat; next, the size of half a date stone, and the largest is the size of the upper part of the thumb. The two smaller cones are suitable for direct moxibustion, while the largest is suitable for indirect moxibustion. (Fig. 142.)

(b) Making moxa sticks: These are much more convenient to use than moxa cones. Simply roll moxa wool (other herbal medicine may be mixed in) into the shape of a large cigarette, using paper made of mulberry bark, or any other that is soft yet strong. (Fig. 143.)

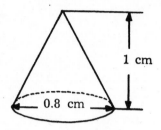

Fig. 142. Moxa cone.

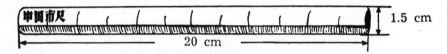

Fig. 143. Moxa stick.

(2) Posture of the patient

The patient should be placed according to the location of the points selected. The patient should be comfortable and able to maintain the position for the required time of treatment.

2. Classification of Moxibustion

Clinically, there are three methods of application; i.e. with moxa cones, with moxa sticks, and with warming needle. (Tab. 15.).

Tab. 15

Moxibustion
- Moxa cones
  - Direct moxibustion
    - Scarring moxibustion
    - Non-scarring moxibustion
  - Indirect moxibustion
    - Ginger insulation
    - Garlic insulation
    - Salt insulation
- Moxa sticks
- Warming needle

(1) Moxibustion with moxa cones may be direct or indirect.

(a) Direct: A moxa cone is placed directly on the skin and ignited. This type may be scarring or non-scarring according to the degree of cauterization.

i. Scarring moxibustion: A small cone is placed on the point and burned, followed by another. This causes a local burn, blister formation, festering, and final healing with scar formation. Indications are certain chronic persistent diseases such as asthma.

ii. Non-scarring moxibustion: A moxa cone is placed on a point and ignited. When half to two thirds of it is burnt and the patient feels scorching, remove and renew it several times. No blister should be formed, and there should be no festering and scar formation. Indications are asthma, chronic diarrhea, indigesion, etc. of the chronic deficient and cold nature. The range of indications is broader than for scarring moxibustion. (Fig. 144.)

(b) Indirect moxibustion: The ignited moxa cone does not rest on the skin. According to the substance insulating the cone and the skin, there are three kinds of indirect moxibustion.

(i) On ginger. Cut a slice of ginger about 0.2 cm. thick, punch numerous holes in it and place it on the selected point, adding a large moxa cone and igniting it. When the patient feels it scorching, remove it and light another. This method is indicated in symptoms of weakness of the stomach and spleen such as diarrhea, abdominal pain, painful joints and symptoms of deficiency of *yang*. (Fig. 145.)

(ii) On garlic: Cut a slice of garlic (a large single clove of garlic is desirable), punch holes in it, put it between the point and the ignited moxa-cone. Renew the cone when the patient feels it scorching. This method is indicated in scrofula, the early stage of skin infections, poisonous insect bite, etc.

Fig. 144. Moxibustion with moxa cone.

Fig. 145. Indirect moxibustion with ginger.

(iii) With salt: Fill the umbilicus with salt to the level of the skin, place a large moxa-cone on top and ignite it. This method is applied mainly in cases of collapse with symptoms of cold limbs and undetectable pulse after severe abdominal pain, vomiting and diarrhea. (Fig. 146.)

(2) Moxibustion using the stick form.

Apply a lighted moxa-stick over the selected point from some distance to cause a mild warmth to the local area until it becomes hot and pink. The moxa-stick may be moved up and down like a sparrow feeding. This method is convenient and can be applied on points where cones are not suitable. (Fig. 147.)

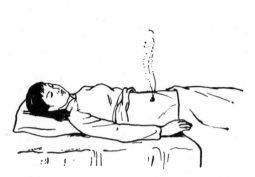

Fig. 146.   Indirect moxibustion with salt.

Fig. 147.   Moxibustion with moxa stick.

(3) With warming needle: With the filiform needle retained in the point, wrap the handle tight in moxa-wool and ignite it to cause a mild heat around the area of the point. This method is suitable for patients for whom a retained needle and moxibustion are indicated, such as those suffering from painful joints due to cold and damp. (Fig. 149.)

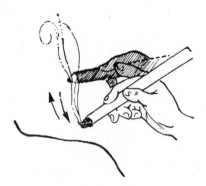

Fig. 148.   "Sparrow-picking" method with moxa stick.

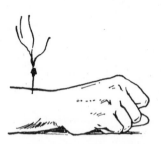

Fig. 149.   A piece of moxa stick stuck on the top of the handle.

3. Precautions and remarks:

(1) If moxibustion is to be applied to the upper and lower parts of the body at one sitting, treat the upper part first. Treat the back before the abdominal aspect, the head and body before the extremities. But consideration should be given to the pathological condition and the number of sites to be treated.

(2) In determining the size of a moxa-cone or how many cones should be used, or the duration of the moxa-stick application, the patient's pathological condition, general constitution and age, and the site where moxibustion is to be applied should be taken into consideration. Generally, 3-5 cones are used for each point, and 10-15 minutes for the application of moxa-stick.

(3) Moxibustion is contraindicated in high fever either due to exogenous factors or deficiency of *yin*.

(4) Scarring moxibustion is not suitable for face and head for cosmetic reasons. Moxibustion should not be applied to the lower abdomen or sacral region of pregnant women. Some ancient medical literature proscribes as not suitable for moxibustion certain points, most of which are close to important organs or arteries. Examples are Jingming (U.B. 1), close to the eyeball, and Renying (St. 9), above a large artery. For further details refer to method in acupuncture and moxibustion.

(5) Moxibustion may leave various degrees of burn in the local area. This ranges from heat sensation and local redness which will disappear of itself, to blister formation. Take care not to let small blisters break, as the fluid will be absorbed without infection. Large blisters, however, should be punctured and drained. If pus is formed, the blister should be dressed to prevent further infection.

APPENDIX: CUPPING

Cupping is the treatment of disease by suction to the skin surface by attaching small jars in which a vacuum is created by introducing heat in the form of an ignited alcohol-soaked cotton ball. The jars may be of bamboo or glass and in various sizes. The rims must be even and smooth.

(1) Indications: Rheumatism, painful joints, sprains, facial paralysis, asthma, etc.

(2) Manipulation: Ignite a cotton ball soaked in 95% alcohol and hold in forceps, thrust it inside the jar, remove it and swiftly cup the jar on the selected area. The sucking up of the skin may generally be allowed to go on for 10-15 minutes. To remove, let air into the jar by holding it in the right hand and pressing the skin at the rim of the jar with the left.

Precautions:

(a) It is not advisable to apply cupping to patients with high fever, convulsion, allergic skin disease, edema, or hemorrhagic tendency, or to the abdominal area of women during pregnancy.

(b) It is undesirable also to apply cupping at articulated areas where the surface is not smooth, on hairy areas or where the skin is loose.

(c) When applying cupping, be sure the fire is strong enough to create a vacuum. Hold the jar with the rim close to the local area and cup it to the skin swiftly and deftly. Therapeutic result depends on the sucking action.

(d) The local area will show blood congestion after cupping, the bruise on the skin surface gradually disappearing within a few days. If minute blisters form, they may also be absorbed after one or two days. However for any large blisters, it is advisable to drain the fluid with a sterilized syringe, and apply gentian violet before dressing.

CHAPTER II

A GENERAL INTRODUCTION TO
ACUPUNCTURE TREATMENT

In treating diseases with acupuncture and moxibustion it is necessary to differentiate the pathological condition according to the basic theory of Chinese traditional medicine and the peculiarities of acupuncture. It is also important to master the basic principle for prescribing points and the application of the specific points.

I. BASIC PRINCIPLES OF TREATMENT
ACCORDING TO DIFFERENTIATION OF
PATHOLOGICAL CONDITIONS

Acupuncture and moxibustion are methods of "treating interior diseases from the exterior". Various diseases may be cured by the application of the methods of reinforcing the deficiency, and reducing the excess, to the points of the body surface. It is imperative, therefore, to have full knowledge of the channel courses, the distribution of points and the indications of each individual channel. Clinical practice requires that before giving treatment the pathological condition, which may be very complicated, should be analysed and summarized according to the "eight principles", the theories of *zang-fu* (internal organs) and the channels and collaterals in order to locate and diagnose the disease. After discovering which channel or which internal organ is affected, investigate further the mechanism of the disease and determine the essential and secondary symptoms so as to decide whether acupuncture or moxibustion, reinforcing or reducing method should be applied.

The basic principle for acupuncture treatment may be stated as follows: Reinforcing method should be employed for *xu* (deficiency) syndrome, reducing for *shi* (excess) syndrome. Swift insertion and withdrawal of needle for heat syndrome, retaining needle for cold syndrome. In deficiency and failing of *yang* (vital function), moxibustion is indicated. Venous pricking to cause bleeding is used for blood stasis of the collaterals. Moreover, *xu* syndrome may be complicated with *shi* syndrome or vice versa, and method of treatment may be reinforcing first and reducing afterwards, or both simultaneously.

II. THE BASIC PRINCIPLE GOVERNING PRESCRIPTION AND COMBINATION OF POINTS

The basic principle for prescribing and combining points is to select points according to the course of the channel, the distribution of points and their indications. There are three ways for selecting points in clinical practice:

1. Selection of Remote Points

After the involved channel and organ are determined, points below elbow or knee of the involved channel are selected. For instance, Zusanli (St. 36) is chosen to treat gastric or abdominal disorders; Hegu (L.I. 4) may be punctured for diseases of the face, etc. Thus, diseases of the face, head, trunk or internal organs may be treated. Selection of remote points also includes choosing points on the lower part of the body to treat diseases of the upper part, and vice versa. This is essentially to select points below the elbow and knee as the principal ones. For neck pain, for instance, Houxi (S.I. 3) is chosen; for the tense type of apoplexy, Yongquan (K. 1); etc. An example of selecting points on the upper part of the body to treat diseases of the lower part is selecting Baihui (Du 20) to treat prolapse of rectum due to chronic dysentery, Renzhong (Du 26) to treat low back pain, etc.

2. Selection of Local Points

For example, Zhongwan (Ren 12) is chosen to treat gastric pain, Shangxing (Du 23) to treat headache, etc. If there is ulcer, wound or scar in the local area, neither acupuncture nor moxibustion should be applied there, but may be applied at points in the adjacent area.

3. Selection of Adjacent Points

For instance, Zhangmen (Liv. 13) is used to treat gastric pain, Fengchi (G.B. 20) in diseases of the eye. For strengthening therapeutic effect local points may be combined with adjacent points, or adjacent points can substitute for local points.

The above three methods of selecting points may be used separately or in combination. For instance the selection of Zusanli (St. 36) and Neiguan

Table 16. Examples for Prescription and Combination of Points

Diseased area	Remote Points		Adjacent Points	Local Points
	Upper Extrem.	Lower Extrem.		
Face & forehead	Sanjian (L.I. 3)	Xiangu (St. 43)	Baihui (Du 20)	Shangxing (Du 23)
Head & temple	Waiguan (S.J. 5)	Xiaxi (G. B. 43)	Fengchi G.B. 20)	Taiyang (Extra) Shuaigu (G.B. 8)
Nape	Houxi (S.I. 3)	Foot-Tonggu (U.B. 66)	Dashu (U.B. 11)	Fengfu (Du 16) Fengchi (G. B. 20)
Eye	Yanglao (S.I. 6)	Guangming (G.B. 37)	Shangxing (Du 23)	Jingming (U.B. 1) Sizhukong (S.J. 23)
Nose	Quchi (L.I. 11)	Lidui (St. 45)	Tongtian (U.B. 7)	Yingxiang (L.I. 20) Nose-Heliao (L.I. 19)
Mouth & cheek	Hegu (L.I. 4)	Neiting (St. 44)	Tianrong (S.I. 17)	Dicang (St. 4) Jiache (St. 6)
Ear	Hand-Zhongzhu (S.J. 3)	Foot-Zulinqi (G.B. 41)	Tianrong (S.I. 17)	Tinghui (G. B. 2) Yifeng (S.J. 17)
Throat	Shaoshang (Lu. 11)	Zhaohai (K. 6)	Yamen (Du 15)	Lianquan (Ren 23) Tiantu (Ren 22)
Chest	Chize (Lu. 5)	Fenglong (St. 40)	Burong (St. 19)	Shanzhong (Ren 17)
Costal region	Zhigou (S.J. 6)	Yanglingquan (G.B. 34)	Ganshu (U.B. 18)	Shidou (Sp. 17) Qimen (Liv. 14)
Hypochondrium		Yangfu (G.B. 38)	Qimen (Liv. 14)	Daimai (G.B. 26) Wushu (G.B.27)
Upper abdomen	Neiguan (P. 6)	Zusanli (St. 36)	Zhongting (Ren 16)	Zhongwan (Ren 12)
Lower abdomen		Sanyinjiao (SP. 6)	Tianshu (St. 25)	Guanyuan (Ren 4)
Lumbar region	Yanglao (S.I. 6)	Weizhong (U.B. 40)	Jingmen (G.B. 25)	Ganshu (U.B. 18) Shenshu (U.B. 23)
Rectum		Chengshan (U.B. 57)	Baihuanshu (U.B. 30)	Changqiang (Du 1) Huiyang (U.B. 35)

(P. 6) of the remote area combined with Zhongwan (Ren 12) of the local area or Zhangmen (Liv. 13) of the neighbouring area may be considered in treating gastric pain. (See table 16.)

The crossing methods of selecting points may also be used i.e. selecting points of the right side to treat disorders of the left, and vice versa. For instance, points may be chosen on the affected side or the healthy side to treat facial paralysis or hemiplegia. Hegu (L.I. 4) of the right hand may be punctured for toothache on the left side, and vice versa.

III. THE APPLICATION OF SPECIFIC POINTS

Specific points are indicated in various diseases. Clinically, they can be selected singly or in combination with other points according to the above basic principle of selecting points.

1. The Application of the Yuan (Source) Points and the Luo (Connecting) Points:

The Yuan (Source) Points are indicated in *xu* syndrome as well as *shi* syndrome of their respective related organs. The Luo (Connecting) Points of the twelve regular Channels are indicated by the symptoms of their respective "externally-internally related channels".

Clinically, these two groups of points can be used separately or co-ordinately. When a channel is affected, the Yuan (Source) Point of that channel may be chosen as the main organs. The Luo (Connecting) Points of its externally-internally related channel combined with it to enhance the therapeutic effect. For instance, functionally, the Lung Channel of Hand-Taiyin and the Large Intestine Channel of Hand-Yangming are externally-internally related. If the Lung Channel is involved, Taiyuan (Lu. 9), the Yuan (Source) Point of the Lung Channel, and Pianli (L.I. 6), the Luo (Connecting) Point of the Large Intestine Channel, may be prescribed. Or, Hegu (L.I. 4), the Yuan (Source) Point of the Large Intestine Channel, and Lieque (L. 7), the Luo (Connecting) Point of the Lung Channel, are prescribed to treat diseases of the Large Intestine Channel. (See Tab. 17.)

Appendix: The Luo (Connecting) Point of Ren Channel is Jiuwei (Ren 15).

The Luo (Connecting) Point of Du Channel is Changqiang (Du 1).

The major Luo (Connecting) Point of the spleen is Dabao (Sp. 21).

Table 17. The Yuan (Source) and the Luo (Connecting) Points

Channel	Yuan (Source) Point	The Luo (Connecting) Point
Lung Channel of Hand Taiyin	Taiyuan (Lu. 9)	Pianli (L.I. 6)
Lung Channel of of Hand-Yingming	Hegu (L.I. 4)	Lieque (Lu. 7)
Stomach Channel of Foot-Yangming	Chongyang (St. 42)	Gongsun (Sp. 4)
Spleen Channel of Foot-Taiyin	Taibai (Sp. 3)	Fenglong (St. 40)
Heart Channel of Hand-Shaoyin	Shenmen (H. 7)	Zhizheng (S.I. 7)
Small Intestine Channel of Hand-Taiyang	Hand-Wangu (S.I 4.)	Tongli (H. 5)
Urinary Bladder Channel of Foot-Taiyang	Jinggu (U.B. 64)	Dazhong (K. 4)
Kidney Channel of Foot-Shaoyin	Taixi (K. 3)	Feiyang (U.B. 58)
Pericardium Channel of Hand-Jueyin	Daling (P. 7)	Waiguan (S.J. 5)
Sanjiao Channel cf Hand-Shaoyang	Yangchi (S.J. 4)	Neiguan (P. 6)
Gall Bladder Channel of Foot-Shaoyang	Qiuxu (G.B. 40)	Ligou (Liv. 5)
Liver Channel of Foot-Jueyin	Taichong (Liv. 3)	Guangming (G. B. 37)

2. The Application of the Back-Shu and the Front-Mu Points

The Back-Shu Points and the Front-Mu Points can be used separately or in combination. Whenever an internal organ is affected, the Back-Shu Point and the Front-Mu Point of that organ can be prescribed. One can either prescribe its corresponding Back-Shu Point, or its corresponding Front-Mu Point, or both simultaneously. For instance: Weishu (U.B. 21) of the back and Zhongwan (Ren 12) of the abdomen may be selected for gastric disorders; or Pangguangshu (U.B. 28) of the sacral region and Zhongji (Ren 3) of the lower abdomen are chosen for disorders of the urinary bladder.

The Back-Shu Points relate to *yang* and can be used in treating visceral diseases as well as diseases of the sense organs which are related to their respective corresponding internal organs. For instance, Ganshu (U.B. 18), the Back-Shu Point of the liver, may be chosen to treat eye disorders, as eye is the "window" of the liver; Shenshu (U.B. 23), the Back-Shu Point

Table 18. The Back-Shu Points and the Front-Mu Points

Internal organs	Back-Shu Point	Front-Mu Point
Lung	Feishu (U.B. 13)	Zhongfu (Lu. 1)
Pericardium	Jueyinshu (U.B. 14)	Shanzhong (Ren 17)
Heart	Xinshu (U.B. 15)	Jujue (Ren 14)
Liver	Ganshu (U.B. 18)	Qimen (Liv. 14)
Gall Bladder	Danshu (U.B. 19)	Riyue (G.B. 24)
Spleen	Pishu (U.B. 20)	Zhangmen (Liv. 13)
Stomach	Weishu (U.B. 21)	Zhongwan (Ren 12)
Sanjiao	Sanjiaoshu (U.B. 22)	Shimen (Ren 5)
Kidney	Shenshu (U.B. 23)	Jingmen (G. B. 25)
Large Intestine	Dachangshu (U.B. 25)	Tianshu (St. 25)
Small Intestine	Xiaochangshu (U.B. 27)	Guanyuan (Ren 4)
Urinary Bladder	Pangguangshu (U.B. 28)	Zhongji (Ren 3)

of the Kidney, can be selected to treat deafness, as ear is the "window" of the kidney.

The Front-Mu Points relate to *yin*. Their therapeutic function is mainly in treating disorders of the internal organs and local areas. For instance: for liver disorders associated with hypochondriac pain, Qimen (Liv. 14) may be prescribed; Tianshu (St. 25) may be prescribed for disorders of the large intestine associated with abdominal pain. (See Tab. 18.)

3. The Application of the Five Shu Points

The Five Shu Points are respectively attributed to the five elements. The order of the five elements in the *yin* channels is wood → fire → earth → metal → water; the order in the *yang* channels is metal → water → wood → fire → earth. According to the inter-promoting relation of the five elements, each channel has a "mother point" and a "son point". For instance, the Lung Channel relates to metal, the "mother" of metal is earth, then the mother point of the Lung Channel is Taiyuan (Lu. 9) which is attributed to earth according to the category of the five elements; the

Table 19. The Five Shu Points of the Yin Channels

	Channel	I (Wood) Jing-Well	II (Fire) Rong-Spring	III (Earth) Shu-Stream	IV (Metal) Jing-River	V (Water) He-Sea
The Three Yin Channels of Hand	Lung Hand-Taiyin	Shaoshang (Lu. 11)	Yuji (Lu. 10)	Taiyuan (Lu. 9)	Jingqu (Lu. 8)	Chize (Lu. 5)
	Pericardium Hand-Jueyin	Zhongchong (P. 9)	Laogong (P. 8)	Daling (P. 7)	Jianshi (P. 5)	Quze (P. 3)
	Heart Hand-Shaoyin	Shaochong (H. 9)	Shaofu (H. 8)	Shenmen (H. 7)	Lingdao (H. 4)	Shaohai (H. 3)
The Three Yin Channels of Foot	Spleen Foot-Taiyin	Yinbai (Sp. 1)	Dadu (Sp. 2)	Taibai (Sp. 3)	Shangqiu (Sp. 5)	Yinlingquan (Sp. 9)
	Liver Foot-Jueyin	Dadun (Liv. 1)	Xingjian (Liv. 2)	Taichong (Liv. 3)	Zhongfeng (Liv. 4)	Ququan (Liv. 8)
	Kidney Foot-Shaoyin	Yongquan (K. 1)	Rangu (K. 2)	Taixi (K. 3)	Fuliu (K. 7)	Yingu (K. 10)

"son" of metal is water, so the "son point" of the Lung Channel is Chize (Lu. 5) which is attributed to water.

The "mother point" of a channel has a tonifying effect and is indicated in *xu* syndrome of its related channel; while the "son point" has a reducing effect and is indicated in the *shi* syndrome of its related channel. Hence the maxim: "Reinforce the 'mother' for *xu* syndrome; reduce the 'son' for *shi* syndrome." For example, when the Lung Channel is involved in *xu* syndrome with symptoms of chronic cough, shortness of breath, low voice, hydrosis and thready weak pulse, then the reinforcing method on Taiyuan (Lu. 9) may be prescribed. On the other hand, if the Lung Channel is involved in *shi* syndrome with abrupt onset of cough, dyspnea, coarse voice, stifling sensation in chest with inability to lie flat, and superficial and forceful pulse, Chizi (Lu. 5 with reducing method may be prescribed. (See Tab. 20, 21, 22.)

Table 20.　The Five Shu Points of the Yang Channels

Channel		I (Metal) Jing-Well	II (Water) Rong-Spring	III (Wood) Shu-Stream	IV (Fire) Jing-River	V (Earth) He-Sea
The Three Yang Channels of Hand	Large Intes. Hand-Yang-ming	Shangyang (L.I. 1)	Erjian (L.I. 2)	Sanjian (L.I. 3)	Yangxi (L.I. 5)	Quchi (L.I. 11)
	Sanjiao Hand-Shao-yang	Guanchong (S.J. 1)	Yemen (S.J. 2)	Hand-Zhongzhu (S.J. 3)	Zhigou (S.J. 6)	Tianjing (S.J. 10)
	Small Intes. Hand-Tai-yang	Shaoze (S.I. 1)	Qiangu (S.I. 2)	Houxi (S.I. 3)	Yanggu (S.I. 5)	Xiaohai (S.I. 18)
The Three Yang Channels of Foot	Stomach Foot-Yang-ming	Lidui (St. 45)	Neiting (St. 44)	Xiangu (St. 43)	Jiexi (St. 41)	Zusanli (St. 36)
	Gall Bladder Foot-Shao-yang	Foot-Qiaoyin (G.B. 44)	Xiaxi (G.B. 43)	Foot-Linqi (G.B. 41)	Yangfu (G.B. 38)	Yangling-quan (G.B. 34)
	Urin. Bladder Foot-Taiyang	Zhiyin (U.B. 67)	Foot-Tonggu (U.B. 66)	Shugu (U.B. 65)	Kunlun (U.B. 60)	Weizhong (U.B. 40)

Each group of the Five Shu Points may also have properties in common. For reference see Chapter I, Part II.

4. The Application of the Xi (Cleft) Points and the Lower He-Sea Points

The Xi (Cleft) Points have the properties of treating acute diseases occurring in their respective related organs. For instance, Kongzui (Lu. 6)

Table 21. The "Mother" and "Son" Points for Reinforcing and Reducing

Channels	Mother Point (Reinforcing)	Son Point (Reducing)
Lung Channel of Hand-Taiyin	Taiyuan (Lu. 9)	Chize (Lu. 5)
Large Intes. Channel of Hand-Yangming	Quchi (L.I. 11)	Erjian (L.I. 2)
Stomach Channel of Foot-Yangming	Jiexi (St. 41)	Lidui (St. 45)
Spleen Channel of Foot-Taiyin	Dadu (Sp. 2)	Shangqiu (Sp. 5)
Heart Channel of Hand-Shaoyin	Shaochong (H. 9)	Shenmen (H. 7)
Small Intes. Channel of Hand-Taiyang	Houxi (S.I. 3)	Xiaohai (S.I. 8)
Urinary Bladder Channel of Foot-Taiyang	Zhiyin (U.B. 67)	Shugu (U.B. 65)
Kidney Channel of Foot-Shaoyin	Fuliu (K. 7)	Yongquan (K. 1)
Pericardium Channel of Hand-Jueyin	Zhongchong (P. 9)	Daling (P. 7)
Sanjiao Channel of Hand-Shaoyang	Hand-Zhongzhu (S.J. 3)	Tianjing (S.J. 10)
Gall Bladder Channel of Foot-Shaoyang	Xiaxi (G. B. 43)	Yangfu (G.B. 38)
Liver Channel of Foot-Jueyin	Ququan (Liv. 8)	Xingjian (Liv. 2)

of the Lung Channel of Hand-Taiyin is effective in hemoptysis; Wenliu (L.I. 7) of the Large Intestine Channel of Hand-Yangming is effective for borborygmus and abdominal pain; Liangqiu (St. 34) of the Stomach Channel of Foot-Yangming is for epigastric pain; Diji (Sp. 8) of the Spleen Channel of Foot-Taiyin is prescribed for menstrual pain. (See Tab. 22.)

Table 22.   The Xi (Cleft) Points

	Channel	Xi-Cleft Point
3 Yin Channels of Hand	The Lung Channel of Hand-Taiyin	Kongzui (Lu. 6)
	The Pericardium Channel of Hand-Jueyin	Ximen (P. 4)
	The Heart Channel of Hand-Shaoyin	Yinxi (H. 6)
3 Yang Channels of Hand	The Large Intes. Channel of Hand-Yangming	Wenliu (L.I. 7)
	The Sanjiao Channel of Hand-Shaoyang	Huizong (S.J. 7)
	The Small Intes. Channel of Hand-Taiyang	Yanglao (S.I. 6)
3 Yang Channels of Foot	The Stomach Channel of Foot-Yangming	Liangqiu (St. 34)
	The Gall bladder Channel of Foot-Shaoyang	Waiqiu (G. B. 36)
	The Urinary Bladder Channel of Foot-Taiyang	Jinmen (U.B. 63)
3 Yin Channels of Foot	The Spleen Channel of Foot-Taiyin	Diji (Sp. 8)
	The Liver Channel of Foot-Jueyin	Foot-Zhongdu (Liv. 6)
	The Kidney Channel of Foot-Shaoyin	Shuiquan (K. 5)
Extra Channels	Yangqiao Channel	Fuyang (U.B. 59)
	Yinqiao Channel	Jiaoxin (K. 8)
	Yangwei Channel	Yangjiao (G.B. 35)
	Yinwei Channel	Zhubin (K. 9)

The Lower He-Sea Points of the *fu* organs usually give satisfactory results in treating diseases of the six *fu* organs, the reason being that the *fu* organs i.e. stomach, large intestine, small intestine, gall bladder, urinary bladder and *sanjiao* are closely related with the three *yang* channels of foot, and each has a Lower He-Sea Point. At the same time the three *yang* channels of foot communicate with the three *yang* channels of hand. In treating diseases of the six *fu* organs, the main points selected are the Lower He-Sea Points. For instance, for gastric pain and acidity, Zusanli (St. 36) is selected; for dysentery or appendicitis, Shangjuxu (St. 37) is used; Yanglingquan (G.B. 34) is for pain in the gall bladder, vomiting, etc. (See Tab. 23.)

Table 23. The Lower He-Sea Points of the Six Fu Organs

Yang Channels of Foot	Fu-Organ	Lower He-Sea Point
Foot-Yangming	Stomach	Zusanli (St. 36)
	Large Intestine	Shangjuxu (St. 37)
	Small Intestine	Xiajuxu (St. 39)
Foot-Shaoyang	Gallbladder	Yanglingquan (G.B. 34)
Foot-Taiyang	Urinary Bladder	Weizhong (U.B. 40)
	Sanjiao	Weiyang (U.B. 39)

5. The Eight Influential Points of the Eight Tissues and the Eight Confluent Points of the Eight Extra Channels

There are eight 'influential' points, each of which has an effect on the diseases of certain tissue. For instance, the Influential Point of the *zang* organ, Zhangmen (Liv. 13), is chosen to treat weakness of spleen, the Influential Point of the *fu* organ, Zhongwan (Ren 12), for borborygmus, vomiting and diarrhea; the Influential point of *qi* (respiratory system), Shanzhong (Ren 17), is used for cough and asthma; the Influential Point of the blood, Geshu (U.B. 17), for vomiting blood, wasting and consumptive diseases; the Influential Point of tendon and muscle, Yanglingquan (G.B. 34), is called on for muscular atrophy and weakness of the joints; the Influential Point of vessels and pulse, Taiyuan (Lu. 9), for weakness of pulse and deficiency of vital energy; the Influential Point of bone, Dashu (U.B. 11), is chosen for painful joints and rheumatism; the Influential

Point of the marrow, Xuanzhong (G.B. 39), for apoplexy, paralysis, etc. (See Tab. 24.)

Table 24. The Eight Influential Points

Tissue	Influential Point
Zang organs	Zhangmen (Liv. 13)
Fu organs	Zhongwan (Ren 12)
Qi (respiratory system; breathing)	Shanzhong (Ren 17)
Blood	Geshu (U.B. 17)
Tendon	Yanglingquan (G.B. 34)
Pulse, vessels	Taiyuan (Lu. 9)
Bone	Dashu (U.B. 11)
Marrow	Xuanzhong (G.B. 39)

The Eight Confluent Points are points in the extremities connecting the eight extra channels and the 12 regular channels. These points have the therapeutic properties for treating diseases of the extra channels and their related regular channels. Four of these eight points are on the upper extremities, while the other four are on the lower extremities. Clinically, these points may be prescribed separately, according to their related channels. For instance, if the Du Channel is affected, Houxi (S.I. 3) may be selected, and if the disease is related to Chong Channel, Gongsun (Sp. 4) may be used. Points of the upper extremities may at times be combined with those of the lower extremities. For example, Neiguan (P. 6) combined with Gongsun (Sp. 4) is indicated in diseases of the heart, chest and epigastric region. Houxi (S.I. 3) combined with Shenmai (U.B. 62) is indicated in diseases of the neck, shoulder, back and inner canthus; Waiguan (S.J. 5) combined with Foot-Linqi (G.B. 41) is indicated in disorders of the mastoid region, cheek and outer canthus; while Lieque (Lu. 7) and Zhaohai (K. 6) in combination are indicated in disorders of the throat, chest and lung. (See Tab. 25.)

Table 25. The Eight Confluent Points of the Eight Extra. Channels

Confluent Point	Regular Channel	Extra. Channel	Indication (portion of the body)
Neiguan (P. 6)	Pericardium	Yinwei	Heart, chest, stomach
Gongsun (Sp. 4)	Spleen	Chong	
Houxi (S.I. 3)	Small Intestine	Du	Neck, shoulder, back, inner canthus
Shenmai (U.B. 62)	Urinary Bladder	Yangqiao	
Waiguan (S.J. 5)	Sanjiao	Yangwei	Retroauricle, cheek, outer canthus
Foot-Linqi (G.B. 41)	Gallbladder	Dai	
Lieque (Lu. 7)	Lung	Ren	Throat, chest, lung
Zhaohai (K. 6)	Kidney	Yinqiao	

CHAPTER III

TREATMENT OF COMMON DISEASES WITH ACUPUNCTURE AND MOXIBUSTION

I. WINDSTROKE (APOPLEXY)

Etiology

The causative factor of this disease is stirring wind arising from hyperactivity of *yang* in liver resulting from exasperation or agitation accompanied with disturbance of the *zang-fu* organs, *qi* and blood, imbalance of *yin* and *yang* and dysfunction of the channels and collaterals. Another factor is endogenous wind caused by phlegm-heat after overindulgence in alcohol and fatty diet.

Differentiation:

There are two types of windstroke according to the degree of severity: The severe type or what is called the *zang-fu* organs being attacked showing symptoms and signs of the channels and collaterals and the viscerae; the mild type or channels and collaterals being attacked, the symptoms and signs pertaining to the channels and collaterals.

(1) The severe type — the *zang-fu* organs being attacked — may be subdivided into (a) tense syndrome and (b) flaccid syndrome.

(a) Tense syndrome: Sudden collapse, coma, staring eyes, fists and jaws clenched, redness of face and ears, gurgling with sputum, coarse breathing, retention of urine, and constipation, wiry and rolling forceful pulse.

(b) Flaccid syndrome: Coma, hands relaxed and mouth agape, eyes closed, pallor, profuse drops of sweat over head and face, snoring. There may be incontinence of feces and urine, cold limbs and feeble pulse. (See Tab. 26.)

Table 26. Comparison of main symptoms and signs of tense and flaccid syndromes of apoplexy.

Tense syndrome	Flaccid syndrome
Eyes open	Eyes closed
Clenched jaws	Mouth agape
Clenched fists	Relaxed hands
Anhidrosis	Hidrosis
Continence of urine, constipation	Incontinence of urine and feces
Wiry, rolling and forceful pulse	Feeble pulse

(2) The mild type, or channels and collaterals being attacked.

Symptoms and signs are mostly those of the sequelae of the severe type, which involve the channels and collaterals. There are also primary cases without affliction of *zang-fu* organs. Manifestations are hemiplegia or deviation of mouth due to motor or sensory impairment.

Treatment:

(1) The severe type — *zang-fu* organs being attacked.

(a) Tense syndrome

Method: To promote resuscitation by applying reducing method to points of the Du Channel and the Jing-Well Points.

Prescription: Renzhong (Du 26) , Baihui (Du 20), the 12 Jing-Well Points of both hands: (Lu. 11, H.9, P.9, L.I. 1, S.J. 1, S.I. 1), Yongquan (K. 1).

Points according to symptoms and signs:

Clenched jaws: Jiache (St. 6), Xiaguan (St. 7), Hegu (L.I. 4)

Gurgling with sputum: Tiantu (Ren 22), Fenglong (St. 40).

Aphasia and stiffness of tongue:Yamen (Du 15), Lianquan (Ren 23), Tongli (H. 5).

Explanation: Renzhong (Du 26) and Baihui (Du 20) regulate the *qi* of the Du Channel, effecting resuscitation. Bleeding the twelve Jing-Well Points of both hands may eliminate heat of the upper portion of the body, thus causing the endogenous wind to subside. Yongquan (K. 1) conducts the heat downward. This method is known as selecting points of the inferior portion of the body to treat diseases of its superior portion.

When the crisis is over, points may be chosen according to symptoms, such as Jiache (St. 6), Xiaguan (St. 7) and Hegu (L.I. 4) for clenched jaws. This method is known as combining the local and distal points according to the courses of the channels, because the Large Intestine Channel and Stomach Channel traverse the cheek. Tiantu (Ren 22) and Fenglong (St.

40) are effective in soothing *qi* (breath) and resolving sputum. Yamen (Du. 15) and Lianquan (Ren 23) are local and adjacent points of the tongue. Tongli (H. 5), the Luo (Connecting) Point of the Heart Channel, may relieve stiffness of tongue because functionally the tongue is related to the heart.

(b) Flaccid syndrome

Method: To recapture *yang* and avert the collapsing state by applying moxibustion to points of Ren Channel.

Prescription: Qihai (Ren 6), Guanyuan (Ren 4), Shenjue (Ren 8).

Explanation: These three points are main points for emergency measures to restore vital function. Continuous indirect moxibustion with salt may offer improvement.

If it is difficult to decide whether the syndrome is of the tense or flaccid type, it is not advisable to bleed the twelve Jing-Well Points of the hand, but it is desirable to apply acupuncture to Renzhong (Du 26) for regaining consciousness, and Zusanli (St. 36) to readjust vital function.

(2) The mild type — channels and collaterals being attacked.

Hemiplegia: This again may be severe or mild, and the attack may be on either side of the body. At the beginning, the affected limbs may be limp. Later, they become stiff, which finally leads to motor impairment. There may be dizziness and dysphasia.

Method: Readjust *qi* (vital function and blood circulation, and remove obstruction from channels and collaterals by puncturing the points of the Yang Channels of the affected side as the main points. Points of the healthy side may be used also. Puncture the healthy side first and then the affected side. Moxibustion may be applied as supplement. The manipulation for acupuncture should be even. (See treatment of the *bi* and *wei* syndromes on pp. 369-373.)

Prescription: Baihui (Du 20), Fengfu (Du 16), Tongtian (U.B. 7).

Upper extremity: Jianyu (L.I. 15), Quchi (L.I. 11), Waiguan (S.J. 5), Hegu (L.I. 4).

Lower Extremity: Huantiao (G.B. 30), Yanglingquan (G.B. 34), Zusanli (St. 36), Jiexi (St. 41).

Explanation: Wind, being a *yang* pathogenic factor, usually invades the upper and exterior parts of the body. Baihui (Du 20), Fengfu (Du 16) and Tongtian (U.B. 7) are used to eliminate pathogenic wind of the upper part of the body. Since *yang* channels dominate the exterior part of the body, points are chosen mainly from these to readjust the *qi* and blood of the body and promote smooth circulation in the channels and collaterals of both the upper and lower parts of the body.

Facial paralysis: (See Treatment of Facial Paralysis on p. 340.)

(3) Prophylactic measures.

Senile patients with deficiency of *qi* and excessive sputum or with manifestations of hyperactivity of *yang* of liver such as dizziness and palpitation may sometimes present symptoms of stiffness of tongue, slurred speech and numbness of finger tips. These are prodromal signs of windstroke. Prophylactic measures are paying attention to diet and daily activities, avoiding over-straining. Frequent moxibustion on Zusanli (St. 36) and Xuanzhong (G.B. 39) may prevent an attack.

Remarks:

Windstroke is similar to cerebrovascular accidents in modern medicine including cerebral hemorrhage, thrombosis, embolism, subarachnoid hemorrhage, etc.

After the acute stage is over, there may be sequelae such as hemiplegia, monoplegia, or aphasia, etc.

II. SYNCOPE

Etiology

Onset of syncope is due mainly to poor health with emotional disturbance and exhaustion. This is because such a condition causes derangement of *qi* of the channels, which in turn hinders the *qi* and blood of the twelve channels in their ascent to the head, prevents the *yang qi* from reaching the extremities and leads the nutrient *qi* and defensive *qi* out of their normal routes of circulation.

Differentiation

Xu type: Shallow breathing, mouth agape, hidrosis, pallor, cold extremities, deep, feeble and thready pulse.

Shi type: Coarse breathing, rigid extremities, clenched jaws, deep and forceful pulse.

Treatment

Method: To promote resuscitation and mental clearness by puncturing points of the Du and Pericardium Channels as the main points. Reducing method for the *shi* type and reinforcing method for the *xu* type.

Prescription: Renzhong (Du 26), Zhongchong (P. 9), Hegu (L.I. 4), Taichong (Liv. 3).

Secondary points:

Xu type: Baihui (Du 20), Qihai (Ren 6), Zusanli (St. 36). Apply acupuncture combined with moxibustion.

Shi type: Laogong (P. 8), Yongquan (K. 1).

Explanation

Renzhong (Du 26) and Zhongchong (P. 9) are points for resuscitation. Hegu (L.I. 4) and Taichong (Liv. 3) may relieve clenching of jaws and mental cloudiness and invigorate circulation of *qi* and blood. Laogong (P. 8) and Yongquan (K. 1) promote a clear mind and dissipate heat. Baihui (Du 20), Zusanli (St. 36) and Qihai (Ren 6) recapture *qi* and re-establish *yang*.

Remarks

(1) This condition includes simple fainting, postural hypotension, sunstroke, hypoglycemia, hysteria, etc. in modern medicine.

(2) Ear acupuncture therapy:

Main points — Heart, Subcortex, Adrenal, Ear-Shenmen.

Method — Strong stimulation.

III. HEADACHE
(Appendix: Trigeminal Neuralgia)

Etiology

The head is where all the *yang* channels of hand and foot meet. Attack of endogenous or exogenous factors may cause headache due to derangement of *qi* and blood in the head and retardation of circulation of *qi* in the channels that traverse the head.

Headache caused by exogenous pathogenic factors will be discussed in the section on the common cold. Here, we deal in detail with headache of endogenous origin, called "head-wind", which is intermittent, protracted and intractable. Pain, in either the right side or the left side of the head is known as one-sided headache. It may be of the *shi* or *xu* type, the former due mainly to hyperactivity of *yang* of the liver and the latter to deficiency of *qi* and blood.

Differentiation

Headache is differentiated according to its locality and its supplying channels. Pain at the occipital region and nape, for example, is related to Urinary Bladder Channel of Foot-Taiyang, pain at the forehead and supraorbital region relates to the Stomach Channel of Foot-Yangming, pain at the temporal region of both sides or only one side relates to the

Gall bladder Channel of Foot-Shaoyang and that at the parietal region is related to the Liver Channel of Foot-Jueyin.

Shi type: Violent boring pain may be accompanied by dizziness, irritability, bitter taste in mouth, nausea, suffocating feeling in chest, hypochondriac pain, sticky tongue coating and wiry pulse.

Xu type: Onset is mostly due to strain and stress. The pain is insidious. It may be agitating or mild and reponds to warmth and pressure. The accompanying symptoms and signs are usually lassitude, palpitation, insomnia, pale tongue and weak pulse.

Treatment

Method: To dispel wind, remove obstruction in the channels and collaterals, and regulate *qi* and blood by puncturing points of the local area combined with points of the remote area. Reducing method for the *shi* type and reinforcing method or tapping with cutaneous needle for the *xu* type.

Prescriptions:

Occipital headache: Fengchi (G.B. 20), Kunlun (U.B. 60), Houxi (S.I. 3).

Frontal headache: Touwei (St. 8), Yintang (Extra.), Shangxing (Du 23), Hegu (L.I. 4), Neiting (St. 44).

One-side headache: Taiyang (Extra.), Shuaigu (G.B. 8), Waiguan (S.J. 5), Foot-Linqi (G.B. 41).

Parietal headache: Baihui (Du 20), Houxi (S.I. 3), Zhiyin (U.B. 67), Taichong (Liv. 3).

Points according to symptoms and signs:

Hyperactivity of *yang* of liver: Xingjian (Liv. 2), Yanglingquan (G.B. 34).

Deficiency of *qi* and blood: Qihai (Ren 6), Zusanli (St. 36).

Explanation:

The above prescriptions are formulated by combining local points with distal points according to the location of headache and the channels affected.

Occiptal headache — points of Taiyang Channels of Hand and Foot.

Frontal headache — points of Yangming Channels of Hand and Foot.

One-side headache — points of Shaoyang Channels of Hand and Foot.

Parietal headache — points of Taiyang Channels of Hand and Foot plus those of the Jueyin Channel of Foot.

These prescriptions have the effect of removing obstruction of channels and collaterals, regulating the *qi* and blood and relieving pain.

Remarks:

1. Headache occurs in various diseases in modern medical consideration: internal medicine, surgery, neurology, psychosis, ear, nose, throat, etc. Acupuncture gives gratifying results in migraine, and in vascular and functional headache.

2. Cutaneous needle tapping and cupping method:

Main points: Area along L_1 to S_4.

Secondary points: Fengchi (G.B. 20), Taiyang (Extra.), Yangbai (G.B. 14).

Method: Tap on area from L_1 to S_4. Then tap on the local area and that where the afflicted channels pass through. In acute pain, Taiyang (Extra.) and Yangbai (G.B. 14) etc. may be tapped until slight bleeding occurs, then apply cupping.

3. Ear-acupuncture therapy

Main points: Subcortex, Forehead, Occiput, Kidney, Gallbladder, etc.

Method: Insert needles and manipulate intermittently. For persistent headache, rotate the needles continuously for 5 minutes to cause strong stimulation. Or, needles can be embedded at the sensitive spots for 1-7 days.

APPENDIX: TRIGEMINAL NEURALGIA

This is a transient paroxysmal burning pain on the facial region which is supplied by the trigeminal nerve.

Treatment

Prescriptions:

Pain at the 1st (ophthalmic) branch: Yangbai (G.B. 14), Taiyang (Extra.), Zanzhu (U.B. 2), Waiguan (S.J. 5).

Pain at the 2nd (maxillary) branch: Sibai (St. 2), Nose-Juliao (St. 3), Renzhong (Du 26), Hegu (L.I. 4).

Pain at the 3rd (mandibular) branch: Xiaguan (St. 7), Jiache (St. 6) Chengjiang (Ren 24), Neiting (St. 44).

Ear Acupuncture:

Main points: Forehead, Sympathetic Nerve, Ear-Shenmen, auricular points corresponding to the painful areas.

Method: Rotate the needles for several minutes, or embed them at the sensitive spots.

IV. DIZZINESS AND VERTIGO

Etiology

Causative factors:

(1) Upward attack of hyperactive *yang* of the liver due to failing of water in nourishing wood (dysfunction of the kidney affecting the liver);

(2) Interior retention of phlegm-damp which causes mental cloudiness, and

(3) *Xu* (deficiency) of *qi* and blood, which causes insufficiency of the "sea of marrow" in the head.

Differentiation

Main symptoms are giddiness, and blurring of vision with a whirling sensation and of things turning, also of a tendency to fall.

(1) Upward attack of hyperactive *yang* of liver: Besides the main symptoms, there appear tinnitus, flushed face, nausea, backache, redness of tongue proper and wiry and rapid pulse.

(2) Interior retention of phlegm-damp: Complications are fullness and suffocating sensation of chest and epigastric region, nausea and vomiting, profuse sputum, anorexia, white and sticky coated tongue, rolling pulse.

(3) *Xu* (deficiency) of *qi* and blood: Complications are listlessness, lassitude, palpitation, insomnia, pulse without force.

Treatment

(1) Upward attack of hyperactive *yang* of liver:

Method: Points from the Jueyin (Liver) Channel and the Shaoyin (Kidney) Channel are selected as the main ones to nourish *yin* and pacify *yang*. Reinforcing and reducing methods may be used at one sitting. The condition of the disease determines the method of choice.

Prescription: Shenshu (U.B. 23), Taixi (K. 3), Ganshu (U.B. 18) Xingjian (Liv. 2), Fengchi (G.B. 20).

Explanation: Application of reinforcing method to Shenshu (U.B. 23) and Taixi (K. 3) strengthens the kidney, while application of reducing method to Ganshu (U.B. 18), Xingjian (Liv. 2) and Fengchi (G.B. 20) pacifies *yang* of the liver.

(2) Interior retention of phlegm-damp:

Method: Resolve phlegm and eliminate damp by applying reinforcing and reducing methods to the Back-Shu, Front-Mu and Luo (Connecting) Points of the spleen and stomach.

Prescription: Pishu (U.B. 20), Zhongwan (Ren 12), Fenglong (St. 40), Neiguan (P. 6), Touwei (St. 8).

Explanation: Application of reinforcing method to Pishu (U.B. 20), the Back-Shu Point of the spleen, and Zhongwan (Ren 12), the Front-Mu Point of the stomach, strengthens the function of the spleen and stomach to eliminate damp. Fenglong (St. 40) the Luo (Connecting) Point of the stomach has the function of resolving phlegm when the reducing method is applied. Touwei (St. 8) is an effective point for dizziness, Neiguan (P. 6) for keeping the stomach in order and stopping vomiting.

(3) *Xu* (deficiency) of *qi* and blood

Method: Points of the Ren, Taiyang (Urinary Bladder) and Yangming (Stomach) Channels are selected as the main points. Apply reinforcing method. Moxibustion may also be used.

Prescription: Guanyuan (Ren 4), Pishu (U.B. 20), Sanyinjiao (Sp. 6), Zusanli (St. 36).

Explanation: Guanyuan (Ren 4) strengthens vital energy. Pishu (U.B. 20), Sanyinjiao (Sp. 6) and Zusanli invigorate the spleen and stomach, sources of *qi* and blood production.

Remarks:

(1) Dizziness and vertigo may be explained as derangement in the sense of equilibrium in modern medicine. Clinically, such illness is mostly present as Meniere's syndrome, labyrinthitis, otosclerosis, hyper- or hypotension, neurasthenia, etc.

(2) Tapping needle method:

Main points: Baihui (Du 20), Taiyang (Extra.), Yintang (Extra.), Huatuo Jiaji (Extra.).

Method: Treat once or twice daily with moderate stimulation. Five to ten treatments constitute a course.

(3) Ear acupuncture:

Main points: Forehead, Heart, Sympathetic Nerve, Ear-Shenmen, Kidney, Endocrine, Adrenal, Occiput.

Method: Select 2-4 points in each treatment. Manipulate the needles intermittently with moderate stimulation. Retain the needles for 15-20 minutes. Treatment may be given daily, three to seven treatments to a course. Needles may be implanted intradermally.

V. FACIAL PARALYSIS

Etiology

Onset of the disease is due to derangement of *qi* and blood and malnutrition of the channels caused by invasion of the channels and collaterals in the facial region by pathogenic wind-cold or phlegm.

Differentiation

Clinical manifestations on the affected side are incomplete closing of the eye, lacrimation, drooping of the angle of the mouth, salivation, and inability to frown, raise the eyebrow, close the eye, blow out the cheek, show the teeth or whistle. There may be pain in the mastoid region or headache. The tongue is coated white. The pulse is superficial.

Treatment

Method: Eliminate the wind and remove obstruction of the collaterals by applying even-movement method to points of the Yangming Channels of Hand and Foot as the main points.

Prescription: Yifeng (S.J. 17), Dicang (St. 4), Jiache (St. 6), Yangbai (G.B. 14), Taiyang (Extra.), Hegu (L.I. 4), Quanliao (S.I. 18), Xiaguan (St. 7).

Manipulation: Select 3-5 points at one sitting. The method of horizontal penetration of two points may be used, such as penetration of Dicang (St. 4) horizontally towards Jiache (St. 6). Treat daily at the beginning.

Points according to symptoms and signs:

Headache: Fengchi (G.B. 20).

Profuse sputum: Fenglong (St. 40).

Difficulty in frowning and raising the eyebrow: Zanzhu (U.B. 2) Sizhukong (S.J. 23).

Incomplete closing of the eye: Zanzhu (U.B. 2), Jingming (U.B. 1), Tongziliao (G.B. 1), Yuyao (Extra.), Sizhukong (S.J. 23).

Difficulty in sniffling. Yingxiang (L.I. 20).

Deviation of the philtrum: Renzhong (Du. 26).

Inability to show the teeth: Nose-Juliao (St. 3).

Tinnitus and deafness: Tinghui (G.B. 2).

Twitching of the eyelid and the mouth: Taichong (Liv. 3).

Tenderness at the mastoid region: Head-Wangu (G.B. 12).

Explanation: Combination of Hegu (L.I. 4) and Taichong (Liv. 3), the respective Yuan (Source) Points of the Large Intestine and Liver Channels, is effective in eliminating pathogenic wind in the head and facial region. Tinghui (G.B. 2) and Head-Wangu (G.B. 12) are useful in eliminating wind and clearing the ear. Jiache (St. 6), Xiaguan (St. 7), Dicang (St. 4), Nose-Juliao (St. 3), Qanliao (S.I. 18), Yangbai (G.B. 14), Tongziliao (G.B. 1), Zanzhu (U.B. 2), Sizhukong (S.J. 23), Jingming (U.B. 1), Yingxiang (L.I. 20) and Renzhong (Du 26) are all local points of the involved channels and have the effect of eliminating wind and invigorating circulation.

Remarks:

(1) This disease is the same as peripheral facial paralysis or Bell's palsy in modern medicine.

(2) In long-standing cases, the warming needle or mild moxibustion may be used. The points are Taiyang (Extra.), Jiache (St. 6), Dicang (St. 4), Nose-Juliao (St. 3) and Xiaguan (St. 7). Two or three points may be used at each treatment, with heat applied to each point for 2-3 minutes.

(3) Cupping. Cupping may be used as an adjuvant method to acupuncture. The affected side may be treated with small cups once every 3-5 days.

VI. SUNSTROKE

Etiology

This is most often due to invasion of summer heat damaging *qi* and *yin* in conditions of extreme fatigue from prolonged labour under hot sun.

Differentiation

Sunstroke may be divided into mild and severe types.

(1) Mild type: Headache, hidrosis, hot skin, coarse breathing, dry tongue and mouth, thirst, superficial large and rapid pulse.

(2) Severe type: Headache, thirst, fast short breathing followed by sudden collapse, loss of consciousness, sweating, deep and forceless pulse.

Treatment

(1) Mild type:

Method: Eliminate summer heat by application of reducing method to points selected from the Du, Jueyin (Pericardium) and Yangming (Large Intestine) Channels as the main points.

Prescription: Dazhui (Du 14), Daling (P. 7), Weizhong (U.B. 40), Hegu (L.I. 4), Quchi (L.I. 11), Jinjin, Yuye (Extra.).

Explanation: Dazhui (Du. 14) eliminates heat. Daling (P. 7) reduces the fire of the heart. Pricking Weizhong (U.B. 40) to cause bleeding dispels summer heat. Hegu (L.I. 4) and Quchi (L.I. 11) are two main points for antipyretic purpose. Pricking and bleeding Jinjin, Yuye (Extra.) may relieve dry mouth and thirst.

(2) Severe type:

Method: Reduce heat and regain consciousness by applying reducing method to points of the Du Channel as the main points. (See also treatment of the tense syndrome of windstroke on p. 332.)

Prescriptions: Renzhong (Du 26), Baihui (Du 20), Weizhong (U.B. 40), Shixuan (Extra.)

Explanation: Renzhong (Du 26) and Baihui (Du 20) promote resuscitation and mental clearness. Weizhong (U.B. 40) and Shixuan (Extra.) reduce heat and summer sultriness.

Etiology

Malaria is known as quotidian malaria, tertian malaria and quartan malaria according to the interval between attacks. In chronic cases there may be a mass in the right hypochondrium.

Onset of the disease is mostly due to derangement of nutrient *qi* and defensive *qi* (vital function) caused by humid heat and damp attacking the Shaoyang Channel complicated with pestilential factor. The main manifestation is alternate chills and fever.

Differentiation

Chills are usually present at the beginning of the seizure, followed by fever with symptoms and signs of headache, flushed face and thirst. After the attack, the fever subsides and there is general sweating. There may be a stifling feeling in the chest and hypochondriac region, a bitter taste in the mouth, yellow, sticky thin coated tongue, wiry and rapid pulse.

Treatment

Method: The treatment mainly aims at regulating the Du Channel and harmonizing the Shaoyang Channels. If chills are the dominant symptom during the attack, acupuncture and moxibustion may be used simultaneously. If fever is the dominant symptom, use acupuncture only. Treatment is given two hours prior to the attack.

Prescription: Dazhui (Du 14), Taodao (Du 13), Foot-Linqi (G.B. 41), Houxi (S.I. 3), Jianshi (P. 5).

Secondary points:

High fever — Quchi (L.I. 11), needling with reducing method.

A mass in the right hypochondrium — Zhangmen (Liv. 13), Huangmen (U.B. 51). Apply acupuncture to the former and moxibustion to the latter.

In grave attack with delirium and mental cloudiness — Prick the twelve Jing-Well Points on the hand (Lu. 11, H.9, P.9, L.I. 1, S.J. 1, S.I. 1).

Explanation: Dazhu (Du 14) and Taodao (Du 13) remove obstruction in the Du Channel and harmonize *yin* and *yang*, while Foot-Linqi (G.B. 41) harmonizes the *qi* of Shaoyang Channels. Houxi (S.I. 3) disperses the exterior heat, and Jianshi (P. 5) eliminates the interior heat. When both the exterior and interior heat subside, the co-ordination of nutrient *qi* and defensive *qi* (vital function) is attained, which checks the disease.

Ear-acupuncture therapy:

Main points: Adrenal, Subcortex, Endocrine, *Sanjiao* and Spleen.

Method: Treatment is to be given 1-2 hours before the attack successively for three days. Retain needles for one hour. For recurrent cases, add the auricular point Spleen.

VIII. THE COMMON COLD

Etiology

Causative factors are exogenus wind-cold or wind-heat which hinders the lung's dispersing action, and low defensive vital function of the superficial portion of the body.

Differentiation

(1) Common cold due to wind-cold: Chills, fever, anhidrosis, headache, nasal obstruction, rhinitis, aching of joints. There may be the complication of itching of the throat, and cough. Tongue coating is thin and white, the pulse superficial and tense.

(2) Common cold due to wind-heat: Fever, intolerance to wind, hidrosis, distending sensation of head, thirst, hacking cough, dry, congested and sore throat, thin and yellowish tongue coating, superficial and rapid pulse.

Treatment

(1) Wind-cold:

Method: To eliminate wind and relieve exterior symptoms by applying reducing method to points of the Du, Taiyang and Shaoyang Channels as the main points.

Prescription: Fengfu (Du 16), Fengmen (U.B. 12), Fengchi (G.B. 20), Lieque (Lu. 7), Hegu (L.I. 4), Fuliu (K. 7).

Points according to symptoms and signs:

Headache: Taiyang (Extra.).

Nasal obstruction: Yingxiang (L.I.20).

Explanation: Fengfu (Du 16), Fengmen (U.B. 12) and Fengchi (G.B. 20) stimulation alleviate headache by eliminating wind and relieving exterior symptoms. Leique (Lu. 7), the Luo (Connecting) Point of the Lung Channel, is used in treating disorders of the head and neck and easing nasal obstruction. Hegu (L.I. 4) and Fuliu (K. 7) cause sweating to enhance the effect of relieving the exterior symptoms. Taiyang (Extra.) and Yingxiang (L.I. 20) are local points used to eliminate pathogenic wind in the head and facial region.

(2) Wind-heat:

Method: To eliminate wind and heat by applying needling with reducing method to points of the Du and Shaoyang Channels as the main points.

Prescription: Dazhui (Du 14), Fengchi (G.B. 20), Waiguan (S.J. 5), Hegu (L.I. 4), Shaoshang (Lu. 11).

Explanation: Dazhui (Du 14) is a point where the Du Channel and all the *yang* channels meet. Fengchi (G.B. 20), Waiguan (S.J. 5) and Hegu (L.I. 4) eliminate wind and heat. Pricking Shaoshang (Lu. 11) to cause bleeding eliminates wind-heat in the Lung Channel and eases the throat.

Prophylaxis:

Application of moxibustion to Fengmen (U.B. 12) or Zusanli (St. 36) daily may prevent the common cold when this disease is prevalent.

IX. COUGH

Etiology

Causative factors may be exogenous or endogenous. Exogenous factors are wind-cold or wind-heat which attacks the lung, preventing it from performing its function of dispersing. Endogenous factors are (1) dryness of the lung due to *xu* (deficiency) of *yin* resulting in impairment of its descending function, and (2) *xu* (deficiency) of the *yang* of the spleen leading to accumulation of damp and formation of phlegm.

Differentiation

(1) Invasion of exogenous pathogenic factors:

(a) Wind-cold type: Chills, fever, headache, nasal obstruction, choking cough. The tongue has a thin white coating the pulse is superficial.

(b) Wind-heat type: Fever without chills, thirst, cough with purulent thick sputum, yellow tongue coating, superficial rapid pulse.

(2) Endogenous factors:

(a) Dryness of the lung due to *xu* (deficiency) of *yin*: Dry cough with no or scanty sputum, dry or sore throat. There may be bloody sputum or even hemoptysis, afternoon fever, malar flush. Red tongue with thin coating, feeble rapid pulse.

(b) *Xu* (Deficiency) of *yang* of spleen: Cough with excessive sputum which becomes severe in winter, anorexia, listlessness, thick sticky slippery white-coated tongue, pulse usually deep and slow.

Treatment

(1) Invasion by exogenous pathogenic factors:

Method: Points are mainly selected from the Taiyin (Lung) and Yangming (the Large Intestine) Channels to activate the dispersing function of the lung and relieve the exterior symptoms. For wind-cold type, acupuncture may be combined with moxibustion, while for wind-heat type use acupuncture only.

Prescription: Lieque (Lu. 7), Hegu (L.I. 4), Feishu (U.B. 13), Chize (Lu. 5).

Explanation: Lieque (Lu. 7) and Hegu (L.I. 4), combination of Yuan (Source) and Luo (Connecting) Points, are used to eliminate wind and relieve exterior symptoms. Feishu (U.B. 13) activates the dispersing function of the lung. Chize (Lu. 5) clears the lung and relieves cough.

(2) Endogenous factors:

(a) Dryness of the lung due to *xu* (deficiency) of *yin*:

Method: The Back-Shu and Front-Mu Points of the lung are taken as the main points to tonify the *yin* and activate the descending function of the lung. Points are punctured superficially. Moxibustion is not advisable.

Prescription: Feishu (U.B. 13), Zhongfu (Lu. 1), Lieque (Lu. 7), Zhaohai (K. 6).

Secondary points:

Hemoptysis: Kongzui (Lu. 6), Geshu (U.B. 17).

Explanation: Feishu (U.B. 13) and Zhongfu (Lu. 1), a combination of Back-Shu and Front-Mu Points, are used to regulate the respiratory tract. Lieque (Lu. 7) and Zhaohai (K. 6), a pair of the Eight Confluent Points, ease the throat through its action in tonifing the *yin* and activating the descending function of the lung. Kongzui (Lu. 6), the Xi (Cleft) Point of the lung, and Geshu (U.B. 17), the Influential Point dominating blood, are used to achieve hemostatic effect.

(b) *Xu* (deficiency) of *yang* of spleen:

Method: The Back-Shu Point of the spleen and the Front-Mu Point of the stomach are taken as the main points to strengthen the spleen and resolve sputum. Apply needling with reinforcing method combined with moxibustion.

Prescription: Pishu (U.B. 20), Zhongwan (Ren 12), Zusanli (St. 36), Feishu (U.B. 13), Gaohuangshu (U.B. 43), Fenglong (St. 40).

Explanation: Pishu (U.B. 20), Zhongwan (Ren 12) and Zusanli (St. 36) strengthen the spleen and stomach to eliminate damp and resolve phlegm. Application of moxibustion to Feishu (U.B. 13) and Gaohuangshu (U.B. 43) activates and gives warmth to the *qi* of the lung.

Remarks:

(1) If cough is accompanied by fever and asthma, see treatment of the common cold and asthma on pp. 344 and 347.

(2) The type of cough mentioned in this section occurs for the most part in the common cold, acute and chronic bronchitis and pneumonia.

(3) Cupping method:

Main points: Fengmen (U.B. 12), Feishu (U.B. 13).

(4) Tapping-needle method: Tap along the Du and Urinary Bladder Channels on the upper part of the back till the skin becomes red or bleeds slightly.

(5) Ear acupuncture:

Main points: Lung, Ear-Asthma.

Method: Treatment is given once daily or every other day. Needles are retained for 30-60 minutes. A course may be 5-10 treatments.

X. ASTHMA

Etiology

There are two main types of asthma: the *xu* type and the *shi* type. *Shi* type asthma results from dysfunction of the lung in descending due to invasion of exogenous wind-cold or disturbance of phlegm-heat. *Xu* type asthma is due to (1) *xu* (weakness) of the lung, or (2) *xu* (weakness) of the kidney which fails to perform its function of receiving *qi* (air).

Differentiation

(1) *Shi* type

(a) Wind-cold: Cough with thin sputum, shortness of breath. Usually there are accompanying symptoms of fever, chills, anhidrosis, white coating on tongue, superficial pulse.

(b) Phlegm-heat: Rapid and coarse breathing, stifling sensation in the chest, thick purulent sputum, thick yellowish coating on tongue, rapid, rolling and forceful pulse.

(2) *Xu* type

(a) *Xu* of lung: Short and quick breathing, weak and low voice, hidrosis, weak pulse.

(b) *Xu* of kidney: Asthma, dyspnea upon exertion, chilliness with cold extremities, deep thready feeble pulse.

Treatment

(1) *Shi* type

Method: For asthma due to wind-cold, points of the Lung Channel are taken as the main points to eliminate wind and cold and soothe asthma. For asthma due to phlegm-heat, points of the Stomach Channel are taken as the main points to resolve phlegm and soothe asthma. Puncture with reducing method for both types. Moxibustion may be added for the former condition.

Prescription:

(a) Wind-cold: Feishu (U.B. 13), Lieque (Lu. 7), Hegu (L.I. 4).

(b) Phlegm-heat: Fenglong (St. 40), Tiantu (Ren 22), Chize (Lu. 5), Dingchuan (Asthma Relief) (Extra.).

Explanation: Feishu (U.B. 13) activates qi of the lung. Lieque (Lu. 7) and Hegu (L.I. 4) eliminate wind and cold. Fenglong (St. 40), a distal point, combined with Tiantu (Ren 22), a local point, pacifies breathing and resolves phlegm. Chize (Lu. 5), He-Sea Point of the Lung Channel, reduces the heat in the lung to soothe asthma.

(2) Xu type

Method: Reinforce the qi (vital energy) of the lung and kidney. Puncture with reinforcing method. Moxibustion is advisable.

Prescriptions:

(a) Xu of lung: Feishu (U.B. 13), Taiyuan (Lu. 9), Zusanli (St. 36).

(b) Xu of kidney: Shenshu (U.B. 23), Mingmen (Du 4), Qihai (Ren 6), Shanzhong (Ren 17).

Secondary points:

Chronic persistent asthma: Shenzhu (Du 12), Gaohuangshu (U.B. 43).

Xu of spleen: Zhongwan (Ren 12), Pishu (U.B. 20).

Explanation: Applying moxibustion to Feishu (U.B. 13) reinforces the qi of the lung. According to the theory of the five elements, both Taiyuan (Lu. 9), the Shu-Stream Point of the Lung Channel, and Zusanli (St. 36), the He-Sea Point of the Stomach Channel, are related to earth. Puncturing these two points is to strengthen the lung (metal) through invigorating the spleen (earth) and stomach (earth). Shenshu (U.B. 23) and Mingmen (Du 4) reinforce the qi (vital energy) of the kidney. Qihai (Ren 6) is an essential point for strengthening qi. Shanzhong (Ren 17), the Influential Point dominating qi (respiration), is for regulating qi and soothing asthma. Application of indirect moxibustion with garlic to Shenzhu (Du 12) and Gaohuangshu (U.B. 43) may relieve chronic asthma. Application of moxibustion to Zhongwan (Ren 12) and Pishu (U.B. 20) strengthens the qi (vital energy) of the spleen.

Remarks:

(1) Asthma here includes bronchial asthma, asthmatic bronchitis, and dyspnea present in some other diseases. Other therapeutic measures besides acupuncture may be considered for symptomatic dyspnea.

(2) Ear acupuncture may be applied during the attack.

Main points: Lung, Kidney, Adrenal, Sympathetic Nerve, Ear-Asthma.

Method: Select 2-3 points each time, or puncture the tender spots. Needles are retained for 30-60 minutes. After 10-15 sittings let 3-5 days elapse before starting another course of treatment.

XI. INSOMNIA

Etiology

Causative factors: (1) *xu* of spleen and blood insufficiency resulting from anxiety, (2) flaring of heart fire due to insufficiency of *yin* in kidney causing disharmony of heart and kidney, (3) upward disturbance of liver fire resulting from mental depression, and (4) retention of phlegm-heat due to gastric indigestion.

Differentiation

(1) *Xu* of spleen and blood insufficiency: Difficulty in falling asleep and disturbed sleep accompanied by palpitation, poor memory, lassitude, listlessness, anorexia, sallow complexion and thready weak pulse.

(2) Disharmony of heart and kidney: Irritability and insomnia accompanied by dizziness, tinnitus, low back pain, seminal emission, leukorrhagia and rapid weak pulse.

(3) Upward disturbance of liver fire: Mental depression, quick temper and dream-disturbed sleep accompanied by headache, distending pain in the costal and hypochondriac region, bitter taste in mouth and wiry pulse.

(4) Dysfunction of stomach: Insomnia accompanied by fullness and suffocating feeling in the epigastric region, abdominal distension, belching and full forceful pulse.

Treatment

Method: Points are mainly selected from the Heart Channel to calm the heart and soothe the mind.

Xu of spleen and blood insufficiency: Apply needling with reinforcing method. Moxibustion is used in combination.

Disharmony of heart and kidney: Apply needling with even-movement method.

Upward disturbance of liver fire: Apply needling with reducing method.

Dysfunction of stomach: Apply needling with reducing method.

Prescription: Shenmen (H. 7), Neiguan (P. 6), Sanyinjiao (Sp. 6).

Points according to different syndromes:

Xu of spleen and blood insufficiency: Pishu (U.B. 20), Xinshu (U.B. 15), Yinbai (Sp. 1, moxibustion with small-sized moxa cones).

Disharmony of heart and kidney: Xinshu (U.B. 15), Shenshu (U.B. 23), Taixi (K. 3).

Upward disturbance of liver fire: Ganshu (U.B. 18), Danshu (U.B. 19), Head-Wangu (G.B. 12).

Dysfunction of stomach: Weishu (U.B. 21), Zusanli (St. 36).

Explanation: Shenmen (H. 7) is the Yuan (Source) Point of the Heart Channel, Neiguan (P. 6) the Luo (Connecting) Point of the Pericardium Channel, and Sanyinjiao (Sp. 6) the Crossing Point of the Liver, Spleen and Kidney Channels. Combining these three points may calm the heart and soothe the mind. Pishu (U.B. 20) and Xinshu (U.B. 15) are used because the spleen controls blood and the heart produces blood. Yinbai (Sp. 1) is the Jing-well Point of the Spleen Channel. Moxibustion using small moxa cones at this point treats dream-disturbed sleep and being startled during sleep. Combination of Xinshu (U.B. 15), Shenshu (U.B. 23), and Taixi (K. 3) may adjust the disharmony of heart and kidney. Combination of Ganshu (U.B. 18), Danshu (U.B. 19) and Head-Wangu (G.B. 12) is to reduce the upward disturbance of the fire of the liver and gall bladder. Weishu (U.B. 21) and Zusanli (St. 36) are used to promote the function of the stomach and relieve distension.

Remarks:

(1) Tapping-needle method: Tap on Sishencong (Extra.) and Huatuo Jiaji (Extra.) lightly from above downward 2-3 times in one sitting. Give treatment once daily or every other day. Ten treatments may be considered as a course. Continue treatment if results are satisfactory.

(2) Ear acupuncture:

Main points: Subcortex, Ear-Shenmen, Kidney, Heart.

Method: Select 2-3 points each time. Needles are retained for 20 minutes or embedded for 2-3 days.

XII. PALPITATION, ANXIETY

Etiology

Causative factors: (1) Deficiency of qi and blood plus mental disturbance due to fright, (2) Disturbance of the heart by stirring of endogenous phlegm-fire, and (3) Perversion of harmful fluid due to dysfunction of the heart. In mild cases, palpitation may be intermittent; in severe cases, there may be continuous and incontrollable violent throbbing of the heart.

Differentiation

(1) Insufficiency of qi and blood: Pallor, shortness of breath, general weakness, disturbed sleep, dizziness, blurring of vision, pale flabby tongue with teeth prints on the border, thready forceless pulse.

(2) Stirring of endogenous phlegm-fire: Irritability, restlessness, dream-disturbed sleep, yellow coating on tongue, rolling rapid pulse.

(3) Retention of harmful fluid: Expectoration of mucoid sputum, fullness in the chest and epigastric region, lassitude, white coating on tongue, wiry rolling pulse.

Treatment

Method: Apply even-movement method to the Back-Shu and Front-Mu Points of the heart as the main points to calm the heart.

Prescription: Xinshu (U.B. 12), Juque (Ren 14), Shenmen (H. 7), Neiguan (P. 6).

Points according to syndromes:

(1) Insufficiency of *qi* and blood: Qihai (Ren 6), Pishu (U.B. 20), Weishu (U.B. 21).

(2) Stirring of endogenous phlegm-fire: Fenglong (St. 40), Yanglingquan (G.B. 34).

(3) Retention of harmful fluid: Guanyuan (Ren 4), Sanjiaoshu (U.B. 22), Zusanli (St. 36), Shanzhong (Ren 17).

Explanation: Xinshu (U.B. 15) and Juque (Ren 14), the Back-Shu and Front-Mu Points of the heart, Shenmen (H. 7), the Yuan (Source) Point of the Heart Channel, and Neiguan (P. 6), the Luo (Connecting) Point of the Pericardium Channel, all have the properties of regulating *qi* and blood of the heart and as tranquilizer. Qihai (Ren 6) strengthens *qi*. Pishu (U.B. 20) and Weishu (U.B. 21) adjust the function of the spleen and stomach, which are the foundation for producing *qi* and blood. Applying acupuncture or moxibustion on Guanyuan (Ren 4), Shanzhong (Ren 17) and Zusanli (St. 36) will strengthen the spleen, invigorate *yang* and eliminate harmful fluid. Sanjiaoshu (U.B. 22) regulates the upper, middle and lower *jiao* and promotes transportation of water. Fenglong (St. 40) and Yanglingquan (G.B. 34) eliminate the phlegm-fire in the stomach.

Remarks:

(1) Palpitation and anxiety described here may be symptoms present in neurosis, functional disorders of vegetative nervous system and cardiac arrhythmia of various origins.

(2) Ear acupuncture

Main points: Ear-Shenmen, Heart, Sympathetic Nerve, Subcortex, Small Intestine.

Method: Select 2-3 points in each treatment and give moderate stimulation. Needles are retained for 15-20 minutes. Treatment is given every other day. 10-15 treatments constitute a course. Allow 3-5 days interval between courses.

XIII. DEPRESSIVE AND MANIC MENTAL DISORDERS

Etiology

Depressive mental disorder is usually caused by retardation of *qi* and accumulation of phlegm resulting from mental depression. Manic mental disorder may be caused by (1) *qi* stasis due to exasperation which elicits fire and causes formation of phlegm, or (2) excessive heat in the stomach hindering the descent of harmful *qi* which results in accumulation of heat disturbing the mind.

Differentiation

(1) Depressive mental disorder: Gradual onset, mental depression and dullness at the initial stage, followed by paraphasia and paraphronia, or muteness, hypersomnia and anorexia. The tongue is thinly or moderately coated. The pulse is wiry and thready.

(2) Manic mental disorder: Sudden onset, preceded by irritability, peevishness, and scarcely sleeping and eating. This is followed by mania demonstrated by shouting, yelling, tearing off clothes, running about, sleeplessness, smashing things and hitting people. The tongue is yellow and sticky. The pulse is usually wiry, rolling and rapid.

Treatment

Method: Points from the Du Channel and Hand-Jueyin (Pericardium) Channel are selected as the main points to calm the heart and mind and restore mental clarity. For depressive mental disorder, apply needling with even-movement method. Moxibustion may be applied according to the condition. For mania, use reducing method in needling.

Prescription: Renzhong (Du 26), Shaoshang (Lu. 11), Yinbai (Sp. 1), Daling (P. 7), Shenmai (U.B. 62), Fengfu (Du 16), Jiache (St. 6), Chengjiang (Ren 24), Laogong (P. 8), Shangxing (Du 23), Quchi (L.I. 11).

Points for maniac cases with extreme heat: Prick the 12 Jing-Well Points on hand (Lu. 11, H. 9, P. 9, L.I. 1., S.J. 1, S.I. 1) till they bleed to reduce heat.

Explanation: Renzhong (Du 26), Shaoshang (Lu. 11) and Yinbai (Sp. 1) are effective for regaining mental clarity, dispelling heat and suppressing madness. Daling (P. 7), the Yuan (Source) Point of the Pericardium Channel, and Laogong (P. 8), the Ying-Spring Point of the Pericardium Channel, are used to reduce the heat in the Pericardium Channel. Shenmai (U.B. 62), Fengfu (Du 16) and Shangxing (Du 23) dispel heat in the Yangqiao Channel and Du Channel to tranquilize the mind. Jiache (St. 6) and Quchi (L.I. 11) dissipate heat from Hand- and Foot-Yangming Channels.

Remarks:

(1) Depressive and manic mental disorders correspond to the depressive and manic types of schizophrenia and psychosis in modern medicine.

(2) Ear acupuncture:

Main points: Sympathetic Nerve, Ear-Shenmen, Heart, Liver, Subcortex, Endocrine, Stomach, Occiput.

Method: Select 1-2 points for each treatment.

XIV. VOMITING

Etiology

Vomiting is due to dysfunction of the stomach in digestion and transportation. The qi of the stomach ascends instead of descends. Causative factors are:

(1) Overeating and retention of cold and fatty food.

(2) Perversion of qi of liver due to anger affecting the function of stomach; and

(3) Weakness of the spleen and stomach.

Differentiation

(1)Retention of food: Epigastric and abdominal distension or pain, acid fermented vomitus, belching, anorexia, constipation, foul gas. The tongue is thickly coated and sticky; the pulse is rolling and forceful.

(2) Invasion of stomach by qi of liver: Vomiting, acid regurgitation, continual belching, distending pain in hypochondriac region. The tongue is thinly coated and sticky, the pulse wiry.

(3) Weakness of spleen and stomach: Sallow complexion, vomiting after eating a very full meal, lack of appetite, slightly loose stools, general lassitude, forceless pulse, thinly coated, sticky tongue.

Treatment

Method: Points of the Stomach Channel are the main points. When retention of food or invasion of the stomach by qi of liver is at fault, needling is given with reducing method. For weakness of spleen and stomach, needling is given with reinforcing method combined with moxibustion.

Prescription: Zusanli (St. 36), Zhongwan (Ren 12), Neiguan (P. 6), Gongsun (Sp. 4).

Secondary points:

(1) Retention of food: Tianshu (St. 25).

(2) Invasion of stomach by *qi* of liver: Taichong (Liv. 3).

(3) Weakness of spleen and stomach: Pishu (U.B. 20).

(4) Pernicious vomiting: Jinjin, Yuye (Extra.).

Explanation: Zusanli (St. 36) is the He-Sea Point of the Stomach Channel and Zhongwan (Ren 12) is the Front-Mu Point of the stomach. The two points used together are effective in readjusting the stomach and subduing the ascending *qi*. Neiguan (P. 6) and Gongsun (Sp. 4), one of the pair-points of the Eight Confluent Points, relieve the feeling of fullness in the chest and stomach. Tianshu (St. 25) stimulation relieves intestinal obstruction. Needling Taichong (Liv. 3) with reducing method activates the function of the liver. Needling Pishu (U.B. 20) with reinforcing method strengthens the spleen. Pricking Jinjin, Yuye (Extra.) to cause bleeding is an empirical method for checking vomiting.

Remark: Vomiting as described in this section means mainly acute and chronic gastritis and neurotic vomiting.

XV. HICCUP

Etiology

Causative factors: (1) Failure of *qi* of stomach to descend caused by irregular food intake and stagnation of *qi* of liver, and (2) ascending of *qi* of stomach caused by attack by cold.

Differentiation

(1) Retention of food and stagnation of *qi*: Epigastric and adbominal distension, hiccups, yellowish sticky coated tongue, rolling forceful pulse. There may be distending pain in the chest and hypochondrium, irritability and wiry forceful pulse.

(2) Attack by pathogenic cold: Slow and forceful hiccups which may be alleviated by hot drinks, white moist tongue coating, slow pulse.

Treatment

Method: Points are mainly selected from the Foot-Yangming (Stomach) Channel to readjust the function of the stomach, subdue the ascending *qi* and relieve hiccups. For cases due to retention of food and stagnation of *qi*, needling with reducing method is advisable. For cases due to cold, acupuncture should be combined with moxibustion.

Prescription: Zusanli (St. 36), Zhongwan (Ren 12), Neiguan (P. 6), Geshu (U.B. 17), Tiantu (Ren 22).

Points for different syndromes:

(1) Retention of food and stagnation of *qi*: Neiting (St. 44), Taichong (Liv. 3), Juque (Ren 14).

(2) Attack by pathogenic cold: Shangwan (Ren 13).

Explanation: Zusanli (St. 36), Zhongwan (Ren 12) and Neiguan (P. 6) relieve the sensation of fullness in the chest and activate qi. Geshu (U.B. 17) and Tiantu (Ren 22) subdue the ascending qi. Neiting (St. 44) readjusts the stomach and relieves stagnation. Taichong (Liv. 3) readjusts the qi of the liver. Juque (Ren 14) eases the chest and diaphragm to check hiccups. Application of moxibustion to Shangwan (Ren 13) warms the spleen and stomach and eliminates cold.

Ear acupuncture

Main points: Ear-Shenmen, Diaphragm, Subcortex.

Method: Give strong stimulation. Needles are retained for an hour.

XVI. EPIGASTRIC PAIN

Etiology

Causative factors: (1) irregular meals which injure the spleen and stomach, (2) affecting the stomach by perversion of liver qi due to mental depression, and (3) xu of the stomach with stagnation of cold.

Differentiation

(1) Retention of food: Distension and pain in the epigastrium, pain aggravated on pressure and after eating, belching with fetid odour, anorexia, thick sticky coated tongue, deep forceful pulse.

(2) Attack on stomach by liver qi: Paroxysmal pain in the epigastrium, distending pain in the hypochondriac region. There may be nausea, acidity, abdominal distension and anorexia. The pulse is deep and wiry.

(3) Xu of stomach with stagnation of cold: Dull pain in the epigastrium, general lassitude, regurgitation of thin fluid, pain which may be alleviated by pressure and warmth, thin white coated tongue, deep slow pulse.

Treatment

Method: The principle of treatment is to pacify the stomach and relieve pain by a combination of local with distal points. For cases due to retention of food or attack on the stomach by liver qi, acupuncture with reducing method is advisable. Needles are retained for 30-60 minutes. For cases with xu of the stomach and stagnation of cold, acupuncture with even-movement method combined with moxibustion is recommended.

Prescription: Zusanli (St. 36), Zhongwan (Ren 12), Neiguan (P. 6).

Points for different syndromes:

(1) Retention of food: Zhangmen (Liv. 13), Neiting (St. 44).

(2) Attack on stomach by liver qi: Taichong (Liv. 3), Qimen (Liv. 14).

(3) *Xu* of stomach with stagnation of cold: Qihai (Ren 6. indirect moxibustion with ginger), Pishu (U.B. 20), Gongsun (Sp. 4).

Explanation: Zusanli (St. 36), the He-Sea Point of the Stomach Channel, and Zhongwan (Ren 12), the Front-Mu Point of the stomach, possess the effect of pacifying the stomach and relieving pain. Neiguan (P. 6), communicating with the Yinwei Channel, relaxes the chest and stops vomiting. Zhangmen (Liv. 13) and Neiting (St. 44) promote digestion and relieve epigastric fullness. Needling Qimen (Liv. 14) and Taichong (Liv. 3) with reducing method may promote the function of the liver, regulate *qi* and relieve distension and pain. Application of moxibustion to Gongsun (Sp. 4) and Pishu (U.B. 20) strengthens the spleen, pacifies the stomach, dispels cold and relieves pain. Indirect moxibustion on Qihai (Ren 6) with ginger is the most suitable method to treat chronic gastric pain due to cold, as ginger and moxa together have the property of dispelling cold.

Remarks:

(1) Epigastric pain described here is a symptom in gastric and peptic ulcer, gastritis, gastric neurosis, and diseases of the liver, gall bladder and pancreas.

(2) Cupping method: Cupping is applied with large or medium-sized cups mainly to the upper abdomen or Back-Shu Points for 10-15 minutes.

(3) Ear acupuncture

Main points: Stomach, Sympathetic Nerve, Subcortex, Duodenum.

Method: Select 2-3 points for each treatment. Needles are retained for 15-30 minutes. 10-15 treatments constitute a course; 2-3 days should be allowed before starting the next course.

XVII. ABDOMINAL PAIN

Etiology

Causative factors:

(1) Accumulation of cold due to invasion of exogenous pathogenic cold, or endogenous cold due to intake of too much cold food;

(2) Retardation of *qi* due to retention of food impairing the function of the stomach and intestines in transportation.

Differentiation

(1) Internal accumulation of cold: Sudden violent pain which responds to warmth, loose stools, white coated tongue, deep tense pulse.

(2) Retention of food: Epigastric and abdominal distension and pain which may be aggravated by pressure, foul belching and acidity. Abdom-

inal pain may be accompanied by diarrhea and relieved after defecation. The tongue coating is sticky; the pulse is rolling.

Treatment

Method: Local and distal points are selected according to the diseased area and the involved channels, with the purpose of dispelling old and relieving stagnation. When cold is accumulated, apply both acupuncture and moxibustion. In cases of retention of food, needling with reducing method is applied.

Prescriptions:

Pain above the umbilicus: Gongsun (Sp. 4), Huaroumen (St. 24), Xiawan (Ren 10).

Pain around the umbilicus: Shuiquan (K. 5), Qihai (Ren 6), Tianshu (St. 25).

Pain in the lower abdomen: Sanyinjiao (Sp. 6), Guilai (St. 29), Guanyuan (Ren 4).

Explanation: As the region above the umbilicus relates to the spleen, Gongsun (Sp. 4), the Luo (Connecting) Point of the Spleen Channel, combined with the local points Huaroumen (St. 24) and Xiawan (Ren 10) may adjust the function of the spleen and stomach. The umbilical region relates to the kidney, so Shuiquan (K. 5), the Xi (Cleft) Point of the Kidney Channel, combined with local points Qihai (Ren 6) and Tianshu (St. 25), is prescribed. The three *yin* channels of foot pass through the lower abdomen, so Sanyinjiao (Sp. 6), the Crossing Point of the three *yin* channels of foot, combined with local points Guilai (St. 29) and Guanyuan (Ren 4), is chosen.

Remark: Various diseases may be accompanied by the symptom of abdominal pain such as disturbance of the organs in the abdominal cavity and urogenital organs in the pelvic cavity of the female, intestinal parasitic diseases and functional disorders, especially acute abdomen, such as acute appendicitis, intestinal obstruction, acute peritonitis and perforation of peptic ulcer. If acupuncture is applied, strict observation of the patient is necessary and other therapeutic measures should be taken when necessary.

XVIII. DIARRHEA

Etiology

Causative factors of acute diarrhea:

(1) Dysfunction of the digestive tract due to unsuitable food intake and invasion of exogenous cold-damp; and

(2) Invasion of damp-heat in summer and autumn.

Chronic diarrhea is due to *xu* (insufficiency) of *yang* of spleen and kidney affecting the function of transportation and transformation.

Differentiation

(1) Acute diarrhea

(a) Cold-damp: Watery diarrhea with abdominal pain and borborygmus, chilliness which responds to warmth, absence of thirst, pale tongue with white coating, deep and slow pulse.

(b) Damp-heat: Diarrhea with yellow, hot, loose and fetid stools, accompanied with abdominal pain, burning sensation in the anus, scanty brownish urine, yellow sticky coated tongue, rolling and rapid pulse. There may be fever and thirst.

(2) Chronic diarrhea

(a) *Xu* (insufficiency of *yang* of spleen: Loose stools with undigested food, epigastric and abdominal distension, anorexia, lassitude, thin whitish coated tongue, thready forceless pulse.

(b) *Xu* (insufficiency) of *yang* of kidney: Slight abdominal pain, borborygmus and diarrhea once or several times each morning at dawn, chilliness in the abdomen and lower extremities, whitish coated tongue, deep forceless pulse.

Treatment

Method: The Back-Shu and Front-Mu Points of the large intestine are the main points for treatment. For cold-damp type, apply needling with even-movement method and combined with moxibustion (or indirect moxibustion with ginger); for damp-heat type, apply needling with reducing method. Apply needling with reinforcing method and combined with moxibustion in chronic cases. Moxibustion may be the main treatment for syndrome of *xu* of *yang* of kidney.

Prescription: Tianshu (St. 25), Dachangshu (U.B. 25), Zusanli (St. 36). Points for different syndromes:

(1) Cold-damp: Zhongwan (Ren 12), Qihai (Ren 6).

(2) Damp-heat: Neiting (St. 44), Yinlingquan (Sp. 9), Hegu (L.I. 4).

(3) *Xu* of *yang* of spleen: Pishu (U.B. 20), Zhangmen (Liv. 13), Taibai (Sp. 3), Zhongwan (Ren 12).

(4) *Xu* of *yang* of kidney: Shenshu (U.B. 23), Mingmen (Du 4), Taixi (K. 3), Guanyuan (Ren 4), Baihui (Du 20).

Explanation: Tianshu (St. 25) and Dachangshu (U.B. 25), the Front-Mu and Back-Shu Points of the large intestine, are effective in adjusting the transporting function of the large intestine and checking diarrhea.

Zusanli (St. 36) is used to strengthen the transporting function of the spleen and stomach. Application of acupuncture and moxibustion to Zhongwan (Ren 12) and Qihai (Ren 6) is effective in giving warmth to the spleen and stomach and dispelling cold. Needling Neiting (St. 44), Yinling-quan (Sp. 9) and Hegu (L.I. 4) with reducing method can eliminate damp-heat in the large intestine. Application of acupuncture and moxibustion to Pishu (U.B. 20), Zhangmen (Liv. 13) and Taibai (Sp. 3), the Back-Shu, Front-Mu and Yuan (Source) Points of the spleen respectively, together with Zhongwan (Ren 12), the Front-Mu Point of the stomach, invigorates the *yang* of the spleen, promotes the transporting function and checks diarrhea. Shenshu (U.B. 23), Mingmen (Du 4) and Taixi (K. 3) may warm and invigorate the *yang* of the kidney. Application of moxibustion to Baihui (Du 20) may raise the lowering *qi* of the spleen and stomach, strengthen *qi* and check diarrhea.

Remark: Diarrhea in traditional Chinese medicine includes diarrhea appearing in acute and chronic enteritis, dyspepsia, intestinal parasitic disease, diseases of the pancreas, liver and biliary tract, disorders of endocrine metabolism as well as neurotic diarrhea.

XIX. DYSENTERY

Etiology

This disease is usually caused by lesion of the stomach and intestines due to invasion of damp-heat or cold-damp and the intake of contaminated food.

Differentiation

The main types of dysentery:

(1) Damp-heat type: Abdominal pain, tenesmus, white and red (or mainly red) mucus in stool. There may be accompanying symptoms of high fever, nausea and vomiting. Tongue is mostly yellow and sticky coated, pulse rolling and rapid.

(2) Cold-damp type: Scanty defecation, mainly white mucus in stool, response to warmth and dislike of cold, usually with accompanying symptoms of fullness in the chest and epigastrium, lingering abdominal pain, tastelessness in mouth, absence of thirst, white sticky coated tongue, deep slow pulse.

(3) Chronic dysentery: Prolonged persistent dysentery or recurrent dysentery. In addition to the common clinical features, there may be lassitude, sallow complexion, chilliness, anorexia, and deep thready pulse.

Treatment

Method: The Front-Mu and Inferior He-Sea Points of the large intestine are the main points to relieve stagnation and promote smooth transportation. For dysentery of damp-heat type, apply needling with reducing method; for that of cold-damp type, apply needling together with moxibustion; while for chronic dysentery, needling is given with both reinforcing and reducing methods and combined with moxibustion.

Prescription: Tianshu (St. 25), Shangjuxu (St. 37), Hegu (L.I. 4).

Points for different syndromes and symptoms:

(1) Damp-heat type: Quchi (L.I. 11), Neiting (St. 44), Yinlingquan (Sp. 9).

(2) Cold-damp type: Zhongwan (Ren 12), Qihai (Ren 6), Sanyinjiao (Sp. 6).

(3) Chronic dysentery: Pishu (U.B. 20), Weishu (U.B. 21), Zhongwan (Ren 12), Zusanli (St. 36).

(4) Tenesmus: Zhonglüshu (U.B. 29).

(5) Prolapse of rectum: Baihui (Du 20).

Explanation: It is recorded in *Neijing* that for diseases of the *fu* organs, He-Sea Points are recommended. So Shangjuxu (St. 37), the Inferior He-Sea Point of the large intestine, Tianshu (St. 25) and Hegu (L.I. 4) are taken as the main points to relieve stagnation in the intestine. Needling Neiting (St. 44), Quchi (L.I. 11) and Yinlingquan (Sp. 9) with reducing method is to eliminate damp-heat. Application of moxibustion to Zhongwan (Ren 12) and Qihai (Ren 6) warms the spleen and stomach to dispel cold. Sanyinjiao (Sp. 6) strengthens the spleen and disperses damp. Applying acupuncture with both reinforcing and reducing methods and frequent moxibustion to Pishu (U.B. 20), Weishu (U.B. 21), Zhongwan (Ren 12) and Zusanli (St. 36) warms the spleen and stomach as well as eliminates intestinal stagnation.

Remark: Dysentery in traditional Chinese medicine includes acute and chronic stages of both the bacillary and amebic types.

XX. JAUNDICE

Etiology

Dysfunction of the spleen and stomach in transporting and transforming leads to internal accumulation of damp which impedes the normal excretion of bile causing a yellowish discoloration of the skin. There are two types of jaundice: jaundice of *yang* type in which damp-heat is dominant, and jaundice of *yin* type in which cold-damp is dominant.

Differentiation

Jaundice is characterized by yellow sclera, skin and urine, yellow with lustre indicating *yang* type while lustreless yellow indicates *yin* type.

Jaundice of *yang* type is usually accompanied with fever, a heavy sensation of the body, thirst, fullness in the abdomen, yellow sticky coated tongue and wiry rapid pulse.

Jaundice of *yin* type is usually accompanied by heavy sensation of the body, lassitude, somnolence, absence of thirst, thick white coated tongue and deep slow pulse.

Treatment

Method: Points are mainly selected from the Taiyin (Spleen), Yangming (Stomach) and Shaoyang (Gall bladder) Channels. Needling with reducing method is recommended for treating jaundice of the *yang* type, as the principle is to dispel damp-heat. In treating jaundice of the *yin* type, the principle is to dispel damp by warming the spleen and stomach. Needling is given with even-movement method combined with moxibustion.

Prescription: Yinlingquan (Sp. 9), Zusanli (St. 36), Riyue (G.B. 24), Danshu (U.B. 19), Yanggang (U.B. 48), Zhiyang (Du 9).

Points for different types:

Yang type: Penetration of Taichong (Liv. 3) towards Yongquan (K. 1), Yanglingquan (G.B. 34.).

Yin type: Pishu (U.B. 20), Zhangmen (Liv. 13).

Explanation: Yinlingquan (Sp. 9) and Zusanli (St. 36) strengthen the spleen to disperse damp. Riyue (G.B. 24), Danshu (U.B. 19), Zhiyang (Du 9) and Yanggang (U.B. 48) are essential points for treatment of jaundice. These four points can be used in alternation. Taichong (Liv. 3) and Yanglingquan (G.B. 34) eliminate heat in the *yang* type of jaundice. Application of moxibustion to Pishu (U.B. 20) and Zhangmen (Liv. 13) in the *yin* type disperses cold-damp.

Remark: Jaundice as described in this section is seen in acute icteric hepatitis.

XXI. HYPOCHONDRIAC PAIN

Etiology

The channel of the liver supplies the costal and hypochondriac region. Emotional depression from various causes may restrain liver function, causing inactive circulation of *qi* in the channel, often with resulting costal and hypochondriac pain. Traumatic injuries such as sprain and contusion may also cause hypochondriac pain due to blood stasis of the collaterals.

Differentiation

Stagnation of qi: Distending pain in the costal and hypochondriac region, fullness in the chest, bitter taste in mouth, wiry pulse. Severity of symptoms varies with emotional state.

Stagnation of blood: Fixed stabbing pain in the hypochondriac region, pain intensified on pressure and at night, purplish petechiae on the tongue, wiry pulse.

Treatment

Method: Points are mainly selected from the Foot-Jueyin Channel and Shaoyang Channels to ease the liver and remove obstruction in the collaterals. Needling with reducing method is to be applied for both the yin and $yang$ types.

Prescription: Yanglingquan (G.B. 34), Zhigou (S.J. 6), Qimen (Liv. 14).
Points for different types:
Stagnation of qi: Ganshu (U.B. 18), Qiuxu (G.B. 40).
Stagnation of blood: Geshu (U.B. 17), Xingjiang (Liv. 2).

Explanation: The Shaoyang Channels supply the lateral aspect of the body, so Zhigou (S.J. 6) and Yanglingquan (G.B. 34) are used to relieve pain by regulating the qi of the Shaoyang Channels. Qimen (Liv. 14), the Front-Mu Point of the Liver Channel, eases the liver and relieves pain in the hypochondrium. Ganshu (U.B. 18) and Qiuxu (G.B. 40) promote the unrestraining function of the liver and regulate the circulation of qi. Sanyinjiao (Sp. 6) and Geshu (U.B. 17) activate blood circulation and remove stasis.

Remarks:

(1) Hypochondriac pain is seen in diseases of the liver and gall bladder, sprain of the hypochondriac region, intercostal neuralgia and costal chondritis.

(2) Ear acupuncture

Main points: Chest, Ear-Shenmen, Liver.

Method: Select 2-3 points on the affected side. Needles are retained for 20-30 minutes. Treatment is given during the attack of pain.

XXII. LOW BACK PAIN

Etiology

Causative factors: (1) Retention of pathogenic wind, cold and damp in the channels and collaterals, (2) xu (deficiency) of qi of kidney, and (3) stagnation of *qi* and blood in the lumbar region due to sprain or contusion.

Differentiation

(1) Cold-damp: Low-back pain usually occurs after exposure to pathogenic wind, cold and damp. Clinical manifestations are heavy sensation and pain in the dorsolumbar region and stiffness of muscles, limiting extension and flexion of the back. The pain may reflex downward to the buttocks and lower extremities, and the affected area usually feels cold. Pain becomes intensified in cloudy and rainy days and is not alleviated by bed rest.

(2) *Xu* (insufficiency) of *qi* of kidney: Onset is insidious, and pain is mild but protracted, with lassitude and weakness of the lumbar region and knee. Symptoms are intensified after strain and stress and alleviated by bed rest.

(3) Trauma: The patient has a history of sprain of the lumbar region. Clinical manifestations are rigidity and pain of the lower back. The pain is fixed and aggravated on pressure and turning of the body.

Treatment

Method: Points are mainly selected from the Du and Foot-Taiyang (Urinary Bladder) Channels to promote the circulation of *qi* and blood, relax the muscles and activate the collaterals. Apply both acupuncture and moxibustion for cold-damp type. In case of *xu* (insufficiency) of *qi* of kidney, apply needling with reinforcing method and moxibustion. For traumatic low back pain, apply needling with reducing method or pricking to cause bleeding.

Prescription: Shenshu (U.B. 23), Yaoyangguan (Du 3), Feiyang (U.B. 58).

Secondary points:

Xu (Insufficiency) of *qi* of kidney: Mingmen (Du 4), Zhishi (U.B. 52), Taixi (K. 3).

Sprain of the lumbar region: Renzhong (Du 26), Weizhong (U.B. 40).

Explanation: Shenshu (U.B. 23) favours the *qi* of the kidney. Yaoyangguan (Du 3) is a local point. Feiyang (U.B. 58), the Luo (Connecting) Point of the Urinary Bladder Channel, is a distal point important for treatment of low back pain. Combination of the above three points gives the effect of relaxing the soft tissues and activating blood circulation. For backache due to cold-damp, acupuncture and moxibustion are applied to Shenshu (U.B. 23) and Yaoyangguan (Du 3) to dispel cold-damp, warm the channels and promote smooth circulation. For low back pain due to *xu* (insufficiency) of the *qi* of the kidney, Mingmen (Du 4), Zhishi (U.B. 52) and Taixi (K. 3) are selected for the purpose of tonifying the essence of the kidney. Renzhong (Du 26) is selected according to the principle of selection of upper points for disorders of lower areas. Pricking Weizhong (U.B. 40) to cause bleeding is an effective method to treat traumatic low back pain and rigidity.

Remarks:

(1) Low back pain may be seen in renal diseases, rheumatism, rheumatoid diseases, strains or traumatic injuries of the lumbar region.

(2) Ear acupuncture

Main points: Kidney, Lumbar Vertebrae, Sacral Vertebrae, Ear-Shenmen, Sympathetic Nerve.

Method: Select 2-3 points for each treatment. Needles are retained for 10-30 minutes. Treat once daily or every other day. Or, needles may be embedded for 3-5 days.

XXIII. EDEMA

Etiology

Obstruction of the water passages in the three *jiao* (the upper, middle and lower portions of the body cavity) due to derangement of the lung, spleen and kidney caused by invasion of the lung by wind and cold or *xu* (insufficiency) of *yang* in spleen and kidney results in overflow of excess fluid.

Differentiation

Shi (Excess) type: Onset is usually abrupt. Generally edema appears first on the head, face or lower extremities. The skin is lustrous. Accompanying symptoms and signs are cough, asthma, fever, thirst, scanty urine and low back pain. The pulse is superficial or rolling and rapid.

Xu (Insufficiency) type: Onset is insidious. Edema first appears on the pedis dorsum or eyelids then over the entire body. Accompanying symptoms and signs are chilliness, pallor, backache, general weakness, abdominal distension, loose stools and deep thready pulse.

Treatment

Method: For edema of the *shi* type, apply acupuncture at points commonly used for strengthening the dispersing function of the lung to promote circulation of water. After the exterior pathogenic factors are eliminated, method of treatment may be similar to that for edema of the *xu* type. That is to select points for warming and tonifying the spleen and kidney and give acupuncture with reinforcing method plus moxibustion.

Prescription:

Shi type: Lieque (Lu. 7), Hegu (L.I. 4), Pianli (L.I. 6), Yinlingquan (Sp. 9), Pangguangshu (U.B. 28).

Xu type: Pishu (U.B. 20), Shenshu (U.B. 23), Shuifen (Ren 9), Qihai (Ren 6), Sanyinjiao (Sp. 6), Zusanli (St. 36), Weiyang (U.B. 39).

Points according to symptoms:

Edema of the face: Renzhong (Du 26).

Constipation with abdominal distension: Fenglong (St. 40).

Edema of the pedis dorsum: Foot-Linqi (G.B. 41), Shangqiu (Sp. 5).

Explanation: Hidrosis is desirable for edema above the waist, Lieque (Lu. 7) and Hegu (L.I. 4) being used to promote perspiration and subsidence of the exterior symptoms by activating the *qi* of the lung. For edema below the waist, diuresis is recommended. Pianli (L.I. 6) and Yinlingquan (Sp. 9) are used to cause diuresis in order to eliminate damp. Pangguangshu (U.B. 28) regulates the function of the urinary bladder for excreting fluid. Application of moxibustion to Pishu (U.B. 20) and Shenshu (U.B. 23) for edema of the *xu* (insufficiency) type eliminates damp and fluid through warming and tonifying the *yang* of both the spleen and the kidney. Moxibustion applied to Shuifen (Ren 9) produces a diuretic effect, while to Qihai (Ren 6) it tonifies the original *qi*. Needling Weiyang (U.B. 39), the Inferior He-Sea Point of *sanjiao*, removes obstruction from water passages. Needling Zusanli (St. 36) and Sanyinjiao (Sp. 6) with reinforcing method strengthens the function of the spleen and stomach to eliminate damp.

Remark: Edema is seen in acute and chronic nephritis, malnutrition, etc.

XXIV. NOCTURNAL ENURESIS

Etiology

Enuresis in children over 3 years of age and in any adult is considered as a disease. The causative factor is insufficiency of the *qi* of the kidney and debility of the urinary bladder in controlling urination.

Differentiation

This is involuntary urination during sleep with dreams several times a night or once in several nights. In protracted cases, there are accompanying symptoms of sallow complexion, anorexia and lassitude.

Treatment

Method: The Back-Shu and Front-Mu Points of the urinary bladder and kidney are the main points for tonification of qi of the kidney. Acupuncture with reinforcing method or moxibustion is recommended.

Prescription: Shenshu (U.B. 23), Pangguangshu (U.B. 28), Zhongji (Ren 3), Sanyinjiao (Sp. 6), Dadun (Liv. 1).

Points for different symptoms:

Enuresis with dreams: Shenmen (H. 7).

Anorexia: Pishu (U.B. 20), Zusanli (St. 36).

Explanation: The kidney and urinary bladder are externally-internally related. The Back-Shu Points of these two organs, together with Zhongji (Ren 3), the Front-Mu Point of the urinary bladder, adjust the function of the two organs. Moxibustion applied to Sanyinjiao (Sp. 6), the Crossing Point of the three yin channels of foot, and Dadun (Liv. 1), the Jing-Well Point of the Liver Channel which curves around the pubic region, can warm and remove obstruction of the channels to enhance the therapeutic effect.

Remarks:

(1) Acupuncture treatment is effective for enuresis due to hypoplasia of the nerve which controls urination. As to enuresis due to organic diseases such as deformity of the urinary tract, occult rachischisis, organic cerebral diseases or due to oxyuriasis, the primary disease should be treated.

(2) Ear acupuncture

Main points: Kidney, Urinary Bladder, Brain Point, Subcortex.

Method: Select 2-3 points for each treatment. Needles are retained for 10-20 minutes. Treatment is given once every other day. Or, needles may be embedded for 3-5 days.

XXV. RETENTION OF URINE

Etiology

Causative factors: (1) Accumulation of damp-heat in the urinary bladder which disturbs its function of excreting urine, (2) traumatic injuries such as falling and contusion, or surgical operation on the lower abdomen in which the qi of the channels is damaged, and (3) insufficiency of the $yang$ of the kidney which results in disability of the urinary bladder to excrete urine.

Differentiation

There are 3 main types according to various causes:

(1) Accumulation of damp-heat in the urinary bladder: Hot scanty urine or retention of urine, distension of lower abdomen, thirst but with no desire to drink. There may be constipation. The tongue is red with yellow coating on the posterior part, the pulse is rapid or thready and rapid.

(2) Damage of the *qi* of the channels: Dribbling urination or complete retention of urine, distension and pain in the lower abdomen, thready rapid pulse, petechiae over the tongue.

Insufficiency of the *yang* of the kidney: Dribbling urination attenuating in force, pallor, listlessness, chilliness and weakness in the lumbar region and knee, pale tongue, thready pulse especially weak at the proximal part.

Treatment

Method: In accordance with the principle of treating acute symptoms first in case of emergency, the Front-Mu Point of the urinary bladder should be chosen as the main point to promote urination. In treating the first two types, needling with reducing method is advisable. For retention of urine due to insufficiency of *yang* of the kidney, needling should be given with reinforcing method plus moxibustion.

Prescription: Zhongji (Ren 3), Sanyinjiao (Sp. 6), Weiyang (U.B. 39).

Points for different types:

Accumulation of damp-heat in the urinary bladder: Yinlingquan (Sp. 9).

Damage of the *qi* of the channel: Xuehai (Sp. 10).

Insufficiency of the *yang* of the kidney: Baihui (Du 20), Guanyuan (Ren 4).

Explanation: Zhongji (Ren 3), the Front-Mu Point of the urinary bladder, combined with Sanyinjiao (Sp. 6) can adjust the function of the urinary bladder. Weiyang (U.B. 39), the Inferior He-Sea Point of *sanjiao*, promotes circulation of water passages. Yinlingquan (Sp. 9) eliminates damp-heat. Xuehai (Sp. 10) activates the channels and collaterals. Moxibustion applied to Guanyuan (Ren 4) strengthens the *qi* of the kidney to promote urination. Application of moxibustion to Baihui (Du 20) is a method of selection of upper points for disorders of lower areas.

Etiology

Seminal emission may be involuntary, or with dreams (nocturnal emission). The former is mainly due to anxiety or sensual indulgence which leads to weakness of the kidney and excess of fire in the heart. Involuntary emission usually results from a long illness or excessive sexual activity causing exhaustion of the essence of the kidney. Loss of *yin* affects *yang* which leads to uncontrolled emission.

Differentiation

(1) Nocturnal emission: "Morning-after" dizziness, palpitation, listlessness, lassitude, scanty yellow urine, red tongue and thready rapid pulse.

(2) Involuntary emission: Frequent emission, pallor, listlessness, pale tongue, deep feeble forceless pulse.

Treatment

Method: For nocturnal emission, apply acupuncture with reducing method to points of the Hand-Shaoyin (Heart) Channel and reinforcing method to points of the Foot-Shaoyin (Kidney) Channel. For involuntary emission, apply acupuncture with reinforcing method plus moxibustion to points mainly selected from the Foot-Shaoyin (Kidney) and Ren Channels.

Prescriptions:

(1) Nocturnal emission: Shenmen (H. 7), Xinshu (U.B. 15), Taixi (K. 3), Zhishi (U.B. 52).

(2) Involuntary emission: Shenshu (U.B. 23), Dahe (K. 12), Sanyinjiao (Sp. 6), Guanyuan (Ren 4), Qihai (Ren 6).

Explanation: For treating nocturnal emission, Shenmen (H. 7) and Xinshu (U.B. 15) are punctured with reducing method to lessen the fire of the heart, and Zhishi (U.B. 52) and Taixi (K. 3) with reinforcing method to tonify the *qi* of the kidney. For treating involuntary emission, Shenshu (U.B. 23), Dahe (K. 12) and Sanyinjiao (Sp. 6) are punctured with reinforcing method to strengthen the function of the kidney in controlling emission. Guanyuan (Ren 4) and Qihai (Ren 6) are two important tonification points of the Ren Channel. Moxibustion applied to these two points can strengthen the original *qi*.

Remark: Ear acupuncture

Main points: Seminal Vesicle, Endocrine, Liver, Kidney.

Method: Select 2-4 points for each treatment. Needles are retained for 10-30 minutes. Treatment is given once daily or every other day. Or, needles may be embedded for 3-5 days.

XXVII. IMPOTENCE

Etiology

Impotence is generally due to damage of *yang* of kidney resulting from repeated seminal emission or excessive sensual activity. It may also be due to damage to *qi* of the heart, spleen and kidney resulting from emotional factors such as fright and worry.

Differentiation

Impotence is characterized by inability of the penis to erect. In case of insufficiency of *yang* of kidney, there may appear pallor, dizziness, blurring of vision, listlessness, soreness and weakness of the lumbar region and knee, frequent urination and deep thready pulse. If it is complicated with damage of *qi* of the heart and spleen, palpitation and insomnia may be present.

Treatment

Method: Apply acupuncture with reinforcing method plus moxibustion to points selected from the Ren and Kidney Channels to tonify the *yang* of the kidney.

Prescription: Guanyuan (Ren 4), Mingmen (Du 4), Shenshu (U.B. 23), Taixi (K. 3), Baihui (Du 20).

Points for damage of *qi* of heart and spleen: Xinshu (U.B. 15), Shenmen (H. 7), Sanyinjiao (Sp. 6).

Explanation: Moxibustion applied to Guanyuan (Ren 4) tonifies original *qi*. Mingmen (Du 4), Shenshu (U.B. 23) and Taixi (K. 3) are used to strengthen the *yang* of the kidney. Moxibustion at Baihui (Du 20) can raise *yang qi*. Xinshu (U.B. 15), Shenmen (H. 7) and Sanyinjiao (Sp. 6) are used to tonify the *qi* of the heart and spleen.

Remark: Ear acupuncture

Main points: Seminal Vesicle, External Genitalia, Testis, Endocrine.

Method: Select 2-4 points for each treatment. Needles are retained for 10-30 minutes. Treatment is given once daily or every other day. Or, needles may be embedded for 3-5 days.

XXVIII. *BI* SYNDROMES (PAINFUL JOINTS)

Etiology

Bi means obstruction of circulation of *qi* and blood, which usually results from invasion of the channels and collaterals by wind, cold and damp due to weakness of defensive *qi* when one is wet with perspiration and exposed to the wind, dwelling in damp places or wading in water. There are different types of *bi* syndromes, such as wandering *bi* (in which wind predominates), painful *bi* (in which cold predominates), fixed *bi* (in which damp predominates) and febrile *bi* (in which wind, cold and damp turn into heat).

Differentiation

The chief symptom of *bi* syndromes is arthralgia. There may be muscular soreness and numbness. In prolonged cases, contracture of the extremities, or even swelling or deformity of joints may be present.

Wandering *bi*: This type is characterized by wandering pain of the joints of the extremities with limitation of movement. There may be chilliness and fever, thin and sticky coated tongue, superficial and rapid pulse.

Painful *bi*: Arthralgia responds to warmth and is aggravated by cold. There is no local inflammation. Thin white coated tongue, deep wiry pulse.

Fixed *bi*: Numbness of the skin and muscles, heavy sensation of the body and extremities, arthralgia with fixed pain, attacks provoked by cloudy or wet weather. White sticky coated tongue, deep slow pulse.

Febrile *bi*: Arthralgia with local redness, swelling and tenderness in which one or several joints are involved. Accompanying symptoms are fever and thirst. Yellow coated tongue, rolling rapid pulse.

Treatment

Method: Local and distal points are selected from the *yang* channels supplying the diseased areas for the purpose of eliminating wind, cold and damp. Wandering *bi* is mainly treated with needling; painful *bi* with moxibustion and needling as adjuvant. For severe pain, the use of intradermal needles or indirect moxibustion with ginger is recommended. Fixed *bi* is treated with both acupuncture and moxibustion. Warming needle is also advisable. Febrile *bi* is treated by needling with reducing method.

Prescriptions:

Pain in the shoulder joint: Jianyu (L.I. 15), Jianliao (S.J. 14), Jianzhen (S.I. 9), Naoshu (S.I. 10).

Pain in the scapula: Tianzong (S.I. 11), Bingfeng (S.I. 12), Jianwaishu (S.I. 14), Gaohuangshu (U.B. 43).

Pain in the elbow: Quchi (L.I. 11), Chize (Lu. 5), Tianjing (S.J. 10), Waiguan (S.J. 5), Hegu (L.I. 4).

Pain in the wrist: Yangchi (S.J. 4), Yangxi (L.I. 5), Yanggu (S.I. 5), Waiguan (S.J. 5).

Numbness and pain in fingers: Houxi (S.I. 3), Sanjian (L.I. 3), Baxie (Extra.)

Pain in the hip joint: Huantiao (G.B. 30), Yinmen (U.B. 37), Femur-Juliao (G.B. 29).

Pain in the knee joint: Lianqiu (St. 34), Dubi (St. 35), Medial Xiyan (Extra.), Yanglingquan (G.B. 34), Xiyangguan (G.B. 33), Yinlingquan (Sp. 9).

Numbness and pain in the leg: Chengshan (U.B. 57), Feiyang (U.B. 58).

Pain in the ankle: Jiexi (St. 41), Shangqiu (Sp. 5), Qiuxu (G.B. 40), Kunlun (U.B. 60), Taixi (K. 3).

Numbness and pain in the toe: Gongsun (Sp. 4), Shugu (U.B. 65), Bafeng (Extra.).

Pain in the lumbar region: Yaoyangguan (Du 3).

General aching: Houxi (S.I. 3), Shenmai (U.B. 62), Dabao (Sp. 21), Geshu (U.B. 17).

Points according to symptoms and signs:

Fever: Dazhui (Du 14).

Deformity of the joint: Dashu (U.B. 11).

Explanation: The above prescriptions are formulated by selection of local points according to the courses of channels to relax the tendons, remove obstruction from channels and collaterals, regulate *qi* and blood and eliminate pathogenic factors.

Remark: *Bi* syndromes are seen in rheumatic fever, rheumatic arthritis, rheumatoid arthritis and gout.

XXIX. *WEI* SYNDROME (PARALYSIS)

(Appendix: Infantile Paralysis)

Etiology

Causative factors: (1) Malnourishment of tendons due to exhaustion of body fluid caused by invasion of the lung by exogenous pathogenic wind-heat, (2) lesion of the tendons due to accumulation of damp-heat which affects the Yangming Channels, and (3) malnutrition of tendons due to loss of the essence and *qi* of the liver and kidney caused by long illness or sexual excess.

Differentiation

Wei syndrome is characterized by muscular flaccidity or atrophy of the extremities with motor impairment.

Heat in the lung: This usually occurs during or after a febrile disease, accompanied by cough, irritability, thirst, scanty brownish urine, red tongue with yellow coating, and thready rapid pulse.

Damp-heat: The accompanying symptoms and signs are sallow complexion, listlessness and cloudy urine. There may be a hot sensation in the soles of the feet with desire to expose them to coolness. Yellow and sticky coated tongue, forceful pulse.

Insufficiency of the essence of the liver and kidney: The accompanying symptoms are soreness and weakness of the lumbar region, seminal emission, prospermia, leukorrhea, dizziness and blurring of vision. Red tongue, thready rapid pulse.

Treatment

Method: Main points are selected from the Yangming Channels to promote circulation of *qi* in the channels and nourish the tendons and bones. When heat in the lung or damp-heat is responsible, needle with reducing method to dissipate heat; moxibustion is contraindicated. In case of insufficiency of essence of the liver and kidney, needle with reinforcing method. Generally, treatment is given only to the affected side. But, as the process of treatment is rather long, crossing method of puncturing may be applied. Puncture the sound side first and then the affected side.

Prescriptions:

Upper limb: Jianyu (L.I. 15), Quchi (L.I. 11), Hegu (L.I. 4), Waiguan (S.J. 5).

Lower limb: Biguan (St. 31), Zusanli (St. 36), Jiexi (St. 41), Huantiao (G.B. 30), Yanglingquan (G.B. 34), Xuanzhong (G.B. 39).

Points for different types:

Heat in the lung: Chize (Lu. 5), Feishu (U.B. 13).

Damp-heat: Pishu (U.B. 20), Yinlingquan (Sp. 9).

Insufficiency of essence of liver and kidney: Ganshu (U.B. 18), Shenshu (U.B. 23).

Explanation: The two prescriptions are based on *Neijing*: Select points only from Yangming for treating *wei* syndrome. Yanglingquan (G.B. 34) and Xuanzhong (G.B. 39), the two Influential Points dominating respectively the tendon and marrow, are added to enhance the effect of nourishing the tendon and bone. Feishu (U.B. 13) and Chize (Lu. 5) are used to dissipate heat in the lung, and Pishu (U.B. 20) and Yinlingquan (Sp. 9) to eliminate damp-heat. Moxibustion alone or combined with acupuncture is applied only after heat subsides. Ganshu (U.B. 18) and Shenshu (U.B. 23) are used to tonify the liver and kidney. As *wei* syndrome requires a long period of treatment, it is necessary to win the patient's co-operation and confidence. Applying tapping-needle method along the channels or over the diseased area is advisable.

Remark: *Wei* syndrome is seen in acute myelitis, progressive myatrophy, myasthenia gravis, periodic paralysis and hysterical paralysis.

Appendix: Infantile Paralysis (Poliomyelitis)

The principle involved in treating infantile paralysis is similar to that for *wei* syndrome. The corresponding Huatuo Jiaji Points (Extra.) can be added. In case of paresis of the extensor, points from the *yang* channels of the extension aspect are advisable; while in those cases with paresis of the flexor, points from the *yin* channels of the flexion aspect may be chosen. During convalescence, acupuncture should be the main treatment, with manipulation light and superficial. Moxibustion may be applied in addition.

XXX. HYSTERIA

Etiology

Hysteria is due to mental disturbance caused by fire resulting from frustration or depression.

Differentiation

Various psychotic symptoms such as melancholy without any assignable reason, paraphronia, suspiciousness, paraphobia, palpitation, irritability, somnolence, etc. There may be sudden onset of suffocating sensation, hiccup, aphonia and convulsion. The pulse is wiry and thready. In severe cases, there may be loss of consciousness and syncope.

Treatment

Method: The Front-Mu and Yuan (Source) Points of the Heart Channel are taken as the main points to tranquilize the mind. Needling is given with reducing method.

Prescription: Juque (Ren 14), Shenmen (H. 7), Sanyinjiao (Sp. 6).
Points according to different symptoms and signs:
Suffocating sensation: Neiguan (P. 6), Shanzhong (Ren 17).
Hiccup: Gongsun (Sp. 4), Tiantu (Ren 22).
Aphonia: Tongli (H. 5), Lianquan (Ren 23).
Convulsion: Hegu (L.I. 4), Taichong (Liv. 3).
Loss of consciousness and syncope: Renzhong (Du 26), Yongquan (K. 1).
Explanation: Juque (Ren 14) and Shenmen (H. 7), the Front-Mu and Yuan (Source) Points of the Heart Channel, together with Sanyinjiao

(Sp. 6) from the Spleen Channel, constitute the main prescription for the purpose of nourishing blood and tranquilizing the mind. Neiguan (P. 6) and Shanzhong (Ren 17) are used to relieve suffocating sensation. Gongsun (Sp. 4) and Tiantu (Ren 22) conduct the qi downward to stop hiccup. Tongli (H. 5) and Lianquan (Ren 23) relieve aphasia. Hegu (L.I. 4) and Taichong (Liv. 3) adjust the liver to relieve convulsion. Renzhong (Du 26) and Yongquan (K. 1) restore consciousness.

Remarks:

(1) Hysteria described in this section corresponds to hysteria in modern medicine. However, there are different types of hysteria, some of which may relate to other diseases in traditional Chinese medicine.

(2) Ear acupuncture

Main points: Heart, Kidney, Subcortex, Ear-Shenmen, Stomach, Sympathetic Nerve.

Method: Select 2-3 points in each treatment. Give strong stimulation.

XXXI. AMENORRHEA

Etiology

Causative factors are various, but the main ones are blood stasis and blood exhaustion. Amenorrhea due to blood stasis is usually caused by mental depression or invasion by cold during menstruation. Amenorrhea due to blood exhaustion most commonly results from deficiency of the Liver, Spleen and Kidney Channels caused by long illness or blood depletion due to multiparity.

Differentiation

(1) Blood stasis: Sudden onset, distension and pain in the lower abdomen aggravated by pressure. There may be a mass on palpation. Deep wiry pulse.

(2) Blood exhaustion: Delayed menstruation gradually decreasing in amount to amenorrhea, usually accompanied by sallow complexion, dry skin, listlessness, anorexia, loose stools, white coated tongue and forceless pulse.

Treatment

(1) Blood stasis type

Method: Points are mainly selected from the Ren, Foot-Taiyin (Spleen) and (Liver) Channels to remove stasis. Needling is given with reducing method.

Prescription: Zhongji (Ren 3), Xuehai (Sp. 10), Sanyinjiao (Sp. 6), Xingjian (Liv. 2), Guilai, St. 29), Ciliao (U.B. 32), Hegu (L.I. 4).

Explanation: Zhongji (Ren 3) is a point where the Ren Channel and the three *yin* channels of foot meet. Ciliao (U.B. 32) and Guilai (St. 29) are local points used to remove blood stasis of the uterus. Hegu (L.I. 4) and Sanyinjiao (Sp. 6) adjust *qi* and blood. Xingjian (Liv. 2) releases *qi* of the liver. Xuehai (Sp. 10) activates blood circulation and promotes menstrual flow.

(2) Blood exhaustion type:

Method: Points from the Ren Channel and Back-Shu Points are the main points used to adjust and nourish the liver, spleen and kidney. Needling is given with reinforcing method. Moxibustion may be used in combination.

Prescription: Guanyuan (Ren 4), Ganshu (U.B. 18), Pishu (U.B. 20), Shenshu (U.B. 23), Tianshu (St. 25), Zusanli (St. 36), Sanyinjiao (Sp. 6).

Explanation: Guanyuan (Ren 4) is a point used for toning. Ganshu (U.B. 18), Pishu (U.B. 20) and Shenshu (U.B. 23) activate the functions of the liver, spleen and kidney. Zusanli (St. 36) and Sanyinjiao (Sp. 6) are distal points of the related channels. Tianshu (St. 25) is an adjacent point used to regulate the spleen and stomach, the sources of *qi* and blood formation.

XXXII. DYSMENORRHEA

Etiology

Dysmenorrhea is generally of two types:

(1) Dysmenorrhea of *shi* (excess) type is due to coagulation of blood in the uterus resulting from emotional disturbance such as obsession, worry, melancholy and anger, or invasion of cold or taking cold drinks during menstruation.

(2) Dysmenorrhea of *xu* (deficiency) is caused by insufficiency of *qi* and blood and dysfunction of the Chong and Ren Channels.

Differentiation

(1) *Shi* type: Premenstrual cramping pain fixed in the lower abdomen and aggravated when pressed. This radiates to the lower back and thighs, gradually diminishing after onset of menstruation; menstrual flow dark purplish in colour with clots, hesitant; pulse wiry.

(2) *Xu* type: Lower abdominal pain at late stage of menstruation or post-menstruation, mild but persistent pain responding to warmth and pressure, menstrual flow scanty and pinkish in colour. In severe cases, there may appear chilliness, palpitation and dizziness. Pulse thready and forceless.

Treatment

(1) *Shi* type

Method: Points are mainly selected from the Ren Channel and the Spleen Channel to activate blood circulation and remove obstruction from the channel. Needling is given with reducing method. For cases cold in nature, moxibustion is advisable.

Prescription: Zhongji (Ren 3), Xuehai (Sp. 10), Diji (Sp. 8), Hegu (L.I. 4), Daju (St. 27).

Explanation: Xuehai (Sp. 10) activates blood circulation. Diji (Sp. 8), the Xi (Cleft) Point of the Spleen Channel, when combined with Hegu (L.I. 4), is indicated in painful menstruation. Zhongji (Ren 3) and Daju (St. 27) are local points to remove blood stasis and relieve pain.

(2) *Xu* type:

Method: Points from the Ren Channel and the Back-Shu Points of the spleen and kidney are taken as the main points to adjust and strengthen *qi* and blood. Needling is given with reinforcing method and combined with moxibustion.

Prescription: Guanyuan (Ren 4), Pishu (U.B. 20), Shenshu (U.B. 23), Zusanli (St. 36), Sanyinjiao (Sp. 6).

Explanation: Moxibustion applied to Guanyuan (Ren 4) warms and strengthens original *qi*. Pishu (U.B. 20) and Shenshu (U.B. 23) regulate and promote the functions of the spleen and kidney. Zusanli (St. 36) and Sanyinjiao (Sp. 6) are distal points used to strengthen the spleen and stomach, sources of blood formation.

Remarks:

(1) Dysmenorrhea usually involves local diseases of the genital system, endocrine disorders or neurological and psychological factors.

(2) Ear acupuncture

Main points: Ovary, Ear-Shenmen, Endocrine.

Method: Manipulate the needles intermittently with moderately strong stimulation until pain is alleviated.

XXXIII. UTERINE HEMORRHAGE

Etiology

Causative factors: (1) Physical or mental strain which injures the spleen, (2) dysfunction of the spleen in conducting blood caused by impairment of liver function due to extreme anger, and (3) dysfunction of the Chong and Ren Channels caused by invasion of the uterus by pathogenic cold or heat.

Differentiation

Uterine hemorrhage may be of abrupt onset, profuse or lingering and scanty, the two conditions possibly occurring alternately. Other symptoms are dizziness, fatigue, low back pain and general weakness.

(1) Heat in the blood: The blood is bright red with foul odour. Irritability, rapid pulse and yellow coated tongue are usual symptoms.

(2) Deficiency of *qi*: The blood is pinkish and dull, there is cold in the lower abdomen, usually with chilliness, pallor of the face and lips, deep slow pulse.

Treatment

Method:

(1) Heat in the blood: Treatment is aimed at elimination of heat to stop the bleeding. Needling is given mainly with reducing method.

(2) Deficiency of *qi*: Treatment is aimed at regulation of the Chong and Ren Channels. Needling is given with reinforcing method plus moxibustion.

Prescription: Guanyuan (Ren 4), Yinbai (Sp. 1).

Points for different types:

(1) Heat in the blood: Taichong (Liv. 3), Rangu (K. 2).

(2) Deficiency of *qi*: Baihui (Du 20), Yangchi (S.J. 4).

Explanation: Guanyuan (Ren 4) regulates the function of the Chong and Ren Channels. Yinbai (Sp. 1), a point of the Spleen Channel, is used to invigorate the function of the spleen in conducting blood. Generally, uterine bleeding can be stopped by applying moxibustion to these two points. Taichong (Liv. 3), the Yuan (Source) Point of Liver Channel, promotes liver function and regulates vital energy, and, when combined with Rangu (K. 2), the Ying-Spring Point of the Kidney Channel, eliminates heat and cools the blood. Applying moxibustion to Baihui (Du 20) raises the *yang qi* of the Du Channel. Yangchi (S.J. 4), the Yuan (Source) Point of the Sanjiao Channel, promotes the function of the Chong and Ren Channels in controlling blood.

Remarks:

(1) Uterine hemorrhage described in this section corresponds to functional uterine hemorrhage due to derangement of the ovaries. Organic diseases of the genital system should be excluded.

(2) Any massive bleeding should first be checked. If bleeding is lingering, observe whether there is blood stagnation. If there are purplish clots in the blood, and abdominal pain is aggravated when pressed and alleviated after bleeding, Hegu (L.I. 4) combined with Sanyinjiao (Sp. 6) can be used to activate blood circulation and remove stagnation.

(3) Ear acupuncture

Main points: Uterus, Subcortex, Endocrine.

Method: Needles are to be retained for 1-2 hours and manipulated intermittently.

XXXIV. LEUKORRHEA

Etiology

Leukorrhea means persistent mucous vaginal discharge in the absence of menstruation. Causative factors are dysfunction of the Chong and Ren Channels and weakness of the qi of the Dai Channel due to insufficiency of qi and blood and downward infusion of damp-heat.

Differentiation

Leukorrhea may be differentiated as white or yellow discharge.

(1) White discharge is due to insufficiency of qi and presence of damp. It is thin, whitish or yellowish, with odour.

(2) Yellow discharge is due to downward infusion of damp-heat. It is pinkish or deep yellow with fetid odour.

Both conditions may be accompanied by low back pain, dizziness and lassitude.

Treatment

Method: Main points are those from the Dai and Spleen Channels for regulating qi and blood and eliminating damp-heat. Acupuncture with reinforcing method plus moxibustion is applied for white discharge and reducing method for yellow discharge.

Prescription: Daimai (G.B. 26), Wushu (G.B. 27), Qihai (Ren 6), Sanyinjiao (Sp. 6).

Points for different symptoms:

(1) White discharge: Ciliao (U.B. 32), Shenshu (U.B. 23), Baihuanshu (U.B. 30).

(2) Yellow discharge: Zhongji (Ren 3), Ligou (Liv. 5), Yinlingquan (Sp. 9).

Explanation: Qihai (Ren 6) is used to regulate the qi of the Chong and Ren Channels. Daimai (G.B. 26) and Wushu (G.B. 27), being the Crossing Point of the Dai and Gall bladder Channels, have the property of strengthening the Dai Channel and are indicated in treating leukorrhea. Sanyinjiao (Sp. 6) regulates the three yin channels of foot to eliminate damp-heat. Shenshu (U.B. 23) strengthens the qi of the kidney and is efficacious for tonic purposes. Ciliao (U.B. 32) and Baihuanshu (U.B. 30), being adjacent to the local area, check leukorrhea. Zhongji (Ren 3), the Crossing Point of the Ren Channel and the Liver Channel, and Ligou (Liv. 5), the Luo (Connecting) Point of the Liver Channel, when used in combination, can reduce the fire of the liver. Yinlingquan (Sp. 9) strengthens the spleen to eliminate damp-heat.

Remark: Leukorrhea as described in this section refers to inflammation of the genital system such as vaginitis, cervicitis, endometritis and infections of the pelvic organs.

XXXV. MORNING SICKNESS

Etiology
Vomiting at the early stage of pregnancy is due in the main to general weakness of stomach qi and reaction to the development of the fetus.

Differentiation
Nausea and vomiting occur after about one month of pregnancy. Vomiting may take place right after food intake or at the sight or smell of food. The accompanying symptoms are fullness in chest, dizziness, blurring of vision and lassitude.

Treatment
Method: The points selected are mainly from the Foot-Yangming (Stomach) and Hand-Jueyin (Pericardium) Channels. These inhibit vomiting by pacifying the stomach qi. Needling is given with even-movement method.

Prescription: Zusanli (St. 36), Neiguan (P. 6), Shangwan (Ren 13).

Explanation: Zusanli (St. 36) calms the ascending qi of the stomach. Neiguan (P. 6) stops vomiting by easing the chest and relieving discomfort. Shangwan (Ren 13), a local point, is indicated in treating fullness in the epigastric region.

Remark: Ear acupuncture

Main points: Liver, Stomach, Ear-Shenmen, Sympathetic Nerve.

Method: Treatment is given once a day. Or, needles may be embedded for 3-5 days. Massaging the points where needles are embedded enhances the therapeutic effect.

XXXVI. LACTATION INSUFFICIENCY

Etiology
Causative factors: (1) Poor health and deficiency of qi and blood, (2) massive loss of blood in childbirth, and (3) mental depression affecting the liver.

Differentiation
Scanty or absence of milk secretion after childbirth, or continuous decrease in quantity during lactation. In the xu type, the accompanying

symptoms are palpitation, lassitude and thin milk. In the *shi* type, there appear fullness in chest, anorexia, retention of milk and hypochondriac pain.

Treatment

Method:

(1) *Xu* type: Needling is given with reinforcing method and combined with moxibustion.

(2) *Shi* type: Needling is given with reducing method. Moxibustion is also advisable.

Prescription: Rugen (St. 18), Shanzhong (Ren 17), Shaoze (S.I. 1).

Secondary points:

(1) *Xu* type: Pishu (U.B. 20), Zusanli (St. 36).

(2) *Shi* type: Qimen (Liv. 14), Neiguan (P. 6).

Explanation: Rugen (St. 18) is a point of the Stomach Channel and also a local point. Shanzhong (Ren 17) is the Influential Point dominating *qi*. Moxibustion applied at these two points warms the *qi* and blood and activates their circulation. Some effect may also be obtained by puncturing these two points horizontally towards the breasts to cause radiating sensation in the local area. Shaoze (S.I. 1), is an empirical point for promoting lactation. Pishu (U.B. 20), the Back-Shu Point of the spleen, and Zusanli (St. 36), the He-Sea Point of the stomach, regulate the function of the spleen and stomach in blood and milk formation. Qimen (Liv. 14), the Front-Mu Point of the liver, regulates the function of the liver to soothe the hypochondrium. Neiguan (P. 6) eases the chest and relieves depression to allow the flow of milk.

XXXVII.   INFANTILE CONVULSION

Etiology

Infantile convulsion may be of the acute or chronic type.

(1) Acute convulsion: Causative factor is endogenous wind elicited by extreme heat due to phlegm caused by invasion of exogenous wind-cold accompanied by accumulation of undigested food in the stomach. Acute febrile disease may also lead to acute convulsion.

(2) Chronic convulsion: This is usually due to weakness of spleen and stomach after chronic wasting disease.

Differentiation

(1) Acute convulsion: High fever, coma, upward staring eyes, clenched jaws, rattles, tetanic contraction, opisthotonos, cyanosis, rapid and wiry pulse.

(2) Chronic convulsion: Emaciation, pallor, lassitude, lethargy with half-closed eyes, intermittent convulsion, cold extremities, loose stools with undigested food, profuse clear urine, deep feeble pulse.

Treatment

(1) Acute convulsion

Method: Elimination of heat and wind and resuscitation by applying needling with reducing method to points of the Du Channel as the main points. Moxibustion is contraindicated.

Prescription: Shixuan (Extra.), Yintang (Extra.), Renzhong (Du 26), Quchi (L.I. 11), Taichong (Liv. 3).

Secondary points for different symptoms and signs:

Coma: Laogong (P. 8), Yongquan (K. 1).

Protracted convulsion: Xingjian (Liv. 2), Yanglingquan (G.B. 34), Kunlun (U.B. 60), Houxi (S.I. 3).

Continuous high fever: Dazhui (Du 14), Hegu (L.I. 4).

Explanation: Pricking and bleeding Shixuan (Extra) eliminates heat. Yintang (Extra.) promotes relaxation and spasmolysis. Renzhong (Du 26) is effective in resuscitation. Quchi (L.I. 11) eliminates the heat of the Yangming Channels. Needling Taichong (Liv. 3) with reducing method calms the wind of the liver. Laogong (P. 8) and Yongquan (K. 1) are important points for emergency which eliminate heat. Xingjian (Liv. 2) and Yanglingquan (G.B. 34) are used for spasmolysis. Kunlun (U.B. 60) is a point of the Urinary Bladder Channel the upper portion of which enters the brain; Houxi (S.I. 3) communicates with the Du Channel. Puncturing these two points in combination is effective in clearing mental cloudiness and relieving convulsion. Dazhui (Du 14), the Crossing Point of all the *yang* channels, and Hegu (L.I. 4), the Yuan (Source) Point of the Hand-Yangming Channel, are used to bring down excess heat in the *yang* channels.

(2) Chronic convulsion

Method: To strengthen the spleen and stomach by applying acupuncture and moxibustion at points of the Ren and Foot-Yangming (Stomach) Channels as the main sites.

Prescription: Zhongwan (Ren 12), Guanyuan (Ren 4), Zusanli (St. 36), Zhangmen (Liv. 13), Yintang (Extra.).

Explanation: Zhangmen (Liv. 13), Zhongwan (Ren 12) and Zusanli (St. 36) are used to readjust the function of the spleen and stomach. Moxibustion on Guanyuan (Ren 4) strengthens the original *qi* (vital force). Moxibustion of Yingtang (Extra.) checks convulsion.

Remarks:

Acute convulsion may imply infection of the central nervous system and toxic encephalopathy, such as epidemic meningoencephalitis and toxic pneumonia. Acupuncture tends to reduce fever and spasmolysis, but immediate diagnosis is imperative in order to give proper timely treatment.

Chronic convulsion results in the main from prolonged chronic vomiting and diarrhea, metabolic disturbance, malnutrition, or chronic infection of the central nervous system. It may also be an after-effect of acute convulsion. Measures should be adopted accordingly.

XXXVIII. INFANTILE DIARRHEA

Etiology

Causative factor is indigestion due to careless nursing and irregular feeding (or contaminated milk) resulting in weakness of the infant's spleen and stomach. It may also be due to exposure to exogenous cold.

Differentiation

Abdominal distension, borborygmus, intermittent abdominal pain relieved after diarrhea which may occur from several to more than ten times a day with strong fetid odour and at times producing stools mixed with milk curd, frequent belching, anorexia. Tongue is sticky coated, pulse deep and forceless.

Treatment

Method: To readjust the function of spleen and stomach by applying acupuncture or moxibustion to points of the Foot-Yangming (Stomach) Channel as the main points. Needling is given with even-movement method. Do not retain the needle.

Prescription: Zhongwan (Ren 12), Tianshu (St. 25), Shangjuxu (St. 37), Sifeng (Extra.).

Secondary points:

Exogenous cold: Hegu (L.I. 4).

Explanation: Zhongwan (Ren 12), the Front-Mu Point of the stomach and also the Confluent Point of the *fu* organs, regulates the *qi* (vital function) of the stomach. Tianshu (St. 25) and Shangjuxu (St. 37), the Front-Mu Point and the Inferior He-Sea Point of the large intestine, when used in combination, adjust the function of the intestines to halt diarrhea. Sifeng (Extra.), the empirical point in the treatment of digestive disturbance of infants, have the effects of promoting digestion, relieving abdominal distension and strengthening the spleen and stomach.

XXXIX. MUMPS

Etiology

Causative factor is accumulation of heat in the Large Intestine and Sanjiao Channels due to invasion of seasonal epidemic factors and upward attack of heat in the stomach.

Differentiation

Onset is chills and fever with redness and swelling of the parotid region on one or both sides. In severe heat, symptoms are thirst, constipation, deep yellow urine, sticky coated tongue and superficial rapid pulse.

Treatment

Method: To disperse heat and wind by applying superficial puncture with reducing method to points of the Large Intestine and Sanjiao Channels as the main points:

Prescription: Waiguan (S.J. 5), Yifeng (S.J. 17), Jiache (St. 6), Quchi (L.I. 11), Hegu (L.I. 4).

Explanation: Waiguan (S.J. 5) eliminates heat from the Sanjiao Channel. Quchi (L.I. 11) and Hegu (L.I. 4) eliminate heat from the Large Intestine Channel. Yifeng (S.J. 17) and Jiache (St. 6) are local points used to remove obstruction from the involved channels supplying the parotid region in order to relieve swelling and pain.

Remark: Pricking the ear apex with a three-edged needle to cause bleeding is also effective in treating mumps.

XL. URTICARIA

Etiology

Causative factor is heat in blood complicated with exogenous wind attacking the superficial layer of the muscles or accumulation of heat in the stomach and intestines due to intake of food to which the patient is unaccustomed.

Differentiation

Abrupt onset with itching wheals of various size. There may be accompanying abdominal pain, constipation and superficial rapid pulse. Acute conditions subside quickly, while recurrences are frequent when the disease is chronic.

Treatment

Method: To disperse wind and eliminate heat in the blood by puncturing with reducing method to points of the Spleen and Large Intestine Channels as the main points.

Prescription: Xuehai (Sp. 10), Sanyinjiao (Sp. 6), Quchi (L.I. 11), Hegu (L.I. 4).

Secondary points:

Abdominal pain: Zusanli (St. 36).

Explanation: Xuehai (Sp. 10) and Sanyinjiao (Sp. 6) eliminate damp-heat in the blood. Quchi (L.I. 11) and Hegu (L.I. 4) relieve itching and wheals through eliminating wind-heat. Zusanli (St. 36) soothes the stomach and intestines to relieve abdominal pain.

Remark: Ear acupuncture

Main points: Endocrine, Lung, Adrenal.

Method: Needles are retained for an hour with intermittent manipulation.

XLI.　ERYSIPELAS

(Appendix:　Herpes Zoster)

Etiology

Causative factor is invasion of the Large Intestine Channel by exogenous wind-heat or damp-heat which infects the blood. The main site of occurrence is the lower limbs, or around the face. It may spread over the whole body.

Differentiation

The onset is chills and fever followed by sudden appearance of deep red cloud-like patches diffusely spreading over the skin with clear demarcation and burning pain. The accompanying symptoms and signs are irritability, thirst, constipation, brownish urine, rapid pulse and thick coated tongue.

Treatment

Method: To eliminate heat in the blood by puncturing with reducing method or pricking to cause bleeding to points of the Large Intestine Channel as the main points.

Prescription: Quchi (L.I. 11), Hegu (L.I. 4), Weizhong (U.B. 40), Quze (P. 3).

Explanation: Quchi (L.I. 11) and Hegu (L.I. 4) eliminate the heat of the Large Intestine Channel. Venous pricking at Weizhong (U.B. 40) and Quze (P. 3) eliminates heat in the blood.

Remark: Erysipelas of the lower limbs may also be treated by pricking the affected area with the three-edged needle or tapping with the cutaneous needle to cause bleeding. Toxic heat may vanish, but care should be taken to avoid infection, and routine sterilization should be applied before manipulation.

APPENDIX: HERPES ZOSTER

Herpes zoster occurs mainly in the lumbar and hypochondriac regions, with small vesicles like beads forming a girdle. Severe burning pain and redness and hotness of the skin mark the disease.

Points for treatment: Quchi (L.I. 11), Xuehai (Sp. 10), Weizhong (U.B. 40).

Needling is done with reducing method. Puncturing the Huatuo Jiaji points (Extra.) corresponding to the site of lesion is also advisable.

XLII. FURUNCLE AND LYMPHANGITIS

Etiology

Causative factors: (1) Endogenous toxicity due to extreme heat of the viscera caused by fatty and spicy food, and (2) stagnation of qi and blood resulting from invasion of toxic exogenous factors in summer when the skin is contaminated by sweat.

Differentiation

Furuncle may occur on the head, face or extremities. It first appears like a grain of millet, with a hard base. Pain or a tingling sensation may be present. A blister or pustula yellowish or purplish in colour and hard as a nail is formed, usually accompanied by chills and fever. If it occurs on the extremities with a red thread-like line running proximally, it is known as red-thread furuncle (i.e., lymphangitis).

Treatment

Method: Apply needling with reducing method or pricking to cause bleeding to points of the Du and Large Intestine Channels as the main points. For lymphangitis, prick with the three-edged needle to cause bleeding at 2-inch intervals along the red line proximally towards the focus.

Prescription: Lingtai (Du 10), Shenzhu (Du 12), Ximen (P. 4), Hegu (L.I. 4), Weizhong (U.B. 40).

Explanation: Lingtai (Du 10) is an empirical point for treatment of furuncle. Shenzhu (Du 12), being a point of the Du Channel, readjusts the qi of all the *yang* channels. Ximen (P. 4), the Xi (Cleft) Point of the Pericardium Channel is effective in treating acute diseases. Hegu (L.I. 4) eliminates the exogenous pathogenic factors from the exterior portion of the body. Weizhong (U.B. 40) is effective in clearing heat and toxin

from the blood. Using these two points together allays inflammation. Pricking to cause bleeding disperses toxin and heat from the blood.

Remark: Another efficacious method for treating furuncle is to prick
and tilt with the three-edged needle the small papules which may appear
alongside the thoracic vertebrae in cases of furuncle. Treatment may be
given once a day.

XLIII. ACUTE MASTITIS

Etiology

Causative factor is retention of milk in the breast caused by mental
depression affecting the *qi* of the liver or stagnation of toxic heat in the
Stomach Channel.

Differentiation

Onset is redness, swelling, heat and pain of the breast, accompanied by
chills, fever, nausea, irritability and thirst. Pulse wiry and rapid.

Treatment

To regulate the *qi* of the Liver and Stomach Channels, relieve depression and eliminate heat by applying needling with reducing method to
points of the Liver, Gall bladder and Stomach Channels. Moxibustion
may be used in combination.

Prescription: Taichong (Liv. 3), Foot-Linqi (G.B. 41), Shanzhong (Ren
17), Jianjing (G.B. 21), Rugen (St. 18).

Secondary points:

Chills and fever: Hegu (L.I. 4), Waiguan (S.J. 5).

Distending pain of the breasts: Yingchuang (St. 16).

Explanation: Taichong (Liv. 3) promotes liver function. Foot-Linqi
(G.B. 41) helps subsidence of swelling of the breast. Shanzhong (Ren 17)
relieves feeling of pressure in the chest. Jianjing (G.B. 21) and Rugen (St.
18) promote circulation of *qi* to stop pain. Hegu (L.I. 4) and Waiguan
(S.J. 5) reduce fever. Yingchuang (St. 16) is punctured obliquely to soften
the lump in the breast and promote milk flow.

Remarks:

(1) The condition may correspond to the early stage of mastitis.

(2) Ear acupuncture

Main points: Chest, Adrenal, Ear-Shenmen, Subcortex.

Method: Puncture two points at each treatment with moderate stimulation. Needles are retained for 30 minutes. Give treatment once daily.

Etiology

Causative factors: (1) Accumulation of damp-heat due to retention of food in the intestines, and (2) stagnation of *qi* and blood due to exposure to extreme heat or cold.

Differentiation

In acute cases the onset is marked by chills and fever, irritability, nausea, abdominal pain with tenderness and aggravated on coughing or sneezing and flexing the right leg. The pain finally localizes in the right lower abdomen. There is constipation, thick sticky coated tongue, and wiry rapid pulse.

Treatment

Method: To disperse damp-heat by puncturing with reducing method with points of the Yangming Channels as the main points. Retain needles for a prolonged period ranging from half an hour to 2 hours, manipulate every ten minutes, and treat every 6-8 hours. When symptoms and signs are alleviated, treatment may be given once daily with needles retained for 30 minutes.

Prescription: Lanwei (Appendix, Extra.) or Shangjuxu (St. 37), Quchi (L.I. 11), Tianshu (St. 25).

Secondary points:

Fever: Dazhui (Du 14), Hegu (L.I. 4).

Vomiting: Neiguan (P. 6), Zhongwan (Ren 12).

Explanation: Lanwei (Appendix, Extra.), an empirical point, and Shangjuxu (St. 37), the Inferior He-Sea Point of the large intestine, are tender spots in appendicitis. Tianshu (St. 25), the Front-Mu Point of the large intestine, removes obstruction and damp-heat from the intestines and subsequently relieves abdominal pain. Quchi (L.I. 11), the He-Sea Point of the Large Intestine Channel, is also effective in eliminating heat. Dazhui (Du 14) and Hegu (L.I. 4) used together allay inflammation. Neiguan (P. 6) and Zhongwan (Ren 12) pacify the stomach and check vomiting.

Remarks:

(1) This disease corresponds to acute simple appendicitis, for which acupuncture treatment is considered effective. If perforation is suspected, other therapeutic measures should be resorted to, the above prescription proving satisfactory in chronic appendicitis. Treatment is given once daily or every other day. Moxibustion may be applied at local points.

(2) Ear acupuncture:

Main points: Ear-Appendix, Ear-Shenmen, Sympathetic Nerve, Subcortex.

Method: In acute conditions treatment is given 1-3 times a day, while in chronic cases it is given once daily or every other day.

XLV. GOITER

Etiology

This is an endemic disease whose causative factors are (1) blood stasis and accumulation of phlegm due to obstruction of qi caused by exasperation, anxiety or mental depression, and (2) stagnation of qi in neck due to invasion of any of the six exogenous pathogenic factors and environmental inadaptability.

Differentiation

Swelling of the neck, which may be accompanied by stuffiness in the chest, palpitation, shortness of breath, exophthalmos and irascibility. Pulse is wiry and rolling.

Treatment

Method: To activate blood and qi circulation and remove stasis and lumps by puncturing with reducing method at points of the Sanjiao, Large Intestine and Stomach Channels as main points.

Prescription: Naohui (S.J. 13), Tianding (L.I. 17), Tianrong (S.I. 17), Tiantu (Ren 22), Hegu (L.I. 4), Zusanli (St. 36).

Secondary points:

Depression of qi of liver: Shanzhong (Ren 17), Taichong (Liv. 3).

Explanation: Naohui (S.J. 13), a point of the Sanjiao Channel, has the effect of dispersing the stagnant qi and phlegm in the goiter because *sanjiao* dominates the qi of the whole body. Tianding (L.I. 17), Tianrong (S.I. 17) and Tiantu (Ren 22) are located at the neck; puncturing the three points promotes the circulation of qi and blood in the local area so as to disperse the stagnant qi and blood. Hegu (L.I. 4) and Zusanli (St. 36) are distal points pertaining respectively to the Hand- and Foot-Yangming Channels which pass through the neck. They are used to direct the circulation of qi and blood.

Remarks:

(1) Goiter as described in this section corresponds to simple goiter and hyperthyroidism.

(2) Ear acupuncture

Main points: Endocrine, Ear-Shenmen, Neck.

Method: Give moderate stimulation. Needles are retained for 30 minutes. Treatment is given once daily or every other day. 10-15 treatments constitute a course.

XLVI. SPRAIN

Etiology

Local congestion caused by obstruction of *qi* and blood in the joint due to awkward posture of the body, sudden twisting or falling during physical exertion.

Differentiation

Local soreness, distension and pain or mild redness and swelling. Movement is limited or impossible.

Treatment

Method: Ashi Points are the main points used to ease the tendons and activate blood circulation. Local and distal points of the involved channels may be combined. Apply needling plus moxibustion to the former and needling to the latter.

Prescription: Ashi Points.

Secondary points:

Neck: Tianzhu (U.B. 10), Houxi (S.I. 3).

Shoulder joint: Jianjing (G.B. 21), Jianyu (L.I. 15).

Elbow joint: Quchi (L.I. 11), Hegu (L.I. 4).

Wrist joint: Yangchi (S.J. 4), Waiguan (S.J. 5).

Hip joint: Huantiao (G.B. 30), Yanglingquan (G.B. 34).

Knee joint: Dubi (St. 35), Neiting (St. 44).

Ankle joint: Jiexi (St. 41), Qiuxu (G.B. 40), Kulun (U.B. 60).

Explanation: Local and distal points selected from the involved channels can promote the circulation of *qi* and blood in the channels and collaterals. Moxibustion on the local points warms and promotes circulation of *qi* and blood so as to relieve swelling and pain.

Remark:

Needling may be applied to the sound side at the area corresponding to the affected area. When manipulating the needle, ask the patient to move the sprained joint. Alleviation or subsidence of pain may be expected.

XLVII. DEAFNESS AND TINNITUS

Etiology

Deafness and tinnitus can be divided into two types: the *xu* and the *shi*. The *shi* type is usually due to upward perversion of the *qi* of the liver and gall bladder which affects the sense of hearing. The *xu* type is usually due to lowering of the *qi* of the kidney, which fails to ascend.

Differentiation

(1) *Shi* type:

Tinnitus: Continuous ringing of the ear unrelieved by pressure.

Deafness: Sudden deafness.

The accompanying symptoms and signs are distension and heavy sensation of the head, nasal obstruction, bitter taste in mouth, hypochondriac pain, sticky coated tongue and rolling rapid pulse.

(2) *Xu* type

Tinnitus: Intermittent ringing of the ear which becomes aggravated after stress and strain and is somewhat alleviated by pressure.

Deafness: Gradually intensified deafness.

The accompanying symptoms and signs are dizziness, blurring of vision, low back pain, lassitude and thready pulse.

Treatment

Method:

(1) *Shi* type: To restore the sense of hearing by puncturing with reducing method at points of the Sanjiao and Gall bladder Channels as the main points.

(2) *Xu* type: To strengthen the liver and kidney by puncturing with even movement plus moxibustion at points of the Kidney and Liver Channels.

Prescription: Yifeng (S.J. 17), Ermen (S.J. 21), Tinghui (G.B. 2), Yemen (S.J. 2), Xiaxi (G.B. 43), Hand-Zhongzhu (S.J. 3).

Secondary points:

(1) *Shi* type:

Upward perversion of *qi* of liver and gall bladder: Xingjian (Liv. 2). Foot-Linqi (G.B. 41).

Sudden deafness: Tianyou (S.J. 16).

(2) *Xu* type:

Lowering of *qi* of kidney: Shenshu (U.B. 23), Mingmen (Du 4), Taixi (K. 3).

Insufficiency of *yin* of liver and kidney: Taichong (Liv. 3), Sanyinjiao (Sp. 6).

Explanation: Yemen (S.J. 2), Xiaxi (G.B. 43), Yifeng (S.J. 17), Ermen (S.J. 21), Tinghui (G.B. 2) and Hand-Zhongzhu (S.J. 3) are selected as the main points because the Hand- and Foot-Shaoyang Channels (Sanjiao and Gall bladder Channels) pass through the ear region. Xingjian (Liv. 2) and

Foot-Linqi (G.B. 41) are used to regulate the *qi* of the Liver and Gallbladder Channels. Tianyou (S.J. 16) is a local point used for treatment of sudden deafness. Shenshu (U.B. 23), Mingmen (Du 4) and Taixi (K. 3) strengthen the *qi* of the kidney. Sanyinjiao (Sp. 6) and Taichong (Liv. 3) nourish the *yin* of the liver and kidney to reduce the *xu* fire (the presence of which is due to insufficiency of *yin*).

Remarks:

(1) Tinnitus and deafness may be present in various diseases, those most often encountered in the acupuncture clinic being due to nerve defects.

(2) Ear acupuncture

Main points: Ear, Internal Ear, Ear-Shenmen, Kidney, Endocrine, Occiput.

Method: Select 2-3 points at each treatment. Needles are retained for 20-30 minutes at each treatment, which is given every other day. 10-15 treatments make a course.

XLVIII. CONGESTION, SWELLING AND PAIN OF THE EYE

Etiology

Causative factors: (1) Invasion of exogenous wind-heat, (2) upward disturbance of fire of liver and gall bladder.

Differentiation

Congestion, swelling, pain and burning sensation of the eye, photophobia, lacrimation and sticky discharge.

(1) Invasion of exogenous wind-heat: Headache, fever, superficial rapid pulse.

(2) Upward disturbance of fire of liver and gall bladder: Bitter taste in mouth, irritability with feverish sensation, constipation, wiry pulse.

Treatment

Method: Distal and local points are used in combination to disperse wind-heat. Needling is given with reducing method.

Prescription: Hegu (L.I. 4), Jingming (U.B. 1), Fengchi (G.B. 20), Taiyang (Extra.), Xingjian (Liv. 2).

Secondary points:

Upward disturbance of fire of liver and gall bladder: Taichong (Liv. 3), Guangming (G.B. 37).

Explanation: Hegu (L.I. 4) and Fengchi (G.B. 20) disperse wind-heat. Jingming (U.B. 1), a point where the Urinary Bladder and Stomach Channels meet, eliminates heat in the diseased area. Xingjian (Liv. 2), the

Ying-Spring Point of the Liver Channel, reduces the heat of the liver. Pricking Taiyang (Extra.) to cause bleeding enhances the effect of reducing heat. Taichong (Liv. 3), the Yuan (Source) Point of the Liver Channel, is selected because the liver is related to the eye. As there is an external-internal relation between the liver and gall bladder, Guangming (G.B. 37), the Luo (Connecting) Point of the Gall bladder Channel, is used to reduce the fire of the liver and gall bladder.

Remarks:

(1) The condition corresponds to acute conjunctivitis in the sense of modern medicine.

(2) Ear acupuncture

Main points: Liver, Eye, Ear Apex.

Method: Treatment is given once daily with needles retained for 15-20 minutes and ear apex pricked to let out 2-3 drops of blood. 3-5 treatments make a course.

XLIX. RHINORRHEA

Etiology

Causative factors: (1) Invasion of the exterior part of the body by wind-cold which, when accumulated, turns into heat blocking the nose, and (2) damp-heat of the Gall bladder Channel which goes upward and accumulates in the nose.

Differentiation

Nasal obstruction, loss of the sense of smell, yellow fetid nasal discharge accompanied by cough, dull pain, cloudiness and heaviness of the frontal region of the head, red tongue with thin yellow coating, wiry rapid pulse.

Treatment

Method: To disperse heat of the lung by puncturing with reducing method at points of the Lung and Large Intestine Channels as the main points.

Prescription: Lieque (Lu. 7), Hegu (L.I. 4), Yingxiang (L.I. 20), Yintang (Extra.).

Secondary points:

Headache: Fengchi (G.B. 20), Taiyang (Extra.).

Explanation: Lieque (Lu. 7) eliminates pathogenic wind by activating the dispersing function of the lung. Hegu (L.I. 4) and Yingxiang (L.I. 20) reduce the heat of the lung by regulating the qi of the Large Intestine Channel. Yintang (Extra), a local point at the nose, has the effect of reducing heat by removing obstruction of the nose. Fengchi (G.B. 20) eliminates the wind and reduces the heat so as to relieve headache. Taiyang (Extra.) is an important point for treatment of headache.

Remarks:

(1) Rhinorrhea as described in this section corresponds to chronic rhinitis and chronic nasal sinusitis.

(2) Ear acupuncture

Main points: External nose, Internal Nose, Forehead.

Method: Give moderate stimulation. Needles are retained for 10-15 minutes. 10-15 treatments make a course.

L. EPISTAXIS

Etiology

Extravasation of blood due to (1) ascending of wind-heat of the lung or fire of the stomach to disturb the nose, or (2) insufficiency of *yin* causing hyperactivity of fire which exhausts the *yin* of the lung.

Differentiation

(1) Excess of heat in lung and stomach: Epistaxis is accompanied by fever, cough, thirst, constipation and superficial rapid pulse.

(2) Hyperactivity of fire due to insufficiency of *yin*: Epistaxis is accompanied by malar flush, dryness of mouth and feverish sensation in palms and soles. In severe cases there may be afternoon fever and thready rapid pulse.

Treatment

Method: To reduce heat and stop bleeding by puncturing with reducing method for the heat-excessive type and even movement for *yin* insufficient type at points of the Large Intestine and Du Channels.

Prescription: Hegu (L.I. 4), Shangxing, (Du 23).

Secondary points:

Heat of the lung: Shaoshang (Lu. 11).

Heat of the stomach: Neiting (St. 44).

Hyperactivity of fire due to insufficiency of *yin*: Taixi (K. 3).

Explanation: The Large Intestine Channel is externally-internally related to the Lung Channel and links with the Stomach Channel, so Hegu (L.I. 4) is used to reduce the heat of the three channels to stop bleeding. The Du Channel is the confluence of all the *yang* channels, and Shangxing (Du 23) is used to reduce the excessive *yang* of the Du Channel which causes hyperactivity of heat. Shaoshang (Lu. 11), the Jing-Well Point of the Lung Channel, is used to reduce the heat of the lung. Neiting (St. 44), the Ying-Spring Point of the Stomach Channel, is effective in reducing fire in the stomach. Taixi (K. 3), the Yuan (Source) Point of the Kidney Channel, has the effect of tonifying *yin* and reducing heat.

Remarks:

(1) Epistaxis may be caused by trauma, nasal diseases or systemic diseases such as diseases of blood, cardiovascular diseases and acute febrile infectious diseases. In addition to acupuncture treatment, other therapeutic measures should be adopted according to its primary cause.

(2) Ear acupuncture

Main points: Internal Nose, Ear-Shenmen, Sympathetic Nerve.

Method: Give moderate stimulation. Treatment is given 1-2 times a day, with needles retained for 15-20 minutes each time. 4-6 treatments make a course.

LI. TOOTHACHE

Etiology

Causative factors: (1) Flaring up of the accumulated heat of the stomach and intestines together with invasion of exogenous pathogenic factors, and (2) flaring up of *xu* fire due to insufficiency of *yin* of kidney.

Differentiation

(1) Wind-heat: Gingival swelling and pain, thirst and preference for cold beverages, constipation, red tongue with yellow coating, rapid pulse.

(2) *Xu* of kidney: Intermittent dull pain, loose teeth, red tongue, thready rapid pulse.

Treatment

(1) Wind-heat:

Method: To reduce heat and relieve pain by puncturing with reducing method at points mainly selected from the Large Intestine and Stomach Channels.

Prescription: Hegu (L.I. 4), Neiting (St. 44), Xianguan (St. 7), Jiache (St. 6) Fengchi (G.B. 20).

Explanation: Hegu (L.I. 4) of the contralateral side is used to disperse the pathogenic heat of the Large Intestine Channel. Neiting (St. 44), the Ying-Spring Point of the Stomach Channel, pertains to water in the five elements, so it is used to reduce the fire of the stomach. Fengchi (G.B. 20) has the effect of eliminating wind and reducing fire. Xiaguan (St. 7) and Jiache (St. 6) are local points.

(2) *Xu* of kidney:

Method: To nourish *yin* and reduce fire by puncturing with even movement at points of the Stomach Channel as the main points.

Prescription: Taixi (K. 3), Jiache (St. 6), Xiaguan (St. 7).

Explanation: Teeth relate to the kidney and are situated where the Stomach Channel and the Large Intestine Channel go through, thus Taixi (K. 3) is effective in nourishing *yin* of the kidney and reducing *xu* fire. Jiache (St. 6) and Xiaguan (St. 7) relieve pain by regulating the *qi* of the channels.

Remark: Toothache as described in this section includes acute and chronic pulpitis, dental caries, peridental abscess and pericoronitis in the sense of modern medicine.

LII. SORE THROAT

Etiology

Sore throat is divided into two types: the *shi* and the *xu*.

(1) *Shi* type: Invasion of laryngopharynx by exogenous pathogenic wind-heat, or flaring up of the accumulated heat of the Lung Channel and the Stomach Channel.

(2) *Xu* type: Flaring up of *xu* fire due to insufficiency of *yin* of the kidney.

Differentiation

(1) *Shi* type: Abrupt onset with chills, fever and headache, congested and sore throat, thirst, constipation, red tongue with thin yellow coating, superficial rapid pulse.

(2) *Xu* type: Gradual onset without fever or with low fever, intermittent sore throat, dryness of the throat which usually becomes aggravated by night, feverish sensation in palms and soles, uncoated red tongue, thready rapid pulse.

Treatment

(1) *Shi* type:

Method: To eliminate wind and heat by puncturing with reducing method at points of the Large Intestine and Stomach Channels as the main points.

Prescription: Shaoshang (Lu. 11), Hegu (L.I. 4), Neiting (St. 44), Tianrong (S.I. 17).

Explanation: Pricking Shaoshang (Lu. 11) to let out a small amount of blood clears the heat of the lung and relieves pain. Hegu (L.I. 4) disperses exterior pathogenic factors of the Lung Channel. Neiting (St. 44), the Ying-Spring Point of the Stomach Channel, reduces heat of the stomach. Tianrong (S.I. 17), a local point used to promote circulation of *qi* and blood in the local area, is efficacious in relieving sore throat.

(2) *Xu* type:

Method: To nourish the *yin* and reduce *xu* fire by puncturing with reinforcing method at points of the Kidney Channel as the main points.

Prescriptions:

    (a) Taixi (K. 3), Yuji (Lu. 10).

    (b) Zhaohai (K. 6), Lieque (Lu. 7).

These two prescriptions may be used alternately.

Explanation: Taixi (K. 3) is the Ying-Spring Point of the Kidney Channel which runs along the throat superiorly. Yuji (Lu. 10) is the Ying-Spring Point of the Lung Channel. Combination of the two nourishes *yin* and reduces fire. Zhaohai (K. 6) and Lieque (Lu. 7), one of the pairs of the Eight Confluent Points, relieve sore throat by reducing *xu* fire.

Remarks:

(1) Sore throat as described in this section includes acute tonsilitis and acute and chronic pharyngitis in the sense of modern medicine.

(2) Ear acupuncture

Main points: Pharynx, Tonsil, Helix 1-3, pricking the small vein in the back of the ear to cause bleeding.

Method: Puncture 2-3 points at each treatment with moderate stimulation. Needles are retained for an hour. Treatment is given once daily. 3-5 treatments make a course. Prick the small vein in the back of the ear to let out a small amount of blood.

APPENDIX

CHAPTER I

EAR ACUPUNCTURE THERAPY

Ear acupuncture therapy is to treat diseases by stimulating certain points of the auricle with needles. Such method of treatment was recorded as early as in the book *Neijing* (500-300 B.C.) and other medical literature of subsequent dynasties. This therapeutic method has long been used by the labouring people. Since China's liberation, medical workers in accordance with Chairman Mao's instruction "Make the past serve the present and foreign things serve China" have inherited and promoted traditional Chinese medicine while also studying foreign materials for making a comprehensive study of ear acupuncture. Repeated practice and constant summing up of experience have greatly broadened the realm of ear acupuncture therapy.

I. RELATIONS BETWEEN THE AURICLE AND CHANNELS, COLLATERALS AND *ZANG-FU* ORGANS

It is held in traditional Chinese medicine that the ear is not a separate organ but closely connected with channels and collaterals and *zang-fu* organs, and is a part of the body as an organic whole. As is pointed out in *Neijing*, the *qi* and blood of all twelve channels and their 365 collaterals ascend to the face and brain, their branches reaching the ear to make auditory function normal. This generalizes the relation between the auricle and channels and collaterals. Specifically, the six *yang* channels respectively enter and go around the ear, i.e., the Small Intestine Channel of Hand-Taiyang, Large Intestine Channel of Hand-Yangming, Sanjiao Channel of Hand-Shaoyang and Gallbladder Channel of Foot-Shaoyang enter the ear, while the Stomach Channel of Foot-Yangming and Urinary Bladder Channel of Foot-Taiyang reach the periauricular region. The six *yin* channels indirectly connect with the ear through the branches of the twelve channels. Besides, among the eight extra channels, the Yangqiao and Yinqiao Channels together enter the retroauricular region and the Yangwei Channel enters the ear after circling the head. *Neijing* claims on the basis of these facts that the ear is the converging site of a number of channels.

Numerous writings concerning the relationship between the ear and *zang-fu* organs have also been found in ancient medical literature. For instance, *Neijing* points out that ample storage of the *qi* of the kidney makes the auditory function of the ear normal; insufficiency of essence in the kidney leads to insufficiency of the brain which gives rise to dizziness and tinnitus. These show a physical and pathological relationship between the ear and *zang-fu* organs.

In normal conditions, a relative balance and co-ordination is maintained among the physiological functions of the various parts of the body. Once an imbalance and inco-ordination are present and channel stasis occurs, reactions can be detected at the corresponding areas on the auricle. Clinically, diseases of various parts of the body can be cured by needling the corresponding auricular points, which may promote free circulation of *qi* and blood in the channels and collaterals and adjust the *zang-fu* organs.

II. ANATOMICAL STRUCTURE OF THE SURFACE OF THE AURICLE

The auricle is composed of a plate of elastic cartilage, a thin layer of fat and connective tissue supplied by numerous nerves. The main nerves are the great auricular and the lesser occipital derived from the 2nd and 3rd cervical spinal nerves, the auriculo-temporal branch of the trigeminal nerve, the posterior auricular branch of the facial nerve and the mixed branch of the vagus and the glossopharyngeal nerves.

For greater clarity, the anatomical structure of the surface of the auricle relating to ear acupuncture are briefly described as follows: (Fig. 150.)

1).

1. Helix

The prominent rim of the auricle.

2. Helix crus

The interior end of the helix, a horizontal prominence.

3. Auricular tubercle

A small tubercle at the posterior upper aspect of the helix.

4. Helix cauda

The inferior end of the helix, at the junction of the helix and the lobule.

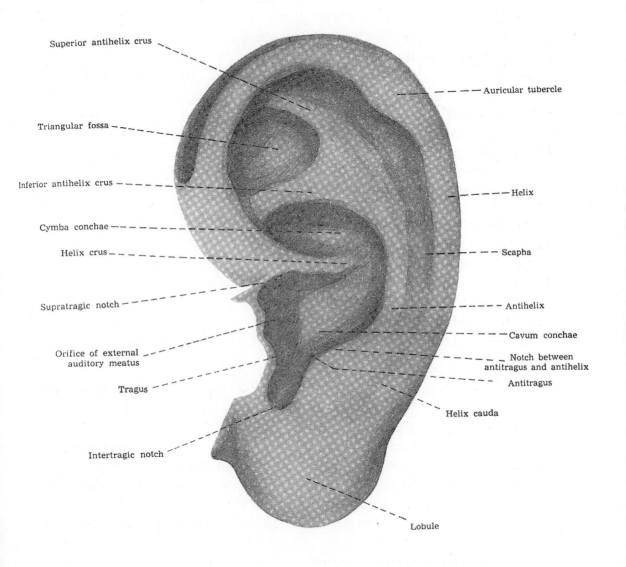

Superior antihelix crus

Triangular fossa

Inferior antihelix crus

Cymba conchae

Helix crus

Supratragic notch

Orifice of external
auditory meatus

Tragus

Intertragic notch

Auricular tubercle

Helix

Scapha

Antihelix

Cavum conchae

Notch between
antitragus and antihelix

Antitragus

Helix cauda

Lobule

Fig. 150.   Anatomy of the surface of the auricle.

5. Antihelix

A curved prominence opposite to the helix. Its upper part branches out into the superior and the inferior antihelix crus.

6. Triangular fossa

The depression between the two crura of the antihelix.

7. Scapha (or scaphoid fossa)

The narrow curved depression between the helix and the antihelix.

8. Tragus

A small, curved flap in front of the auricle.

9. Supratragic notch

The depression between the helix crus and the upper border of the tragus.

10. Antitragus

A small tubercle opposite to the tragus and inferior to the antihelix.

11. Intertragic notch

The depression between the tragus and the antitragus.

12. Notch between the antitragus and antihelix

13. Lobule

The lower part of the auricle where there is no cartilage.

14. Cymba conchae

The concha superior to the helix crus.

15. Cavum conchae

The concha inferior to the helix crus.

16. Orifice of the external auditory meatus

The opening in the cavum conchae shielded by the tragus.

III. AURICULAR POINTS

Auricular points are specific points on the auricle to which stimuli are given for treatment of disease. When disorders occur in the internal organs or other parts of the body, various reactions may appear at the corresponding parts of the auricle, such as tenderness, decreased resistance to electric current, morphological changes and discoloration. In making a diagnosis, these phenomena can be taken into consideration. Application of stimuli to the sensitive sites serves to prevent and treat disease. These sites are also referred to as tender spots, spots with increased conductance, or sensitive spots.

1. Distribution of auricular points

Auricular points are distributed on the auricle in a certain pattern. Generally speaking, points that are located at the lobule are related to the head and facial region, those on the scapha to the upper limbs, those on the antihelix and its two crura to the trunk and lower limbs, and those in the cavum and cymba conchae to the internal organs. (Fig. 151.)

2. Location of commonly used auricular points and their indications

The following is a table showing the location of commonly used auricular points and their indications.

IV. CLINICAL APPLICATION OF EAR ACUPUNCTURE

At present, ear acupuncture is used for prevention and treatment of disease, and for acupuncture analgesia. Its application for the latter purpose is to be discussed in Chapter II of the Appendix, which section will deal mainly with its application to clinical practice.

1. Rules for selection of points

(1) Selection of points according to the diseased area. That is, auricular points corresponding to the diseased areas are selected for treatment, e.g. Pt. Stomach for gastralgia, Pt. Shoulder for shoulder pain.

(2) Selection of points according to the theories of *zang-fu* and channels and collaterals. That is, on the basis of the physiology of the *zang-fu* organs, courses of circulation of channels and collaterals and their external-internal relationship, corresponding auricular points are selected for treatment. E.g., Pt. Lung can be selected for skin diseases because the lung dominates the skin and hair; Pt. Small Intestine for palpitation as the heart is externally-internally related to the small intestine; Pt. Gall bladder for temporal headache as the temporal region is supplied by the Gall bladder Channel of Foot-Shaoyang.

(3) Selection of points in terms of modern medicine. That is, auricular points are selected with physiological and pathological consideration, e.g., Pt. Endocrine is selected for irregular menstruation, Pt. Sympathetic Nerve for abdominal pain.

In addition, auricular points can be selected according to the cardinal symptoms of a disease, e.g., Pt. Ear Apex for redness, swelling and pain of the eye, Pts. Helix 1-6 for sore throat.

The above rules can be followed separately or in combination. The principle of choosing less points but with precision is advisable. Generally, points of the affected side are used. Rarely, points of both sides or only the healthy side are used. If necessary, ear acupuncture may be combined with ordinary acupuncture to enhance therapeutic effects.

2. Technique of ear acupuncture

Along with the popularization of ear acupuncture therapy, different methods have been developed on the basis of puncture with filiform

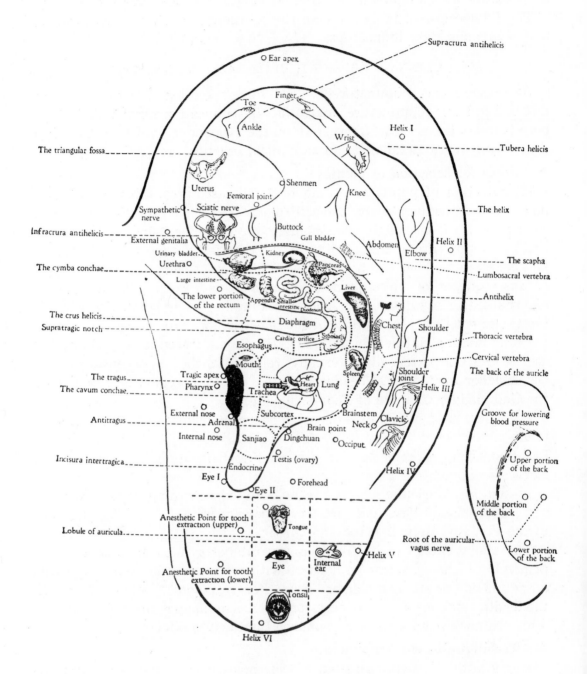

Fig. 151. Distribution of auricular points.

Area Auricular	Name of Point	Location	Indication
Helix crus	Diaphragm	On the helix crus	Hiccup, jaundice
	Lower Portion of Rectum	On end of helix, near supratragic notch	Constipation, diarrhea
	Urethra	On helix, at level of lower border of inferior antihelix crus	Frequency and urgency of micturition, retention of urine
	External Genitalia	On helix, at level of upper border of inferior antihelix crus	Impotence, eczema of the perineum
Helix	Ear Apex	At tip of auricle when folded towards tragus	Acute conjunctivitis, hypertension
	Helix 1-6	Region from lower border of auricular tubercle (Helix 1) to midpoint of lower border of lobule (Helix 6) is divided into five equal parts. The points marking the divisions are respectively Helix 2, 3, 4 and 5.	Acute tonsillitis

Auricular Area	Name of Point	Location	Indication
	Finger	In scapha, superior to auricular tubercle	Pain at corresponding part of body
	Wrist	In scapha, level with auricular tubercle	
	Elbow	Between Pt. Wrist and Pt. Shoulder	
Scapha	Shoulder	In scapha, level with supratragic notch	
	Clavicle	In scapha, level with notch between antitragus and antihelix, slightly lateral to helix cauda	
	Shoulder Joint	Between Pt. Shoulder and Pt. Clavicle	
	Toe	At posterior upper corner of superior antihelix crus	
Superior antihelix crus	Ankle	At anterior upper corner of superior antihelix crus	
	Knee	At origin of superior antihelix crus, level with upper border of inferior antihelix crus	

Auricular Area	Name of Point	Location	Indication
Inferior antihelix crus	Buttocks	Posterior half of upper border of inferior antihelix crus	Pain at corresponding part of body
	Sciatic Nerve	Anterior half of upper border of inferior antihelix crus	Sciatica
	Sympathetic Nerve	At junction of inferior antihelix crus and medial border of helix	Diseases of digestive and circulatory systems
	Abdomen	On antihelix, level with lower border of inferior antihelix crus	Adbominal pain, dysmenorrhea
	Chest	On antihelix, level with supratragic notch	Chest pain, intercostal neuralgia
	Neck	At junction of antihelix and antitragus, near scapha	Strained neck
Antihelix	Spinal Column { Lumbosacral Vertebrae, Thoracic Vertebrae, Cervical Vertebrae }	Curved line of medial border of antihelix corresponds to vertebral column. The line is divided into 3 parts by drawing two horizontal lines respectively from Pt. Lower Portion of Rectum and Pt. Shoulder Joint. The upper, middle and lower parts are respectively locations of Lumbosacral, Thoracic and Cervical Vertebrae.	Pain at corresponding part of body

Auricular Area	Name of Point	Location	Indication
Triangular fossa	Ear-Shenmen	At bifurcating point of superior antihelix crus and inferior antihelix crus	Insomnia, dream-disturbed sleep, inflammation, pain
	Uterus (Seminal Vesicle)	In triangular fossa, at midpoint inferior to border of helix	Irregular menstruation, leukorrhea, dysmenorrhea, impotence, nocturnal emission
Tragus	External Nose	In centre of lateral aspect of tragus	Rhinitis
	Pharynx & Larynx	Upper half of medial aspect of tragus	Pharyngitis, laryngitis, tonsillitis
	Internal Nose	In medial and inferior aspect of tragus	Rhinitis, maxillary sinusitis
	Tragic Apex	At upper tubercle on border of tragus	Toothache
	Adrenal	At lower tubercle on border of tragus	Hypotension, pulselessness, shock, asthma, inflammation
Notch between antitragus & antihelix	Brain Stem	At junction of antitragus and antihelix	Headache, vertigo

Auricular Area	Name of Point	Location	Indication
Concha Cymba	Ear-Asthma	At apex of antitragus	Asthma, bronchitis, mumps
	Brain Point	At midpoint of line connecting Pt. Ear-Asthma and Pt. Brain Stem	Enuresis
Antitragus	Subcortex	On interior wall of antitragus	Insomnia, dream-disturbed sleep, inflammation, pain
	Testis (Ovary)	A part of Pt. Subcortex, at lower part of interior wall of antitragus	Epididymitis, irregular menstruation
	Forehead	At anterior inferior corner of lateral aspect of antitragus	Headache, dizziness, insomnia
Crus of helix Periphery	Occiput	At posterior superior corner of lateral aspect of antitragus	Headache, neurasthenia
	Taiyang	At midpoint of line connecting Pt. Forehead and Pt. Occiput	Unilateral headache
	Esophagus	At anterior two-thirds of inferior aspect of helix crus	Dysphagia
Anthelix	Cardiac Orifice	At posterior third of inferior aspect of helix crus	Nausea, vomiting

Auricular Area	Name of Point	Location	Indication
Periphery of helix crus	Stomach	At area where helix crus terminates	Gastralgia, vomiting, dyspepsia
	Duodenum	At posterior third of superior aspect of helix crus	Duodenal ulcer, pylorospasm
	Small Intestine	At middle third of superior aspect of helix crus	Dyspepsia, palpitation
	Large Intestine	At anterior third of superior aspect of helix crus	Diarrhea, constipation
	Appendix	Between Pt. Large Intestine and Pt. Small Intestine	Acute simple appendicitis
	Urinary Bladder	On lower border of inferior antihelix crus, directly above Pt. Large Intestine	Enuresis, retention of urine
Cymba conchae	Kidney	On lower border of inferior antihelix crus, directly above Pt. Small Intestine	Lumbago, tinnitus, impaired hearing
	Liver	Posterior to Pt. Stomach and Pt. Duodenum	Hepatitis, hypochondriac pain, eye diseases
	Spleen	Inferior to Pt. Liver, close to border of antihelix	Abdominal distension, dyspepsia
	Pancreas & Gall bladder	Between Pt. Liver and Pt. Kidney	Pancreatitis, dyspepsia, diseases of bile duct

Auricular Area	Name of Point	Location	Indication
	Mouth	Close to posterior wall of orifice of external auditory meatus	Facial paralysis, ulceration of the mouth
	Heart	In centre of cavum conchae	Hysteria, palpitation, arrhythmia
Cavum conchae	Lung	A U-shaped area superior, inferior and posterior to Pt. Heart	Cough, asthma, urticaria
	Trachea	Between Pt. Mouth and Pt. Heart	Cough
	Endocrine	In cavum conchae, near intertragic notch	Dysmenorrhea, irregular menstruation
	Sanjiao	In middle of four points of Mouth, Endocrine, Subcortex and Lung	Constipation, edema
Intertragic notch	Eye 1 Eye 2	On both sides of intertragic notch, the anterior being Eye 1 and the posterior Eye 2	Glaucoma, myopia, hordeolum
	Toothache 1	At postero-inferior corner of 1st section of lobule*	Toothache, anaesthetic point for tooth extraction
Lobule	Toothache 2	In centre of 4th section of lobule	
	Eye	In centre of 5th section of lobule	Eye diseases

Auricular Area	Name of Point	Location	Indication
	Internal Ear	In centre of 6th section of lobule	Tinnitus, impaired hearing
	Tonsil	In centre of 8th section of lobule	Tonsillitis
	Groove for Lowering Blood Pressure	At back of ear, in groove between lateral border of protuberance of cartilage and helix	Hypertension
Back of auricle	Upper Portion of Back of Auricle	On protuberance of cartilage at upper portion of back of auricle	Back and low back pain, skin diseases
	Middle Portion of Back of Auricle	At midpoint of line connecting the two points of upper and lower portion of back of auricle	
	Lower Portion of Back of Auricle	On protuberance of cartilage at lower portion of back of auricle	
	Root of Auricular Vagus Nerve	At junction of back of auricle and mastoid, level with helix crus	Gastralgia, headache, asthma, biliary ascariasis

* In order to facilitate location, the lobule is divided into 9 sections. First, draw a horizontal line at the cartilage border of the intertragic notch. Draw two parallel lines below it to divide the lobule into three equal parts transversely. Then divide the second parallel line into three equal parts with points and draw two vertical lines from the points crossing the three horizontal lines to divide the lobule into nine sections. These sections are numbered anteroposteriorly and superoinferiorly in the order of 1, 2, 3, 4, 5, 6, 7, 8 and 9. (See Fig. 151.)

needles, such as imbedding needles and needling with electric stimulation. Among them, puncture with filiform needles is most widely used clinically. The technique is described as follows:

(1) Probing of the sensitive spot: After points are prescribed, it is necessary to probe for the sensitive spots at the areas where the selected points are located. The commonly used methods are the following.

a. Probing for the tender spot: Probe with a blunt needle around the selected point on the auricle from the rim towards the centre. When marked tenderness is located, press hard to mark the spot for applying acupuncture.

b. Probing by electric apparatus: That is to observe the changes in electric resistance, capacity and potential at the areas of the selected auricular points with a special apparatus. At present, the most commonly used method is to determine the conductant point by the skin resistance. The conductant points on the auricle are usually effective spots for application of stimuli in acupuncture treatment.

(2) Aseptic procedure: Auricular points are swabbed with 75% alcohol or 2% iodine.

(3) Insertion of needle: Stabilize the auricle with the left hand. Hold a filiform needle of 0.5 or 1 *cun* with the right hand and insert it swiftly into the point avoiding penetration of the ear. There is generally a sensation of pain, but sometimes of hotness, distension, soreness or heaviness, any of which usually signify satisfactory therapeutic result.

(4) Retention of needle: Needles are usually retained for 20-30 minutes, but in acute inflammatory cases, severe pain and paroxysmal seizures, needles are retained for 1-2 hours or even longer and intermittently manipulated to enhance stimulation.

(5) Removal of needle: After the needle is removed, press the puncture hole with a dry, sterile cotton ball to avoid infection.

(6) Course of treatment: Treatment is given once every day or every other day. Ten treatments make a course. The interval between courses is 5-7 days.

3. Remarks

(1) Strict antisepsis is necessary to avoid infection. Needling is contraindicated if frost-bite or inflammation is present at the auricle. In case of inflammation of the punctured hole or distension and pain in the auricle, timely and appropriate measures should be taken.

(2) Ear acupuncture is not advisable for women during pregnancy if there is a history of miscarriage. Aged and asthenic patients with hyperten-

sion and arteriosclerosis should be given proper rest before and after needling so as to avoid accident.

(3) If ear acupuncture is indicated for a patient who is overtired, hungry, asthenic or under mental tension, give the treatment with the patient in reclining position to prevent fainting. Should fainting occur, treat it in the same way as in ordinary acupuncture.

(4) If sudden pain, soreness or distension occurs with retained needle at an area not within that of the disease being treated, it is advisable to lift the needle a little or remove it so that the abnormal feeling disappears.

(5) In treating a patient with sprain or motor impairment of the extremities, it is necessary after the needle has caused heat from congestion in the auricle to ask the patient to move the affected limb, or apply massage or moxibustion to the affected part in order to enhance the therapeutic effect.

4. Examples of selection of points for common diseases

(1) Headache   Subcortex, Forehead, Occiput or Taiyang.

(2) Hypertension   Groove for Lowering Blood Pressure, Heart, Ear-Shenmen.

(3) Insomnia   Ear-Shenmen, Heart, Forehead or Occiput, Subcortex.

(4) Hysteria   Heart, Subcortex.

(5) Gastralgia   Stomach, Duodenum, Sympathetic Nerve or Root of the Auricular Vagus Nerve, Abdomen.

(6) Hiccup   Diaphragm.

(7) Diarrhea, constipation   Large Intestine, Lower Portion of Rectum, Spleen, Sympathetic Nerve.

(8) Asthma   Ear-Asthma, Lung, Adrenal.

(9) Tertian malaria   Adrenal, Subcortex, Endocrine.

(10) Acute sprain or contusion   Auricular points corresponding to the affected area, Subcortex, Ear-Shenmen.

(11) Sprained neck   Neck or Cervical Vertebrae, tender spots round Pts. Shoulder and Clavicle.

(12) Sciatica   Sciatic Nerve, Buttocks, Ear-Shenmen or Subcortex.

(13) Biliary ascariasis   Gall bladder, Liver, Duodenum, Sympathetic Nerve or Root of Auricular Vagus Nerve.

(14) Acute simple appendicitis   Appendix, Large intestine, Sympathetic Nerve.

(15) Acute orchitis   Testis, External Genitalia, Liver.

(16) Pain in wound after surgical operation Subcortex, Ear-Shenmen, auricular points corresponding to incised area.

(17) Dysmenorrhea   Uterus, Endocrine, Liver.

(18) Enuresis, retention of urine   Urinary Bladder, Kidney, Urethra.

(19) Herpes zoster   Auricular points corresponding to the affected areas, Adrenal.

(20) Urticaria   Lung, Liver, Spleen.

(21) Flat wart   Ear-Shenmen, Lung, auricular points corresponding to the affected areas.

(22) Acute conjunctivitis   Ear, Liver or Ear Apex.

(23) Hordeolum   Eye, Liver, Eye 1, Eye 2.

(24) Acute tonsillitis   Tonsil, 2-3 points from Helix 1-6.

(25) Impaired hearing Internal Ear, Kidney.

CHAPTER II

A BRIEF INTRODUCTION TO ACUPUNCTURE ANALGESIA

Acupuncture analgesia is a new analgesic method developed on the basis of relieving pain by needling. It combines Chinese traditional and Western medicine and has the following advantages:

1. It is safe to use in a great variety of indications.

Up to the present, acupuncture analgesia has been used in millions of surgical operations without mortality or undesirable side effect such as accidentally happens with drug anaesthesia. Acupuncture analgesia does not elicit such postoperative complications as respiratory tract infection, functional disorders of the gastrointestinal tract, abdominal distension, retention of urine, etc. It is safe for use in aged and debilitated patients or those with cardiac, pulmonary, hepatic and renal insufficiency.

2. Reduced embarrassment of physiological function promotes early recovery.

Because physiological function of the human body can be regulated by channel reaction through puncturing certain points, physiological disturbances induced by any pain that may occur in surgical operation can be avoided under acupuncture analgesia as the medical workers are able to take immediate measures according to any subjective signs of the conscious patient. Blood pressure, pulse and respiration rate remain stable in most cases during operation, and physiological function remains normal after operation. The patient regains appetite and ambulatory activity soon after operation, and the wound heals satisfactorily, all of which are conducive to early recovery.

3. Active co-operation of the patient ensures operative results.

The patient under acupuncture analgesia is mentally alert and able to communicate with the surgeons, who can judge operation results as it proceeds. During thyroidectomy, for instance, the patient's phonation may be tested; in total laryngectomy, the patient's swallowing movement can be examined; in eye surgery for correction of strabismus, eyeball movement may be observed; and in laminectomy for decompression of the spinal cord, it is possible to localize the focus accurately and examine the voluntary movement of the extremities. These are definite advantages in surgical operation.

4. The method is simple, convenient and suited for mass use.

Acupuncture analgesia requires only simple apparatus. No special equipment or environment is requied, only skillful selection of points and mastery of manipulation technique. It is especially applicable in rural or isolated areas enabling patients to undergo emergency surgery without delay.

I. PRINCIPLES OF SELECTING POINTS FOR ACUPUNCTURE ANALGESIA

Since acupuncture analgesia is effective through stimulating certain points of the body surface, the selection of points and needle manipulation to produce appropriate stimulus to the points are crucial in acupuncture analgesia.

Three methods commonly used in selecting points:

1. According to the theory of channels

There are two:

(1) Selection of points according to the channel courses.

It is considered in traditional Chinese medicine that the twelve regular channels which distribute over the body connect interiorly with the viscera and exteriorly with the extremities and joints. Each of the channels has its own pathway and connects to the others according to an exterior-interior relation. Selection of points according to the distribution of the channels is illustrated in an old saying: "Where a channel traverses, there the place is amenable to treatment." That is, select points the channel of which traverses the site of the operation.

(2) Selection of points according to differentiation of symptoms and signs.

Traditional Chinese medicine attaches great importance to the concept of the integrity of the human body. When any portion of the human body is affected by disease, various symptoms and signs may be manifested through the channels that portion connects. In treating diseases with acupuncture, it is important to apply the theory of the *zang-fu* organs and that of the channels to differentiate symptoms and signs. The selection of points depends upon this differentiation, the rule applying in selecting points for acupuncture analgesia as well. That is before selecting points, first differentiate the symptoms and signs of a disease and find out their relation with the *zang-fu* organs and the channels. Consideration should also be given to the responses that may be elicited in the operative procedure. Next, plan the prescription carefully. For instance for chest operation, Ximen (P. 4) and Neiguan (P. 6) of the Pericardium Channel of Hand-Jueyin may be selected, because patients undergoing this kind of operation are likely to experience palpitation, shortness of breath and irritability in the preoperative period or during the operation. According to the theory of Chinese traditional medicine, these symptoms are due to disturbances of the heart, while Ximen (P. 4) and Neiguan (P. 6) have the effect of soothing, tranquilizing and adjusting the function of the heart.

2. Selection of points according to segmental innervation

Clinical practice and scientific experiments with acupuncture analgesia show that the nervous system plays a role in suppressing pain and the regulative effect of acupuncture analgesia. Actually, it is based on the fact that the functional integrity of the nervous system is an essential condition for the production of needling response and that the analgesic effect can be induced by such response that the method of selecting points according to segmental innervation is established. And, based on the segmental innervation relation between the puncturing site and the operative site, there are 3 ways to select points, i.e., (1) selecting points in the adjacent segmentation, or in an area that is supplied by the same spinal nerve or an adjacent nerve that supplies the operative site; (2) selecting points in a remote segmentation, that is in an area that is not supplied by the same or adjacent spinal nerve of the operative site; (3) stimulating the nerve trunk within the same segmentation, that is to stimulate directly the peripheral nerve which supplies the operative site. For instance, Hegu (L.I. 4) and Neiguan (P. 6) are points of the adjacent segmentation for analgesia in thyroidectomy, while Neiting (St. 44) and Zusanli (St. 36) are points in remote segmentation. Neck-Futu (L.I. 18) is regarded as a point for direct stimulation of the cutaneous cervical nerve plexus, known as stimulating the nerve trunk within the same segmentation.

The implication of selecting points in the adjacent and remote segmentations in acupuncture analgesia is different from that of selecting the neighbouring and distal points in acupuncture therapy. In the latter, the relative distance between the location of the points chosen and the affected area to be treated is implied only. Selecting points far from the affected site is known as the method of selecting remote points, while selecting points near the affected site is known as the method of selecting adjacent points. Neither method is related with segmental nerves. For example, for analgesia in thyroidectomy, Hegu (L.I. 4) and Neiguan (P. 6) are chosen as adjacent points according to segmental innervation; but from the point of view of the distance between these points and the neck, they are considered distal points.

3. Selection of auricular points

That is to select the corresponding auricular areas according to the operative site and its involved internal organs. For example, Point Stomach is chosen for subtotal gastrectomy.

Auricular points are also selected according to the theory of the *zang-fu* organs. For example, lung dominates skin and hair, and Point Lung is often chosen for various operations; while kidney dominates bone, and Point Kidney is often selected for orthopaedic surgery. Moreover, reaction-points on the auricle may be chosen, such as tenderness, reducing of electro-resistance, or the appearance of deformation and discoloration when a certain internal organ or area of the body is affected. According to therapeutic experience, Point Shenmen and Sympathetic Nerve are efficacious for sedation and suppressing pain and are frequently used in acupuncture analgesia.

II. MANIPULATION METHOD

Hand manipulation and electropulsating stimulation are the most popular at present.

1. Hand manipulation

This is basic. Even if electro-acupuncture is applied, it has to start with hand manipulation, the electro-apparatus not being connected until the patient feels the needling response. Hand manipulation is to lift-thrust and rotate the needle with the thumb, index and middle fingers holding the handle of the needle after it is inserted at the point in order to apply mechanical stimulus. Rotation alone of the needle may be done, or lift-thrust and rotation alternately. For points of the auricle, only rotation of the needle is allowed since the auricle is too thin to apply the lift-thrust method. Generally, the degree of rotation on points of the body is 90°-360°, the depth for lift-thrust manoeuvre is 0.6-1.0 cm and the frequency of rotation varies between 1 and 3 times per second.

2. Electric stimulation

After the desired needling response is obtained by hand manipulation, the output wire of the electric acupuncture apparatus is attached to the handle of the filiform needle, and the current turned on.

The electric stimulus usually used for acupuncture analgesia is continuous, sparse and dense, or intermittent electric pulsating, mostly in the form of biphasic spike or rectangular wave 0.5-2 msc. in width. But the biphasic sinusoid or irregular sound wave may also be used. The frequencies of electric pulse are of two kinds: 2-8 times per second and 40-200 times per second. The stimulation force should be adjusted according to the patient's tolerance. Generally, acupuncture analgesia requires powerful stimulation which may be increased gradually up to the highest limit, that is the limit which the patient can stand.

3. Induction and Retaining of the Needle

Acupuncture analgesia demands an induction period. That is, after the needle is inserted and a needling reponse is obtained, hand manipulation or electric stimulation is applied continuously to cause a constant needling effect with a suitable stimulating degree and a desirable period of time. Generally, the induction period is about 20 minutes. By means of induction, the patient may adapt himself to the stimulus of acupuncture analgesia. At the same time, it plays an active role in regulating the function of various internal organs of the body, preparing the patient for surgical operation.

During intervals within the operative period when the operative stimulus is slight, hand manipulation may be stopped or the current for electric stimulation cut and the needles allowed to remain in place. Before the operation proceeds to a stage of vigorous stimulation, it is necessary to continue the lift-thrust and rotation manoeuvre or electric stimulus to maintain and strengthen the analgesic effect of the acupuncture.

III. REMARKS

1. It is important preoperatively to understand the patient's attitude to surgery under acupuncture analgesia and do explanatory work when necessary. The patient must have confidence in the method, and any misgivings should be dispelled by explaining the procedure so as to gain the patient's co-operation.

2. In order to know the patient's response to acupuncture and tolerance to pain in the preoperative period, it is also necessary to test the patient's pain threshold after needling. This may serve as a guide in administer-

ing an appropriate method of acupuncture analgesia and power of stimulation.

3. According to the different conditions of patients and different types of operations, some preoperative adjuvants may be applied. Usually 25-100 mg Dolantin is given intramuscularly 30 minutes prior to operation. When it is necessary to cut the nerve, or aching pain and discomfort occur in certain locations, 0.5-1% procaine for local infiltration or nerve blockage may be administered.

4. In performing a surgical operation under acupuncture analgesia, the surgeon must observe the principle of being precise, accurate, light and deft in his technique.

5. As yet, acupuncture analgesia in surgery still has its drawbacks. In some instances and during certain stages of some operations, it does not yet produce total analgesia. In abdominal operations, it fails to give complete and satisfactory relaxation of the abdominal muscles and prevent the unpleasant response to retraction of the internal organs. Further study and practice should help to solve such problems.

IV. SOME EXAMPLES OF SELECTING POINTS FOR ACUPUNCTURE ANALGESIA

1. Head region
Cranial operation: Xiangu (St. 43), Foot-Linqi (G.B. 41), Taichong (Liv. 3), Quanliao (S.I. 18). All on the diseased side.

2. Eye region
(1) Detached retina:
   a. Hegu (L.I. 4), Zhigou (S.J. 6). Both on the diseased side.
   b. Auricular points: Forehead towards Eye 1, Eye 2.
Yangbai (G.B. 14) towards Yuyao (Extra.).
All on the diseased side.
(2) Operations of trichiasis for entropion: Hegu (L.I. 4). Bilaterally.
(3) Correction of strabismus:
   a. Hegu (L.I. 4), Zhigou (S.J. 6), Yangbai (G.B. 14) towards Yuyao (Extra.), Sibai (St. 2) towards Chengqi (St. 1). All on the diseased side with electric stimulation.
   b. Hegu (L.I. 4), Zhigou (S.J. 6), Houxi (S.I. 3), Jingmen (G.B. 25), All on the diseased side.
(4) Cataract couching:
   a. Hegu (L.I. 4), Waiguan (S.J. 5) towards Neiguan (P. 6). Both on the diseased side.

b. Hegu (L.I. 4), Zhigou (S.J. 6). Both on the diseased side.

(5) Enucleation of eyeball: Hegu (L.I. 4), Waiguan (S.J. 5), Houxi (S.I. 3). All on the diseased side. If the eyeball is sensitive, administer 1% dicaine for surface anaesthesia during the operation.

(6) Iridectomy: Hegu (L.I. 4), Waiguan (S.J. 5), Neiting (St. 44). All bilaterally. At the first two points, give hand manipulation. For the last one, retain the needle after needling sensation is produced.

(7) Shortening of sclera:

a. Hegu (L.I. 4), Zhigou (S.J. 6), Yangbai (G.B. 14) towards Yuyao (Extra.), Sibai (St. 2) towards Chengqi (St. 1). All on the diseased side with electric stimulation.

b. Hegu (L.I. 4), Zhigou (S.J. 6). Both on the diseased side with electric stimulation.

(8) Replantation of pterygium:

a. Auricular points: Eye, Liver. Both on the diseased side.

b. Auricular points: Ear-Shenmen, Eye, Eye 1. All on the diseased side.

(9) Dacryocystectomy and dacryocystotomy for discharging of pus:

a. Hegu (L.I. 4), Taichong (Liv. 3). Both on the diseased side.

b. Hegu (L.I. 4), Zanzhu (U.B. 2), Yingxiang (L.I. 20). All on the diseased side.

(10) Exenteration of orbit: Hegu (L.I. 4), Zhigou (S.J. 6). Both bilaterally. Auricular points: Forehead towards Eye 2, Ear-Shenmen towards Sympathetic Nerve. Both bilaterally.

3. Jaw

(1) Resection of tumour in parotid glands: Fenglong (St. 40), Yangfu (G.B. 38), Fuyang (U.B. 59), Xiangu (St. 43), Taichong (Liv. 3), Xiaxi (G.B. 43). All bilaterally. Needles are retained after needling sensation is produced.

(2) Operations in the submaxillary region: Fenglong (St. 40), Yangfu (G.B. 38), Fuyang (U.B. 59), Taichong (Liv. 3), Gongsun (Sp. 4). All on the diseased side.

(3) Operations of the mandible: Fenglong (St. 40), Yangfu (G.B. 38), Fuyang (U.B. 59), Taichong (Liv. 3), Gongsun (Sp. 4), Neiguan (P. 6). All on the diseased side.

(4) Plastic operation of the tempromandibular joint: Fenglong (St. 40), Yangfu (G.B. 38), Fuyang (U.B. 59), Taichong (Liv. 3), Gongsun (Sp. 4), Hegu (L.I. 4). The first four points on both sides and the last two on the diseased side.

(5) Mixed tumour of the palate: Hegu (L.I. 4), Neiguan (P. 6), Gongsun (Sp. 4).

4. Ear region
(1) Radical mastoidectomy:

a. Waiguan (S.J. 5), Yanglingquan (G.B. 34). Both bilaterally with electric stimulation.

b. Hegu (L.I. 4), Zhigou (S.J. 6). Both on the diseased side. Auricular points: Ear-Shenmen, Lung, Kidney, Ear. All on the diseased side. In the induction period use the auricular points only.

(2) Operation to expose the tympanic cavity: Hegu (L.I. 4), Houxi (S.I. 3), Waiguan (S.J. 5). All on both sides.

(3) Tympanotomy: Hegu (L.I. 4). Bilaterally or on the diseased side.

5. Throat
(1) Total laryngectomy:

Auricular points: Ear-Shenmen towards Sympathetic Nerve, Forehead towards Ear-Asthma, Adrenal. Hegu (L.I. 4), Zhigou (S.J. 6). All on the left side.

(2) Tonsillectomy:

a. Auricular points: Throat, Tonsil. Both bilaterally.

b. Hegu (L.I. 4). Bilaterally.

6. Nose
(1) Lateral nasal incision: Hegu (L.I. 4), Zhigou (S.J. 6), Nose-Juliao (St. 3) towards Sibai (St. 2). All on the diseased side.

(2) Radical maxillary sinusotomy: Hegu (L.I. 4), Zhigon (S.J. 6). During the induction period, Nose-Juliao (St. 3) towards Dicang (St. 4) is added.

(3) Radical frontal sinusotomy: Yangbai (G.B. 14) towards Zanzhu U.B. 2), Nose-Juliao (St. 3) towards Sibai (St. 2), Hegu (L.I. 4), Zhigou (S.J. 6). All on the diseased side.

(4) Polypectomy:

a. Hegu (L.I. 4) or Yingxiang (L.I. 20). Bilaterally or on the diseased side.

b. Auricular point: External Nose. Bilaterally or on the diseased side.

7. Neck Region
Resection of thyroid adenoma: Hegu (L.I. 4), Neiguan (P. 6).

8. Chest region
(1) Separation of mitral valve: Neiguan (P. 6), Hegu (L.I. 4), Zhigou (S.J. 6). All on the diseased side.

(2) Resection of pericardium: Hegu (L.I. 4), Neiguan (P. 6). Both bilat-erally.

(3) Pneumonectomy:

    a.   Binao (L.I. 14). On the diseased side.

    b. Waiguan (S.J. 5) towards Neiguan (P. 6). On the diseased side.

9.   Abdominal region

(1) Gastric operations: Zusanli (St. 36), Shangjuxu (St. 37). Bilaterally or on the diseased side.

(2) Splenectomy: Hegu (L.I. 4), Neiguan (P. 6), Zusanli (St. 36), San-yinjiao (Sp. 6), Taichong (Liv. 3). All on the diseased side.

(3) Appendectomy:

    a. Shangjuxu (St. 37), Lanwei (Appendix, Extra.), Taichong (Liv. 3). All bilaterally.

    b. Hegu (L.I. 4), Neiguan (P. 6), Gongsun (Sp. 4). All bilaterally.

(4) Herniorrhaphy: Zusanli (St. 36), Weidao (G. B. 28). Both bilaterally.

(5) Cesarean section: Zusanli (St. 36) Sanyinjiao (Sp. 6), Daimai (G.B. 26), Ncimadian (Extra., located at midpoint of the line joining Yinling-quan (Sp. 9) and internal malleolus). All bilaterally.

(6) Panhysterectomy with resection of appendixes of uterus: Yaoshu (Du 2), Mingmen (Du 4), Daimai (G.B. 26), Zusanli (St. 36), Sanyinjiao (Sp. 6), Zhongliao (U.B. 33) or Ciliao (U.B. 32). All bilaterally.

(7) Tubal ligation: Zusanli (St. 36), Foot-Zhongdu (Liv. 6). Both bila-terally.

10.   Perineum

Operations in perineum:

    a. Dachangshu (U.B. 25). on the diseased side with electric stimula-tion.

    b. Auricular points: Lung, Lower Portion of Rectum. Both on the diseased side with electric stimulation.

11.   Lumbodorsal region

(1) Spondylodesis:

    a. Hegu (L.I. 4), Neiguan (P. 6), Huizong (S.J. 7), Zusanli (St. 36), Chengshan (U.B. 57), Kunlun (U.B. 60), Yangfu (G.B. 38). All bilaterally.

    b. Auricular points: Ear-Shenmen, Lung, Kidney, Thoracic Ver-tebrae, Lower Back. All on the diseased side.

(2) Nephrectomy:

    a. Hegu (L.I. 4), Neiguan (P. 6), Zusanli (St. 36), Sanyinjiao (Sp. 6), Taichong (Liv. 3). All on the diseased side.

b. Auricular points: Ear-Shenmen, Lung, Waist, Ureter. All on the diseased side.

12. Four extremities

(1) Reduction of shoulder joint:

　　a. Auricular points: Shoulder towards Shoulder Joint, Ear-Shenmen, Sympathetic Nerve, Kidney. All on the diseased side.

　　b. Hegu (L.I. 4), Bizhong (Extra.). Both bilaterally.

(2) Amputation of forearm: Chize (Lu. 5), Qingling (H. 2), Sanjiaoji (Deltoideus, Extra.), Jianqian (Extra.) towards Jianhou (Extra.) All bilaterally.

(3) Internal fixation of fractures of neck of femur with three-flanged nail: Zusanli (St. 36), Fenglong (St. 40), Fuyang (U.B. 59), Waiqiu (G.B. 36), Xuanzhong (G.B. 39), Sanyinjiao (Sp. 6), Qiuxu (G.B. 40), Xiangu (St. 43). All on the diseased side with electric stimulation.

(4) Amputation of lower portion of leg:

　　Auricular points: Ear-Shenmen, Lung, Kidney, Sciatic Nerve towards Sympathetic Nerve. All on the diseased side with electric stimulation.

INDEX OF THE
ACUPUNCTURE POINTS

*(361 Regular Points and 20
Extraordinary Points)*

Dubi (犊鼻 , St. 35)

Duiduan (兑端 , Du 27)

Dushu (督俞 , U.B. 16)

Ear-Heliao (耳和髎 , S.J. 22)

Erjian (二间 , L.I. 2)

Ermen (耳门 , S.J. 21)

External Xiyan (外膝眼 , See Dubi)

Feishu (肺俞 , U.B. 13)

Feiyang (飞扬 , U.B. 58)

Femur-Futu (股伏兔 , St. 32)

Femur-Juliao (股居髎 , G.B. 29)

Femur-Wuli (股五里 , Liv. 10)

Femur-Zhongdu (股中渎 , G.B. 32)

Fengchi (风池 , G.B. 20)

Fengfu (风府 , Du 16)

Fenglong (丰隆 , St. 40)

Fengmen (风门 , U.B. 12)

Fengshi (风市 , G.B. 31)

Foot-Linqi (足临泣 , G.B. 41)

Foot-Qiaoyin (足窍阴 , G.B. 44)

Foot-Tonggu (足通谷 , U.B. 66)

Foot-Zhongdu (足中都 , Liv. 6)

Fuai (腹哀 , Sp. 16)

Fubai (浮白 , G.B. 10)

Fufen (附分 , U.B. 41)

Fujie (腹结 , Sp. 14)

Fuliu (复溜 , K. 7)

Fushe (府舍 , Sp. 13)

Fuxi (浮郄 , U.B. 38)

Fuyang (跗阳 , U.B. 59)

Gall Bladder (胆囊 , Extra.)

Ganshu (肝俞 , U.B. 18)

Gaohuangshu (膏肓俞 , U.B. 43)

Geguan (膈关 , U.B. 46)

Geshu (膈俞 , U.B. 17)

Gongsun (公孙 , Sp. 4)

Guanchong (关冲 , S.J. 1)

Guangming (光明 , G.B. 37)

Guanmen (关门 , St. 22)

Guanyuan (关元 , Ren 4)

Guanyuanshu (关元俞 , U.B. 26)

Guilai (归来 , St. 29)

Hand-Wangu (手腕骨 , S.I. 4)

Hand-Wuli (手五里 , L.I. 13)

Hand-Zhongzhu (手中渚 , S.J. 3)

Hanyan (颔厌 , G.B. 4)

Head-Linqi (头临泣 , G.B. 15)

Head-Qiaoyin (头窍阴 , G.B. 11)

Head-Wangu (头完骨 , G.B. 12)

Hegu (合谷 , L.I. 4)

Henggu (横骨 , K. 11)

Heyang (合阳 , U.B. 55)

Houding (后顶 , Du 19)

Houxi (后溪 , S.I. 3)

Huagai (华盖 , Ren 20)

Huangmen (肓门 , U.B. 51)

Huangshu (肓俞 , K. 16)

Huantiao (环跳 , G.B. 30)

Huaroumen (滑肉门 , St. 24)

Huatuo Jiaji (华陀夹脊 , Extra.)

Huiyang (会阳 , U.B. 35)

Huiyin (会阴 , Ren 1)

Huizong (会宗 , S.J. 7)

Hunmen (魂门 , U.B. 47)

Jiache (颊车 , St. 6)

Jianjing (肩井 , G.B. 21)

Jianli (建里 , Ren 11)   Liangmen (梁门 , St. 21)

Jianliao (肩髎 , S.J. 14)   Liangqiu (梁丘 , St. 34)

Jianneiling (肩内陵 , See Jianqian)   Lianquan (廉泉 , Ren 23)

Jianqian (肩前 , Extra.)   Lidui (厉兑 , St. 45)

Jianshi (间使 , P. 5)   Lieque (列缺 , Lu. 7)

Jianwaishu (肩外俞 , S.I. 14)   Ligou (蠡沟 , Liv. 5)

Jianyu (肩髃 , L.I. 15)   Lingdao (灵道 , H. 4)

Jianzhen (肩贞 , S.I. 9)   Lingtai (灵台 , Du 10)

Jianzhongshu (肩中俞 , S.I. 15)   Lingxu (灵墟 , K. 24)

Jiaosun (角孙 , S.J. 20)   Lougu (漏谷 , Sp. 7)

Jiaoxin (交信 , K. 8)   Luoque (络却 , U.B. 8)

Jiexi (解溪 , St. 41)   Luxi (颅息 , S.J. 19)

Jimai (急脉 , Liv. 12)   **M**eichong (眉冲 , U.B. 3)

Jimen (箕门 , Sp. 11)   Mingmen (命门 , Du 4)

Jinggu (京骨 , U.B. 64)   Mouth-Yinjiao (口龈交 , Du 28)

Jingmen (京门 , G.B. 25)   Muchuang (目窗 , G.B. 16)

Jingming (睛明 , U.B. 1)   **N**aohu (脑户 , Du 17)

Jingqu (经渠 , Lu. 8)   Naohui (臑会 , S.J. 13)

Jinjin, Yuye (金津, 玉液 , Extra.)   Naokong (脑空 , G.B. 19)

Jinmen (金门 , U.B. 63)   Naoshu (臑俞 , S.I. 10)

Jinsuo (筋缩 , Du 8)   Neck-Futu (颈扶突 , L.I. 18)

Jiquan (极泉 , H. 1)   Neiguan (内关 , P. 6)

Jiuwei (鸠尾 , Ren 15)   Neiting (内庭 , St. 44)

Jizhong (脊中 , Du 6)   Nose-Heliao (鼻禾髎 , L.I. 19)

Juegu (绝骨 , See Xuanzhong)   Nose-Juliao (鼻巨髎 , St. 3)

Jueyinshu (厥阴俞 , U.B. 14)   **P**angguangshu (膀胱俞 , U.B. 28

Jugu (巨骨 , L.I. 16)   Pianli (偏历 , L.I. 6)

Juque (巨阙 , Ren 14)   Pishu (脾俞 , U.B. 20)

Kongzui (孔最 , Lu. 6)   Pohu (魄户 , U.B. 42)

Kufang (库房 , St. 14)   Pushen (仆参 , U.B. 61)

Kunlun (昆仑 , U.B. 60)   **Q**ianding (前顶 , Du 21)

Lanwei (Appendix 阑尾 , Extra.)   Qiangjian (强间 Du 18)

Laogong (劳宫 , P. 8)   Qiangu (前谷 , S.I. 2)

Qichong (气冲 , St. 30)

Qihai (气海 , Ren 6)

Qihaishu (气海俞 , U.B. 24)

Qihu (气户 , St. 13)

Qimai (瘈脉 , S.J. 18)

Qimen (期门 , Liv. 14)

Qinglengyuan (清冷渊 , S.J. 11)

Qingling (青灵 , H. 2)

Qishe (气舍 , St. 11)

Qiuxu (丘墟 , G.B. 40)

Qixue (气穴 , K. 13)

Quanliao (颧髎 , S.I. 18)

Qubin (曲鬓 , G.B. 7)

Quchai (曲差 , U.B. 4)

Quchi (曲池 , L.I. 11)

Quepen (缺盆 , St. 12)

Qugu (曲骨 , Ren 2)

Ququan (曲泉 , Liv. 8)

Quyuan (曲垣 , S.I. 13)

Quze (曲泽 , P. 3)

Rangu (然谷 , K. 2)

Renying (人迎 , St. 9)

Renzhong (人中 , Du 26)

Riyue (日月 , G.B. 24)

Rugen (乳根 , St. 18)

Ruzhong (乳中 , St. 17)

Sanjian (三间 , L.I. 3)

Sanjiaoshu (三焦俞 , U.B. 22)

Sanyangluo (三阳络 , S.J. 8)

Sanyinjiao (三阴交 , Sp. 6)

Shangguan (上关 , G.B. 3)

Shangjuxu (上巨虚 , St. 37)

Shanglian (上廉 , L.I. 9)

Shangliao (上髎 , U.B. 31)

Shangqiu (商丘 , Sp. 5)

Shangqu (商曲 , K. 17)

Shangwan (上脘 , Ren 13)

Shangxing (上星 , Du 23)

Shangyang (商阳 , L.I. 1)

Shanzhong (膻中 , Ren 17)

Shaochong (少冲 , H. 9)

Shaofu (少府 , H. 8)

Shaohai (少海 , H. 3)

Shaoshang (少商 , Lu. 11)

Shaoze (少泽 , S.I. 1)

Shencang (神藏 , K. 25)

Shendao (神道 , Du 11)

Shenfeng (神封 , K. 23)

Shenmai (申脉 , U.B. 62)

Shenmen (神门 , H. 7)

Shenque (神阙 , Ren 8)

Shenshu (肾俞 , U.B. 23)

Shentang (神堂 , U.B. 44)

Shenting (神庭 , Du 24)

Shenzhu (身柱 , Du 12)

Shidou (食窦 , Sp. 17)

Shiguan (石关 , K. 18)

Shimen (石门 , Ren 5)

Shiqizhui (Seventeenth Vertebra 十七椎 , Extra.)

Shixuan (十宣 , Extra.)

Shousanli (手三里 , L.I. 10)

Shuaigu (率谷 , G.B. 8)

Shufu (俞府 , K. 27)

Shugu (束骨 , U.B. 65)

Shuidao (水道 , St. 28)

Shuifen (水分 , Ren 9)

Shuigou (水沟 , See Renzhong)

Shuiquan (水泉 , K. 5)

Shuitu (水突 , St. 10)

Sibai (四白 , St. 2)

Sidu (四渎 , S.J. 9)

Sifeng (四缝 , Extra.)

Siman (四满 , K. 14)

Sishencong (四神聪 , Extra.)

Sizhukong (丝竹空 , S.J. 23)

Suliao (髎素 , Du 25)

Taibai (太白 , Sp. 3)

Taichong (太冲 , Liv. 3)

Taixi (太溪 , K. 3)

Taiyang (太阳 , Extra.)

Taiyi (太乙 , St. 23)

Taiyuan (太渊 , Lu. 9)

Taodao (陶道 , Du 13)

Tianchi (天池 , P. 1)

Tianchong (天冲 , G.B. 9)

Tianchuang (天窗 , S.I. 16)

Tianding (天鼎 , L.I. 17)

Tianfu (天府 , Lu. 3)

Tianjing (天井 , S.J. 10)

Tianliao (天髎 , S.J. 15)

Tianquan (天泉 , P. 2)

Tianrong (天容 , S.I. 17)

Tianshu (天枢 , St. 25)

Tiantu (天突 , Ren 22)

Tianxi (天溪 , Sp. 18)

Tianyou (天牖 , S.J. 16)

Tianzhu (天柱 , U.B. 10)

Tianzong (天宗 , S.I. 11)

Tiaokou (条口 , St. 38)

Tinggong (听宫 , S.I. 19)

Tinghui (听会 , G.B. 2)

Tongli (通里 , H. 5)

Tongtian (通天 , U.B. 7)

Tongziliao (瞳子髎 , G.B. 1)

Touwei (头维 , St. 8)

Waiguan (外关 , S.J. 5)

Wailing (外陵 , St. 26)

Waiqiu (外丘 , G.B. 36)

Weicang (胃仓 , U.B. 50)

Weidao (维道 , G.B. 28)

Weiguanxiashu (胃管下俞 , Extra.)

Weishu (胃俞 , U.B. 21)

Weiyang (委阳 , U.B. 39)

Weizhong (委中 , U.B. 40)

Wenliu (温溜 , L.I. 7)

Wuchu (五处 , U.B. 5)

Wushu (五枢 , G.B. 27)

Wuyi (屋翳 , St. 15)

Xiabai (侠白 , Lu. 4)

Xiaguan (下关 , St. 7)

Xiajuxu (下巨虚 , St. 39)

Xialian (下廉 , L.I. 8)

Xialiao (下髎 , U.B. 34)

Xiangu (陷谷 , St. 43)

Xiaochangshu (小肠俞 , U.B. 27)

Xiaohai (小海 , S.I. 8)

Xiaoluo (消泺 , S.J. 12)

Xiawan (下脘 , Ren 10)

Xiaxi (侠溪 , G.B. 43)

Xiguan (膝关 , Liv. 7)

Ximen (郄门 , P. 4)

Xingjian (行间 , Liv. 2)

Xinhui (囟会 , Du 22)

Xinshu (心俞 , U.B. 15)

Xiongxiang (胸乡 , Sp. 19)

Xiyan (膝眼 , Extra.)

Xiyangguan (膝阳关 , G.B. 33)

Xuanji (璇玑 , Ren 21)

Xuanli (悬厘 , G.B. 6)

Xuanlu (悬颅 , G.B. 5)

Xuanshu (悬枢 , Du 5)

Xuanzhong (悬钟 , G.B. 39)

Xuehai (血海 , Sp. 10)

Yamen (哑门 , Du 15)

Yangbai (阳白 , G.B. 14)

Yangchi (阳池 , S.J. 4)

Yangfu (阳辅 , G.B. 38)

Yanggang (阳纲 , U.B. 48)

Yanggu (阳谷 , S.I. 5)

Yangjiao (阳交 , G.B. 35)

Yanglao (养老 , S.I. 6)

Yanglingquan (阳陵泉 , G.B. 34)

Yangxi (阳溪 , L.I. 5)

Yaoshu (腰俞 , Du 2)

Yaoyan (腰眼 , Extra.)

Yaoyangguan (腰阳关 , Du 3)

Yemen (液门 , S.J. 2)

Yifeng (翳风 , S.J. 17)

Yinbai (隐白 , Sp. 1)

Yinbao (阴包 , Liv. 9)

Yindu (阴都 , K. 19)

Yingchuang (膺窗 , St. 16)

Yingu (阴谷 , K. 10)

Yingxiang (迎香 , L.I. 20)

Yinlian (阴廉 , Liv. 11)

Yinlingquan (阴陵泉 , Sp. 9)

Yinmen (殷门 , U.B. 37)

Yinshi (阴市 , St. 33)

Yintang (印堂 , Extra.)

Yinxi (阴郄 , H. 6)

Yishe (意舍 , U.B. 49)

Yixi (譩譆 , U.B. 45)

Yongquan (涌泉 , K. 1)

Youmen (幽门 , K. 21)

Yuanye (渊腋 , G.B. 22)

Yuji (鱼际 , Lu. 10)

Yunmen (云门 , Lu. 2)

Yutang (玉堂 , Ren 18)

Yuyao (鱼腰 , Extra.)

Yuzhen (玉枕 , U.B. 9)

Yuzhong (彧中 , K. 26)

Zanzhu (攒竹 , U.B. 2)

Zhangmen (章门 , Liv. 13)

Zhaohai (照海 , K. 6)

Zhejin (辄筋 , G.B. 23)

Zhengying (正营 , G.B. 17)

Zhibian (秩边 , U.B. 54)

Zhigou (支沟 , S.J. 6)

Zhishi (志室 , U.B. 52)

Zhiyang (至阳 , Du 9)

Zhiyin (至阴 , U.B. 67)

Zhizheng (支正 , S.I. 7)

Zhongchong (中冲 , P. 9)

Zhongfeng (中封 , Liv. 4)

Zhongfu (中府 , Lu. 1)

Zhongji (中极 , Ren 3)

Zhongliao (中髎 , U.B. 33)   Zhongwan (中脘 , Ren 12)

Zhonglüshu (中膂俞 , U.B. 29)   Zhouliao (肘髎 , L.I. 12)

Zhongquan (中泉 , Extra.)   Zhourong (周荣 , Sp. 20)

Zhongshu (中枢 , Du 7)   Zhubin (筑宾 , K. 9)

Zhongting (中庭 , Ren 16)   Zusanli (足三里 , St. 36)

Errata

Page	Line	Originals	Corrections
36	4 from bottom	essential qi	pectoral qi (zong qi)
37	8		add "thus there comes such sayings, 'qi is the commander of blood,' and 'Blood is the mother of qi'"
45	4 from bottom	may by due to	may be due to
46	13	excessive sweating	spontaneous sweating
53	2 from bottom	automatic sweating	spontaneous sweating
62	5	superficial and forceful	superficial and tense
64	16	syndromes of yin xu	syndromes of yang xu
82	14	porton	portion
125	17	Between the eyeball and the midpoint of the infraorbital ridge	midway between the eyeball and the infraorbital ridge
315	6 from bottom	symptoms of weakness	the syndrome of
315	8 from bottom	and symptoms of	the syndrome of
323	line 4	lung channel of Hand-ying ming	Large Intestine Channel of Hand-Yangming
326	13	chizi (LU 5)	Chize (Lu 5)
326	Table 20 Line 1 Column 3	Rong-spring	Ying-spring
337	7	and reponds to	and responds to
351	9	Xinshu (UB 12)	Xinshu (UB 15)
369	5	damage to qi	damage of qi
371	5	lianqiu (St 34)	Liangqiu (St 34)
394	11 from bottom	Xianguan (St 7)	Xiaguan(St 7)
415	4 from bottom	Ear	Eye

图书在版编目（CIP）数据

中国针灸学概要/北京中医药大学等编.
－2版.北京：外文出版社，2005
ISBN 7-119-00240-6
I.中… II.北… III. 针灸学-英文 IV. R245

中国版本图书馆 CIP 数据核字（2004）第 137572 号

责任编辑　贾先锋
封面设计　蔡　荣
印刷监制　韩少乙

中国针灸学概要

北京中医药大学

上海中医药大学

南京中医药大学

中国中医研究院针灸研究所　编

*

©外文出版社
外文出版社出版
（中国北京百万庄大街 24 号）
邮政编码　100037
外文出版社网址 http://www.flp.com.cn
外文出版社电子信箱: info@flp.com.cn
sales@flp.com.cn
三河市汇鑫印务有限公司印刷
中国国际图书贸易总公司发行
（中国北京车公庄西路 35 号）
北京邮政信箱第 399 号　邮政编码　100044
1980 年（16 开）第 1 版
1993 年第 2 版
2005 年第 2 版第 2 次印刷
（英）
ISBN 7-119-00240-6
09800（精）
14-E-1506S